# The Coming of the Welfare State

# The Coming of the
# WELFARE STATE

*Maurice Bruce*

*Professor, Director of Extramural Studies,*
*University of Sheffield*

B. T. BATSFORD LTD London

This edition is dedicated to
my Mother on her eightieth birthday
and to the memory of my Father

*First published 1961*
*Second edition 1965*
*Third edition 1966*
*Reprinted 1967*
*Fourth edition, reset, 1968*
*Reprinted 1972*

© Maurice Bruce, 1961, 1965, 1966, 1968

Made and printed in Great Britain by
C. Tinling & Co. Ltd, London and Prescot
for the publishers B. T. Batsford Ltd
4 Fitzhardinge Street, London W1

ISBN 0 7134 1359 X

*Legislative opinion is itself more often the result of facts than of philosophical speculations.*

A. V. Dicey, 1905

*The scheme proposed . . . is in some ways a revolution, but in more important ways it is a natural development from the past. It is a British revolution.*

The Beveridge Report, 1942

*In many ways the development of the welfare state in Britain is the result of walking long enough without any clear indication of where we wanted to get to.*

D. C. Marsh, *The Future of the Welfare State*, 1964

# Preface

This book is an attempt to show how the Welfare State of the present day has grown out of the needs of the English people and out of the struggle for social justice. Two themes run through it. The first is that of the acceptance of community responsibility, through the 'poor law', and, later, by other means, for the less fortunate members of society. This was first given statutory expression under Queen Elizabeth I and was then based on the parish. The story of the poor law from the sixteenth century until its final abolition in 1948 is the story of the slow widening of the area of responsibility, from the parish, through the Union (1834) to the Local Authority (1930), and eventually, under the Unemployment Assistance Board of 1934 and the National Assistance Board of 1948, to the nation as a whole. This widening of the area of responsibility was matched by a similar widening of the range of services provided, from simple 'out-relief' and the more complex issues of 'setting the poor on work' to National Assistance and Full Employment; from the apprenticing of poor children to the provision of a State system of education; from the care of the sick to the environmental health services of the nineteenth century and the National Health Service of today. The transformation of the country brought about by the industrial revolution was, of course, a decisive challenge to the modest system of relief then existing, and provided, in time, both opportunity and resources for a completely new range of services.

The widening of both the area of responsibility and the range of services has been an essentially practical response to the problems and conditions of English society as it developed and became more self-conscious. The practical approach, typically English as it is, is our second theme.

Underlying these themes, of course, has been the problem of resources, both in finance and in administration. Throughout the long period we have to consider there has been a constant struggle over the raising of the resources required for the services at the time considered necessary. Not until the present century, with its dreadful example of two wars of national survival, has it been accepted that in the last resort the resources of the nation can and must be used for what the Elizabethans called the 'common weal', which is at once the basis and the essence of the Welfare State.

How far, in fact, the nation's resources actually are used, or should still further be used, is a matter of current controversy, but changes continue to take place under our eyes at a pace which would have seemed impossible even in quite recent times. With the Welfare State, therefore, as with other aspects of British life at the present time, particularly in the Commonwealth, one is conscious of the span and movement of history. To what we are trying to do, past generations, in their own strivings and endeavours, have contributed so much. And when one recalls that it was only in 1948 that the Elizabethan poor law finally vanished from the statute-book, history becomes very much a matter of current concern.

The subject is, of course, a vast one, and it has not been possible to do much more than drive a highway through it, drawing attention to points of particular interest and importance en route. Much has been bulldozed or squeezed out. What has been attempted, however, has been not only to show what the Welfare State amounts to and how it has developed, but what has been thought at various times about the services it incorporates and the problems it has sought to solve. In addition, something has been said of the general movement of events, political, social and economic, of which the growth of welfare forms part.

Except in explanation of German influence on Lloyd George's proposals, only passing references have been made to social policy in other countries, either in the British Dominions or elsewhere. Until the second half of the nineteenth century British poor-law policy, with what was developing from it, grossly inadequate though it seems now, was not only outstanding but unique. Thereafter the lead was not maintained, though some allowance has to be made for the legacy of the pioneer of the industrial revolution. What has finally emerged, however, incomplete though it still is, can stand comparison with any other system, and has been gained without the sacrifice of political liberty. Political liberty and social justice, indeed, have grown together: what has been created has been essentially the achievement of a whole people. To it have contributed many individuals, many organisations, many interests: for only a few of them is there space for a direct reference in the pages that follow. Whenever an Act of Parliament is mentioned, therefore, the various pressures that have brought it into being, often only after a long period of discussion and agitation, must be considered as understood. Further, if the passage of an Act is the climax of one process, it must be seen as only the beginning of another: it is effective administration, with the underlying support of the courts, that converts good intentions into actions. In one respect, therefore, the evolution of the Welfare State is the evolution of social administration, from the amateur J.P. and overseer of the poor, through Queen Victoria's 'red-tapist, narrow-minded' bureaucrat, to the trained official of today. If less is said of this than of other aspects it is not for lack of recognition of its significance.

Reference throughout the book is almost entirely to English experience. It is essentially the English story which is traced, and, although there is, of course, very much in common with Scotland and Ireland, there are many differences, especially in Scottish traditions and administration. It has been thought best, however, to drive the one road, while recognising the great activity of many Scots, especially in the health services, on and around it. The distinctive references to Scotland and

Ireland are therefore few: the author hopes that his fellow citizens of the United Kingdom in those countries will excuse the omissions that have been made under the demands of concentration and in the interests of clarity.

As far as possible contemporary evidence has been used throughout the book to substantiate or illustrate the points made. The debt to other writers on aspects of the history of welfare policy will be obvious enough to the reader and is duly acknowledged, whether in the text or in the list of references.

Parliamentary reports and papers have also been drawn on, together with other contemporary material, including in some cases the novels which have often reflected the commonly held views and prejudices of the day. No doubt it is rash of a historian to venture into the field of social policy, where sociologists, economists and psychologists have so much to offer. The historian, however, is concerned with the questions, what happened, and how and why, and these are the questions that the book tries to answer.

# Preface to the Fourth Edition

Advantage has been taken of the reprinting of the book to make a number of additions and corrections, to insert, in response to many requests, the source of every quotation, and to bring the references themselves and the suggestions for further reading up to date.

Thanks are due to many friends in Britain, the United States and Japan for their interest in the book and their help with it. British indebtedness is too widespread to specify, though an exception must be made for the book's publishers, and especially Sam Carr and Patrick Connell, for their constant encouragement and support. Among American friends mention must be made of Bentley Gilbert, whose own work is covering much of the same ground in far greater depth; among Japanese, Joju Akita, author of a Japanese translation. One of the pleasures arising from the book has been the extension of a circle of friends literally all round the world.

MAURICE BRUCE

*University of Sheffield*

*Note to new impression.* Advantage has been taken of another reprint to make further additions and corrections.

# Contents

# 1 | The Ground Surveyed

The *coming* of the Welfare State is a title deliberately chosen. The historical process considered in these pages might equally well be styled the *making* of the Welfare State, but for the suggestion of deliberate process and purpose that such a title might produce. No-one, not even Beveridge himself, ever planned the Welfare State, nor has it been the direct outcome of any political or social philosophy. It has been, in fact, no more than the accumulation over many years of remedies to specific problems which in the end have reached such proportions as to create a new conception of governmental responsibility. Care for the unfortunate has been a feature of English administration, through the Poor Law, since the sixteenth century. The industrial revolution (to use the convenient term which everyone understands despite the technical objections to it) added immeasurably, in a period of expanding population, to the problems and tensions of a society which, though it was increasing in numbers and resources, had outgrown its capacity to cope, and was compelled to improvise. Nineteenth-century social legislation was a process of improvisation which in the end opened the way to new notions of society and government. Its inspiration was in part Christian concern for fellow men, in part the humanism of the late eighteenth century and the social legacy of the French Revolution, and in part—for long, the least part—the socialism which, repudiating as inadequate its idealistic past, endeavoured to find scientific remedies for the injustices of industrial society. Set against the movement for reform was the prevailing doctrine of *laissez-faire*, which was rather more, however, an attitude of mind than a conscious political or economic creed. It can easily be shown that a perfect state of *laissez-faire* never in fact existed. By the time that the old mercantilist restrictions, against which Adam Smith and others had inveighed, had finally been removed, new social restraints were being devised, though for long the significance of the new measures was obscured by the ignorance of the right hand of Victorian government as to the activities of the left. Not until the twentieth century was the process of collectivisation recognised for what it was, not until then was it realised that the wealth created by industrialisation could be directed, through the power of the State, to the alleviation of misery which industrialisation itself had done so much to intensify. In modern parlance, technical maturity had been achieved, and consideration for the welfare of those who had benefited least could be entertained: in W. W. Rostow's words, 'the emergence of the Welfare State is one manifestation of a society's moving beyond technical maturity'.[1] Hence the reforms of the Liberal Government of the productive years before 1914, though much must be attributed to the efforts of individuals, both in politics and outside, and to the chances of the political process. Thenceforward development was steady, if slow. How it would have gone but for the further chance of the Second World War, following as it did the long years of depression, it is impossible to say. It was the national unity of the war, the shared sacrifices of all classes, that rounded off the process, under the inspiration of the lead given by Beveridge in his report of 1942, *Social Insurance and Allied Services*. Since then prosperity and full employment, the hallmarks of the Affluent Society, have created new conditions, in which, in a famous phrase coined by Harold Macmillan in a speech at Bedford in 1957 (and often since misquoted), 'most of our people have never had it so good'. If for most people conditions have never before been so good, gaps have nevertheless remained, and on both counts it has had to be asked whether the services created to cope with past deficiencies were necessarily appropriate to the new circumstance. The process of adaptation to changing needs and conditions has therefore continued, often amid heated debate.

Debate has long turned on the issue of individual and collective responsibility. Originally it was on moral grounds. It was held that all could support themselves and should: those who did not were the failures of society and to be treated as such. Gradually, however, the ground shifted. It was increasingly realised that the problem was a practical one. Many, under existing conditions of economic development, could not support themselves adequately against all the accidents of life, and means had to be devised to provide protection, whether through insurance, as in the great scheme of 1911, or through outright benefits, as with old age pensions in 1908. This was the empirical approach, which was then extended. Now, with a more widespread prosperity than has ever before been enjoyed, the issue of personal responsibility has been revived in some quarters, though less now on the moral than on the practical grounds of the general level of well-being under conditions of full employment. On the whole the Conservative Party, while accepting the reforms of 1945–8 and the protection they afford to those in need, has laid more stress on individual responsibility; the Labour Party, true to its fundamental doctrines, has been more concerned to preserve the collective responsibility established as a result of wartime, and earlier, experience. Much has been accepted on both sides that would earlier have seemed inconceivable. Thus, Conservatives have accepted, and done much to develop, a national system of health insurance, the National Health Service, which aims at providing for all, whatever their personal means, medical attention such as few, in the face of the cost of modern treatment, could afford for themselves unaided. (Conservative policy, has, however, aimed at making some charges, especially on prescriptions:

the abolition of prescription charges was one of the first steps of the Labour Government of 1964, though harsh economic circumstances soon restored them.) More recently, Labour has been willing to reconsider such services as Family Allowances which changing conditions since 1945 have rendered less essential to many families than pre-war experience suggested. Generally there is agreement that more attention should be devoted now to those who, for one reason or another, have benefited least from contemporary affluence. To that extent at least Labour has been willing to compromise with the principle of universal coverage to which pre-war experience of the 'means test' approach had given particular significance. On both sides, of course, there are those who would press further their party's particular viewpoint. Some Conservative elements argue in almost pure nineteenth-century terms for a return to an unregulated market economy, some Labour idealists for a more thorough-going Socialism. On both sides there are also those with little interest in what does not directly concern themselves: Arthur Seaton, the voice of 'Labour anarchy' in Alan Sillitoe's *Saturday Night and Sunday Morning*, has probably not been alone in complaining of a system of government 'that puts stamps all over your phizzog . . . and what's more makes you buy 'em so's they can keep on doing it'.

Our concern here is not with the rights and wrongs of the debate but with its resolution over the years up to the time in 1948 when, after many modifications, an old system of social provision was finally put aside and a new one took its place. The conditions under which the new system came into operation have, however, been startlingly different from those for which it was intended. In particular, the degree of full employment has been far greater, despite wartime promises about 'the maintenance of a high and stable level of employment', than could have been imagined possible in the immediate post-war years. Unemployment, so long of necessity a matter of urgent concern to the whole country, has not been the problem which the economic dislocations of the Second World War and the experience of the years immediately following the First had led everyone to expect: one of the major problems of all projects of national welfare, which had dominated thought and policy for half a century, has proved less intractable than ever before. Its place has been taken by another problem of long standing, the maintenance of old people in retirement, now intensified by the increasing number of the elderly, the steady pressure of inflation and the higher standards of living generally enjoyed throughout the community.

When that pioneer of the Welfare State, Sidney Webb, died in 1947 an American magazine commented on the irony of the fact that so much of what he and his 'other one', Beatrice, had long worked for was being achieved only under the difficult economic conditions of a Britain weakened by two world wars. The Webbs, were they still with us, would undoubtedly disown much of what the Welfare State has come to represent, but it is indeed true that the 'break-up of the old poor law', urged so many years before in the famous Minority Report on the Poor Law of 1909, which they largely drew up, was not finally achieved until

1948. The National Assistance Act of that year, with its formal abolition of the last remnants of the poor-law system, can be regarded as symbolic of the completion of a new conception of society's duty to its members, of the final triumph of collective welfare over individual alms. Yet an American commentator could reasonably take the view in 1947 that Britain was now too poor to carry the welfare schemes which the Webbs had spent their careers in advancing. In fact, however, the conditions in which the Welfare State has operated have been markedly different not only from those of 1909 or of the unhappy years between the wars, but even from those anticipated by Beveridge in that other famous Report of 1942, which stands with the Minority Report of 1909 as one of the great milestones on the road towards the Welfare State. Full employment and a greater degree of general prosperity than has ever before been known have blunted the edge of the problems which the changes made in social policy in the years from 1945 to 1948, themselves based on the Beveridge proposals of 1942, were intended to relieve.

Like the General Staff of many an ironic comment, the Welfare State, indeed, fights today the problems of yesterday, and the reason is not far to seek. When problems have been studied and reported upon, and public opinion is prepared for measures to remedy them, the ripe moment for action is probably already past. Politicians are primarily not social reformers but manipulators of the political machine, and their concern must be rather more with what can be carried than with what is necessarily most desirable.

Looked at more broadly, the development of the Welfare State might be related not only to an increasing social consciousness and concern over a century and a half but to the gradual creation of a margin of national wealth that permitted a wider diffusion of the benefits of industrialisation. To quote W. W. Rostow again, Britain in the nineteenth century 'took its technological virtuosity as given, and, at a decorous rate, proceeded to explore at the margin, objectives beyond'.[2] The age of mass consumption, though it was slow to come to the pioneer of industrial development, did eventually arrive, and the economic organisation on which it was based has made possible a raising of standards all round. Earlier generations, lacking social protection, paid the price of capital creation founded on their toil, though, as we shall see, governments intervened early, and, if only moderately, at least against all the theories of *laissez-faire*, to effect some improvement in the worst conditions. A fully-shared collective responsibility came only slowly, however, and was finally given expression in the legislation of 1945–8 that reflected the possibilities of the organisation of the national wealth for common purposes that had been one of the revelations of the Second World War.

**The Establishment of the Welfare State**    The legislative reforms which were carried between 1945 and 1948 were inspired from many sources, but had their immediate origin in the Beveridge Report which, although almost a private, and certainly a very personal, document, made recommendations which gave point to much of the deep-felt desire in the country for a better order of things.

Two years after the appearance of the Report, in 1944, the government took its own first steps towards post-war reconstruction and a new conception of social welfare. A White Paper on Social Insurance was issued, with acknowledgements to Beveridge's preparation of the ground, and this was followed by the establishment of a new Ministry of National Insurance (originally to be styled the Ministry of *Social* Insurance), which was intended both to absorb existing services and to offer new ones. A little earlier there had appeared proposals for a radically new National Health Service, and these were followed by the White Paper on Employment Policy, which committed the Government, in a famous phrase, to 'the maintenance of a high and stable level of employment after the war'. At the same time a great Education Act was passed and the national education system, which had started with modest beginnings in elementary education in 1870, and had been since 1899 under the supervision of a nominal 'Board', was at last put in the charge of a fully-fledged Ministry.

In the next year, 1945, the year of victories, came the first of the new services with the Family Allowance Act, and in 1946, an *annus mirabilis* of legislation, the National Insurance Act, the National Insurance (Industrial Injuries) Act and the National Health Service Act. Two years later there followed the Children Act and the National Assistance Act, which explicitly brought to an end the poor law and completed the framework and foundations of the Welfare State.

Of these great measures only one, that providing for family allowances, could be regarded as entirely new, though even that was not altogether without precedents in unemployment insurance. The other measures were extensions and enlargements of existing provisions, though with the admission of new principles that vastly extended their range and made them truly national in operation as in name.

**The Origins of the Welfare Services**    The oldest in origin of the services was workmen's compensation, which had begun on a very modest scale, and without any assistance from national funds, in 1897, and which was the logical, if tardy, corollary of the long series of Factory Acts which protected the hours and conditions of work of the industrial worker. The first, very modest, attempts by Parliament to grapple with the problem of unemployment had been made in 1905, and the first national contribution towards the relief of poverty due to unemployment had been made in the following year. In 1908 had been instituted, again on a modest scale, the State system of old age pensions, non-contributory until 1925, when they were greatly enlarged and extended in scope and placed on a contributory basis. Old age pensions had been the first of the major social reforms of the Liberal Ministry that had taken office in 1905 and been given a great vote of electoral confidence in the 'landslide' General Election of 1906. In 1909, the year after the introduction of old age pensions, there had followed the establishment of Labour Exchanges to encourage labour mobility and of Trade Boards to suppress 'sweated labour'.

In the same year had come the famous 'People's Budget', sponsored by Lloyd George as Chancellor of the Exchequer. In the budget of 1907 Asquith as Chancellor had cautiously introduced new principles with old age pensions and the beginnings of graduated taxation. These principles Lloyd George, now Chancellor of the Exchequer under Asquith as Prime Minister, carried much further in 1909, dramatically using graduated taxation, in his own words, 'to wage implacable warfare against poverty and squalidness'.[3] Coinciding as it did with the appearance of the Majority and Minority Reports on the Poor Law, the 'People's Budget', however limited its immediate effects, introduced an approach to social problems from which henceforth there could be no going back. Furthermore, it brought to a head a long-standing conflict with the House of Lords, which, after many bitter passages, culminated in the passing of the Parliament Act of 1911, under the protection of which Lloyd George pushed through the National Insurance Act in the same year. This Act instituted for all below a certain income-level, though in the case of unemployment at first only in certain trades, a national system of insurance for sickness and unemployment, with a triple system of contributions, from employed, employer and the State.

**The Administration of the Local Services**   The administrative machinery available for the conduct of the various services that were being devised half a century ago was a typically English combination of the established and the *ad hoc*: not until 1944, with the creation of the Ministry of National Insurance, was a more logical system introduced, though even then it remained incomplete. It was only in 1966 that a Ministry of Social Security was established to deal with National Insurance and its related benefits together. Workmen's compensation on its inception in 1897 became the responsibility of the Home Office, which since 1834 had been supervising the related service of the factory inspectorate under the Factory Acts. The factory inspectors remained under the Home Office, despite the setting-up of the Ministry of Labour in 1916, until 1940, when Ernest Bevin, as Minister of Labour and National Service, insisted on their passing into his charge.

The Trade Boards and Labour Exchanges set up in 1909 were commended to the care of the Board of Trade, which in 1911 also assumed responsibility for unemployment insurance: all three services were transferred in 1916 to the newly established Ministry of Labour.

**Poor Law and Health—the Environmental Services**   The government department which in 1909 still had the widest responsibilities in the field of welfare was the Local Government Board, set up in 1871 to co-ordinate the central direction of sanitary, public health and poor-law services throughout the country. Poor-law administration in its nineteenth-century form dated from 1834, though it was firmly based on the Elizabethan system of poor relief and on the Law of Settlement and Removal of 1662, intended to tie the poor to their parishes. The sanitary and public health services were in the first place an offshoot of the reformed poor law of 1834. It was the 1842 report of the Poor Law Commissioners on *The Sanitary Condition of the Labouring Population* which first shocked opinion into a recognition of the misery and squalor of life in the rapidly growing industrial centres, and by revealing the need for the improvement of living conditions eventually led to the establishment of preventive and positive health services and to the complete reconstruction of local government.

In the same year that saw the report on sanitary conditions, appeared another which also presented a horrifying picture of industrial conditions, the first report of the Royal Commission on the Employment of Children, which described conditions in mines and is well known for its telling illustrations. Already the Factory Act of 1833 had begun to check abuses in the employment of children in factories and had led to the appointment of the first factory inspectors. As more came to be known, the hours and conditions of work of women, young people and children were subjected to control, and working conditions generally were gradually improved, side by side with improvements in housing and sanitary conditions made under other legislation.

The first Public Health Act was passed in 1848. This gave powers to local authorities for the protection of public health and made the first, unsatisfactory, experiment of a central directing influence in a 'General Board of Health', but it was not until 1871 that a properly constituted central department to control local government and public health was established. Then, however, the new department assumed responsibility not only for these services but also for the central control of the poor law, and the combination proved a most unfortunate one. The poor law was conceived of as essentially a deterrent service, and the Local Government Board soon acquired an unhappy reputation for restraining any undue enthusiasm among local authorities for the improvement of their services.

In 1875, however, before the cold hand of poor-law administration had made itself felt, was passed the first great Public Health Act, the climax of mid-Victorian concern with sanitary conditions and the foundation of a system that was to be superseded only by the Public Health Act of 1936. The 1875 Act, it has justly been said, stands with the Reform Act of 1832 and the Education Act of 1870 as one of the formative measures of the nineteenth century.

To the situation created in 1871 must be attributed in the first place the insignificant part played by the Local Government Board in the reforms of the years from 1906, though not a little was due also to the acquiescence in the established restrictions of the President of the Board who was the Liberals' greatest disappointment, the former labour leader John Burns (President, 1905–14). Something must be allowed also for the contempt felt for Burns by Lloyd George (President of the Board of Trade, 1905–8; thereafter Chancellor of the Exchequer) and by his successor at the Board of Trade, Winston Churchill, no less than for the ambition of these two formidable figures to make their mark politically.

Hence, quite apart from any logic in existing arrangements, the placing of labour exchanges, trade boards and unemployment insurance under the Board of Trade. Hence, too, the far more significant decision to administer the medical side of National Health Insurance through specially established Insurance Commissioners, a decision taken deliberately by Lloyd George in 1911 in spite of all the obvious disadvantages of a split in the public provision for health. These disadvantages were not altogether overcome by the establishment in 1919 of the Ministry of Health, which absorbed all the existing health services. They lingered until 1951, when the Ministry of Local Government and Planning (soon to become the Ministry of Housing and Local Government) took over the central responsibility for local government and the sanitary services, leaving the Ministry of Health to concentrate on the great scheme of medical care founded in 1946 and put into effect in 1948.

**The Coming of Positive Health Services**   The double provision for health service from 1911 to 1919, through the Local Government Board and the Insurance Commissioners, was the more unfortunate since another government department, the Board of Education, had begun to assume some responsibility for the health of schoolchildren. In 1904 a specially appointed Inter-Departmental Committee on Physical Deterioration had been set up, as part of the national grand inquest on the conduct of the South African War, to consider the reasons for the rejection of a large proportion of recruits to the Army. The Committee considered evidence on the health and physique of the people and made recommendations on such matters as the compulsory appointment of medical officers of health, overcrowded housing, smoke abatement, the sale of cigarettes to children, physical education in schools, the medical inspection of schoolchildren and the provision of meals to the underfed among them. All these recommendations were in time to be carried out, though it was not until the Housing Act of 1935 that overcrowding was at last legally defined, while smoke abatement had to wait even longer for attention.

In 1906, however, the Liberal Government arranged for the provision of school meals to necessitous children and in the following year for the medical inspection of all children in local authority schools. The feeding of schoolchildren was objected to by the Local Government Board as an invasion of its poor-law responsibilities, but the new service was both an indication of a need and an example of the ways in which parallel services were now springing up. A further illustration of this parallelism is to be found in the variety of provision for deprived, destitute and delinquent children, with whom the Local Government Board, the Board of Education, the Home Office and a number of voluntary societies were variously concerned. It was from the Home Office, which had already produced since 1906 the Borstal system and the probation service, that there came in 1908, under the inspiration of Herbert Samuel as Under-Secretary, the Children Act, the first comprehensive statute on the care of children and the precursor of the great constructive Act of 1948: among other things, the 1908 Act introduced Juvenile Courts and forbade the sale of cigarettes to children. Since the end of the poor law in 1948 the Home Office has retained its special responsibility for the care of children, partly because of a long-standing connexion which goes back beyond 1908 into the nineteenth century, partly because of the unhappy association of the deprived with the delinquent, though the direct responsibility for the care of deprived children rests today with the local authorities.

The Education (Administrative Provisions) Act of 1907 which established the school health service has well been described as marking the beginning of the *personal* health services. It was the first step towards a positive conception of health, as against the preventive approach of the environmental health services which had been started in the 40s and had reached their climax in the Public Health Act of 1875 and the Housing Act of 1890. Much had been done by the early years of the twentieth century to develop the environmental services, and one of the few measures carried by the Local Government Board under John Burns was the Housing and Town Planning Act of 1909, which finally prohibited the construction of back-to-back houses, those plagues of the industrial centres which are only now disappearing, through slum clearance measures, half a century and more later. The Act also carried out the recommendations of the Physical Deterioration Committee of 1904 with regard to the compulsory appointment of Medical Officers of Health, and made the first tentative approaches towards a policy of town planning, though the approaches were so tentative as to be ineffectual. Not until the Second World War did town and country planning, the crown of the environmental services, become a real possibility, and by that time the disadvantages of inaction had become only too apparent.

**The Positive Approach—'Social Welfare' and Insurance**    It will be clear from this preliminary sketch that even before 1945 much had been done, however unsystematically, to advance social welfare. In particular, the foundations of services that were later to expand almost out of recognition were laid in the years from 1906 to 1911. The leading economist of the day, Alfred Marshall, called Lloyd George's budget of 1909 a 'social welfare budget', and the social purposes of the insurance scheme of 1911, with its contributions from government and employers as well as from the individual worker, were at once recognised in the coining of the phrase 'social insurance'. It was, indeed, both 'social' and 'insurance', both a method of insurance against social ills and, to a very limited extent, a means for the transfer of wealth by taxation for social ends. Lloyd George claimed that his budget taxed, though only lightly, 'the pleasures of the few in order to spare the sorrows of the myriad', and Winston Churchill, in an equally characteristic phrase, saluted Liberalism as 'the cause of the left-out millions'.

The nineteenth century had concentrated upon environment, improving the conditions of work and living which had impeded progress. Now a more positive approach was being developed, not merely in matters of health. The change is significant, but hardly less so is the shrewd acceptance of the insurance principle. This gave the new policy respectability, and removed, or at least mitigated, the notion that the 'left-out millions' were actually getting something for nothing. At the same time it put personal protection through insurance on a national basis, with contributions from the State and the employer to make it a social service. The State was able to guarantee more than double the insurance payments that a friendly society, for instance, could offer: hence Lloyd George's famous phrase, 'ninepence for fourpence'.

**National Insurance**   Owing to a possible confusion with socialism, particularly unwelcome among conservatives, 'national' rather than 'social' insurance was the phrase adopted, though as late as 1944 it was intended that 'social' should be the qualifying adjective, and 'social security' was at last formally accepted in 1966, though it still includes 'national' insurance. 'National' had this justification in 1911, that it recognised the creation of a new national service in preference to the inadequate personal arrangements for insurance that were all that were hitherto available to even a minority of workers. It had the further justification in 1944 that the coverage was at last to be truly national: the whole nation was to be included, even to the self-employed and those not needing to work.

**Social Investigations and their Influence**   But for the services that have been built up since the Liberal victory of 1906 the great tasks of 1944–8 could hardly have been carried through so smoothly. Much is owed, in particular, to the civil service pioneers, Bradbury, Braithwaite, Morant and others, who with few precedents to guide them achieved in 1911–12 the enormous task of erecting national insurance. Still more is due to all those who, during the previous hundred years and especially in the later years of the nineteenth century, had been investigating social problems and revealing their findings to a shocked and startled public.

Outstanding among private investigators, of course, were such pioneers of social enquiry as Charles Booth and Seebohm Rowntree. Earlier enquirers, such as Edwin Chadwick, who had been responsible for the 1842 report on working-class conditions, and John Simon, had stressed the appalling effect of unsavoury environment, and their efforts had brought improvements in environment, in housing and working conditions and in the sanitary services, which had seemed to many to be enough to ensure the health and physical well-being without which prosperity could never be achieved. By the end of the century, however, the significant change from the environmental to the positive approach was taking place. Investigations showed that low wages, large families, irregularity of employment and actual unemployment kept a startlingly high proportion of workers below the poverty line. The view was still held that no man who genuinely wanted work could fail to find it, that every man in work could, if he cared, provide through the much-vaunted principles of thrift for the accidents of sickness, unemployment and poverty-stricken old age. Hence the somewhat penal conception of the poor law, with the workhouse little better than a prison, and the pauper dependent upon public relief deprived of his voting rights, a penalty that was not finally removed until 1918. It was recognised, of course, that there were unfortunate cases of people who had genuinely striven to work and save and who had yet been forced by circumstances into destitution. For these the charitable societies were intended to provide, and, when it began to be realised that their resources were inadequate, attempts were made to provide work through public authorities.

**The Unemployed Workmen Act, 1905**  These attempts were first given parliamentary encouragement by the Unemployed Workmen Act of 1905, passed, be it noted, by a Conservative government, though its provisions had been tentatively anticipated as far back as 1886 by Joseph Chamberlain when President of the Local Government Board.

The Unemployed Workmen Act, which was largely the work of Walter Long, until recently President of the Board, was intended at first to do hardly more than provide for the disposal of voluntary funds through local committees. It achieved little, and, though it was not repealed until 1929, its significance has been overlooked in the long and unhappy record of unemployment between the wars. But it was a seminal measure, important as a recognition of the fact that unemployment was something more than a purely personal problem to be overcome by an individual's adaptability or thrift, or left to the tender mercies of the poor law. It recognised implicitly that the problem was a social one, to be dealt with by social action, and the fact was driven home in 1906 when, private charity proving inadequate, government money was made available for distribution. Long himself claimed that the Act had been devised to remedy the 'national crime' by which men genuinely lacking work were left with no help except the poor law, but Lloyd George rightly saw that Long was building better than he knew: 'the Tories don't realise what they have let themselves in for', he wrote to his brother William.[4] What they had let themselves in for, of course, was not merely the unemployment insurance of 1911, to which the workman had to contribute, but the whole conception of social action against low standards of living, which led by way of 'the dole' in the 20s and Unemployment Assistance in the 30s to the reforms of 1944-8.

**Old Age Pensions and the 'Deserving Poor'**  It was partly also because of the conception of the 'deserving poor' that old age pensions were introduced in 1908: they were explicitly denied to anyone who had 'habitually failed to work' or to provide for the future through a friendly society or similar organisation. Not until 1919, when an Amending Act was passed, was this limitation removed and the idea fully banished that there was a moral issue at stake, that some of those in need of help were morally better entitled to it on grounds of past work and thrift than others. Walter Long in his work for the unemployed had spoken of his concern for 'respectable men'; Gerald Balfour, who succeeded him at the Local Government Board for a few months in 1905 before the Conservative Government fell, of the 'élite of the unemployed'.[5] In the case of the elderly it was realised that many who had sought to make provision for old age had been unable to do so. What was not realised was that the whole notion of the 'deserving' was rather a projection of nineteenth-century ideas on the morality of work and thrift than a reflection of the facts. The idea that unemployment was beyond the control of any individual, however moral, was beginning to creep in, and was to be given forceful presentation by William Beveridge in the first of his famous and influential writings, the *Unemployment: A Problem of Industry* of 1909. The idea that it might not after all be possible for everyone unaided to provide for the other vicissitudes of life, including the ills incidental to old age, was also becoming accepted.

**'Social Pity' and the Working Classes**   The fundamental error of the pre-1914 period lay in its failure to take working-class opinion into its confidence, a failure that had been deplored by Alfred Marshall as long ago as the early 90s.[6] Lloyd George's coming into office coincided with a growing social unease, in-inspired in part by the reports of social investigations and of such official bodies as the 1904 Committee on Physical Deterioration, and in part by an increasing awareness of the incidence of unemployment, which had grown rapidly after the war boom of 1899–1902. Lloyd George felt himself, as he put it in 1911, 'carried forward on a tide of social pity that was only waiting for a chance of expression'.[7] No Minister before had had even his limited experience of working-class life, but there was a general desire to do something about the economic conditions of the working classes, even as earlier their living and working conditions had been improved. What the recipients of this interest really thought of it, and what they really wanted for themselves, few troubled to enquire, except to hope that socialist agitation might be checked by timely reforms. Working men had been largely enfranchised in the towns since 1867, and in the rural areas since 1884, while many of them had become members of the new local government bodies set up in the counties and county boroughs in 1889, in urban and rural districts in 1895 and in London in 1900. The Labour Representation Committee, out of which the Parliamentary Labour Party was to develop, was formed under Keir Hardie's lead in 1900, and was to return twenty-nine M.P.s to Westminster in 1906, but except through the sympathetic interest of Liberals in social problems the working classes had singularly little influence on legislation. Something was done by them, as in Poplar, where George Lansbury was a councillor and a member of the local Board of Guardians, to temper the austerities of the poor law, and Lansbury himself was appointed a member of the Royal Commission on the Poor Law, for which, naturally, he signed the Minority, not the Majority, Report. But no real effort was made to take working men into confidence and to discover their views and reactions. Thus, *The Times* could confidently assert in 1901 that rate-aided school meals would tempt parents to starve their children at home, and it needed the Report on Physical Deterioration of 1904 to swing opinion in favour of the measure.[8]

**Labour and the Welfare State**    National government, in fact, was still a matter for the governing classes; the welfare services were provided *for* the people, not by them. Labour Councillors gradually took their share of local government, Labour Ministers held office during the First World War and there was even a precariously balanced first Labour Government in 1924. But not until 1929 was Labour actually in power, though it was soon to be swept away in 1931 by the economic storms that tossed whole regions of the world into strange, and in some cases terrible, ways. Not until 1945 did a Labour Government have scope for putting its ideas into practice, and by then many of the ideas of earlier days had been so much discussed as to be commonplace. Considering that nationalisation of the railways had been urged by Winston Churchill as Liberal policy in 1906[9] and that of the mines recommended by the Sankey commission of 1919, there was little that was revolutionary in the carrying of these two measures, and it is significant that they have been acquiesced in by the whole nation—too readily acquiesced in, perhaps, in view of the many problems of the efficient conduct of State enterprise that had to be solved. The greatest achievement of the 1945–51 Government lay less in its samples of nationalisation than in the firm rounding-off of half a century's constructive work of welfare, and the final shaping of the Welfare State on the lines first laid early in the century on the basis of nineteenth-century experience and investigation.

It would be too much, of course, to suggest that there were no changes of substance, no policies that went beyond mere logical development. The means test based on the household, so bitterly associated with the unemployment assistance of the 30s, had already been largely abolished in 1940, under Labour influence, but there were the last vestiges of the shame and taint of the poor law to remove. The Labour Government of 1945 was, in any case, as determined to use the financial resources of society to prevent any recurrence of the distress of the years between the wars as it was to control the physical resources of the country for the general well-being: hence, for instance, the nationalisation of the Bank of England and the maintenance of wartime controls, which prevented a recurrence of the disastrous economic collapse that followed the return to 'normality' after 1919. The Government was sustained, too, by a crusading zeal that was the legacy not only of the war but of the unhappy memories of the inter-war years. Yet so much of what came to be done had been anticipated in the National Health, Social Insurance and Employment Policy White Papers of 1944, drawn up by the Coalition Government in which Labour Ministers shared; anticipated too, and more dramatically, in the Beveridge Report of 1942, the reception of which, as a vision of better things in the midst of a holocaust, was an indication of what the majority of British people felt. What the Labour Government manifestly did do was to ensure that the wartime plans were put into effect with amendments and improvements, but with none of the qualifications about 'attractive schemes which turn out to be economically impossible' (to quote a 1942 memorandum of Winston Churchill) which might otherwise have been introduced, and with the minimum relaxation of the controls necessary for the orderly return to peacetime conditions. Stafford Cripps made the first 'bonfire of controls' in 1948, but it was the Conservatives, with their greater interest in 'free enterprise', who after their victory in 1951 began a more thorough easing of the system, though even then, with the need for full employment still accepted as paramount, the economy did not cease to be a 'managed' one to an extent unthinkable before 1940, when the two political parties had united for the preservation and reconstruction of the country. As Beveridge insisted, 'Social Security is not a political question at all. It is neither Socialist nor Capitalist. It is simply common sense.'[10]

The 'National Minimum'   Beveridge's basic aim in 1942 was 'the minimum income needed for subsistence', to be guaranteed by the State through insurance whenever the individual's earnings were interrupted or were inadequate for his family responsibilities. This aim was based on the investigations into the conditions and causes of poverty which had been made between the wars: it was, in fact, in the words of the White Paper on Provision for Old Age of 1958, 'a projection of the state of the nation as it was before the war'. Yet it looked back to Seebohm Rowntree's original investigations into conditions in York in 1899 and to Charles Booth's even earlier ones in London. It looked back also to Beveridge's own experiences before the first war and to his association, as one of their bright young men, with the Webbs and their gospel of a 'national minimum of civilised life'. It looked back no less, though somewhat ironically in view of the reserve accorded to the Beveridge Report in some official circles in 1942, to the appeal made by Winston Churchill as a junior minister in 1906 for 'a line below which we will not allow persons to live and labour'.[11]

This line has not, however, been drawn since 1944 in the sense in which Beveridge spoke of a minimum of *subsistence*. A line of sorts has been drawn, which varies from service to service, but the principle of a subsistence level, however defined, has never been explicitly accepted, and with the steady increase in the cost of living has fallen further and further behind what has in practice been provided. A minimum of economic security is guaranteed by unemployment and sickness insurance, by family allowances and by retirement pensions, as old age pensions are now called, but it has not at any time been adequate, without other resources, for subsistence. For the many without other resources National Assistance (since 1966, Supplementary Benefits), once thought a passing need or one for use only in emergency, has remained an essential, if barely adequate, support. In other respects, of course, something more than a minimum is provided. Thus, the health and education services, though still far from developed to the full standard of which they are capable, are of considerably more than minimal value. Somewhere in between come such services as housing.

Certain of the services are based on insurance, which for the lower wage-earner at least are a form of regressive taxation which has borne heavily upon him. Insurance has the advantage of guaranteeing benefits as of right and without the interposition of a means test, and since 1959 graduated contributions, pensions and benefits have been introduced to bring the traditional flat-rate payments to some extent into line with changed economic conditions. Other services, however —the medical services, family allowances and national assistance—draw upon national taxation, and are therefore truly a social service with an element of transfer of wealth.

**The Emergence of the Welfare State**    What all that has been so far achieved amounts to can hardly be expressed in any phrase more explicit or descriptive than 'the Welfare State'. It is, for instance, certainly not Socialism. Equally it is hardly a system that can have been foreseen, except in particular details: the *ad hoc* nature of much of the legislation and administration, the long delays in the remedying of recognised deficiencies while political conditions worked themselves out, the gaps still existing, the lack of a coherent and unifying plan, all reveal the typical empirical approach of the English. In certain direction, notably in retirement pensions, health services and education, the deficiencies are still considerable. On the other hand, the unexpected conditions of an exceptionally high level of employment since 1945 have protected the welfare services from the stresses that were most to be feared and which might yet expose other serious inadequacies.

Nevertheless, by one means or another the welfare of all is to a considerable extent ensured by legislation and the mobilisation of society's resources. The picture is a somewhat confused one, but a working pattern of some kind has emerged. The White Paper of 1944, to which passing reference has already been made, described social insurance, in a miracle of understatement, as 'essentially a mosaic of detail'. This has since been more vigorously expressed as 'a hotchpotch of administrative units, a tangle of legislative complexity and a jungle of vested interests'.[12] It would seem in fact that the welfare system resembles only too faithfully the political system which brought it into being. It has grown awkwardly and irregularly and in response to varied needs and pressures: it is still far from complete and it is still growing. Indeed, as this book originally took shape a new National Insurance Bill was passing through Parliament, and on the very day on which these lines were written a change in National Assistance was announced to avoid any suggestion that applicants should come, as in the bad old days of the poor law, 'cap in hand'.[13] The change might be regarded as reflecting the last dying flicker of the poor law and the means test, and as symbolising the approach that has characterised the welfare services since 1944 as the social rights of citizens in contrast to the alms and doles of earlier periods.

It is of the essence of the English parliamentary system that while forms are preserved the spirit and aims can change almost without limit. The forms were devised over a long period of aristocratic rule, when there were at least the 'two nations' of Disraeli's famous phrase, and when the majority were 'people', not citizens. These very forms, however, proved themselves capable, if at first slowly and hesitantly, of providing the means for the increasing association of the people with the government as citizens, and for the improvement of their conditions. In the process social as well as political attitudes have almost imperceptibly been modified out of recognition. The degradation of the poor law, for instance, which was at one time as strongly expressed on one side as felt on the other, has been transformed into a concern lest anyone should fear to lose his self-respect 'by exercising the rights which a Christian and civilised society gives of ensuring that no one should fall below the levels that Parliament has laid down'.[14] Years later, the point has still to be made: from its inception in 1966 the Ministry of Social Security has stressed that the supplementary benefits which have succeeded National Assistance are a *'right'*, and has appealed to people to claim them.[15]

The significant word here is 'right': there is no privilege to be abused or withheld on grounds of morality or petty tyranny. Democracy has been established and a revolution, albeit a silent one, achieved. During the nineteenth century the power of the State was feared and interference with economic processes regarded, in a doctrinaire spirit though with some historical warrant, as not merely dangerous but futile. As late as 1894 the Royal Commission on Labour could hold that 'many of the evils to which our attention has been called are such as cannot be remedied by any legislation, but we may look forward with confidence to their gradual amendment by natural forces'.[16] Yet there was in practice, and to an increasing extent, a good deal of State intervention the full implications of which, in the face of the prevailing dogma of individualism, were hardly grasped. The past hundred years, and especially the past fifty, have shown that, given the resources and the detailed information that earlier governments could never have acquired, the power of the State can be used to enlarge freedom, nay, that it is even a condition of freedom. The position has been neatly expressed by Morris Ginsberg: 'There is now general agreement that there is much that the State can do which is not only consistent with liberty but essential to it. The limits are practical. They turn upon such questions as what sort of things *can* be achieved by the use of legal sanctions and cannot be achieved without them, what can best be done by individuals . . . and what things of importance would remain undone, if the State did not do them.'[17] This conception of the relationship between individual liberty and collective responsibility was beginning to be realised by practical experience and in practical terms in the early years of the present century. Hence such preliminary measures as the Unemployed Workmen Act and the sequence of Liberal legislation that followed. The over-idealised individual idealism of the nineteeenth century, already wearing thin, was gradually replaced by a modest collectivism. Speaking at Swansea in 1908 Lloyd George said: 'The day will come that this country will shudder at its toleration of that state of things when it was rolling in wealth . . . in so far as poverty is due to conditions over which the man has no control, then the State should step in to the very utmost limit of its resources.'[18]

Winston Churchill, hardly even a moderate collectivist, echoed these sentiments at Birmingham in the following year: 'There is no country where the organisation of industrial conditions more urgently demands attention. Wherever the reformer casts his eye he is confronted with a mass of largely preventable and even curable suffering.'[19]

Discussing the 'People's Budget' at Leicester in the same year Churchill justi- fied the policy of the Liberal Government as 'the first conscious attempt on the part of the State to build up a better and a more scientific organisation of society for the workers of this country'.[20] It was a high claim, but not unjustified, and although much remained to be done it was perhaps the first step that counted. But it must be emphasised that it was a step taken for practical reasons, on the basis of practical knowledge, and so it has continued. There is little evidence, at any stage in the evolution of the Welfare State, of the direct influence of a political philosophy setting out to remake society. If there has been anything of a revolu- tion, in thought or practice, it has been, as Beveridge suggested in his 1942 report, a characteristically British one, 'a natural development from the past'.[21]

**Poverty and Plenty**    What had become clear when the first remedies were being applied to the problems of society in the early years of the present century was the startling antithesis between great wealth and great  poverty, between the resources that industry and commerce had brought to Britain and the standard of living of a great part of its people. Something had to be done to mobilise social resources for social improvements, and not merely through private charity, long since shown to be inadequate in scale and indiscriminate in effects. Those who were troubled by the power that collectivism was putting into the hands of the State were soon to have their understanding enlarged by the unprecedented mobilisation of national resources for a war of national survival. Looking back with hindsight, we can say that after 1918, although the issue was still hotly debated, it was not really possible to claim that the nation's resources, adequately deployed, were not equal to its needs, social as well as political. Hence the revo- lution in economic thought associated with the name of J. M. Keynes, though the still greater strain of the Second World War was needed to clinch the argu- ment.

**The Final Lessons**    The conditions of millions of unemployed in the 20s and, even more, in the 30s was wretched enough, especially in the unhappily-styled 'depressed areas'. Yet, although the machinery for assistance was still inadequate, it did exist, even if still too much dominated by lingering 'poor law' concepts and still receiving too small a share of the national resources. There was also a slow but significant education of opinion, to which many influences and individuals contributed, not least the Labour Party, which alone had a consistent, if not necessarily altogether relevant, body of doctrine to support a case for change. From 1939, under the combined shock of total war, of the revelations of evacuation and of the impartially distributed sufferings of bombardment, which spared no classes, this process of education was sharply speeded up. Not only the disquieting condition of evacuated mothers and children, but the unexpected revelation of proudly-concealed poverty among old people, what *The Times* in 1940 called 'the remarkable discovery of secret need',[22] stirred public feeling. It was suddenly realised that what had hitherto been done was still far from enough. Already by 1942, when the Beveridge Report appeared, a change so radical had taken place as almost to connote a new approach. 'Dunkirk, and all that the name evokes', it has well been said, 'was an important event in the war-time history of the social services.'[23] Again, it was the practical challenge that brought the response, this time a response that was to be both enduring and more nearly adequate. It was Lloyd George's 'social pity', carried forward to new heights by disturbing revelations of need, and by a sense of national unity, of '*one nation*', such as had never before been experienced.

**What, then, is the Welfare State?**   If, then, we seek to understand the Welfare State, we had best take it for what it is, the sum of efforts over many years to remedy the practical social difficulties and evils of a modern system of economic organisation which grew with but little regard for the majority of those who became involved in it, and which, indeed, insisted, as in the poor-law system of 1834, that developments must be left to take their course. The origins of many of the social problems which have had to be tackled are to be found in the conditions under which modern industry arose. To that extent the Welfare State is the practical British answer to the practical problems of industrial development and mass society which, though Britain was the pioneer, every people in the world now has to face. The very conditions of industry, its massing of people and its creation of wealth and power, brought problems with which the world was not familiar on such a scale, though at the same time they provided the means for their own remedying. Less complex societies have always had to endure poverty, and plenty has been scarce enough throughout the course of history. It was industrial development that produced the paradox of poverty in the midst of plenty.

**Sixteenth-century Origins**   In England, industrial civilisation as it developed had at its command a political machine of great adaptability and a system of relief for poverty which, inadequate though it was, was unique of its kind. Both had their origin in the sixteenth century. To the last years of Elizabeth I can be traced the beginnings of the issue of responsible government over which the Civil War was fought, and which was to be decisive for the future political development of the country, though the issue was already implicit in the situation created by

Henry VIII. To her last years also, though, again, there were precedents from her father's time, can be traced the origins of National Assistance in the great Poor Law Acts passed as the result of a long period of unemployment and scarcity in 1598 and 1601. In the sixteenth as in the twentieth century depression and poverty, different though their origins were over the centuries, challenged Englishmen to find an enduring remedy. It is no accident of history that part at least of the last Poor Law Act passed in this country, the Act of 1930, presented by a Labour Government, was word for word at one with the Elizabethan statutes. In the final Report of the Royal Commission on Unemployment Insurance of 1932, which preceded the Unemployment Assistance out of which National Assistance was to grow, appears the significant comment that, for all the variety of the arrangements made since 1601, 'the broad effect of subsequent statutory enactments . . . has been rather to refashion the administrative machinery for carrying out the duties laid down in the Elizabethan Statute than to amend the purposes or scope of Poor Law assistance'.[24]

The story of the Welfare State is the story of the carrying-out of those duties, and of their enlargement and modification under the stresses of conditions unimaginable to the Elizabethan legislators, until the final abolition of the whole conception of a poor law in 1948, and the erection of a new system of social responsibility that was still not without its obligations to the aims and ideals of the Englishmen of an earlier Elizabethan age.

**Origins of the Name**    A word finally on the phrase, the Welfare State. Its origin is uncertain, though Welfare Services and Agencies were so called in the early years of the present century, when the People's Budget of 1909 in Britain was styled the 'Welfare Budget' and the Germans were applying the term *Wohlfahrtstaat* to the system of social insurance inaugurated by Bismarck in the 1880s. It was not until the late 1930s, however, that the growing concern of democratic governments with the welfare of their citizens under the strain of economic depression caused the term *Welfare State* to be coined, probably by the internationally known Oxford scholar Alfred Zimmern, who used it to point the contrast with the Power State of the Fascist dictators.[25] The term is first found in print, in this sense, in Archbishop William Temple's book of 1941, *Citizen and Churchman*, and was soon to be given a wider connotation and circulation in Britain by the Beveridge Report of 1942, though objected to by Beveridge himself and other purists, who preferred the idea of a *Social-Service State*. From Britain it penetrated to the United States, where it first attained prominence in 1949,[26] and soon came to be used principally in a pejorative sense by critics of the Fair Deal who were in fact still haunting the political battlefields of the 1930s. Though not perhaps in general public use, as a term denoting the aims and methods of modern democratic government, it would seem, for all its imperfections, to have become generally accepted, in both countries, and its very acceptance is significant for an understanding of modern conceptions of government and society.[27]

# 2 | Background and Beginnings

**Poor-Law Principles, 1598–1930** The Elizabethan poor-law system was laid down by Elizabeth I's ninth parliament in 1598 and re-enacted by her last parliament in 1601. With various amendments, the most significant of which was the Poor Law Amendment Act of 1834, which set the poor law on its nineteenth-century footing, it remained the law of England until 1948. The National Assistance Act of that year opened with the blunt and challenging statement, 'the existing poor law shall cease to have effect', and thereby brought to an end a system which had endured through 350 years.

How much the fundamental principles of poor relief remained unchanged through this long period can be seen by comparing the text of the Elizabethan statute with that of the last poor law act passed in this country, that of 1930. *The Acte for the Releife of the Poore* of 1598 consolidated and extended laws passed earlier in Elizabeth's reign (and originating in 1536, in her father's reign) for raising local taxes (rates) and appointing in every parish 'overseers of the poor' for the purpose of,

(a) 'setting to work of the children of all such whose parents shall not be thought able to keep and maintain their children', together with 'all such persons, married or unmarried, as, having no means to maintain them, use no ordinary and daily trade of life to get their living by';

(b) providing a convenient stock of materials 'to set the poor on work';

(c) 'the necessary relief of the lame, impotent, old, blind and such other being poor and not able to work';

(d) 'the putting out of children to be apprentices'.

Section 15 of the Poor Law Act of 1930 re-stated these aims for the guidance of the local authorities which, under the Local Government Act of 1929, had superseded the boards of guardians of the 1834 system and the still earlier overseers of the poor. The wording was that of 1598, suitably edited, the local authorities being empowered to,

(a) set to work all such persons, whether married or unmarried, as have no means to maintain themselves, and use no ordinary and daily trade of life to get their living by;

(b) provide such relief as may be necessary for the lame, impotent, old, blind and such other persons as are poor and not able to work;

(c) set to work and put out as apprentices all children whose parents are not, in the opinion of the council, able to keep and maintain their children.

**Breaches in the Poor-Law System**  By 1930 a number of welfare services had been developed, both out of the poor-law system and independently of it. Some of these, notably education and the environmental health services, were already in the hands of the local authorities; others, such as national insurance and old age pensions, which bore directly upon the poor law, were administered by the central government. And already there were breaches in the poor-law system. The Unemployed Workmen Act, or, rather, the decision in 1906 to use public money to implement it, was to some extent the first such breach, since, contrary to the principles of local taxation for the relief of the local unemployed laid down in the Elizabethan statutes, it provided grants from national funds. More important was the decision in 1908 to provide old age pensions. These amounted to little in themselves, being given only to the most needy and limited in amount, but critics rightly saw in them an abrogation of poor-law principles.

National insurance against unemployment and sickness from 1911 was not so much a breach as a side-stepping of the poor law, preventing the insured from being compelled to turn to it. The extension of benefits, in the depression of the 20s, to unemployed whose insurance backing had been exhausted—the 'transitional benefits' which were popularly known as 'the dole'—were, however, yet another breach. These transitional benefits were given statutory recognition by the Unemployment Act of 1934, which set up the Unemployment Assistance Board, and not only were they given in place of poor-law assistance, but they were administered nationally. The reason for taking unemployment assistance out of the hands of the local authorities was the simple one that only a national service could both spread the burden and equalise rates of relief. The areas worst hit by unemployment had under the old arrangements to bear the heaviest financial burden and some of them were thought to be too generous in their aid. The breach in the poor law was nonetheless real, however, for being based on practical and, indeed, on political, considerations.

A still further breach was made in 1940, when 'supplementary pensions' were granted to old age pensioners with inadequate means, who had hitherto had to rely on poor-law relief, on a 'means test' basis, from the local authorities to supplement their meagre pensions. The unexpectedly large number of applications for these 'supplementary pensions' in 1940 was evidence of the dislike of the poor law and the means test among many who were nevertheless in want.

**Family Responsibility and the 'Means Test'**  The 'means test' was a device for enforcing family contributions for the relief of applicants for public assistance, which had been associated with the poor law from its very beginnings, but which received its name, and its notoriety, from its strict use in the 1930s to enforce economy in the granting of assistance to the unemployed.

The Poor Law Act of 1598 had contained the condition that 'the parents or children of every poor and impotent person, being of sufficient ability, shall at their own charges relieve and maintain every such poor person', and the duty was extended to grandparents in 1601. This definition of family responsibility was maintained and even further extended during the centuries, and the Poor Law Act of 1930 re-asserted the long-established liability in explicit terms: 'It shall be the duty of the father, grandfather, mother, grandmother, husband or child of a poor, old, blind, lame or impotent person . . . if possessed of sufficient means, to relieve and maintain that person.'

The Unemployment Act of 1934, in providing for the unemployed who had exhausted their insurance benefits, adapted this family liability to the new problem by assessing available means on a household instead of on a personal basis. A household is an uncertain and variable entity, and the use of it to assess and test means often led to the break-up of families. The procedure was bitterly resented and, when in 1940 a more generous policy was adopted towards old age pensioners, further changes were obviously called for, changes in which we can detect the influence of the Labour Ministers who had been resisting the means test for years and who now formed part of the wartime government under Winston Churchill.

These further changes came in the following year with the Determination of Needs Act of 1941, which explicitly abandoned the household means test, and substituted for it a 'test of personal need'. It directed that in assessing claims for assistance, 'the resources of members of the household, other than the applicant, the husband or wife of the applicant, and any member of the household dependent upon the applicant, shall not be regarded as resources of the household', though it insisted that within certain limits non-dependent members of the household should be obliged to contribute to household expenses.

**The Passing of the Poor Law**    The change of policy was a momentous one: it reversed not only recent policy but some of the very principles of the Elizabethan poor law. In commending the Determination and Assessment of Needs regulations to the House of Commons, Ernest Bevin, as Minister of Labour and National Service, recalled the bitter controversy over the means test, and quoted with approval the comment that the poor law was at last as good as buried: 'the only thing now left of Queen Elizabeth was one toe sticking out of the ground.'[1]

It is, indeed, true that with the test of family means greatly restricted, the unemployed given assistance from central funds and the elderly receiving supplementary pensions, the scope of the poor law had been narrowed almost out of existence. Seven years later, with the National Assistance Act of 1948, it disappeared altogether. The 'existing poor law' being declared abolished, a new statement of legal liability for family maintenance was made, placing it on as reasonable a basis for the twentieth century as the Act of 1598 had done for the sixteenth. It was held that a man was liable for the maintenance of his wife and children, a woman for that of her husband and children: the legal liability of children for their parents was removed. At the same time the National Assistance Act made regulations 'as to the rendering out of moneys provided by Parliament, of assistance to persons in need', and thereby completed the transfer of assistance from a local to a national responsibility. Thus, just 350 years later, was completed the long process that had begun in 1598.

**The Poor Law in History**    The English poor law was unique, especially in the long scope of its operation. It was preserved over the centuries in the first place by the slowness of evolution of English society, with its lack of revolutionary breaks such as marked the history of certain other countries. Yet it owed its preservation also to its flexibility, which made it possible to vary its operation in different periods, and to its firm base in local life, which enabled it to continue whatever the variations in governmental policy and control. It was in fact part of the very basis of the local organisation of society, an accepted part of the system that kept society steady, checking, however ineffectively, the distress that might have led to social upheavals and setting out to enable everyone to do his duty, in the words of the book of common prayer, in that state of life unto which it should please God to call him—which is preceded in the catechism by the significant undertaking 'to learn and labour truly to get mine own living'. It was widely believed in the early nineteenth century that it was the poor law which had seen the country through the struggle with revolutionary France, and after the developments of that century it was held by many as sacred as the constitution: it had done so much, Walter Long claimed in a speech in 1904, with no suspicion of irony, 'to make the British people what they were'.[2]

The poor law was the first of the welfare services and from it much else was to develop during the nineteenth century. Its principles, and their origins in sixteenth-century conditions, therefore call for some examination before we consider their application in the changing conditions of the seventeenth and eighteenth centuries and under the challenge presented by the industrial revolution, out of which the Welfare State has emerged.

**The Basis of the Poor Law**    Assistance to the less fortunate members of society, which, beginning with poor relief, has grown into the vast modern system of the social organisation of welfare, was not, of course, the creation of the sixteenth century. The duty of charity has long been prescribed, and has equally long been associated with concern for the social and political dangers that might arise from distress. Cynics, indeed, have suggested that care for the unfortunate has not infrequently inspired the double hope that while bringing rewards in the next world it might check social disturbances in this. It was, in fact, a combination of compassion and fear of disturbances that brought about the Elizabethan poor-law system, a combination of social amelioration and police deterrence that might be said to be the ultimate basis of the Welfare State.

The prime duty of government, after defence, is the maintenance of order, the 'Queen's Peace' in both Elizabethan ages, without which all else is impossible. But the preservation of the peace quickly goes beyond the mere pursuit and punishment of the disorderly. There is only too much experience in history of the 'restoration of order' which leaves things fundamentally disorderly, and therefore stores up trouble for the future. English experience in the nineteenth as in the sixteenth century showed that, while revolt might be checked by force, by the exercise of the police power of the State, unrest reflected social stresses and injustices that called for attention. Walter Long, justifying the Unemployed Workmen Act to the Royal Commission on the Poor Law in 1907, spoke with feeling, if somewhat ungrammatically, of unemployed 'respectable men', 'who lost all heart and confidence and turned, not I think unnaturally, to the counsel given them by those who wished them to believe that the entire blame for all that was going on was due to the condition of society'.[3] There is reflected here not only a sincere concern for men in difficulties but also something of the alarm which many others felt at the rising tide of socialist agitation.

A similar combination of fear and feeling can be detected in the preamble to the Elizabethan statute of 1598 concerned with rural unemployment, which arose from the same anxious concern with the times that produced the measures for the relief of the poor: 'whereas a good part of the strength of this realm consisteth in the number of good and able subjects . . . and of late years more than in time past there have been sundry towns, parishes and houses of husbandry destroyed and become desolate, wherof a great number of poor people are become wanderers, idle and loose, which is the cause of infinite inconvenience . . . .'[4]

The nineteenth century, like the sixteenth again, was a period of social and economic upheaval, which produced new and unfamiliar problems for governments to deal with according to such lights as they possessed. Walter Long was very far from being a collectivist, but as President of the Local Government Board from 1900 to 1905 he had realised that the established remedies for dealing with poverty were inadequate to help the workman temporarily out of employment through no fault of his own. His policy was to attempt to deal with the effect rather than with the cause, but that was natural enough in his day and age. There was, in any case, little enough knowledge as to the true causes of unemployment, and what there was could hardly have been swallowed by a conservative landowner.

**Economic and Social Stresses in the Sixteenth Century**   So it was with the governing classes of the sixteenth century, landowners in an agricultural and trading community that was already feeling the first slight stresses of industrial development. They were conscious of changes around them, of the pressure of economic forces which they could not comprehend, and of the resulting unsettlement. Much has been written of the enclosure and 'engrossing' (i.e. amalgamating) of arable land for sheep and cattle in the fifteenth and sixteenth centuries occasioned by the demand for meat for a rising population and for the wool on which the great cloth industry of East Anglia and the West Country, and, later, the still greater industry of the North, were to be built. Economic historians have disputed the degree of depopulation that actually took place, and some have played down the bitter complaints voiced by Sir Thomas More early in the sixteenth century, by Bishop Latimer in the middle years and by such men as Sir Robert Cecil and Sir Francis Bacon in the 90s, against the effects of enclosures. True it is that the process was not general and that the worst effects were probably over by the beginning of the century. Nevertheless, the sixteenth century was very conscious of the uprooting from the land of many peasants, who in a largely static society, in which mobility was discouraged, literally had nowhere to turn. The unemployed land worker, the victim of the 'redundancy' of his day, had hardly more chance of recovering his independent status in the sixteenth century than an unemployed workman in a depressed area in the twentieth, and their problems were not dissimilar. Whatever the order of magnitude of the problem, whether few or many were uprooted, the effect on each locality, in a period when society was still organised on narrow and local lines, was serious enough. As R. H. Tawney has pointed out, economic readjustment was difficult in small isolated communities, 'where most men have never seen more than a hundred separate individuals in the course of their whole lives, where most households live by tilling their great-grandfather's fields with their great-grandfather's plough'.[5]

The stresses of agricultural change were intensified by the growth of population, which probably increased by about one-third during Elizabeth I's reign. Neither the land nor the country's nascent industries could cope with such an increase, and by the beginning of the seventeenth century a condition of *relative* over-population must have existed.[6] Many people flocked to the towns, and especially London, which now began its phenomenal expansion, increasing threefold between 1558 and 1625, greatly to the alarm of the government. Futile efforts were indeed made to check urban growth and force people back on the land. To these problems were added the distress caused by the break-up of many traditional feudal households through economic stress, the fluctuations of the growing cloth trade, which affected employment among the workers in wool, and the devaluation of money through the influx of silver from the Spanish Indies, the two last being economic disturbances which contemporaries, with their unsophisticated outlook, could hardly grasp as possibilities, least of all understand. Add to these more modern difficulties the scourge of epidemic disease, particularly in the dense warrens of London, and the constant doubts about the harvest—especially the fear of a succession of bad harvests—which have haunted men from the earliest times, and much of the background of the Elizabethan poor law system is revealed. Economic distress was endemic in the sixteenth century, but it was the triad of wet summers and bad harvests between 1594 and 1597, with food riots in 1596, that brought the poor law in its final form (see note, page 56).

**The Parish and Mobility of Labour**   People evicted from the land, or without work in times of scarcity, naturally turned to begging and to wandering in search of work or alms. Mobility of labour, however, is a modern conception, associated with, and, indeed, arising from, the great movements of people that created the modern centres of population in areas of factory industry. In the sixteenth century, as in earlier periods, everyone had his 'country' to which he was bound by birth. The natural unit and centre was the parish, in which a man was born, christened and married, and in which, for the most part, he died and was buried. It was in the parish that he could look for help in times of need. Did he take to wandering, it was to his parish that he was likely to be returned, especially if in need. The first check on mobility, in fact, was the police power which kept a man literally in his place. This had long existed by common custom and was first given statutory form by an Act of 1572, principally aimed at the removal of paupers who had flocked into towns. The later Act which finally established the 'Law of Settlement' for all parishes was passed in 1662, in the early years of Charles II's restoration.

**'In Terror of the Tramp'**   Wanderers were feared in the sixteenth century as likely to be thieves and rogues, and if in any number to cause more serious trouble, perhaps even political disturbances. At a time when the only police authority was the parish constable, who, as Shakespeare caricatured him in *Much Ado*, might be good for nothing but a laugh, when there were no regular troops and the nearest civil power might be such men as the local Justices of the Peace could bring together, mobility of labour was to be feared rather than encouraged. As Tawney has said, the sixteenth century lived in terror of the tramp.[7]

**The 'Rogues and Poor'**   Hence the succession of statutes against vagabonds passed since the 'Black Death' as long ago as 1348–9 had raised in an acute form the problem of keeping an adequate labour force on the land. Encouragement was given to the provision of alms for those unable to work, but what were later to be called the 'able-bodied poor' were to be compelled to work, if necessary by whipping and even sterner measures. The sixteenth century was well advanced before it was realised, as modern industrial society later came to realise at the end of the nineteenth century, that there were men 'genuinely seeking work' (to use the twentieth-century phrase) who yet could not find it.

Still more, lives were narrow and consumer goods scarce: there was little enough incentive to steady work. The parliamentary leaders who framed the poor law, notably such men as Sir Robert Cecil and Sir Francis Bacon, realised that the fault lay partly in economic conditions, though they hit on what were probably the least significant, if the most obvious—the enclosures for sheep-farming. Hence the attack on enclosures, which caused one M.P., the noted Puritan, Sir Francis Hastings, to exclaim impatiently in 1597 that more attention was being paid to them than to the 'rogues and poor'.[8] It was easier to lay the blame on the workless themselves as 'rogues and poor', even as in the nineteenth century there was a tendency to ascribe their condition to their own idleness, improvidence and drunken habits. Yet as Cecil himself pointed out in the Parliament of 1601, what were the dispossessed men to do? If they crowded into towns they could be turned out, and if they wandered abroad 'they are within the danger of the Statute of the Poor to be whipt'.[9]

'Setting the Poor on Work' The remedy was to find them work. In 1576 an Act was passed 'for setting the poor on work and for avoiding of idleness': from then until the twentieth century efforts were made to find work which might usefully, and even profitably, be done. Hence the 'workhouse', though the name did not become common until later. The 1576 Act also prescribed 'houses of correction' for rogues and idlers. Such a house had first been established by the corporation of London in 1555, at the old royal palace of Bridewell, a name which was therefore to pass into popular speech. Already 'abiding places' for the poor, the charitable 'hospitals' of earlier periods, were being provided for the impotent who for one reason or another could not earn their living, and these were made obligatory by the Act of 1598. Thus, provision was made for the three classes of the poor, for the impotent in 'abiding places', later to be known as poorhouses, for the able-bodied unemployed, as we should call them, by work at home or, later, in workhouses, and for the unregenerate idlers in houses of correction. Technically, the three classes and methods of provision were distinct, and much emphasis was to be placed by later reformers upon the need for distinction and 'classification'. In practice, however, the three were to be confused, to a large extent because it was obviously simpler, however undesirable, to treat all three under the one head and roof. By the nineteenth century, indeed, the workhouse, poorhouse and house of correction had in practice become one. The punitive spirit triumphed, as we shall see, so that, as the name of 'Bridewell' had come to bear a hateful connotation for many, the prison-like workhouses of the period after 1834 came to be characterised, most significantly, as *Bastilles*.

Long before this, however, it had become apparent that the attempt to provide work had failed. The Act of 1576 directed that a store of materials should be provided on which the poor might work. This was re-enacted in 1598 and was continued, with varying degrees of seriousness but with consistently little success, until the early years of the nineteenth century. It was soon discovered that such work as was done cost considerably more than if done in a more normal manner, and brought little return to pay for the maintenance of the poor workers, while if it had been productive it would have competed with ordinary labour. On this last point Daniel Defoe wrote in 1704 his influential pamphlet, *Giving Alms no Charity and employing the poor a grievance to the Nation*: 'to set poor people at work on the same thing that other poor people were employed on before, and at the same time not increase the consumption, is giving to one what you take from another.'

The 1834 report on the poor law was equally scathing on the cost and quality of the work done: 'The superintendent of pauper labourers has to ascertain, not what is an average day's work, or what is the market price of a given service, but what is a fair day's work for a given individual, his strength and habits considered; at what rate of pay for that work, the number of his family considered, he would be able to earn the sum necessary for his and their subsistence; and lastly, whether he has in fact performed the amount which . . . it appears that he ought to have performed. It will easily be anticipated that this superintendence is very rarely given; and that . . . in fact no work is done.'[10]

In fact, it did become easier to require no work. Where it was required it was only too often stone-breaking, oakum-picking and similar tasks, which were easily found, of limited value and not in competition with normal labour. From this, under the conditions of the 'reformed' poor law of 1834, with its emphasis on deterrence, were derived the degrading stone-yards which by the twentieth century were all that was left of the Elizabethan intention to 'set the poor on work'.

**The Elizabethan System**    The great advance in policy and practice made by the Elizabethans lay, however, in the acceptance, slowly and seemingly reluctantly, that punitive measures were not enough, that society was compelled to accept, and not only to accept but to enforce, some responsibility for its less fortunate members and for their support. Earlier statutes had enjoined upon all the duty of charity, but by gradual stages in 1572, 1576 and 1598 the Elizabethans, in a spirit of idealism tempered with realism,[11] established for the first time what was intended to be adequate local machinery for the maintenance of the poor.

**Government, Commons and 'Common Weal'**    The debates in the formative parliament of 1597-8 have been vividly preserved for us in the *Journals* collected by the notable seventeenth-century antiquarian Sir Simonds D'Ewes. They are of particular interest for our theme since the important measures that followed were thrashed out in committees of the House of Commons, and reflect a significant advance in the process of the 'winning of the initiative' by the Commons, which was to become, in the following century, the basis of a new and revolutionary conception of responsible government. Concern with social and economic conditions was so widespread, and so much affected the general welfare —in Elizabethan language, the 'common weal'—that the House of Commons was able to take the lead in devising legislation, though the Queen's closest advisers in the House, particularly Sir Robert Cecil, naturally played a leading part in the debates and committees.[12]

Tudor government was paternal and looked to controls and restrictions for preventing distress, to the regulation of wages and conditions of service, the protection of employment, the ensuring of food to the poor in times of scarcity and the prevention of profiteering, with the poor law as the last resort but recognised as increasingly needed. The attitude was generally shared, but there were already in 1598 portents of what was to come in a speech from a Member who wanted economic forces to work themselves out. 'Men are not to be compelled by penalties, but allured by profit',[13] he argued, and the sentiment was to be echoed by Sir Walter Raleigh in the next parliament, in 1601, during a discussion on the encouragement of corn-growing: 'I think the best course is to set it at liberty, and leave every man free, which is the desire of a true English man.'[14] The words have a familiar ring even today. Under Tudor conditions the conception of the common weal determined that there should be some restriction of freedom under the control of the royal government. When that control was broken half a century later, in the Civil War, more was to be heard of the kind of opinion that Raleigh reflected, and the results were to be seen in the working of the poor law, as in so much else.

**The Act of 1598**   The aim of the laws passed by the parliament of 1597–8 was, while punishing vagrancy, first to prevent distress by striking at its causes, in so far as they were understood, and by 'setting the poor on work'; secondly, to relieve distress where it was unavoidable. Enclosures were to be checked, and what were later to be called the 'non-able-bodied poor', who could not work, were to be relieved in 'abiding houses', the children among them being apprenticed so that they could learn a trade and come to support themselves, though in practice this often meant no more than that they were bound to the land as labourers or to householders as domestic servants. The 'able-bodied poor' were to be dealt with in two different ways, as in the legislation of 1576, those willing to work being provided with materials, the others, the idle and vagrant, being punished and sent to houses of correction.

**Local Administration—Justices and Overseers**   For all this, machinery was set up which, with modifications in 1834, was destined to stand the test of time for well over 300 years, until 1929. Attempts had been made since 1536 to raise local funds through local officials for the relief of the local poor, at first by charity and then, from 1572, by levying local taxes (these were, in fact, less taxes than compulsory alms). Now all this was put on a secure basis by requiring that 'overseers of the poor' should be appointed in each parish, under the general direction of the Justices of the Peace, those governmental maids of all work of the Tudors. The overseers were to provide for the poor and to tax the parishioners for the purpose. By a significant addition, which was, however, little used, the Justices, in cases where a parish was unable to raise enough money for the relief of its own poor, could levy taxes to spread the expense over the hundred in which the parish was situated, or even, if necessary, over the county.

This is not the place to consider the evolution and functions of that very English institution, the Justices of the Peace, which by this time had considerable local responsibilities for the maintenance of order and local administration that went far beyond mere police powers. Each measure for the relief of the poor passed since 1572 had looked to the J.P. for its enforcement, and he had numerous other duties affecting the well-being of the poorer classes. In times of shortage he had to secure food for them at reasonable prices, and under the 'Statute of Apprentices' of 1563 he was responsible for the regulation of wage-rates, the honouring of contracts of service and the supervision and enforcement of the apprenticeship system. All this was part of the Elizabethan system for the common weal, which the poor law was intended to supplement: how effectively it was carried out in practice was, of course, another matter.

**Central Control—the Privy Council**   The Justices were at once local leaders and unpaid royal officials. They were constantly reminded of their duties by letters from the Privy Council, were informed of the statutes that they had to enforce and were called upon to make returns of the action taken by them. If the administration of the poor law was to be local, there were the Justices to see that the law was carried out, and the Privy Council to ensure that the Justices did their duty. Without this machinery of enforcement, for all the zeal of parliament, the poor law, even had it been set in motion, could never have been maintained. Without it, what the Webbs, with their enthusiasm for sound administration, scathingly called, in their history of *The Old Poor Law*, 'the somewhat pretentious deliverance of Parliament, in its litter of statutes' of 1597–8, could have little effect. As the earlier attempts at poor relief had shown, fine sentiments and the best of principles were no alternative to firm administration. It was the Queen's Privy Council which attended, under her sharp eye, to the day-to-day business of government. Parliament, however much it might be trying to take the initiative when it did meet, met but rarely and only at the sovereign's orders. Forty years were to pass before, in 1640, a Parliament was able to seize the initiative so firmly as to refuse to recognise the royal power to send it packing when its deliberations gave displeasure.

**The Poor Law Launched**   While Crown and Parliament were at one, however, the poor-law system could operate under good auspices, and it was duly re-enacted in 1601. It was spasmodically enforced in the last years of Elizabeth, under James I and, more consistently and vigorously, during the years after 1629 when Charles I was striving to govern the country firmly and efficiently but without that reliance upon Parliament in the last resort which, though he did not realise it, had been one of the major secrets of Elizabeth's shrewd strength. By that time the poor law was coming to be accepted, albeit reluctantly in view of its cost, as a customary duty, and even without pressure from the centre it continued to be applied during the Civil War and Commonwealth. Whether in this first half-century or so it achieved very much may, however, be doubted. A recent investigation, both of overseers' accounts and of Justices' returns to the Council, made by an American historian, W. K. Jordan, has suggested that, although the poor-rate was increasingly levied, its incidence was slight. There is evidence that it was taken seriously enough by Puritan J.P.s during the Interregnum, and especially during the dearth years of the late 1640s,[15] but in the main until the rapidly changing conditions of the Restoration period it was, in fact, hardly more than the last resort in times of exceptional difficulty.[16]

**Private Charity**    What did much more to relieve poverty in this half-century, indeed, was private charity, and especially bequests, and for these Elizabethan legislation had also made due provision. The Acts of 1572, 1598 and 1601 had all been accompanied by measures encouraging and protecting bequests for a wide variety of charitable purposes, and the codified statute of 1601 has remained the basis of the law of charitable uses. Bequests in large numbers provided for such purposes as direct relief, almshouses, hospitals, workhouses, apprenticeships, loans for the establishment of craftsmen in business, marriage dowries and, most obvious today, in its many survivals, the education which was held to be the best preventive of poverty. From a detailed survey of bequests in about one-third of England from the end of the fifteenth century to the middle of the seventeenth it has been estimated that a total sum of more than three million pounds was left during the period for charitable purposes, nearly half of it between the last years of Elizabeth's reign and the Civil War, while by 1660 the annual income must have been of the order of £127,000.[17]

The visible evidence of this charitable activity is to be seen up and down the country in many colleges, grammar schools and almshouses still deriving income from trusts established more than three centuries ago. About one-third of the trusts surveyed by W. K. Jordan have a continuous history to the present day, their original capital value of some three-quarters of a million pounds having now increased to more than ten millions.[18] Here, rather more than in the levying of rates for poor relief, is to be found the evidence for the early seventeenth century's concern with distress. The provision was unequally spread, and, as in that other great period of charitable giving, the Victorian age, the assumption was too readily made that private charity was able to do most of what was required for all who were deserving of consideration and assistance. Nevertheless, the concern was real, as is clear from the surviving sermons and pamphlet literature of the period, the mute records of what once so greatly agitated men's minds and dominated their thoughts and arguments. The duty of charity, John Donne preached at St. Paul's in 1628, was 'a doctrine obvious to all': the Christian who ignored it was guilty of oppressing the weak and poor.[19] And this was a constant theme with writers and preachers.

**Changing Conditions and Attitudes in the Seventeenth Century**    Yet, with the victory of the Parliamentary forces in the Civil War, and the triumph of the

Puritan spirit which had been striving for nearly a century for the soul of Protestant England, something of a change of attitude gradually took place. The Tudor paternalism and care for the common weal which Charles I, with indifferent skill and still less success, had striven to sustain had passed for ever, and with it had gone the possibility of imposing uniformity by royal authority through the Privy Council. Administrative nihilism was henceforth to be increasingly the rule of social policy,[20] though this did not necessarily always mean local ineffectiveness. Not until the nineteenth century was government to begin to interfere actively again: an age of individualistic freedom, foreshadowed by Raleigh in 1601, was at hand, even though it was not to be fully realised or to receive explicit recognition, at the hands of Adam Smith, for another hundred years.

The change can be illustrated from the fate of the Statute of Apprentices of 1563, with its provision for the fair regulation of wages by the Justices of the Peace. Although it remained on the statute-book until it was repealed by two Acts in 1813 and 1814, as far as wage-regulation was concerned it had largely become a dead-letter by the middle of the eighteenth century. The rising cotton industry, since it had been unknown in Elizabethan times, was not within its jurisdiction, and an Act of 1757 specifically withdrew the woollen industry from its control. This measure, 'almost an economic revolution', as it has justly been called, might be regarded as the beginning of *laissez-faire* in practice.[21] Henceforth, apart from a few last flickers of regulation before 1813, wages were left to the free bargaining of employer and employed. Not until 1909, with the institution of the Trade Boards for 'sweated' labour, did the State again intervene in matters of wages.

The change can also soon be seen in the increasing impatience with the poor as feckless obstacles to the steady progress of economic improvement. By a not insignificant coincidence, within only a few months of the execution of Charles I in 1649 the complaint was being heard that, if the poor were to be provided for, it was to be only in the next world, for Parliament was suspected of planning to make for them 'a Bridewell of this world to serve as a Purgatory to the next'.[22] 'Bridewell', indeed, was the key-word, for it was the blurring in practice of the distinction between the genuinely unemployed and the merely idle, between the workhouse, the poorhouse and the house of correction, that was largely to characterise poor relief during the next two centuries and a half.

**Puritans and *Laissez-faire***  The hardening of attitude was but an aspect of the new spirit of individualism and enterprise which was already active in Elizabethan England, and which the Civil War years had brought to dominance. The leadership of Parliament had already been assured by 1641, as the Restoration of 1660 was to show when it picked up the threads broken by the Civil War in 1642. But the Civil War had justified with success the religious and social doctrines of the Puritans and the strivings of an individualist creed. Central control had been discredited under Charles I and rendered still more unpopular by the rule of Cromwell, the follies of James II and the long shadow of the autocracy of Louis XIV in France. Even without the political revolution, which reached its climax in 1688–9, the steady growth of trade and industry, soon to gather pace, would in any case have placed an unbearable strain on the central control of social and economic conditions. The examples of Spain and France, at this period and later, provided evidence enough of the stifling effect both of centralisation and of despotic rule in times of change and growth. In England there were other, and more constructive, factors at work: new ideas were stirring and new practices taking shape. This is not to say that there was any abrupt break, that the fading away of the 'Tudor Experiment in Government' after 1640 marked a rift in policy or practice. Indeed, recent investigations in the records of particular localities have shown how much of continuity there was, how responsible and effective much local administration remained even without the spur of stimulus from the centre.[23] Yet there was a change, and one that proved significant at a time of new movements in commerce and industry. If Puritanism was overthrown in Church government in 1660, its spirit and influence were to remain: the seventeenth century conflicts left an enduring mark on English history. The notion has been popularised that Puritanism was the midwife of a capitalist economy, that it encouraged self-interest and self-reliance at the expense of social responsibility More recent studies have qualified this interpretation, and have shown that Puritans were as keenly alive to the needs of their fellows, and as paternalistic in their care for them, as their Elizabethan fathers. 'God hath given (riches) to us', wrote a distinguished moderate churchman, Edward Reynolds, towards the end of the Interregnum, 'to do good with . . . for the good of our souls and the comfort of our poor brethren',[24] and this was a constant theme of sermons and homilies. The typical Puritan, in fact, was an honest, conscientious, hard-working, God-fearing, frugal small man, whose principles taught him to do his duty by God and man equally. He loathed on the one side the indulgent slackness of Roman Catholic practice, with its saints' days and unproductive monasteries, and was therefore fearful of High Church tendencies in Anglicanism. At the same time he detested the prodigality of the nobility and gentry of his own country and despised the idle tendencies of so many of the labouring poor. Busy labour, he held, was a protection against sin, and the Reformation was the basis of English enterprise in sea-power and trade.[25] 'If thou be upright and diligent in thy lawful calling', another divine, William Perkins, had written 60 years earlier, 'thou shalt finde sufficient for this life',[26] and a Puritan's 'calling', one commentator has reminded us, 'was not a summons to egotistic activity of any kind; it meant the performance of a man's duties in all his social relations'.[27] Perkins urged that everyone should 'apply himself to the uttermost of his power to do all he can for the good of his country; and he must so deale that he may be helpfull to all with whom hee deales, and hurtfull to none'.[28] A sermon preached before the House of Commons in 1643 similarly held that every man was to 'contribute his abilities of what kind soever to be serviceable to the community'.[29] The Puritan ideal, indeed, was not acquisitiveness, but this calling to work and service, the basis of order and true discipline in society. Work was 'the primary and elemental form of social discipline, the key to order, and the foundation of all further morality'.[30] Hence the denunciation of all idleness and dissipation. Raleigh had argued that 'hunger and poverty make men industrious',[31] a notion that was to die hard, but the Puritan view was rather that it was an inner urge that drove men on, a desire to justify themselves before God and their fellows. This, at a time when England's industrial and commercial resources were undergoing their first development, was of moment for the future. As has well been said, there is the closest connection between the Protestant ideology of hard work and the economic needs of English society.[32] Labour, provided that it was not of a degraded kind, therefore possessed dignity and social value, and the steady pursuit through it of self-advantage would redound to the advantage of all. 'It is an undeniable maxim', ran a pamphlet of 1656, 'that everyone by the light of nature and reason will do that which makes for his greatest advantage. . . . The advancement of private persons will be for the advantage of the public.'[33] More than a century later Adam Smith was to enshrine this conclusion in his famous simile of the 'invisible hand', which leads on the individual who 'intends only his own gain . . . to promote an end which was no part of his intention',[34] an argument which England's successes in war and peace would seem by then amply to have justified. Inevitably, however, there developed an impatience with poverty, a tendency to regard worldly success as a mark of moral worth. 'No question', wrote a Puritan pamphleteer in 1654, 'but (riches) should be the portion rather of the godly than of the wicked . . . for godliness hath the promise of this life as well as of the life to come.'[35]

**Morality and Poverty** From this, again, it was an easy step to the view that there was some moral obloquy attaching not merely to wickedness but to lack of success. To be poor in the sense of having to turn to others for help—that is, to be a 'pauper'—unless one were of the 'impotent poor' who could not work, was to be morally deserving of reproach. To be 'unemployed' (though the word itself did not appear until the nineteenth century) in an expanding economy was evidence of vicious or idle habits or both. Thus, the philosopher John Locke, in a report prepared for the Board of Trade in 1697, ascribed the burden of pauperism to 'the relaxation of discipline and corruption of manners', and proposed the disciplining of the poor by 'the restraint of their debauchery . . . by the suppressing superfluous brandyshops and unnecessary alehouses'.[36] The preoccupation with intemperance was to remain for more than two centuries a constant theme in the moral reprobation of pauperism. It was by no means always unjust, though in an age when gentlemen regularly drank themselves into a stupor few critics took account either of the example set the poor or of the living conditions which spirits alone made endurable to many. The consumption of brandy, as an import and a product of the hated French, was discouraged by excise duties from the end of the seventeenth century (hence the now legendary activities of smugglers), and the local product, gin, was favoured to help the farmers dispose of their wheat. There followed the appalling indulgence in gin in the first half of the eighteenth century, long remembered for the phrase 'drunk for a penny, dead-drunk for twopence', and brutally satirised in Hogarth's engraving *Gin Lane* (1751). The gin traffic seemed to justify Locke's criticism and excited disgust that never quite faded. Agitation, in which Hogarth took part, led in 1751 to a stiff duty which checked consumption and the ravages it caused: 'glorious beer' by comparison, at a time when clean drinking water was hardly to be had in towns, was almost what was later to be called a 'temperance beverage'. Yet until the end of the nineteenth century, as *Punch* cartoons, for instance, show, gin and poverty were to be regarded as inseparables. In truth, indulgence in drink arose as much from the emptiness and frustrations of life as from dissipation, emptiness particularly in pre-industrial conditions, frustration no less from the powerlessness of the worker in the face of industrial development over which he had no control.

Defoe in 1704, in *Giving Alms no Charity*, made more of idleness encouraged by alms than of drunkenness: 'the reason why so many pretend to want work is that they can live so well with the pretence . . . they would be made to leave it and work in earnest.'[37] These were not by any means the only opinions in circulation: indeed, there were many more understanding and more charitable views published. But these opinions represent the prevailing trend, which was powerfully to affect policy not only in the eighteenth century but also in the nineteenth.

**'The Beneficent Wisdom of Providence'**    With this view of poverty, which, except in the case of the impotent, deserved no intervention, went a corresponding resistance to State intervention in economic matters and a keen regard for individual activity. The cloth merchants of 1756, arguing against the Statute of Apprentices, maintained that 'trade is a tender plant that can only be nursed up by liberty',[38] and Adam Smith's 'invisible hand' appeared twenty years later. By the middle of the nineteenth century this notion had been carried to such lengths that, to quote a notable example, Richard Whateley, Archbishop of Dublin, could republish lectures delivered in 1831, when he was Professor of Political Economy at Oxford, in which he dwelt on 'the beneficent wisdom of Providence, in directing towards the public good the conduct of those who, even when not basely selfish, are yet not impelled . . . by patriotic motives'.[39] What had been a conscious service to God and His people had become almost a convenient device for justifying personal aggrandisement under the most exalted auspices.

**Religion and the Rise of Capitalism**    All this was in marked contrast to earlier precepts, though perhaps not always so very far removed from earlier practice. How from the teaching both of the medieval church and of early Puritanism, and from the conception of the common weal, these views developed was shown by R. H. Tawney in a famous study, *Religion and the Rise of Capitalism*. Puritanism was a body of doctrine of stern ideals, but 'the loftiest teaching cannot escape from its own shadow': 'To urge that the Christian life must be lived in a zealous discharge of private duties—how necessary! Yet how readily perverted to the suggestion that there are not vital social obligations beyond and above them. . . . In emphasizing that God's Kingdom is not of this world, Puritanism did not always escape the suggestion that this world is no part of God's Kingdom.'[40] Fortunately, there were other aspects of Puritanism to insist on social obligations, as when a preacher at St. Paul's in 1658 charged his congregation, 'Remember . . . it is your duty to consider the ability which God hath given you, to weigh the necessitous condition of the objects set before you, and accordingly to extend your bounty to the honour of God, the discharge of your consciences, the regaining of your credit and the relief of the needy.'[41] This was Puritan doctrine at its best, and there were other religious doctrines, too, to inspire social responsibility, especially as the consequences of *laissez-faire* later came to be realised. In particular, of course, there were the more radical views about society and property which had been flung up by the heart-searching of the Civil War, and which were never to disappear from English life. They coloured the preaching of the dissenting sects after the Restoration, and were to inspire Methodism in the eighteenth century. From them were to flow much of the charitable impulse on the one side and of the trade-union and friendly-society activity on the other that were to mark the nineteenth century and to restore in time the concept of the common weal.

**The Eighteenth Century**   For a great part of its length, however, the eighteenth century was a period of sterner views. Not until well into the second half of the century did a serious concern with the condition of society begin to emerge, and from that much was to come in the nineteenth century. In part, of course, there was a decline in religious feeling, due to the spread of toleration, which took a good deal of the fire out of intolerance and charitable concern alike. The struggle of Anglicanism and Puritanism in the Civil War, and the triumph, first of Puritanism and then, in the Restoration, of a restored Anglicanism, had shown the need for accommodation. The result was the more easy-going attitude of the eighteenth century, bordering on indifference and disregard. It became all the more easy for the narrower Puritan conceptions of self-interest and superiority over the less fortunate to override social obligations and degenerate into a concern for appearances.[42]

As a result the poor began to be seen as a burden rather than as an object of concern and charity. Hence the strictures of Locke and Defoe, which have already been quoted. At the same time the financial burden of poor relief was beginning to be seriously felt. The dislocations of the Civil War period, the demobilization of soldiers and sailors and economic stresses in the early 1660s re-created the problem of uprooted wanderers which had so much exercised the Elizabethans, and private charity was no longer adequate to the task. If each parish was responsible it was important for it to know for whom it was responsible. By the same token it was anxious to disclaim any responsibility that could not legally be pinned to it. Combined with the sterner view of the poor, this led to harsh and even brutal treatment of helpless and unfortunate people.

**The Act of Settlement, 1662** The responsibilities of parishes were given legal definition by the 'Act for the Better Relief of the Poor' of 1662, better known as the Act of Settlement and Removal, which was to provide 'the pivot around which the administration of poor relief was to swing for nearly two centuries'.[43] The Act made it possible for anyone not possessing property, if he were living outside his own parish and unable to guarantee that he would never become at some time a charge on the parish in which he actually resided, to be removed to his native parish, the parish in which he had a 'settlement' and which was legally obliged to provide relief for him in case of need.

**Settlements and Removals** 'Settlements' were gained in various ways, by birth, marriage or apprenticeship, or by living within the parish for a certain period as an accepted parishioner (a condition difficult of achievement), or by being engaged for employment for a complete year (a condition usually evaded by giving employment for a slightly shorter period). The conditions were complicated, and were rendered more so, as time went on, by new Acts and by judicial interpretation of disputed cases. Adam Smith, in one of his few references to the poor law, complained that 'it is often more difficult for a poor man to pass the artificial boundary of a parish, than an arm of the sea or a ridge of high mountains',[44] and to Thomas Malthus, writing in 1798, 'the whole business of settlements is utterly contradictory to all ideas of freedom . . . a most disgraceful and disgusting tyranny'.[45] Not until 1795 was the reasonable limitation enacted that only those actually in need of poor relief should be removed, though even then unmarried mothers as well as rogues and vagabonds were excluded. In practice it had not often happened that an able-bodied man in good health was removed, unless he had a large family. Moreover, by long custom, embodied in an Act of 1697, it was possible for a man to leave his parish with a certificate testifying to his 'settlement' and thereby insuring any place to which he might move against his becoming 'chargeable'. The practice even grew up in such cases, if relief did become necessary, of sending it to the individual from his parish of settlement, thereby avoiding the expense of removal.

But for these loopholes the new industrial centres could hardly have developed as they did. Nevertheless, as long as the parish was the unit of responsibility, some definition of its duties had to exist. In 1846 the Poor Removal Act, passed to help to reconcile landowners and farmers to the repeal of the corn laws, set a limit of five years to the period in which a pauper, living where he had no legal settlement, could be removed back to his parish of settlement: this measure greatly encouraged the drift from the countryside to the industrial centres. Not until 1865, however, was the responsibility of the individual parish extended to the Unions of parishes set up in 1834, though at the same time the period of removability was limited to one year. This still left the Union of settlement unlimited responsibility for the cost of relief, even if a pauper could not be returned to it, but in 1876 this difficulty was eased by a further Act which made it possible to gain a new settlement after only three years' residence. Removals declined, but in the early years of the twentieth century, as the Poor Law Commission showed in 1909, they were still being made at the rate of some 12,000 a year.[46] They later declined further, but the Poor Law Act of 1930 still included legal provision for settlement and removal, though within the larger areas of the local authorities, and it was not until the country at large legally and finally became the area of responsibility, with the disappearance of the poor law in 1948, that the ideas underlying the Act of 1662 ceased to apply.

Meanwhile, especially in the eighteenth century, the settlement laws fell most heavily upon those least able to bear them, the old, the sick, the large family or the unmarried mother-to-be, who was often hurried out of a parish in the last stages of pregnancy lest her bastard child gain a settlement by birth. The parish records that have come down to us show how large a part the investigation of settlements played in local affairs, and how often, for instance, they involved forced marriages,[47] while the Webbs have described the incidence of removals, the 'mournful and onerous "general post" of indigent folk, men, women and children, in all states of health and disease, perpetually criss-crossing the kingdom under expensive escort',[48] though they probably overstated the position.

**Saving the Rates**    The worst feature of the application of the laws, even if an understandable one, was the anxiety in parishes to keep down the rates, an anxiety which gave an edge to the prevailing contempt for the poor. 'The whole history of the administration of poor relief', it has been said, 'is the history of a long struggle between the moral and financial responsibility for the Poor . . . a struggle in which the desire to keep the rates low was the victor.'[49] Here is one of the enduring themes of parochial poor-law history, and, indeed, of the local government history which succeeded it. There is only too much evidence in the eighteenth century of the discouragement of marriage among poor parishioners lest their children, born with a settlement, should become a charge: this inevitably had a deplorable effect on moral standards and led to innumerable illegitimate births. Equally serious was the opposition to cottage building and the frequent demolition of cottages to reduce the number of poorer folk who might gain a settlement by residence: some of the housing difficulties of the nineteenth century were later to be ascribed to this policy. At times, however, the anxiety to save the rates could even attain, however logically, the depths of the ludicrous. A case is recorded in which it was solemnly argued before the Justices which of two parishes was liable for a pauper whose house, and even whose bed, stood on the actual parish boundary—the decision being that the settlement went with the man's head as he lay in bed![50]

**The Standards of the Age**  For cases such as these the Act of Settlement was responsible, even though it had given logical definition to long-existing practice. It is, of course, important not to seek in an earlier period the ideals and standards of a later age. The treatment of the dependants and misfits of society, and of those unable to help themselves, was still harsh, or, at best, careless, enough in the eighteenth century. Criminals, prisoners for debt, the mentally ill, children and even animals were treated in a manner that shocks later generations. Where harshness might be lacking, as in the treatment of many of the poor and sick, carelessness, indifference, faulty understanding, or even slack administration, did much harm. The unfortunate George III, in his bouts of mental illness, now shown to be probably the result of a physical malady, porphyria,[51] presumably had the best attention that the age could offer, but the treatment he endured was appallingly crude by later standards. Even worse was the treatment of the mentally-ill in Bedlam (the old Bethlehem Hospital), where they were regarded as a public show.

**The New Humanitarianism**  Fielding's novels and Hogarth's engravings give us a vivid picture, touched by humanity, of social conditions in the middle years of the eighteenth century. These two were among the pioneers of the new humanitarianism that was to colour the later years of the century and to inspire reform in the nineteenth century. To Dr. Johnson, himself a humane man with a deep interest in social problems, 'a decent concern for the poor is the true test of civilization', and there were not lacking individuals to carry on the charitable enterprise of earlier periods. Fielding himself and his brother John did notable social work as magistrates in Westminster, Hogarth joined with Handel in supporting Captain Coram's famous "Foundling Hospital" for abandoned babies, Jonas Hanway (the pioneer of the umbrella) strove for years to improve the conditions in which pauper children were brought up, and John Howard led the movement for prison reform which has left us his name in the 'Howard Reform League', while throughout the country new hospitals, some 40 in all, including in London Guy's and St. George's, were built by endowment or private subscription.

**Child Labour**  Yet the endeavours of these pioneers served but to mitigate the dreary round of social problems: solid reform was to come only later. Much was accepted as normal and natural that later periods disavowed. Defoe, for instance, in his travels throughout the country in the 1720s was touched with enthusiasm at seeing quite small children earning their living by working at home, and it is clear from many accounts that children's wages were essential, as they had long been and were long to continue to be, in very many homes. It is a mistake to

imagine that the lot of children of working-class parents, as revealed by the investigations into factory conditions in the 1840s, was necessarily any less happy, or
their work any harder, than in the eighteenth century. What the factories did was
to concentrate the conditions and thus expose them, and that to a generation
more alive to social problems. Adequate wages, family allowances, an extensive
system of national education and a change in the attitude to children were needed
before the nation could insist that all its children should be allowed to develop
their powers in the common interest, and these have been finally achieved only in
our own day. Apart from limitations on work in industry from 1833 and compulsory education from 1870, indeed, the first intervention by the State between
parent and child, outside the poor law, came only in the last decade of the nineteenth century, with the Custody of Children Act of 1891. The view of children as
an investment gradually faded but survived well into the twentieth century.

**Wage Standards**   For the most part, whether children were earning or not,
low wages were gradually regarded in the eighteenth century as advantageous.
Life was so narrow for many workers that in good times, as many contemporary
observers complained, the tendency was to take any margin in leisure rather
than in cash. Hence the appeal for the early industrial workers, before the stern
discipline of the modern large-scale factory was imposed, of 'St Monday', by
which the week-end was extended and some spice of excitement added to life.[52]
This did but confirm the common view that the poor were idle and would be more
so if they could: as Arthur Young wrote in 1771, in a well-known passage in his
*Tours*, 'everyone but an idiot knows that the lower classes must be kept poor, or
they will never be industrious'. A few years later George Crabbe, the Suffolk
poet, in *The Village* (1783) wrote feelingly of heartless employers of an old
labourer, who,

> . . . *when his age attempts its task in vain,*
> *With ruthless taunts, of lazy poor complain.*

It was a common, indeed a general, complaint, and in the circumstances of the
age not without warrant. Yet there were those who saw further, and even argued,
as did Adam Smith, for instance, for the incentive of higher earnings.[53] In truth,
the prevailing attitude, while based on the common human failing of scorn for
those of apparently inferior status, also reflected demographic conditions that
were passing. The first half of the eighteenth century had been in the main a
period of labour shortage. Only in the second half did the population begin to
expand and the labour force to increase, while at the very same time the introduction of machinery was raising industrial output. It was no longer so necessary,
therefore, to bear hard upon the poor to make them industrious. There were also
movements of thought and opinion to strengthen humanitarian impulses, but
they had their setting in these more favourable demographic and economic conditions and thereby became the more effective.[54] Even Young was to modify his

views to some extent,[55] though he in his brusque impatience and Crabbe with his human sympathy represented a dichotomy of opinion that was long to endure. With many other arguments to sustain it, the debate was to continue into the twentieth century, a meaningless wrangle until the economic forces governing employment were better understood.

**Apprenticeships and the Factories**  If low wages kept the working poor industrious, many were the efforts still being made to set the pauper on work. In particular, of course, the duty of apprenticing pauper children was observed. This had a double motive. An apprentice was maintained during his years of service, and might be expected to maintain himself thereafter, while apprenticeship of any kind brought a 'settlement' with it. To apprentice a pauper child, therefore, was to be rid of him for good. No training for a craft was necessarily called for: pauper children were usually put on the land or in domestic service or sent to sea or to serve as drudges to craft workers. In the later years of the century, as northern industry expanded and clamoured for more labour, the factories came as 'a godsend to the parish overseers'.[56] Loads of children, nominally apprentices, could now be sent from London in particular northwards. They were not necessarily badly treated, for there were humane employers, but callous and, even more, careless treatment was common enough. And such was the influence of the Act of Settlement that a manufacturer employing pauper 'apprentices' might arrange to have them housed not by his factory and home but in the next parish, so that if unemployment came he might avoid their being chargeable to his rates.

**The First 'Factory Act'**  This employment of helpless children in what Matthew Boulton, the pioneer of industrial power, called in 1786 'the most slavish part of our Business',[57] stirred consciences and roused feelings, not always entirely disinterested, perhaps, on the part of more humane employers, against the worst exploiters. It was a manufacturer and employer of large numbers of 'apprentices', Sir Robert Peel, father of the greater Sir Robert of early Victorian politics, who introduced in 1802 the first 'Factory Act', the *Health and Morals of Apprentices Act*, to protect apprentice labour. The Act had little effect, for powers of enforcement were lacking until the appointment of inspectors under the wider Act of 1833, but its significance lies in its revelation both of the depths to which the Elizabethan concern for the training of the young had sunk under new conditions and of the coming of a new attitude, which was in time, if tardily, to affect the whole industrial scene. 'It is not the least of Britain's debts to the Elizabethan poor law', it has been said, 'that this rider to it . . . got on to the statute book early in the century.'[58] Nor did this concern for the factory apprentice stand alone. Many attempts were made in the later years of the eighteenth century to protect 'apprentices' in other occupations, notably in chimney-sweeping, though for lack of powers of enforcement they also did not achieve much for some time.

**The Inadequacy of Parish Administration**    The abuse of the Elizabethan apprenticeship laws in the eighteenth century was but one aspect of the inadequacy of the poor-law system under changing conditions. In particular, it was evident that the parish was far too small a unit of administration. Few parishes could afford an adequate provision for the poor of all types, and even if they could there were no means of guaranteeing effective administration. The unpaid overseers were only too often reluctant and incompetent, or even corrupt, and the prevailing attitude towards the poor did not encourage any spirit of devotion to their service. Many devices were adopted for deriving some profit from the labour of the able-bodied poor, but the eventual result was only a drift towards the use of forced labour either, in effect, to penalise poverty or to deter applications for relief. The best that could be said of the practice of some workhouses in 1732, for instance, was that 'they that pick oakum are continually refreshed with the balsamic odour of it',[59] a point on which the pickers might have had other views.

**Parish Unions**    The key to the whole problem, as the report of 1834 on the existing system was to show, was to be found in the inadequacy of local administration and in the great variety in practice, the result of the lack of central direction and trained officials. Central direction and control, for reasons already suggested, were unthinkable in eighteenth-century conditions, and even the nineteenth century, with its greater awareness of social problems, was to see much resistance to centralisation as opposed to English traditions. Owing to the legacy of seventeenth-century experience, both in England and abroad, officials were similarly disliked as suggestive of military rule and foreign tyranny. Experiments were made during the eighteenth century to achieve more effective local organisation by combining parishes to provide adequate workhouses, and these were given legislative sanction by an Act of 1723: in this, as in many other instances, the initiative came from the locality, not from the centre. When workhouses were built, relief was frequently made conditional upon willingness to enter them, and this condition was even given legislative sanction. Thus the eighteenth century 'stumbled on the idea of the workhouse test', which was to play so prominent a part in nineteenth-century poor-law policy.[60] In 1756 a further Act authorised an ambitious East Anglian experiment for combined workhouses and poorhouses, serving a number of parishes under 'Incorporated Guardians of the Poor', and employing paid officials. After the first flush of enthusiasm had waned, however, these various experiments failed one after another. Too much depended on sustained local interest, and in any case the ventures affected only a small part of the country. The result was usually but to add another to the collection of what the nineteenth century was to call the 'general mixed workhouses', in which all types of paupers, old, young, sick, mad, able-bodied, lonely and bereaved were indiscriminately jumbled together, evidence of the vanity of human wishes and of what Crabbe called in *The Village* 'the cold charities of man to man'.

**'Gilbert's Act', 1782**   Even as Crabbe was writing, however, the new humanitarian trend of the period produced something that was intended to make a new approach. In 1782, after many endeavours, Thomas Gilbert, M.P. for Lichfield, successfully introduced a Bill ('Gilbert's Act') for the establishment of unions of parishes to set up 'workhouses' for the non-able-bodied poor, with the able-bodied excluded and given either work or relief until work could be found, which in practice, of course, meant out-relief of an unlimited period. The principle of separating the two major classes was sound, though it did not go far enough, but the consequences were unexpectedly dire. Crabbe complained in *The Borough* (1810) of 'the pauper-palaces' in which, though they fared better than outside, the helpless poor were confined in 'a prison with a milder name'. He asked, too, as many were to ask when old age pensions came to be discussed some 80 years later, why the aged poor should be shut away, unlike old horses which were turned out to grass in freedom:

> *But has the labourer, has the seaman done*
> *Less worthy service, though not dealt to one?*
> *Shall we not then contribute to their ease,*
> *In their old haunts, where ancient objects please?*

**'Out-relief' and Wages**   This, as we shall see, was the argument that was eventually to help to win old age pensions. Under Gilbert's Act, however, it was to the able-bodied poor, the unemployed, that, for want of a better remedy, out-relief was given. In practice not only was out-relief given but supplementation of wages when these were recognised as inadequate for the support of a family. This had been a customary practice for some time in certain parts of the country, but it was now to become a major item in the administration of the poor law, and eventually the immediate cause of the new Act of 1834. Only a dozen years after the passing of Gilbert's Act, circumstances conspired to make it the standard practice, at least in the rural southern counties.

**The 'Speenhamland System'**   In the 1790s a series of bad harvests, combined with a rise in prices due to the war with revolutionary France, led to distress and disturbances,[61] an alarming combination in view of the horror with which the revolutionary aims of the French were regarded. Numerous were the remedies proposed, though any increase of wages was keenly deprecated lest it should prove impossible to lower them when prices fell again and the poor chose to be industrious. The influential and operative remedy, the spontaneous reaction to England's first serious wartime inflation, was the decision of the Berkshire Justices at Speenhamland in 1795 to supplement wages from the rates on a sliding scale in accordance with the price of bread and the size of the family concerned. This historic 'Speenhamland system' was given legislative sanction in the following year, when the 'workhouse-test' legislation of 70 years earlier was repealed, and received the blessing of the Prime Minister, Pitt: 'This will make a large family a blessing, not a curse, and thus will draw a proper line of distinction between those who are able to provide for themselves by their labour, and those who, having enriched their country with a number of children, have a claim upon its assistance for support.'

That the measure was, in fact, one of relief to employers rather than employed, that it tied workers still more to the land at a time when there was 'redundancy' in the rural counties and great need of labour in the industrial areas, when, indeed, the rapid spread of enclosures for improved farming was forcing some men off the land, all this was far from clear to those who, with a mixture of motives, but with much real concern, approved the policy of 1795. It was to become clear, however, before 1834, and was to make an ominous impression on poor-law administration in the nineteenth century. In the meantime, whatever the long-term disadvantages, the Speenhamland policy did at least prevent utter destitution and starvation in the long years of high prices before the wars ended, and it was some evidence of the genuineness of concern at distress that it was the price of wheaten bread, not long since still a luxury for the poor, that set the standard of relief.[62]

*Note to page* 38. For a useful and informative study of the background of the Elizabethan Poor Law see J. Pound, *Poverty and Vagrancy in Tudor England* (1971).

# 3 | The Impact of the Industrial Revolution

**England in the 1830s** Let pass an interlude of forty years. The curtain rises again upon the England of the 1830s, the England of the first reform era. Much, very much, has happened, and more is on the way. Our object now is not to trace the course of events, but to take our bearings in the new scene, which is still in many respects an old one, but at the same time is beginning to wear a face familiar to the mid-twentieth-century observer.

Could we for a moment conceal from our gaze everything in our cities and industrial towns constructed since about 1840 we should still see much that was familiar.[1] The concentrations of population are now much larger, but in their centres, and in the mining areas and the industrial valleys of Lancashire and the West Riding, a great deal of housing and industrial building is much as it was. Not far from where this was originally written, modern bulldozing equipment was at the very time of writing razing to the ground back-to-back housing dating from the 1830s and 40s, and modern blocks of flats have risen in its place. Soon little will be left of the industrial relics of the late Georgian and early Victorian period but barrack-like factory buildings, some gaunt, some more elegant structures; faintly neo-classical nonconformist chapels, and gothic-revival churches built with parliamentary funds. Ironically, the position has been reached at which if even the finest and most significant relics of the early days of industrialisation are to be preserved for posterity a conscious effort has to be made. Indeed, 'industrial archaeology' has already become a reputable and popular pursuit. Much that was recently despised has become significant historical material—at least, when cleared of the sooty accretions of a century or more of polluted air—or agreeably quaint matter for a folk museum, and some of the earlier industrial buildings are far from lacking in architectural grace. Industrial housing, however, is on the whole best swept away. A good deal of it was bad by any standards, and standards themselves varied from decade to decade and place to place. Much of it, of course, was better than what had preceded it, and in many places construction was very solid, as slum-clearance schemes in our own day have discovered. On the other hand, from 1793 to 1815 wartime restrictions, rising prices and higher taxation (including the long-established duties on windows, glass, timber and bricks, which were to endure until the middle years of the nineteenth century) had conspired to raise building costs, and standards therefore suffered. Houses were in any case always too small and too closely crowded together while, though many of them soon outlived their usefulness, the need for yet more of them long remained so great as to prevent their being replaced without, in the end, government intervention. All but the best-built houses age rapidly, as, no doubt the experience of the present century will in turn show us, and living standards rise faster in housing than in almost anything else.

What gave so much of their grim character to many industrial centres in the first half of the nineteenth century were the crowded masses of housing, much of it hurriedly constructed, that were put up near to the factories and workshops which were increasingly clamouring for labour. The very crowding itself was evidence of what was happening during the period when England was assuming its modern shape. First there was a great increase of population, an increase that had begun in the eighteenth century and was to continue into the twentieth; secondly there was the extraordinarily rapid development of the industrial and commercial centres, dragging people into them and crowding them together, regardless of comfort and convenience and sanitary conditions, in order to keep turning the myriad wheels that were increasingly being driven by steam power. But for industrial development based on steam, England, with this growing population, would have suffered the fate of Ireland or Italy and been compelled to look to emigration to keep its people alive. Yet the consequences of the crowding of urban areas were serious at a time when the machinery of government was both antiquated in form and quite inadequate in scope to deal with the problems created. Until environmental conditions were improved, the growing towns were more than ever what, in the words of one contemporary observer, towns always had been, 'graves of the human race'.[2]

**The Growth of Population**    The population of England in the time of Elizabeth I, when, as already recorded, most people can have known little but their own limited surroundings, was probably not much more than three million. No census was taken until 1801, but it has been calculated that the population had increased to five million in 1660 and to about seven million in 1760. The census of 1801 gave a return of nearly nine million and thereafter regular returns were made every 10 years. By 1831 the total was nearly 14 million, and by 1851 almost 18 million. England in the middle of the nineteenth century was still a quiet place by present-day standards, but the population had doubled in 50 years and was to double again in the next 60. The two highest proportionate increases took place in the two decades 1811–21 and 1821–31, being 18 and 16 per cent, respectively. Scotland was growing at the same rate. Her population of 1,600,000 in 1801, despite the appeal of the 'high road to England', which Dr Johnson had lauded, and of those longer routes to the colonies overseas, which Scots did so much to build up, was to be almost doubled by 1861, and her greatest proportionate increases also came in the years 1811-31. Here is some measure of the very size of the problem that confronted Great Britain in the years that followed Waterloo.

The causes that touched off the startling increase in population admit of no simple explanation. Around the middle of the eighteenth century a decline in epidemics, combined with a long series of good harvests, both lowered the death-rate and to some extent stimulated the birth-rate. Contemporaries were certainly aware that conditions were improving and standards of living rising: more plentiful supplies of food would in themselves account for much. Little credit can be given to any improvements in medical knowledge and treatment but, as the spread of hospitals showed, there was more concern and care, while the popularity of the new-fangled cotton clothing improved personal hygiene. Such mortality figures as have been calculated are conjectural, but it has been estimated that the death-rate in London fell from 1:25 to 1:40 between 1700 and 1821, while the proportion of children who died before they were five declined from 75 to 41 per cent during the eighteenth century. Losses were still great, and were indeed to be increased for a time by industrial conditions, but there was a marked improvement, as the census of 1801 testified, an improvement buttressed by a steady increase in births. Industrial developments, modest though they yet were, probably contributed to the rising birth-rate, for the prospects of employment, together with freedom from the traditional constraints of apprenticeship, encouraged early marriage. Arthur Young's advice after a visit to the manufacturing areas—'Away! my boys—get children, they are worth more than ever they were'[3]—is well-known, and, if the population explosion in the North is any evidence, would seem to have been taken. Once the expansion of population had begun it was literally, one may say, self-generating, and for the first time in human history the process was to be unchecked by catastrophe.[4] Before long, medical and sanitary science and assured supplies of food were to restrain the ravages which so often in the past had brought expansion to a tragic halt.

Yet despite the beginnings of an industrial population the country was still mainly agricultural. Until the middle of the nineteenth century about half of the population was still rural, but the towns were building themselves up and were attracting more and more of the rural increase. By the end of the century the average Englishman was no longer a countryman, or a townsman who had the countryside at the end of the road, but a city dweller whose glimpses of the country were rare. After the actual increase of population the feature of nineteenth-century development that most impressed contemporaries was what one late Victorian observer justly called 'the stupendous growth of cities'.[5]

**Industry and Trade**  London in 1801, with little short of 900,000 people, was already large, but by 1831 its population had increased to 1,500,000 and the figure was almost to be doubled again in the next 30 years. Glasgow, with 77,000 in 1801, had reached 200,000 in 1831 and was similarly to be doubled by the 60s. Manchester between 1801 and 1851 rose from 100,000 to 400,000, Liverpool from 77,000 to little short of 400,000, Birmingham from 73,000 to nearly 250,000, Leeds from 54,000 to 173,000. And the ceaseless activity of these swarming millions was reflected in the output of industry. Exports boomed in the years of war with France, and were valued at 38 millions in 1805 and 51 millions in 1815, the year of final victory. Thereafter there was a decline until the 30s, but from 1836 to 1844, with occasional setbacks, the total value stood at about 50 millions, after which it began to climb, with ups and downs, until 1854, when it finally passed the 100-million mark.

The first manufacture to be stimulated by the new forms of power was cotton spinning. Between 1812 and 1835, for instance, the number of steam-operated spindles increased from five million to more than 11 million, and contemporaries marvelled at the wonders of machinery; 'wonderful people!—whirr! whirr! all by wheels!—whiz! whiz! all by steam!', as A. W. Kinglake's apocryphal Pasha exclaimed ecstatically in *Eothen*. 'The fine spinning mills at Manchester are the triumphs of art and the glory of England', ran a hardly less enthusiastic comment of 1835, 'in the beauty, delicacy and ingenuity of the machines they have no parallel. . . . It is delightful to see from 800 to 1,000 spindles of polished steel, advancing and receding in a mathematical line, each of them whirling all the time upon its axis.'[6] Dickens later in *Hard Times* was to decry this uncritical and admiring aestheticism, which, struck by their glittering windows and the smooth working of their machines, saw the factories only as 'Fairy palaces' and recked little of their effect on their inmates.[7]

The increase in the production of cotton goods was reflected in their export, £17,500,000 in 1830 and double that amount by the early 50s. Coal, which made steam-power possible, was also being produced in increasing quantities. Already by 1800 10 million tons a year were being extracted, and by 1830 the total was more than half as large again. Exports began in the 30s, reaching one million tons by 1837 and three million by 1850. A new England was taking shape, an England which would have been impossible without the great outpacing of death by birth and survival, and without which the flood of new lives would have perished miserably or been forced overseas.

**Thomas Malthus**   What contemporaries thought of what was happening was first expressed by Thomas Malthus in the famous *Essay on the Principle of Population*, the first version of which appeared in 1798. During the eighteenth century population had been thought to be decreasing, but Malthus raised the alarm, which was apparently to be justified by the startling results of the first census in 1801, with his warning of the disproportionate pressure of population upon the means of subsistence. The striking success of the book over many years was evidence of the increasing concern after 1801 with the growth of population. Malthus fastened in particular upon the poor law as it was applied from 1795, and blamed this growth upon what he called 'the population raised by bounties', which he saw as tending only to starvation and ruin. The increased cost of poor relief, which doubled from four to eight million pounds between 1802 and 1818 and was still seven millions in 1832, seemed to justify the vision of impending disaster, and prepared opinion for the abrupt reversal of poor-law policy in 1834.

It was the gloomy prognostications of Malthus that helped to give the new study of Economics its title as the 'dismal science', coined by its inveterate critic, Carlyle. The remedy which Malthus himself advanced was the voluntary checking of population by late marriage, and he wished to see popular education developed to bring the lesson home to the poor. Not until poor-law encouragement of marriage was brought to an end and the poor learnt through education 'that they are themselves the cause of their own poverty', he maintained, would everyone realise that his duty was 'not to bring beings into the world for whom he cannot find the means of support'.[8]

**Disraeli and *The Two Nations***    Malthus was widely read, but the growth of population went unchecked. From 1837, when the Registrar General's office was established and began the publication of vital statistics, the process came to be better understood. Opinion swung to the view that the worst fears could be averted by importing food from abroad more freely: hence the repeal of the corn laws in 1846. Disraeli was one of those who resisted this blow to the landowning interest, but in his famous political novel of the 40s, *Sybil, or The Two Nations*, first published in 1845, he recorded much of what was then being discussed. In a telling comparison between the influx of new lives and the barbarian invasion of the Roman Empire, he reflected, too, the awed reception accorded to the stream of impressive statistics, with all its implications for the nation's life and livelihood: "'tis the most solemn thing since the Deluge. What kingdom can stand against it?... What are your invasions of the barbarous nations, your Goths and Visigoths, your Lombards and Huns, to our Population Returns?'[9]

**'The Condition of England'**    It was not in the control of population that Disraeli sought the remedy for the problems of his times. *Sybil*, like his other works of the period, was a political manifesto which boldly faced the difficulties even if the remedies it proposed were somewhat wide of the mark. It was the 'condition of England' question with which he was concerned, the conditions of life of the people, not their numbers, though those very numbers, he suggested, might compel attention and bring improvements more speedily than Reform Bills or other political devices. 'I speak of the annual arrival of more than three hundred thousand strangers in this island', said the superior workman of *Sybil*, Walter Gerard: 'How will you feed them? How will you clothe them? How will you house them? They have given up butcher's meat; must they give up bread? And as for raiment and shelter, the rags of the kingdom are exhausted, and your sinks and cellars already swarm like rabbit warrens'.[10] Here, in the 40s, was the first suggestion of that policy of *Sanitas Sanitatum, Omnia Sanitas*, which Disraeli was to make his watchword in a famous speech at the Free Trade Hall, Manchester, in 1872, two years before the election which brought him to power at the age of 69. The phrase had, in fact, been coined in a speech at Aylesbury in 1864, but it crystallised much of Disraeli's thought on social problems, and with *Sybil* brought him an enduring reputation as a social reformer which, in the event, his own achievements as Prime Minister hardly justified. (The social legislation of his Ministry, notably the Public Health, Trade Union and Artizans' Dwelling Acts of 1875, the Education Act of 1876 and the Factory and Workshops Act of 1879, were entirely the work of his colleagues, R. A. Cross, G. Sclater Booth, C. E. Adderley and Lord Sandon.) In the 40s, as investigations were dramatically revealing, there was already only too strong a case for a policy of *sanitas sanitatum*. It was from this period, indeed, that sanitation became, with good reason, a mid-Victorian obsession, almost a panacea for all ills, political hardly less than personal, and the starting point of significant developments in social policy.

**Housing, Crowding and Sanitation**   Could we turn back the clock and revisit a town at any time before the middle of the nineteenth century, the offensive reek of close-packed, ill-washed humanity and of all its rubbish and waste would make the first assault on our senses. 'I smell you in the dark', said Dr Johnson to Boswell in Edinburgh in 1773, though the phenomenon was far from peculiar to 'Auld Reekie'. Until the middle years of the eighteenth century little had been done at all to improve the amenities of towns. Growth was haphazard, of building regulations there was none, and in the new industrial centres, in particular, houses were crowded together and families crammed into them, with no regard for anything but high rents on the part of the landlord and proximity to work for the tenants. In the words of an enlightened employer of 1839, the early manufacturers were 'too much absorbed with the doubtful success of their own affairs to look after the necessities of their workpeople'.[11] From about the middle years of the eighteenth century 'Improvement Commissioners' for the lighting, paving, cleaning and policing of many towns had been established by special Acts of Parliament, but their creation was haphazard and their powers were limited. From the sixteenth century had been inherited the Commissioners of Sewers, but their function was limited to surface drainage and it was illegal to deposit household refuse in the 'sewers', which acquired their modern connotation only through mid-Victorian sanitary reform. It was only through this reform, too, that piped water became the accepted commonplace necessity of life.

**Dirt and Disease**   By the 1830s industrial crowding had reached such a pitch that, despite such efforts as were made by Improvement Commissioners, many towns were becoming in their older parts what a report on the condition of Sheffield bluntly described as 'a putrid bog or morass'.[12] The results were seen in the terrible cholera outbreak of 1832 and in the sudden increase in the death-rate, during the decade, from 20 to 30 per 1,000 in the main industrial centres. Medical men had long been urging the need for improvements and a series of reports now revealed the startling truth. 'The people of England', as one historian has said, 'appeared for the first time to acquire a sense of sight and smell and realise that they were living on a dungheap.'[13]

A number of circumstances combined to force upon public attention what the Webbs have aptly called 'the devastating torrent of public nuisances',[14] but, local stirrings of sympathy apart, first in importance was the realisation that the nuisances were proving both a direct and an indirect charge upon the nation. The causation of epidemic disease did not begin to be understood until the 60s, but the relation between dirty conditions and disease had long since become too obvious to be disregarded and was being confirmed by careful survey and by the statistics provided by the Registrar General through the registration of the causes of death. 'Without exception', declared the Sheffield report already quoted, 'the filth track, the cholera track and the fever track are identical.' Once this blunt analysis had been made manifest and accepted, remedies were soon to be found, though their application in practice was to prove a slow process, partly because medical science was not yet sufficiently advanced to be able to provide any explanation of the spread of disease: Pasteur's pioneer work on bacteria still lay in the future. Yet, even if no satisfactory explanation could yet be offered, the recognition of the connection between dirt and disease, at a time when it was all too easy to hold the poor responsible for their conditions, and when disease, in any case, was still widely accepted as an unavoidable infliction of divine providence, is not to be underestimated. Opinion was shocked into horror and action through recognition of the startling fact that, in the forceful phrase of one of the great pioneers of public health, the population was being 'poisoned by its own excrement'.[15]

**Cholera and the Poor Law**  Fortunately for the readier acceptance of the critical approach, bad conditions did not merely affect those who were compelled to live in them. They suffered most directly, but their more fortunate fellow-citizens had to foot part at least of the bill, for sickness and death brought poverty and poverty was a charge upon the rates. Moreover, disease knew no class distinctions, and although it might normally be restricted to the most wretched parts of towns, virulent epidemics might sweep through whole communities and strike down even the wealthy. This was what happened in 1831–2, when the first epidemic of Asiatic Cholera swept over the country, having crossed the world from Bengal since it had begun its ravages there in 1817, and entered England through the port of Sunderland late in 1831. More than 13,000 people died out of 71,000 attacked, over one-third of the deaths occurring in London. Typical of the effects in the provinces was the Sheffield visitation, which attacked 1,300 people, of whom 400 died, among them the Master Cutler of the year: the dread event was commemorated in a monument which still holds a warning finger aloft on the edge of the old part of the city. It was, of course, water-borne infection, whether of cholera or of typhoid, that struck most indiscriminately, though it was not until later that the connexion with water, first established empirically by Dr John Snow for cholera in 1849, was finally proved; some years, indeed, after the husband of the Queen herself had died of typhoid in 1861. Not until 1884 did Robert Koch at last succeed in isolating the cholera bacillus, and trace its origin to Bengal. Hardly less important than water as a carrier of infection, of course, was the common fly, which bred in filthy conditions and seemed to justify the long-held view that infection was air-borne and arose from stenches (hence the very word *malaria* for another disease). Not until the passing of horse traffic did the fly cease to be a serious menace to health.

Cholera, which appeared again in 1848-9, 1853-4, 1866 and even, mildly, as late as 1893, was epidemic, though the very horror of its arrival, the suddenness with which it struck down its victims and the high proportion of them who suffered an agonising death, all served to heighten concern, and acted as a spur to sanitary reform.[16] (Epidemic influenza, which in 1847 caused nearly as many deaths as cholera in 1832, was far less dreaded.[17]) 'One visible Blessing seems already to be coming upon us through the alarm of the Cholera', wrote Dorothy Wordsworth at the end of 1831, when the first visitation was being fearfully awaited: 'Every rich man is now obliged to look into the miserable bye-lanes and corners inhabited by the Poor; and many crying abuses are ... about to be remedied.'[18]

The attack of 1848-9, with some 80,000 deaths, 15,000 of them in London, was the worst, and was aggravated, no doubt, by the new railways, which aided the rapid spread of infection. Later appearances, with the gradual improvement of sanitary conditions, were less severe: the last wave, in 1893, brought only 135 deaths. Less dramatic, though still more deadly in total effect, however, were the endemic fevers, which in 1838, for instance, killed more than 56,000 people, typhoid alone, it was graphically calculated at the time, accounting for more than double the number of the Allied dead at Waterloo.[19] And to the deaths from fever had to be added an even greater number of cases of illness, which it was thought must amount to a quarter of a million, many of them resulting in extreme poverty and therefore in charges upon the poor rates. To the filth diseases as causes of illness and death must be added, of course, the occupational diseases which were often the tragic, if hopelessly accepted, result of industrial processes, and which were intensified by the conditions created by the coming of steam-power and factory working, grinder's and potter's 'asthma', lead-poisoning and the like.

The incidence of fatal disease was startling. Analysis of the Registrar's returns for 1838, for instance, showed that, as between industrial and rural areas, in the former the number of deaths in all classes of the population was greater for the age group under 20 than for the range 20-60 years.[20] Only in the labouring classes was this also true of rural areas, but, whereas in those areas the proportion was 2:1, in the industrial areas it was 3:1. Another calculation showed that the percentage of adult deaths ascribed to epidemic disease was more than twice as great among the crowded industrial population than among the gentry and professional classes, while there was an average lower expectation of life of 8–10 years among industrial workers. The deaths of heads of families from filth diseases before the age of 45, it was estimated, threw 43,000 widows and 112,000 orphans upon the poor law.[21] Expressed in terms calculated to startle and shock, 'the annual loss of life from filth and bad ventilation is greater than the loss from death or wounds in any wars in modern times'.[22]

The conclusion drawn was irresistible that 'all epidemics and all infectious diseases are attended with charges on the poor rates',[23] that 'much of the evil which preventive measures . . . must provide against, is presented to the Board of Guardians in the shape of claims to relief on the ground of destitution occasioned by sickness.'[24]

It was in fact a combination of concern for the welfare of the overcrowded workers with care for the level of the rates that moved men to action and opened the way for the environmental services. The first cause was the new poor-law system of 1834, which, instituted to lower the cost of poor relief and to raise the position of the country labourers degraded by the long-continued operation of the 1795 system, soon revealed that without improvements in environment poor relief would rapidly become as heavy a burden as ever, though now in the industrial rather than in the rural areas. This had already become clear by 1838, when, as the result of an epidemic in East London, the fourth annual report of the Poor Law Commissioners included a survey of the physical causes of fever which might be prevented by sanitary measures.

**Edwin Chadwick and Sanitary Reform**   Among those who made this survey was a notable doctor, James Kay, afterwards famous, as Sir James Kay-Shuttleworth, for his pioneer work in education. Kay was a Lancastrian, trained in medicine at Edinburgh, who came back to his native county to practise in Manchester. There he made investigations into social conditions in the cotton industry which he published in 1832 as a grim study of *The Moral and Physical Condition of the Working Classes*. Having joined the staff of the Poor Law Commissioners in 1835, he worked first in East Anglia, where he further developed his already strong views on the need for education, and then in London. It was in London that, together with another Edinburgh doctor, Neil Arnott, a pioneer of smokeless fires, he prepared for the Commissioners a hardly less grim picture of the insanitary conditions of much of London.

The moment was ripe for these revelations since the administration of the poor law had struck an unexpected snag. If, aware of the likely effect of dirty conditions upon health and therefore upon the rates, the poor-law officials endeavoured to improve conditions, the cost was likely to be disallowed as a charge upon the rates. After the reaction against eighteenth-century carelessness in matters of public finance the nineteenth century was obsessed with the power of the audit. Boards of Guardians in thickly populated areas were constantly faced, therefore, with the tragic irony of false economy. The man above all others who determined that the point should be driven home was that remarkable and powerful, if disagreeable and tactless, personality, Edwin Chadwick (1800–90), the driving spirit of poor-law reform, now Secretary to the Commissioners, and destined to become the force behind sanitary reform and the protection of the public health.

Of Chadwick's leading part in the 1834 reform of the poor law we must speak in the next chapter. Much of the report on which it was based was his work and he had early realised the necessity for 'collateral aids' to reform, among which he was almost alone at the time in reckoning the health and living conditions of the poor. Hence his interest, in 1838, in bringing forward evidence of the relation-ship between insanitary conditions, illness and poverty, and in the encouragement of sanitary measures as an actual means of economy in poor-law administration. He it was who set Kay and Arnott to their task, and who in the following year printed in the Commission's report further evidence provided by Dr Southwood Smith, of the London Fever Hospital, which showed, among other startling facts, that, of 77,000 cases of pauperism investigated, 14,000 had been caused by fever.[25] These investigations were limited to London, but in 1839 it was decided to ex-tend them throughout the country, and the result was the appearance in 1842 of Chadwick's *magnum opus*, the *Report on the Sanitary Condition of the Labouring Population*, which was to determine his future career and prove the starting-point of the health services.

Chadwick had a flair for punching his points home, and the effectiveness of his choice and presentation of material was shown in the reception of the report, which was almost a best-seller. The report itself was based on evidence from all over the country, but the appeal throughout was to the economy which sanitary improvements could achieve. If disease led to higher rates, Chadwick had already pointed out in the 1838 report, 'the amount of burdens thus produced is fre-quently so great as to render it good economy on the part of the administrators of the poor laws to incur the charges for preventing the evils'.[26] As examples were quoted in the 1842 report ingenious calculations of the direct cost of preventable illness, £46,000 a year in Glasgow, £25,000 in Dundee.[27] Time was to show, of course, that mere sanitary improvement was far from enough. In fact Chadwick by his revelations had initiated the process of a century that was to culminate in the National Health Service. What most shocked opinion into action, however, were the revelations of conditions, in Chadwick's graphic phrase, 'almost as bad as that of an encamped horde, or an undisciplined soldiery'.[28] He had rightly seized, indeed, upon the fact that as a result of their much too rapid growth the industrial centres were little better than standing camps—worse than camps, in fact, since there was no possibility of moving on. And even if the will to improve were present, the means in civic administration were largely lacking: considerable improvements in both local and central government had to come before adequate services could be provided. Great improvements were necessary, too, in the quality of administrators. Chadwick was one of the first of the great civil servants, and, though his defects of character gave the whole class a bad name, he pointed the way to the reforms which began with the establishment of the Civil Service Commission in 1855, and still more with the introduction of entry by competitive examination in 1870. Above all, he insisted on the need for properly qualified and trained expert administrators, challenging the traditional reliance upon the unpaid amateur: much of the bitterness of his career, indeed, turned on this point. To Chadwick, as he constantly insisted, government was a matter of science, and sanitary reform was the aspect of government in which, as he was one of the first to show, scientific methods were indispensable. At the same time he showed nothing but scorn for the medical science of his day, insisting that it could not and did not cure, and that the remedy lay, in any case, in prevention.

**Public Ignorance** The shock of Chadwick's revelations in 1842 was all the greater because of the profound ignorance among the well-to-do of the condition of their less fortunate fellows. It has always been true that one half of the world has not known how the other half lives. Early Victorian England set great store by the Bible, and the injunction, *For the poor shall never cease out of the land: therefore I command thee saying, Thou shalt open thine hand wide* (Deuteronomy, 15, 11), could be only too readily accepted as a justification for regarding the whole problem of poverty as insoluble, and for passing it off with a shrug—or with that 'dignified conclusiveness—not to add a grand convenience' which Dickens held up to ridicule in the 'peculiar flourish' with which Mr Podsnap swept unpleasant truths behind him in *Our Mutual Friend*.[29] Even a century later, in the times of depression in the 1920s and 30s, for all the improved means of communication, the true state of the depressed areas was hardly appreciated outside them. Chadwick in 1842 noted the astonishment with which his account of conditions in many working-class areas was received 'by persons of the wealthier classes living in the immediate vicinity, to whom the facts were as strange as if they related to foreigners or the natives of an unknown country'.[30]

**Squalor and Degradation** Indeed, the working-class areas, and especially the worst of them, the 'slums', as they were coming to be called, were an unknown country, the *Darkest England*, to a later period, of 'General' William Booth of the Salvation Army, who, when he published his famous book in 1890, deliberately parodied the title of Stanley's recent best-seller, *In Darkest Africa*. The old conception of the poor as shiftless and feckless was strengthened by the squalor of their living conditions. Worse still, the physical degradation induced by these conditions seemed to stamp the slum-dwellers as a race apart. The drunkenness which was the easy way of escape from miserable surroundings, the immorality and incest that were stimulated by overcrowding, the desperate hopelessness that was engendered by dirt and misery and that made people apathetic and seemingly indifferent to the finer feelings, all contributed to the impression that Dickens reflected in the well-known passage between Rosa Dartle and Steerforth in *David*

*Copperfield*: '"Are they really animals and clods and beings of another order? I want to know *so* much." "Why, there's a pretty wide separation between them and us", said Steerforth with indifference. "They are not to be expected to be as sensitive as we are . . . they have not very fine natures, and they may be thankful that, like their coarse rough skins, they are not easily wounded."'[31]

This was written in 1850, but is characteristic of the opinions of many over a long period, and point was lent to it by the way in which, amid appalling conditions, families somehow existed and survived, a miracle that, as shown below, was still exciting wonder half a century later.[32] Under the pressure of misfortune, a Scottish doctor, A. P. Alison, wrote in 1840, the poor 'lower their habits': 'Those who have not been accustomed to observe them, are not aware how much reduction of comfort the family of a labouring man, disabled or deprived of employment, may undergo, and not only life be preserved, but the capacity for occasional and precarious employment continue.'[33] At much the same time a clergyman working in Liverpool, where, owing to the incidence of cellar-dwellings, some of the worst conditions were to be found, recorded the impression that had been made even upon him: 'I have seen life under forms which took from it all that, in my eyes, made it happy, hopeful or even human . . . which made it necessary for me to rouse up all the strength of my previous reasoning and convictions, in order to convince myself that these were really fellow-beings.'[34] Yet cellar-dwellings were but the unavoidable result of the crowding into too limited an area of a great influx of population, much of it from the miserable squalor of peasant Ireland, and most of it at so low a standard of living that even a cellar-dwelling in the rapidly expanding cotton towns was preferable to stagnation and starvation at home. But if this was the impact upon a man devoted to Christian social work the less charitably inclined could take refuge in the view that degraded conditions were the result of personal degradation, and it was precisely this view that Chadwick and his colleagues resisted, even as others later were to resist the view that unemployment was explicable solely in terms of personal failure. 'The removal of noxious physical circumstances and the promotion of civic, household and personal cleanliness', wrote Chadwick in the 1842 report, 'are necessary to the improvement of the moral condition of the population.'[35]

**Housing Conditions**    And not only cleanliness was involved, though Chadwick himself always laid the greatest stress upon it. Decent housing conditions were essential, as he showed in quotations from evidence submitted for the report. From Bedford, for instance, came the observation: 'A man who comes home to a poor, comfortless hovel after his day's labour, and sees all miserable around him, has his spirits more often depressed than excited by it. He feels that, do his best, he shall be miserable still, and is too apt to fly for a temporary refuge to the alehouse or beer-shop.'[36] 'Experience sufficiently demonstrates', Dr Alison commented from his own observations, 'that, among people in this climate, reduced to a certain point of depression or destitution, the temptation to drown care in intoxicating liquors . . . is very seldom permanently resisted.'[37] Two Lancashire manufacturers, brothers in partnership, who had built cottages for their work-people, urged that 'the domestic comforts of the labouring classes should be more attended to': 'comfortable dwellings exercise a powerful influence in producing and confirming habits of sobriety and virtue.'[38] Dr Southwood Smith quoting, in a later report of 1844, examples of the most terrible results of overcrowding in promiscuity and incest, described the 'unhumanizing' effects of squalor in terms which, with the dreadful experience of Hitler's concentration camps behind us, we could not presume to challenge: 'If from early infancy you allow human beings to live like brutes, you *can* degrade them down to their level.'[39]

This was also the view of Dr John Simon when, as first Medical Officer of Health for the City of London, he began his investigations into insanitary condi-tions during the cholera epidemic of 1848–9 and saw for himself how the poor lived: 'There are swarms of men and women, who have yet to learn that human beings should dwell differently from cattle . . . people may relapse into the habits of savage life, when their domestic condition is neglected and when they are suffered to habituate themselves to the uttermost depths of physical obscenity and degradation.'[40] Forty years later Beatrice Webb was driven to the same con-clusion by her experience of living in the East End of London: 'Anyone ac-quainted with the sights and sounds and smells of the quarters of great cities in which destitution is widely prevalent . . . learns to recognise a sort of moral malaria, which undermines the spiritual vitality of those subjected to its baneful influence and, whilst here and there a moral genius may survive . . . gradually submerges the mass of each generation as it grows up, in coarseness and bestiality, apathy and cynical scepticism'.[41]

In these comments, rather than in the casual superiority of Steerforth and Miss Dartle, common though that in fact was, lay the explanation of much that shocked and horrified the Victorians. Chadwick's first concern was with the cost to the nation of disease and squalor, and Disraeli in *Sybil*, only a few years after the appearance of the 1842 report, obviously had the kind of evidence it provided in mind in making the point that 'nothing was so expensive as a vicious popula-tion'.[42] Once it was accepted, however, that a remedy could be found, something more than economy was involved. The middle years of the nineteenth century were years of reluctant fumbling after remedies that both cost and interfered little, until gradually it was borne in upon the nation that to repair the evils, aggravated as they were by the steady growth of population, called for more thoroughgoing measures than had been expected.

Alton Locke, in Charles Kingsley's novel of 1850, represented, in his bitter repudiation of his mother's suggestion that his physical frailty was 'God's will', both the current obsession with sanitary improvement and the reforming zeal of his creator, as a Christian Socialist, for more thoroughpaced changes: 'I think it was the will of the world and of the devil, of man's avarice and laziness and ignorance. . . . A sanitary reformer would not be long in guessing the cause of my unhealthiness.'

**Industrial Injuries and the Poor Law**    Chadwick pinned his faith to cleanliness and sanitation, but the springs of many later measures for housing, town-planning, preventive medicine, and even employer's liability for industrial accidents, are to be found in his pages. On this last point, indeed, he appealed as usual to the economy in poor relief which greater precautions against accidents might bring, but he also urged that pressure should be brought to bear upon the self-interest of employers: 'If the branch of industry were charged with the pecuniary consequences of the losses assumed to be necessarily incident to it, generations would not be allowed to pass away in fear, recklessness and misery, without the early adoption of those means of prevention which self-interest would then stimulate.'[43]

In fact, although factory inspectors were by this time being appointed and their duties were gradually to be widened in the 40s and 50s to check dangerous working conditions, it was to be at least another generation before, in 1880, the Employers' Liability Act extended the limited protection afforded to employees against accidents and in 1897 the Workmen's Compensation Act at last made compensation for death or injury a charge upon industry, as Chadwick had desired. The long delay was typical of the resistance to what Chadwick and his colleagues saw as self-evident truths. Many powerful interests were involved and there was great reluctance to allow the State's power of interference to increase. If Adam Smith was right, all would turn out well in the end and State interference was therefore not merely unnecessary but positively harmful: as one M.P. complained of the Employers' Liability Act in 1880, 'this is the most revolutionary measure ever brought into this House against the trading community of the country'.[44]

**Air Pollution**    Air pollution provides one of the most striking examples of delay in tackling an only too evident evil. Chadwick, drawing in his report on the experience of a number of witnesses, pointed to the serious effects of industrial smoke upon health and comfort.[45] There were long-standing laws against the nuisance, but as the magistrates were also in many cases the manufacturers responsible, and were now tending to move their residences to pleasant suburban and rural surroundings, little was done, and the smoke nuisance has remained one of the worst and most enduring legacies of industrial development based on coal.

**'Mere Boys . . .'**    Chadwick did his utmost to stir his readers into protest and activity. If they could not be moved by considerations of economy, he urged them to realise that the high incidence of death through disease among heads of families put the power of agitation into the hands of 'mere boys, who were furious and knew not what they were about',[46] and, it might be added, lacked not only the experience and maturity but also the family responsibilities which might enjoin calm and caution. It was an argument calculated to be effective at a time when Chartism and trade-unionism, strikes and mob violence were much in evidence.

**Housing Reform**   Despite his promptings, however, it was to be many years before Chadwick's recommendations were put into effect, and then only as the inadequacy of half-measures came to be realised. More than 40 years after his strictures on housing, for instance, the 1885 Report of the Royal Commission on the Housing of the Working Classes was echoing much that he had said: 'It is quite certain that the working classes are largely housed in dwellings which would be unsuitable even if they were not overcrowded.'[47] Not until 1890 was an effective Housing Act passed, and by that time much accommodation, originally of poor enough quality, had degenerated still further: as a Liverpool journalist and social reformer wrote in 1856, 'Houses are not like wine or cheese—they do not improve with keeping'.[48] But it was not until after the First World War that adequate public provision for new housing began to be made, and not until the 1930s that a real attack began on the still further degenerated slums. For three quarters of a century after the appearance of the 1842 report Chadwick's insistence upon sanitary reform dominated the scene. More stress was laid on the removal of insanitary conditions than on the creation of good conditions, which, it was conveniently and confidently thought, could be left to private enterprise in housing. The cost of compensation for the destruction of old housing and of the re-housing of people who could afford only low rents was, in fact, an almost insuperable obstacle until Treasury subsidies were forthcoming from 1919. Although some municipal housing was undertaken before 1914, the council estates and blocks of flats that are now a normal feature of municipal activity were, therefore, mainly a development of the 1920s. The process of improvement was painfully slow, but in housing, as in so many other aspects of social life, it was only gradually that reluctance to see State intervention increase was overcome. To ban deleterious conditions, or even to remove them when banned, was one thing, positively to replace them with other conditions was quite another. Once better health was assured for the working classes it was assumed that their earning power, now greater and more sustained, would enable them to save enough either to build for themselves or at least to encourage the speculative builder to undertake the task for them, though Chadwick wished to see more employers creating homes for their workpeople.[49] It needed the immense pressure for new building after the First World War to drive home the practical lesson that private enterprise was not equal to the task, and that without subsidies even the minimum standards now regarded as essential could not be guaranteed to the poorest. It had taken nearly 80 years, however, 80 years of changing conditions and continued revelations, of the gradual acceptance of a broader and more positive conception of the State, together with the upheaval of a great war, to apply to the problems of a growing population in an industrial era the remedies with which Chadwick had been among the first to concern himself.

**Moral Improvement—and its Results**   As we shall see, even as it was believed that once the debilitating effects of squalid environments were removed health and vigorous activity would ensue, so it was held that with health and vigour would come an improved moral condition which would ensure prosperity. For the weaklings and the failures there must be the marginal defence of the poor law, but as moral and physical conditions improved even that would cease to be necessary; the poor would provide their own margin, their own insurance against the ills and accidents of life. Once squalor was checked by law and regulations, thrift would have its chance and friendly societies, savings banks and building societies would see to the rest. This was the comfortable doctrine of the nineteenth century, which continued to be held even after its obvious limitations had been realised and a greater degree of social responsibility was already being accepted. The attitude of society towards problems of housing, poor relief and unemployment was at bottom, therefore, one and the same, as the series of reports written by Chadwick between 1838 and 1842 early made plain.

**The Children's Employment Commission, 1840**   Much of what Chadwick reported was confirmed by other investigations that were being made as he prepared his material (see note, page 88). In 1842 appeared the first report of a Commission set up two years earlier to enquire into the employment of children. This dealt with conditions in mines and was followed in 1843 by evidence on certain other industries. Again the public was aghast at the revelations. Small children were shown to be employed for long hours and, in the mines, in lonely darkness underground; older children and women, even women in pregnancy, toiled at heavy tasks that taxed their strength. These things were literally shown by the skilful use of striking illustrations drawn from the life, an innovation insisted on by Dr Southwood Smith, who argued that pictures would impress even those unwilling to wade through the fat volumes of evidence. Everywhere there was revealed a woeful lack of education and deplorable standards of living. Looking through the evidence today one can feel the shock administered to the Commissioners—and to the readers of their reports—by the constantly repeated admissions on the part of child workers of ignorance of the simplest items of general knowledge and of the bare facts of religious teaching. A case quoted in one report of a boy who claimed to know the name of God only as an expletive was not untypical, and, commonplace though it was, was clearly quoted to shock the God-fearing.

The worst evils were not always the direct fault of employers, but arose from the low standards of wages, which made it necessary for all to work. Children were a liability until they could earn. A Derbyshire report recorded frankly that the sole anxiety of some parents seemed to be 'how to make all they could of their children': when a child was on the way there was real concern lest it prove a girl and therefore have, in time, less earning power.[50] Employers, however, took little or no interest in the children employed and made few attempts to check brutal treatment of them. As Chadwick had noted, there was little knowledge or understanding among the classes. Even local clergy, it was recorded in one mining area, could give little information to the Commissioners, for they themselves 'rarely have an opportunity of even seeing, much more conversing with, either the colliers or their children (except now and then at Sunday school)'.[51]

Part of the difficulty lay in sheer poverty. The comment was frequently made, for instance, that people would not come to church as even their best clothes were too shabby for Sunday display. Under these conditions morality and education could not but suffer. Life was hard, accidents were common, especially in the pits, and death generally came tragically early. 'The seeds of painful and mortal disease are very often sown in childhood and youth', was the concluding observation of the report on mining, 'each generation of this class of the population is commonly extinct soon after fifty.'[52] Here was additional evidence of that preponderance of young people which Chadwick had already noticed. The ability to earn early while physical powers were at their best, even if those powers were being overstrained, the lack of discipline and of example from the older generation, the ignorance and the harsh conditions of life, all seemed to presage some terrible outbreak. 'The morals and habits of the children in Sheffield are much worse than they were 20 years ago', complained Ebenezer Elliot, the 'Corn Law Rhymer'; 'thoughtful men see a coming catastrophe which is too probably destined to cast the horrors of the first French Revolution utterly into shade.'[53] This was strong measure, but it reflected a widespread concern at the possibilities of agitation and revolution, which found expression in much of the literature of the time, not least in Carlyle's *French Revolution*, with its lurid impressions of mob violence.[54] Disraeli, from his own observations and a study of the Commissioners' reports, underlined the restlessness and fierce independence of contemporary youth in *Sybil* with his picture of life in his town of 'Wodgate', hardly exaggerating the ignorance which the reports had revealed in the faith of his filemaker Sue, in 'our Lord and Saviour Pontius Pilate, who was crucified to save our sins, and in Moses, Goliath and the rest of the Apostles'.[55]

**The Wastefulness of Industry** As the burden of Chadwick's reports had been the waste and costliness of disease and the economy to be effected by governmental interference to remedy the worst conditions, so the Children's Employment Commission stressed the need both for the protection of the young against abuses which heavily mortgaged the future of the race and for their education in the interests of morality and public order. What the investigations of the 30s and early 40s had revealed, in fact, was that, Christian charity and fellow-feeling apart, the country could not afford the wastefulness that seemed unavoidable in a system of economic development that believed too uncritically in Adam Smith's 'invisible hand'. Coal-owners and manufacturers regarded all interference as unnecessary and ruinous and believed that it would force them out of business. 'Labour, like many other commodities', argued a Barnsley linen manufacturer in 1834, 'will find its own level, and requires no legislative enactments',[56] and the record of Lord Londonderry, for instance, as a great coal-owner, in opposing State interventions in the mines, was a particularly ignoble example of doctrinaire economic perversity. Two generations later, at the time of the 'People's Budget' of 1909, Lloyd George, unconsciously echoing the anti-Norman sentiments that were one of the themes of *Sybil*, was to pour scorn on the noble coal-owners who behaved as if coal had been introduced into the country in 1066 for the exclusive benefit of the aristocracy.[57] Earlier, in the 50s, Dickens, in *Hard Times*, had derided, in the person of Josiah Bounderby, those who held that any concessions to the working classes would lead to their demanding 'to be set up in a coach and six, and to be fed on turtle soup and venison, with a gold spoon'.[58] In the 30s and 40s, however, legislative interference with property and freedom of contract was abhorrent, and it was only the revelations of the actual conditions of life and work endured by so many, who, from their sex or their youth, could not be regarded as able to make or enforce a reasonable contract, that shocked the country into protective measures. Contemporary economists were opposed to interference by the State, and had no conception yet of the law of diminishing returns. Not until 1860 was it openly admitted, by manufacturers and economists alike, on the basis of experience, that State regulation of conditions of work so far from bringing ruin actually contributed to prosperity by improving the efficiency of the workers.

Industrial England in the 30s and 40s, indeed, was a crude place, ignorant, despite the glamour with which casual visitors surrounded the 'fairy palaces', of the forces it was creating. For the first time in history industrialisation and the creation of capital for its continued development were proceeding at a great pace. None realised it, though all saw, and many deplored, the price that was being paid in human misery and degradation. As Thomas Arnold, a shrewd and penetrating observer, wrote in 1832 in his *Letters on the Social Condition of the Operative Classes*, 'We have been living, as it were, the life of three hundred years in thirty'.[59]

**Industrialisation and Reform**   From the vantage point of the twentieth century we can see what was happening, and we realise, as the early Victorian observer could not, the difficulties in the change-over from an agrarian to a predominantly industrial civilisation without which the ever-teeming millions could not have been supported. Somehow the capital had to be raised for the basic development of industry and transport which would prove the foundation of a later, more general, prosperity, and as in the U.S.S.R. in our own day it was the poorest who paid the price. What the U.S.S.R. has done since 1917, with greater understanding and speed, but not necessarily with much less suffering or many fewer mistakes, England had to do blindly and fumblingly in the nineteenth century.[60] The remedies for the evils uncovered by the reports that were published were slow to apply, but from the early 40s the more obvious evils were at least being revealed. The remedies proposed dealt, it is true, with symptoms rather than with the disease, but more could hardly have been expected. To Chadwick and others sanitary reform and administrative improvements were the answer. To the Chartists it was political reform, and it was only the Socialists, now beginning to formulate their more scientific doctrines in contrast to earlier idealist hopefulness, who saw the need for a radical change in the economic ordering of society. From the 40s onwards the problem was increasingly to be posed—how far must reform go to achieve decency, dignity and prosperity for all? The Welfare State is the slowly evolved, and still rather muddled, answer.

To those who investigated factory conditions, educational opportunities, the limitation of the hours of work for women and young people, a ban on the employment of young children and insistence on safety precautions were the measures most needed. All of these, it was maintained, could be achieved without upsetting the delicate balance of the laws of supply and demand or interfering with personal liberty: indeed, all were necessary if the country were not to be plunged into greater misery.

**Factory Acts**  Already, some measures for the defence of the defenceless had been passed. The first statutory intervention on behalf of any of the children working in factories had been, as mentioned in the previous chapter, the Health and Morals of Apprentices Act of 1802. This, however, was limited to pauper apprentices in cotton factories, and for lack of an adequate inspectorate proved largely a dead letter. In any case, as steam-power was increasingly applied to factories and they came, in consequence, to be developed in towns rather than where simple water-power was available, in the country, the growing populations provided ample supplies of 'free' children. In 1818, after a Commission of Enquiry, Sir Robert Peel was able to add to his earlier Act another, limiting hours of work for all children in cotton factories to 12 and prohibiting employment under the age of nine. Again, however, there was no inspectorate. In 1831 the limitation of hours was extended to all young people under 18, though an attempt to include the woollen mills was defeated. By this time some 30,000 children under 13 were at work in cotton-mills, and twice that number of young people between 13 and 18. Numbers engaged in woollen and worsted mills were smaller, but were increasing as steam-power came to be applied to them also. The traditional domestic processes in both cotton and wool were being superseded, first in spinning and then, with slow and, for the handloom weavers, fateful inexorability, in weaving. Admiring observers saw production concentrated and increasing, with machinery reducing human labour and cutting costs by making it possible to employ women and children. Once prosperous handloom weavers saw ruin approaching and had no choice but to send their children to the factories. In the words that Disraeli put into the mouth of the weaver, Warner, of *Sybil*: '. . . the capitalist has found a slave that has supplanted the labour and ingenuity of man. Once he was an artisan: at the best, he now only watches machines; and even that occupation slips from his grasp, to the woman and the child. The capitalist flourishes, he amasses immense wealth; we sink lower and lower; lower than the beasts of burthen; for they are fed better than we are, cared for more'.[61] To the dispossessed domestic worker the process of change did certainly look like this. To be redundant is never a pleasant position; to be redundant in a society that disregarded the fact of redundancy, that in its ignorance of what was really happening was unaware of the tragedies that underlay the cold facts of economic readjustment in an age of increasing prosperity, was doubly unfortunate. Improvement was to come only with social amelioration, and, no less, with the further development of industry that took up the slack.

**Oastler and 'Yorkshire Slavery'**    It was the condition of children in the woollen and worsted mills that in 1830 roused one of the most fervent of contemporary agitators, Richard Oastler, to his famous passionate protest against *Yorkshire Slavery* in the Bradford mills, 'those magazines of British infantile slavery'. The campaign against negro slavery was then at its height, following the earlier prohibition of the British slave-trade, and Oastler drew a telling picture of children hurrying to work in the early morning through streets still littered with posters from an anti-slavery meeting of the previous night: '. . . the very streets which receive the droppings of an "Anti-Slavery Society" are every morning wet by the tears of innocent victims at the accursed shrine of avarice'.[62] With Oastler were to be associated in the campaign for better conditions in the factories that now began such eminent local figures as the Yorkshire factory-owner, John Wood, who had brought him into the movement, the Bradford clergyman George Bull ('Parson Bull') and one of the leading Lancashire cotton-spinners, John Fielden. Their first Parliamentary champion was the ardent Tory philanthropist, Michael Sadler, who in 1831 introduced a Bill to forbid the employment of children under 9 in all mills and to reduce the hours of work for those between 9 and 18 to ten hours a day. This ten-hour bill was regarded by many as so impossible of attainment as to invite ridicule, and it was not until 1847 that it at last became law, though even then under conditions which seriously limited its effectiveness.

**The Ten-Hour Bill**    Sadler's case for the Bill was based not only on the unhappy conditions of the young workers but on the general disparity of power and resources between employers and employed. Such little regulation of conditions as had existed in the past had already ceased and economists were arguing, in the spirit of *laissez-faire*, that it was to the general interest that employers and workmen should make the best terms they could with each other as free agents. One of the leading economists of the time, Nassau Senior (1790–1864), first Professor of Political Economy at Oxford and, as a member of the Poor Law Commission, the author, with Chadwick, of the 1834 Report, even resisted the very notion of reduction of hours of work on the grounds that it was only in the last hour that any profit was made, an argument from pure, but ill-founded, theory that time was to stand on its head.[63] In the same spirit a mill-owner argued against Sadler's Bill that it would leave him and other manufacturers no alternative but to 'lock up their mills and abandon the trade'.[64] Such arguments were to be used at every stage against legislative interference, and as regularly to be disproved: in the long run humane instincts were to prove more effective and more soundly based than economic arguments founded on too limited a knowledge of the effects of industrialisation. Freedom and enterprise were needed, but it was gradually to appear in practice that, given more effective instruments of government, with all the modern apparatus of inspection, reports, committees of enquiry and statistical returns, State interference was not only compatible with freedom and enterprise but essential to them. This, of course, was the case of the great philosopher of reformed government, Jeremy Bentham (1784-1832), from whom Edwin Chadwick and so many others learned the principles of their craft.

Sadler's view was that the scales were weighted against the worker. 'The employer and the employed do not meet on equal terms in the market of labour', he said when introducing his Bill in the Commons. 'On the contrary, the latter, whatever his age and call him as free as you please, is often almost entirely at the mercy of the former.'[65] Statutory limitation of the hours of work of adult men was to be unthinkable for many years, and was not, in fact, to be adopted until the twentieth century, but in practice, owing to the dependence of the mills on younger workers, limitation of the hours of their labour meant shorter hours for adults as well. Hence the enthusiasm in the factory areas for Sadler's Bill, which made of the ten-hour day something of an industrial Magna Carta.

**The Act of 1833** The introduction of the Bill was followed by the setting-up of a committee of enquiry, with Sadler as chairman, which began the startling revelations about conditions of child labour. Under Sadler's direction it produced a powerful report, distinctly partisan in tone, which was strenuously opposed by the manufacturing interests and led to a further investigation, the Factories Inquiry Commission of 1833, in which Chadwick played a leading part and which, in the event, though hastily prepared, largely confirmed Sadler's case. The first effective Factory Act, drafted by Chadwick himself, followed. It was no Ten-Hours Act, but it did at least exclude children under 9 from the mills, limit the hours of work of those under 13 to nine, and under 18 to twelve (which then also became, in practice, the limit of the adult working day). It also endeavoured to provide, as a condition of employment, that children should receive some schooling and work in shifts to render that possible, though this condition was to prove unenforceable. Most important of all, however, inspectors were appointed to see that the law was obeyed, and, although at first they were very few in number and their powers were narrowly restricted, their influence was to tell strongly, as the years passed, in favour of improved conditions.

**Ashley Cooper and the Children's Employment Commission**   Sadler was not in Parliament for this Act, as he had lost his Leeds seat to Macaulay in the first election of the reformed House of Commons. His health had in any case been affected by his labours for the factory workers, and he died in 1835. He was succeeded as the Parliamentary leader of the factory movement by the man who was to prove the greatest of all the philanthropists and social reformers of the nineteenth century, another high-principled Tory who was, like himself, no democrat but who also spent his life in remedying social abuses—Antony Ashley Cooper (1801–85), Lord Ashley and, from 1851, 7th Earl of Shaftesbury.

Ashley took the lead in the movement for the ten-hour day, which he was to dominate until 1850. In this, as in so many other aspects of mid-nineteenth-century social life which he tackled—his care for housing, for the young chimney-sweeps, for the welfare of 'ragged children', for the reform of the lunacy laws and for the moral welfare of the people, on behalf of which, for instance, his religious zeal caused him to stop Sunday posts and bands in the parks—he softened, in the words of his most notable biographers, 'the savage logic of the Industrial Revolution'.[66] In 1840 he took what proved to be a most significant step by calling for an enquiry into the working of the 1833 Act and into conditions in other branches of industry. The result was the Children's Employment Commission, and the shatteringly revealing reports, already referred to, which it produced in 1842 and 1843. Shocked opinion hastened to extend in several directions the protection already afforded in the cotton and woollen districts. The first Mines Act (1842) forbade the employment of women and girls underground and set a minimum age of 10 for boys. It was followed, after delays due to disagreements between the Church and the Nonconformists over educational provision, by an Act of 1844 which limited in all textile factories the hours of work of children under 13 to six and a half, and those of all girls and, significant addition, of all women to twelve. There was no interference with the hours worked by men, but it had at last been recognised that women and children could not be regarded as able to protect themselves against exploitation, though true to the principles of negative restriction nothing was done, for instance, to help the women displaced from coalmines to find other employment, and much misery resulted.

The Act of 1844 also, and for the first time, insisted on the fencing of machinery, a much resisted measure which reflected Chadwick's exposures and was in time to owe much of its effectiveness to the zeal and care of the factory inspectorate.

**The Ten-Hours Act Passed**   Three years later, in 1847, after delays caused by the preoccupations of politicians with the Irish famine and repeal of the corn laws, came the Ten-Hours Act, introduced by Fielden, since Ashley, who had sat for a protectionist seat which he characteristically felt obliged to resign when it was decided to adopt free trade in corn, was temporarily out of the House of Commons. Once passed, however, the Act was almost immediately frustrated by the device of employing children in relays, thereby keeping their hours of work within the letter of the law without risking any limitation of adult hours, a gloss upon the device of shift-working which Chadwick himself had introduced into the Act of 1833. This evasion of the Act's requirements, soon to receive the reluctant stamp of legal approval, was a blow to the workers' hopes. Yet there was a gain, if a smaller one than had been so long struggled for, and the importance and necessity of the Acts of 1844 and 1847 are clear from the fact that in the cotton mills alone at this time nearly 20,000 children under 13 were employed, more than 80,000 between 13 and 18 and nearly 100,000 women over 18, as against 80,000 men. Not until 1874 did the ten-hour day become a reality. In 1850, when it had become clear that the purpose of the 1847 Act had been defeated, a compromise, agreed to by Ashley at the cost of his following among the industrial workers, established a ten and a half-hour day as the price for the prohibition of the relay system. By 1874, when the extra half-hour was at last removed, this limitation of working hours had been extended beyond the textile industries. Already in 1860, when the first extension was made, some of those who earlier had led the resistance to the Factory Acts openly recanted in Parliament: the earlier Acts, one of them candidly admitted, 'had contributed to the comfort and well-being of the working classes, without materially injuring the masters'.[67]

Government and People   This change of heart and mind still lay, in the 30s and 40s, in the future, however, though its ultimate cause was the shock to opinion of the revelations made by the various reports produced in the years around 1840. Power, wrote Disraeli in Sybil in 1845, 'has only one duty—to secure the social welfare of the PEOPLE',[68] and, although it may be debated how far Disraeli's career lived up to the dictum, it was from the revelation of these years that the active concern of the State with the welfare of the people, under the conditions of industrial civilisation, had its first cautious origins.

It was to be some time, of course, before the people were admitted to partnership. Not until 1867 was the average working-man granted the franchise, and the step was then regarded, in a famous phrase, as 'a leap in the dark'. Disraeli's view of the relationship between government and the governed, however great his concern for the people's welfare, was, like Ashley's, paternalistic. The condition of the people was to be improved, but as a favour and a defence, not as a right, and once conditions were improved political agitation and the desire for sweeping social changes would, it was assumed, altogether cease. Government could do something to improve matters, could impose a negative check on evils: after that it was to the working of the laws of economics, of supply and demand, of thrift and self-help, that the people must look. Economists stated the position firmly in the 30s: economic conditions, they maintained, were controlled by laws 'as immutable as those of gravity':[69] 'The laws according to which wealth is created, distributed, and consumed, have been framed by the Great Author of our being, with the same regard to our happiness which is manifested by the laws that govern the material world.'[70]

Nassau Senior, though his views did not go quite so far, stressed the limited possibilities of interference. 'The capital, on which the miracles of civilisation depend', he argued, was 'the slow and painful creation of the economy and enterprise of the few, and of the industry of the many', and if the many demanded too much it could only too easily be destroyed:[71] 'We *now* know that to attempt to provide by legislative interference, that, in all the vicissitudes of commerce and the seasons, all the labouring classes, whatever be the value of their services, shall enjoy a comfortable subsistence, is an attempt which would in time ruin the industry of the most diligent and the wealth of the most opulent community.'[72]

Unfortunately the 'lower classes' (unconscious seekers, we may say now, after twentieth-century conditions) were not aware of the limitations to legislative interference. 'They grossly miscalculate the number and value of the prizes in the lottery of life; they think they have drawn little better than blanks', and they look to the State to redress the balance: 'Men, whose reasoning faculties are either uncultivated or perverted by their feelings or their imagination, see the great power of the State, and do not perceive its limits.'[73] 'Reasoning faculties uncultivated or perverted by feelings and imagination', this was the critique of the working class's hopes and the justification, in Senior's view, of their exclusion from political power. It was a commonplace of political and economic argument that, could the workers achieve, or see the State achieve on their behalf, the control of economic forces that they sought, the results would be disastrous to them, for capital would flee abroad or dry up, and their last state would be worse than their first.

Yet time after time it was shown that these desperate prognostications were unwarranted. The despair of the critics of the Factory Acts of the 30s and 40s had by 1860 become relief and commendation, though that did not prevent the same kind of argument from being trotted out, adapted to changing circumstances and no less sincerely held. 'Owlish prophets dazzlingly disproved' was the very characteristic jibe at the long-silent critics of the Ten-Hours Act of 1847 with which, 60 years later, Winston Churchill challenged those who prophesied ruin from the Act of 1908 which at long last limited hours of work for all miners.[74]

**Fear of the People**   Part of the difficulty in the early nineteenth century lay in a suspicion and fear of the industrial workers, a relic of the terror of the mob, kept alive by memories of the French Revolution. This was not finally to disappear until the significance of the striking contrast between orderly Chartism in Britain and revolutionary risings abroad was brought home in the 'Year of Revolutions', 1848. *Punch*'s cartoon of the meeting of the classes at the Crystal Palace in 1851—*Whoever thought of meeting you here?*—signalised the arrival of a new attitude, which was not seriously to be disturbed by the violence of crowds in political and economic agitation in the 60s and 80s.

**The People Unknown**    Fear of the mob was, of course, enhanced by the lack of a properly trained police force. Such a force was instituted in London by Peel in 1829, but there was no general provision before the 40s and 50s. Until then the ultimate weapon on the side of law, order and property was the clumsy one of the soldiery, who, as shown, for instance, at the 'Peterloo' affair at Manchester in 1819, could not distinguish between sober protest and revolutionary agitation. A further factor, as already suggested, was sheer ignorance, the fear of the unknown masses swarming in the squalid slums of the industrial centres. To the ignorance which Chadwick noted in 1842 can be added comments from the first report of the Children's Employment Commission of the same year which reveal the surprise felt by investigators at the unexpected revelation of decent sober men struggling to maintain standards of upright conduct among difficult conditions. The very commissioner who found the clergy of the Derbyshire mining areas unhelpful because of their lack of contact with the miners and their families could record, with appreciation, that many of the miners were Methodist preachers and would not allow swearing or unseemly conduct around them. With a touch that sounds a note not unfamiliar from many observations since, he adds to his report the comment that 'I must say I now entertain a much higher opinion of the colliers (both men and children) than I did from hearsay'.[75] There were similar comments, too, from all over the country. Southwood Smith, like the Fat Boy in *Pickwick*, might 'want to make your flesh creep' with his accounts of sexual licence, and shocking headlines might prove as effective in the nineteenth century as in the twentieth in rousing opinion, but his were extreme cases. Beatrice Webb likewise recorded, from her experience in East London in the 8os, cases of incest arising from overcrowding,[76] but more typical then, as throughout the century, was the comment of the Royal Commission on the Housing of the Working Classes in 1885 that the standard of morality even in the crowded quarters was 'higher than might have been expected'.[77]

**Attitudes of the People**    In truth, there was little enough understanding of the actual situation of the working classes. Sympathy might be stirred for those living under the most wretched conditions, but for the aspiration of the rest there was little consideration. If they were in work, they were above the need for consideration: if for any reason they were out of work it was assumed that they had made adequate provision for hard times. That they might lay a reasonable claim to a greater share of what they helped to produce was regarded as preposterous: that they might claim it all was considered as but the lunatic notion of professional agitators. It was too easy, and dangerously convenient, to dismiss all claims, in the sweeping manner of Mr Bounderby, as preposterous and extravagant and to insist that society had no obligations but to protect the destitute and the weak, to improve sanitary conditions and to pass laws for the better regulation of factories. Yet from the 30s there was an increasing class of better-paid wage-earners, as much above the poorest as below the employing and professional classes. It was a class that still found life a struggle and that was still liable to be affected by serious depressions of trade; a class that was concerned to increase its share of the prosperity which its industry was bringing to the country. At the same time, however, it was a class that, being above the immediate and obvious distress that caught sympathetic attention, tended to be ignored or complacently regarded as amply rewarded for its services. Charles Booth, in his studies of the London working classes towards the end of the century, criticised the general blurring of a fundamental distinction between the various grades of the working classes: '. . . it is not by welding distress and aspirations that any good can be done'.[78] This, however, was a lesson that was only slowly learnt. Wages were religiously regarded as too much a product of blind economic forces to be susceptible to regulation. If a man did not get on the fault was his. As Dickens put it in *Hard Times*, the successful employer's case was, 'What I did you can do':

Any capitalist who had made sixty thousand pounds out of sixpence, always professed to wonder why the sixty thousand nearest Hands didn't each make sixty thousand pounds out of sixpence, and more or less reproached them every one for not accomplishing this little feat'.[79]

**The Attitudes Criticised** The quotation neatly sums up a common attitude. The workers were regarded by many not as individuals with rights and claims on society but as mere instruments of productivity. 'Hands' was, indeed, the general term for them: they were, as Dickens said in bitterness, a race 'who would have found more favour with some people, if Providence had seen fit to make them only hands, or, like the lower creatures of the seashore, only hands and stomachs'.[80] Like most of Dickens's social criticism, this when it was written in the early 50s was probably not quite as valid as it would have been earlier. Twenty years before, Thomas Arnold, in his *Letters on the Social Condition of the Operative Classes*, had spoken out, from his own knowledge of conditions, in almost identical terms: 'A man sets up a factory, and *wants hands*. . . . What he wants of his fellow creatures is the loan of *their hands*. . . . These *hands* are attached to certain mouths and bodies which must be fed and lodged, but this must be done as cheaply as possible . . . because the comfort and enjoyment of the human being is quite independent of the serviceableness of his *hands*.'[81]

Nearer to Dickens's *Hard Times* the Royal Commission on Education in Wales, where in the remote valleys attitudes changed slowly, complained no less bitterly in its report in 1847 of employers who cared less for their workers than for their cattle: '. . . they use and regard them as so much brute force instrumental to wealth, but as nowise involving claims on human sympathy.'[82]

This was the other side of the medal from the 'hidden hand': it was comforting to reflect with Archbishop Whately that the 'beneficent wisdom of Providence' was directing towards the public good even the conduct which Arnold and many others condemned. To Arnold it was 'a national crime, a crime in the civil government, a crime in the church, a crime in all the wealthy and intelligent parts of the English people' that more was not done for the welfare of the owners of the hands. The much quoted scriptural text, *The poor shall never cease out of the land*, he exclaimed indignantly, did not mean that they should form the greater part of the population.[83] Thomas Carlyle in *Past and Present* (1843) similarly castigated the well-to-do for their indifference and, to the argument that it was impossible, owing to the laws of economics, to pay better wages, countered with 'it is impossible for us to believe it to be impossible': '. . . the world has been rushing on with such fiery animation to get work and even more work done, it has had no time to think of dividing the wages; and has merely left them to be scrambled for by the Law of the Stronger, law of Supply-and-demand, law of Laissez-faire, and other idle Laws and Un-laws.'[84]

**Chartism and Acquiescence**    The truly amazing phenomenon, for which no simple explanation will suffice, was that although improvements came so slowly there was no movement of revolt. The one popular movement, Chartism, was on the whole too orderly and too diverse to prove a serious menace: it suffered its first real check in the early 40s and subsided completely in 1848, though its inspiration was afterwards to be felt in many more constructive movements. 'By Heavens', said the Chartist leader, George Harney, in 1849, 'the patience—or, rather, the suicidal apathy—of the masses is wonderful and pitiable.'[85]

Harney was a pioneer of Socialism, indeed, a Marxist almost before Marx himself. To him as to many another fervent Chartist the political reforms demanded in the Chartist programme, the 'People's Charter' of 1838—annual parliaments, the vote for all men, equal electoral districts, removal of the property qualification for M.P.s, the secret ballot and payment of M.P.s—at first seemed to promise the means by which conditions could be improved. As he said in late life, reviewing the struggles of earlier years, 'When I was young the reform and regeneration of Britain seemed comparatively easy . . . give [people] knowledge and recognise their rights as men and citizens and the march of regeneration would be swift and sure.'[86] Swift and sure, alas, the process was not. Chartist activity was in fact in no sense a revolutionary movement, but simply an almost spontaneous gesture of protest on the part of the working classes against the worst evils of industrialisation and the meagre prizes, 'little better than blanks', which were all that they drew from the industrial lottery. As a movement of general protest it was given an edge by the economic distress of 1837–42 (the true 'hungry forties', though the phrase is a later invention) and 1847–8, and it was in these periods that it was most active. The movement was never, however, a united one: it varied greatly between different parts of the country and represented a diversity of interests. Factory workers protesting against their conditions of work, handloom weavers struggling to avert their inevitable fate and agricultural workers striving to overcome poverty and the new poor law, all were drawn into it. Its militancy was provided to no small extent by the Irish, who were pouring into England in great numbers and inevitably entering the labour market at the bottom. Many of them drifted into handloom weaving, and there was little in common between them, the increasingly skilled factory workers and the depressed rural labourers. With improving conditions the movement declined and the bitter lesson was learnt that, just and reasonable though its programme was, it had had no real chance of success. Harney and others turned to Socialism, but it was to self-improvement through trade unions and co-operative societies that most workers, at least among the more skilled, looked for better conditions after 1848. Political reform was not a major issue again until the 60s, nor did Socialism become one until the 80s, though this is not to say that there was quiescence or acquiescence: for some years, however, the pressures were contained.

What, in fact, the Chartists were mainly concerned to achieve was a mitigation of the worst evils of industrialisation, which they naïvely hoped might come through political reform. 'If a man asks what I mean by universal suffrage', a Chartist leader proclaimed at Manchester in 1838, 'I mean to say that every working man in the land has the right to a good coat on his back, a good hat on his head, a good roof for the shelter of his household ... and as much wages as will keep him in the enjoyment of plenty.'[87] Despite the seeming inconsequence, the inner logic of this remark is clear enough, and was to be justified by developments. As the industrial workers, through the suffrage and trade unionism, gained respect as citizens, they themselves achieved 'respectability', the Victorian synonym for independence, steadiness of conduct and moderate prosperity, and the State found it both possible and politic, without any concessions to Socialism, to give increasing attention to their needs.

**Trade Unionism**  What contemporaries thought of the trade unionism that, with slowly increasing prosperity, was in time to do more for the industrial workers than protective legislation is shown in *Sybil* and *Hard Times*. Disraeli and Dickens were interested and sympathetic observers, but neither understood—or could be expected to understand—the needs of the working classes or the impulses that moved them, and their writings reflect the attitudes and prejudices of the anxious and sensitive middle-class readers to whom they appealed. To Disraeli, characteristically, a trade union was a colourful and mysterious secret force, entrance to which was through the awe-inspiring initiation that takes place in *Sybil*.[88] To Dickens it was the meeting-place of honest men who, as in the *Men and Brothers* chapter of *Hard Times*, were there made the tools of dangerous and bigoted demagogues.[89] The Combination Laws passed under the shadow of the French Revolution had been repealed in 1824, though they were re-enacted in the following year with some exceptions in favour of trade-union activity, and in 1834 the 'Tolpuddle Martyrs' had been transported for administering a union oath, only to be pardoned, however, two years later. Not until the 70s did the unions receive legal recognition and protection, and they were long regarded with acute suspicion as an attempt to interfere with the free operation of economic laws. Even the best of employers resented and resisted attempts to organise the workers; indeed, the best resented them all the more as evidence of ingratitude to their paternal care. To take only one characteristic instance, though a striking one, a South Wales coal-owner, who once rebuked his son for taking the colliery doctor fishing when his services might at any moment be required, could yet declare in 1853, during a dispute over wages: 'I was and am thoroughly determined that [the works] shall stop if I am not to be Master and the Sole Arbiter of what wages I can afford to give.'[90]

**The Attitude of Labour** 'Blackleg' labour, of course, was in demand for strike-breaking and was easily supplied, whether from the poorer agricultural counties of Britain or from what a Scottish manufacturer in 1835 described as 'the boundless mines of labour in Ireland'.[91] Labour was a commodity like any other, it was maintained, and, if for any reason adequate and acceptable supplies were not at hand in England, Ireland in particular could fill the gap, regardless of whether there was the assurance of a permanent gap to fill. Irish labour could check extravagant claims by English workers: it was always possible, it was said, 'to put on the screw of the Irish competition',[92] as, indeed, is done by John Thornton in Mrs Gaskell's novel of the times, *North and South*.[93] What was not understood, both now and later, was that unlike other commodities labour could not be turned off at will. Manufacturers could, and did, take the view that the poor law would provide for workers whom for one reason or another they could no longer employ, but, as we shall see, the poor law was regarded with dread by the working classes, who failed to see why when through no fault of their own they fell out of work they had to undergo the indignity of poor-law assistance. Chartism itself was, in fact, to no small extent a protest against the reformed poor law of 1834, and its principles were aimed at achieving a system of government more sympathetic to the needs of the workers.

**John Stuart Mill** How those needs affected a particularly close observer can be seen in the case of John Stuart Mill (1806–73). Mill admits in his *Autobiography* that in his early years he had accepted the conventional views of his day, regarding private property and inheritance as 'the *dernier mot* of legislation' and any State interference with the accident that 'some are born to riches and the vast majority to poverty' as nothing short of 'chimerical'. The only hope for the poor lay in the Malthusian remedy of education leading to 'voluntary restraint on population'. After 1848, however, Mill realised that that this was not enough, and became an advocate of an idealistic Socialism under which 'they who do not work shall not eat', whatever their class in society.[94] Few others went so far, but from the end of the 40s onwards, with some of the worst evils being checked by legislation and—unexpectedly—no still worse ills resulting, the necessity for State intervention was increasingly, if grudgingly, conceded.

**The Resistance to Centralisation** For long there stood in the way of State intervention the traditional opposition to anything that smacked of centralisation, a distant echo of seventeenth-century storms. This opposition, as Chadwick found to his cost, was strong, if not fierce. As late as 1885 the Royal Commission on the Housing of the Working Classes could complain that much housing legislation was simply disregarded by local authorities, who 'condemned without a trial' anything that they suspected as tending to centralisation.[95] Ten years earlier resistance to attempts to check the appalling infant mortality of the Lancashire homes where mothers worked regularly in the mills had been led, in the name of constitutional liberty, with a proclamation of the sanctity of the family: 'I would far rather see even a higher rate of infant mortality ... than intrude one iota further on the sanctity of the domestic hearth. ... That unit, the family, is the unit upon which a constitutional Government has been raised which is the admiration and envy of mankind.'[96] This was an extreme statement but it represented the common doctrine of the age, which has never perhaps been more tellingly described than by Dickens in the scene in *Our Mutual Friend* in which Mr Podsnap with his characteristic sublime gesture brushes aside criticism of the operation of the poor law: 'I see what you are driving at. I knew it from the first. Centralization. No. Never with my consent. Not English.'[97]

**The Significance of State Intervention**   This opposition to central control, though something of a rearguard action, has been an enduring element in English life, and to no small extent the long struggle with the conditions produced, and the problems posed, by the new industrial civilisation has been a threefold conflict of individual freedom, local autonomy and central authority. 'Scarcely a single Englishman in 1833', one historian of the period has written, 'either foresaw or desired that profound growth in the role of the central government which marked the beginning of a welfare state.'[98] It was a new world that was first seriously considered in the 30s and 40s, a world which the easy-going methods of earlier periods lacked the means to control, and to which, indeed, their very casualness had contributed both for good and for evil. For most of the people of these islands a whole new way of life was coming into existence, symbolised, as many contemporaries realised, by the discipline of the factory bell. The all-powerful machine was the solvent of society. By concentrating and disciplining those who were compelled to serve it, it both exposed their wretchedness and in time provided them with the strength and discipline to help themselves to overcome it. At the same time the very nature and extent of the problems raised increasingly demanded the intervention of the State. Whether that was to end in the full control of Socialism or in some less complete system by which the resources created by industrialisation could be exploited for the general welfare was to be the major theme of social policy in the next hundred years.

**The Industrial Population**   Out of an amalgam of handworkers, agricultural labourers, children and Irish immigrants was created the industrial population of today. Kay-Shuttleworth, then simple Dr J. P. Kay, described the process as he saw it in the 30s in the case of a Buckinghamshire labourer transplanted with his family to the modest but more prosperous conditions of industrial Lancashire: '. . . the parents seem almost bewildered with the restless energy of the neighbours—astonished at the punctuality required—shocked with the abrupt manners of their fellow operatives.'[99] This was the contrast of North and South as Mrs Gaskell also described it (though her South was an idealisation), the contrast that existed before it was blurred by increasing industrialisation, by the rapid application of steam-power and by the unity imposed by the ceaseless activity of the railways (whirr! whirr! all by wheels;—whiz! whiz! all by steam!), the idols and supreme symbols of the steam age. It was not only the unaccustomed manners and unfamiliar surroundings that caused bewilderment. It was the punctuality, the strict attention to time-keeping that made men the slaves no longer of the variations of sun and seasons but of the clock, the machine and the mysterious processes of supply and demand. As Kay observed with concern, 'the persevering labour of the operative must rival the mathematical precision, the incessant motion, and the exhaustless power of the machine'.[100] Much advantage was in time to come of the change, but its first effects were bewildering and painful to simple folk. Kay noted that, while the transplanted parents were bewildered, the children rapidly adapted themselves, as children will. Yet the shock to the parents of the new manners, the new people and the new social disciplines is easily felt. And it was to be some time before the industrial workers, with other Buckinghamshire peasants breathing down their necks and ready to step into their place, and the Irish pressing behind them, could make head against the new discipline.

**The Railways and Population Changes**   Before the coming of the railways the movements of population that created the new industrial areas were in the main limited in range to some score or so of miles. The move from Buckinghamshire that Kay described was an exceptional measure of poor-law relief. The railways, however, widened and speeded the process even as they widened and speeded the exchange of goods and ideas. They therefore contributed not a little, as the years passed, to the characteristic developments of an age of which they were themselves so characteristic a development. They were drawn to the new towns and further assisted their growth. At the same time the incongruity between their sleek efficiency and the squalor they served did not fail to catch the attention of contemporaries. The first great burst of railway construction, though it was to be completely outshone by the second, in the 40s, came between the opening of the Liverpool–Manchester line in 1830 (heralded by George Stephenson's successful experiment with the *Rocket* in the previous year) and of the London–Birmingham line eight years later. With all else that was going on during them, these years of the 30s, we may therefore say, mark the beginning of modern England. The iron network then laid down still carries our goods and passengers; the investigations that were then first made into the conditions of life under industrial conditions are, we can see now, the cautious beginnings of the Welfare State. And, as we have endeavoured to show, there were not a few at the time who demanded that the same skill and urgency which were applied to problems of railway engineering should be applied no less to the new problems that were plaguing society. A report on the conditions of Sheffield in the 40s, when the second railway boom was at its height and sanitary legislation was being hotly debated, saw the dichotomy and claimed for that legislation recognition as a glory of the age more striking even than the marvels of the railways: 'The present railway movement will doubtless convey to future ages strong proofs of expanded intellect, applied to the production and distribution of wealth . . . but the fact that sordid money-getting speculation is one of the principal causes of the movement will also become matter of history. The efforts made to effect a national system of sanatory (*sic*) reform proceed from a much higher motive . . . that of disinterested philanthropy, and its permanent results on the economy of human life will make it the glory of the age in which we live.'[101]

That the philanthropy existed we cannot doubt, though we may be a little un-certain as to its necessarily being always and completely disinterested. The experience of the 30s had, however, shown, as Thomas Arnold, for one, had brought out in his *Letters* of 1831–2, that industrial expansion was no great cause for satis-faction in itself. Other values clamoured for consideration, and those values the pioneers of sanitation and factory reform were the first to bring to practical atten-tion. A century later Beveridge, in his Social Insurance report of 1942, pointed to the 'five giant evils' that barred the way to progress—Want, Disease, Ignorance, Squalor and Idleness.[102] Something has been said in this chapter of the first exposure, in the 1830s and 40s, of the evils of Disease and Squalor. We must turn now to Want and Idleness and the measures that were taken to grapple with them.

*Note to page* 72. In fact, for his own report, Chadwick drew on material that was being gathered by the Chilaren's Employment Commission.

# 4 | The Victorian Poor Law

## 1 *The Poor Law of 1834*

**Political Changes** If the fourth and fifth decades of the nineteenth century saw the first startled realisation of the conditions which industrial development was creating, they saw also the beginnings of the readjustment of the processes of government to the new demands. The reform of the House of Commons, long agitated and at last achieved in 1832, recognised the existence of new major centres of population by transferring representation from parts of the country, mostly in the south and west, which had declined in importance, to such growing towns as Manchester, Birmingham, Leeds, Bradford, Huddersfield, Sheffield, Bolton, Oldham, Sunderland and Stoke, towns which, though not the creation of the Industrial Revolution, were being magnified almost out of recognition by it and which were now represented in Parliament for the first time. At the same time the franchise was settled on a regular basis throughout the country and, though it was still restricted and associated with property-holding, it acknowledged the existence of new classes and interests. With the increasing recognition of social problems that was to come, the reform of representation and franchise inevitably led to an increase of government activity in legislation and to the increasing absorption of parliamentary time by government rather than, as in the past, by private members' business. The process, it is true, was a slow one: until his death in 1865, for instance, the popular and jaunty Palmerston, whose long ministerial career began in 1807 and culminated in his being Prime Minister, in his 70s, for almost the whole period from 1855 to 1865, could maintain that the best government was the one that legislated least. By 1865, however, the pace of legislative activity was already quickening and the further extensions of the franchise that took place in 1867 and 1884 served to hasten the process. Gladstone's first administration, from 1868 to 1874, and Disraeli's second, from 1874 to 1880 (his first had lasted for only a few months in 1868), mark the watershed of English legislation, and justified in their achievements Palmerston's prophetic comment that his own death would free Gladstone for 'strange doings'. Henceforth it was to the government that the public looked for legislative change, and it was to public support, as expressed in the House of Commons, that the government looked in its legislative projects. Political agitation that had hitherto, of necessity, taken extra-parliamentary forms, as in the case of Chartism, the Anti-Corn-Law League and the campaign for the Ten-Hour Bill, increasingly found expression both in and through the political parties that were now to be organised to win support for legislative programmes.

**Municipal Reform**   Two important measures had followed the carrying of the First Reform Bill in 1832. In 1834 the poor law had been reorganised and in the following year the municipal corporations, which were re-established as elected town councils. No more than the reform of the House of Commons did the changes in municipal government in 1835 in themselves ensure progressive administration. Indeed, one of the aims of the municipal reformers was by abolishing corruption and jobbery to make local government cheaper. Not until much later, on the whole, did the local councils become the vehicles of active policies of municipal improvement. In the meantime everything depended upon local activity and enterprise and on the willingness of the authorities either, as in the case of Liverpool, to seek private statutory powers, or, as with Birmingham under Joe Chamberlain in the 70s, to make adequate use of the permissive powers granted under public statutes. In any case the Act of 1835 did not affect the industrial centres unless they were already incorporated: Manchester, Birmingham and Bolton, for instance, received their charters only in 1838, Sheffield, Bradford and Oldham theirs in the 40s. Nevertheless, the municipal reforms were an important advance, not least because the franchise for the new councils was on a household basis, and therefore much more nearly democratic than for Parliamentary elections, though whether this affected the quality of representation must, for many reasons, be doubted.

*Ad hoc* **Bodies**   Local government in the counties, however, remained in the hands of the J.P.s until the more thoroughgoing reforms of 1888, though old duties were increasingly taken from them and new ones committed to the care of specially created bodies. It was tacitly recognised from the 30s that the machinery of both municipal and county administration, even with the changes in the former, was inadequate to the new demands upon government unless, indeed, there was to be such a central control of local activity as was anathema to the English tradition. To this is to be ascribed the creation of compromise *ad hoc* authorities, such as the Guardians of the Poor and, later, the School Boards, which were independently elected and, although subject to central direction, restricted in scope to particular tasks. The further arguments in favour of such authorities were the avoidance of political party intrigue in the municipalities, a factor of some importance in the case of the School Boards, and the lack, until later in the century, of qualified officials in local government service. It is difficult, in these days of a well-established and highly qualified service, to appreciate the significance of this latter point: in the words of the Webbs, '. . . there was, in 1835, no body of trustworthy, trained, professional officials. The specially characteristic modern vocations, whether of engineers, architects, surveyors, accountants, and auditors;

or of teachers, nurses, sanitary inspectors and medical officers of health; or even of draughtsmen, bookkeepers, clerks and policemen, were as yet only beginning to be developed.'[1] Under these circumstances an *ad hoc* body, grappling as best it could under the eyes of government inspectors, another significant administrative innovation, was for the time being the most effective instrument for particular tasks. It made possible the experimentation in the combination of central direction with local control that was demanded by English tradition, if it were to stand up to the test of problems far greater than it had ever before tackled, without succumbing altogether to the burden. This process of experiment, one may say, proved in the event one of the major tasks of the nineteenth century, and was to be of decisive significance for the future. The principle of inspection in the interests of efficiency and uniformity was, indeed, fundamental, 'the crowning feature of the new state', it has well been said, 'the magical formula that was to preserve the autonomy of local government yet ensure that the worst evils of society would be alleviated'.[2]

**The Poor Law**    The attempt to reconcile local control, in all its variety of needs and interests, especially as between rural and industrial areas, with the demands of national policy, was nowhere more marked than in the field of social policy, in the pioneer service of the poor law. The poor law had for so long been the preserve of local administration, or, more truly, of local maladministration, or sheer *ill*-administration. Now, for more than a century from the first efforts made in 1834 to match it to the needs of the times, it was to be a major preoccupation of the nation, as, indeed, it had already been for so long. At the same time, as more was learnt about the conditions and problems of industrial civilisation, it was to prove, with the concern for sanitation and factory conditions, the fount of much else in social policy and social action.

**The Case for Reform**    The case for a new approach to the perennial problem of poor relief lay in the early 1830s in the disorganisation and disrepute of the prevailing system, still operating on the lines described in chapter 2, with the modifications introduced in the 1790s to meet the economic stresses caused by the combination of bad harvests and the war with revolutionary France. The total cost to the country of the poor-rates, which had amounted in 1776 to $1\frac{1}{2}$ million and in 1802 to $4\frac{1}{4}$ millions, was still in 1832 seven millions, despite the passing of the war crisis and a fall in prices. The total, it is true, represented only a small part of the national income, probably no more than two per cent, but it amounted to one-fifth of the national expenditure and to people who had no means of assessing the national income it loomed appallingly large and seemed to threaten the economic foundations of society. Moreover, by keeping many able-bodied workers, especially in rural areas, dependent upon the public charity of the Speenhamland system with its allowances in supplementation of wages, it degraded their condition, robbed them of respect and made it wellnigh impossible for them either to have their wages adjusted to changing conditions or to escape to the greater promise of other areas. The worst evils, were, indeed, the maintenance of low wages, the immobility of labour and the destruction, in many cases, of any but the narrowest relationship between employer and employed. More men were kept available than were strictly required and although this suited some employers it created an artificial situation that was in fact a heavy burden on everyone concerned at a time when the demands of industry for labour matched the surplus rural population. Most of the ideals that had marked, however inadequately, earlier attempts to deal with the problem of the poor had disappeared in the general degradation of conditions. The Norfolk and Suffolk Unions created under Gilbert's Act, Dr Kay noted sadly in 1836, had come to be little more than 'a conspiracy among the employers for the reduction of wages',[3] and labourers complained only too often that they were treated 'like potatoes in a pit—only taken out for use when (the farmers) can no longer do without us'.[4] Indeed, with parish relief so readily available, it was customary to put men off in times of bad weather so that their wages could be saved.

The 'Labourers' Revolt', 1830   Parliamentary committees had considered the burden of poor relief in 1817 and 1824, but, concerned lest any sudden change of policy should provoke revolutionary agitation through despair, had found no acceptable remedy. Then in 1830 had come the shock of the 'Labourers' Revolt', the last violent protest in English history against rural conditions. The risings, spontaneous outbreaks of rick-burning, rioting and machine-smashing, had been confined to precisely those southern counties in which the Speenhamland system was best known, and were unmistakable evidence of its inadequacy in the face of continued economic stress. After 1830 it was clear that something had to be done, and it was to the reforming administration of Lord Grey, which in 1832 carried out the changes in Parliamentary representation, that the task fell. In the same year the Government set up a major commission of enquiry to look into the operation of the poor law and consider what alterations were necessary. It was, as the event showed, a step of the first importance both for social policy and for the very organisation of government.

The Royal Commission of 1832   The significance of the 1832 Poor Law Commission lay as much in its form and composition, its methods and its administrative proposals as in its actual recommendations for changes in the operation of the poor law. It was in the first place a Royal and not a Parliamentary Commission. That is to say that, unlike the committees of 1817 and 1824, it was not appointed by Parliament from its own ranks. The members of the Commission were nominated by the Crown from outside Parliament and were intended to conduct a fact-finding enquiry free from any suspicion of party bias or advantage. The device was an unusual, indeed almost a new, one, but it proved so successful that it became the standard method for the investigation of major national problems calling for legislative action, particularly in the field of social policy. Cynics have often pointed out that the device has at times seemed to degenerate into a useful means for postponing or avoiding legislation, while the need in matters of contention to make a Commission widely representative has led to disagreement resulting either in a report so general and innocuous as to be useless or in the appearance of majority and minority reports. The Royal Commission on Labour of 1891–4 might be regarded as a principal example of the former type, the Commission on the Poor Laws of 1905–9 as the supreme example of the latter. The 1832 Commission, however, both reported speedily and saw its recommendations converted into legislation as the Poor Law Act of 1834.

The method of appointment of the Commission also determined its working practice. It was to have Assistant Commissioners to carry its enquiries throughout the country and was therefore to base its findings on real knowledge. Moreover, the publication of its evidence, eventually achieved, though only in an incomplete form, in 12 volumes, was intended to secure the interest and support of public opinion. Like the agitation for parliamentary reform the Commission therefore marked a break with the long years of conservative reaction against the tide of revolutionary ideas which had been stirring men's minds since before the French Revolution. English institutions in these years had been almost idealised as 'the wisdom of our ancestors'. The 1832 Commission, however, subjected to stern enquiry the system of poor relief handed down from the palmy days of Queen Elizabeth, now seen only dimly through a fog of almost mystical reverence, and demanded that it should perform in a manner suited to contemporary needs the demands of contemporary society. By its very nature, therefore, the Commission represented a new approach to problems of government, a demand for scientific enquiry and a refusal to accept traditional methods at their face value, which were especially associated at the time with the teaching and inspiration of Jeremy Bentham.

**Bentham and Utilitarianism**   Bentham's was indeed one of the major influences upon the Commission. Several of its members, and especially Edwin Chadwick, who was appointed an additional Commissioner in 1833, were among his favourite disciples. Bentham's teaching was directed, in the famous phrase of his first work, *A Fragment on Government* (1776), towards 'the greatest good of the greatest number', to be achieved on strictly utilitarian lines, testing institutions solely for their serviceability to that end. He was thus the founder (though not the sole founder) of that brand of radical thought, Utilitarianism, or, to call it by its later name, Philosophical Radicalism, which, by synthesising and giving a philosophical and schematic unity to the reforming urge of the age, became the inspiration of the changes that, with some preliminaries in the 1820s, began in 1832. As Bentham himself said of the *Fragment*, 'this was the very first publication by which men at large were invited to break loose from the trammels of authority and ancestor-wisdom'. But Bentham was no revolutionary. He argued the case for the radical reform of institutions, to bring them into line with current needs, but provided that when suitably reformed they could promote the greatest good of the greatest number he was not only content to preserve them but was concerned to make them more efficient. Adam Smith, another Utilitarian, had argued that there was a natural harmony between the self-seeking of the individual and the well-being of society, the notion embodied in his image of the 'invisible hand'. Bentham was inclined to accept this notion in matters of economics, but in politics he believed rather that men should be guided, through the adoption of wise institutions, with manhood suffrage, annual parliaments and the abolition of privilege, to seek the expression of the principle of the greatest good and to give it effect. He was therefore in favour of governmental intervention in matters of poor relief, public health and education, which could not safely be left to purely individual efforts, and recognised the need for centralised government departments to control policy and overcome local opposition and differences. He was opposed to any notion of abstract rights, and would not agree, therefore, that a poor man had any 'right' to relief such as seemed to be assured by the Elizabethan system and its Speenhamland gloss. He believed, however, that as work led to prosperity and therefore happiness it was in the interests of the greatest number to help those in need to preserve their fitness for work. He even sketched, in characteristic turgid phrasing, a ministry of 'Indigence Relief'. Though his philosophy, like that of Adam Smith, was individualist, he recognised the limits of individualism and the necessity for some measure of State intervention in the defence of individualism itself. In his writings, in fact, are to be found the roots of both the extreme individualism and the developing collectivism that were to characterise the nineteenth century.

**Contemporary Views**   The prevailing attitude to the poor law at the time of the Commission's appointment was essentially Malthusian. Attention was concentrated not on the fundamental causes of poverty, which were hardly appreciated, still less understood, but on its most striking manifestation in the conditions of the rural workers, with parish allowances in relief of wages and additional payments for their children. It was believed that the administration of the poor law inherited from Elizabethan times had become too lax and that it was this laxity that was not only ruining the country through the financial burden of the poor-rates, but was demoralising the poor themselves by encouraging them to live at the community's expense and produce children for whom they could not provide. There was general agreement that provision must be made for the aged, the sick, the disabled and the children who could not support themselves. Indeed, the Commission itself paid hardly any attention at all to the case of these 'impotent poor', devoting to them little more than one of the 362 pages of its Report. It was the help given to the able-bodied that was regarded, in the Commission's words, as 'the master evil of the present system',[5] and as urgently calling for reform. There were many who demanded, with Malthus, the complete abolition of this relief, regarding it not only as ruinous to the country and morally degrading to the recipients but as tantamount to the robbery of the working classes as a whole. The common view of wages at this time was that they were drawn from a 'Wages Fund', which formed a fixed part of the return on capital available for wages, taxes and alms. Anything paid in poor relief, or even in charity, was therefore so much less available for actual wages. The logical corollary was that poor relief should not be given, and that it should be left to the normal working of economic laws to provide work and maintenance for all the able-bodied. This was not, however, the view of the Commission, which considered rather that the refusal of all relief would lead to begging and crime, whereas with proper safeguards the giving of public relief could be beneficial both to the individual and to society. Yet, implicit in this opinion was the view that in time poor relief, except for the impotent, would largely cease to be necessary. If it could not be abolished outright, it could at least be rendered less harmful, and, with the improvement in general conditions that could be expected to follow, it would eventually cease to be significant. This was to become, and was long to remain, accepted opinion. As late as 1895, for instance, the Royal Commission on the Aged Poor could resist the provision of old age pensions on the grounds that 'pauperism is becoming a constantly diminishing evil, ultimately to disappear before the continuous progress of thrift and social well-being',[6] while the standard history of the Poor Law, published a few years later, considered that the Commission of 1832 might have taken the risk of abolishing relief 'in the certain expectation that the unimpeded course of industrial progress has sufficient powers of absorption'.[7]

**The Report of 1834**    The Report of the 1832 Commission, which appeared in 1834, though it represented in its approach an advance in social and political enquiry, was produced in a hurry in response to the demands of a Government that was anxious to introduce remedial legislation. The evidence it presented, in the form of lively case-studies, was intended rather to support a predetermined case than to provide the evidence for a considered judgment. It was in fact what the Webbs have called 'good copy': 'What the Assistant Commissioners brought back from their tours was, in the main, an extraordinarily full collection of particular instances of maladministration . . . picturesque details of the action of particular parish officers; and amusing anecdotes of their peculiarities.'[8] This it was which, together with the unhesitating confidence of the Commission's recommendations and the general realisation of the unsatisfactory state of the poor law, made the Report the immense success that it was and the enduring influence that it was to remain. Tawney has well described it in *Religion and the Rise of Capitalism* as 'that brilliant, influential and wildly unhistorical report' which was to prove 'one of the pillars of the social policy of the nineteenth century'.[9] Unhistorical it certainly was, both in its treatment of the Elizabethan system and in its analysis of current problems. Its concentration on the abuses of the Speenhamland system revealed an imperfect and inadequate grasp of contemporary conditions and it was too easily satisfied with evidence that dependence on poor relief was due to 'indolence, improvidence, or vice'—the traditional view which has been described earlier—'and might have been averted by ordinary care and industry'.[10] It overlooked, as opinion was long to overlook, the possibility of genuine unemployment and it made no allowance, for instance, for sickness as a cause of extreme poverty. It was, indeed, only when the incidence of sickness and its relationship with claims for relief struck Chadwick and others later that it was realised that the problems of poor relief were rather more complex than had been realised. Hence the revelations that then led to Chadwick's report of 1842 on *The Sanitary Conditions of the Labouring Population*, described in the previous chapter. To some extent much of the reforming legislation that followed was aimed at filling the gaps in the Poor Law Report of 1834.

**The Report and the Industrial Areas**   In its concentration on abuses the report also overlooked the particular problems of the industrial areas, which were by no means to be explained in the same way as those of the poverty-stricken rural slums. From this there followed the great difficulty that was experienced in applying the reformed poor law to the north after 1834, and the bitter opposition which it roused, summed-up in the characterisation of the workhouses as 'Bastilles'. The glib reasoning of the report took no account of the phenomenon of industrial depression, and the fury with which attempts to apply it were greeted was little short of revolutionary: indeed, it gave an edge to Chartist agitation in many centres. In the event the Commission's recommendations were never carried out in their full vigour in the industrial areas: in fact, in view of the widespread nature of industrial depression, they could not have been. It was to be a very long time, however, before the true nature of industrial unemployment was understood.

**The 'Principles of 1834'**   The fundamental principles on which the Commissioners based their report were, first, the refusal of poor relief to the ablebodied except on terms which would prove them to be so utterly without the means or the hope of independent support as to be willing to accept any conditions to avoid the real risk of starvation, and secondly, the fixing of those terms and conditions so as to keep the position of the relieved person below that of the poorest independent worker. The first principle aimed at preventing fraud; the second, the famous principle of 'less eligibility', at encouraging a return to normal work at the first opportunity. In both were to be seen the influence of Bentham, exercised largely, though not wholly, through Chadwick, who was responsible for the section of the Report which described the remedies proposed. Bentham had taught that men were governed by the 'two sovereign masters, *pain* and *pleasure*', and that according to the principle of utility they would decide their conduct and weigh alternatives in the light of their expectation of these. From this it followed, in the Poor Law Report, that if relief were given only on severe terms it would not be sought except in cases of serious need. Further, the principle of 'less eligibility', though obvious enough, as the Report showed, as a check on fraud, owed much to Bentham's plan for a model penitentiary, the *Panopticon*, in which the convicts were to be kept in a condition which 'ought not to be made more eligible than that of the poorest class of subjects living in a state of innocence and liberty'. The corresponding passage in the Report, which was written by Chadwick, who was an ardent advocate of the principle, argued that the situation of the man in receipt of relief 'shall not be made really or apparently so eligible as the situation of the independent labourer of the lowest class'. The parallel is obvious.[11]

**The 'Workhouse Test'**    The application of these two principles implied a third, that of the 'workhouse test'. The enquiries of the Assistant Commissioners had made only too clear the great variety in the treatment of the poor throughout the country, and the many opportunities for fraud and corruption. What was needed was a simple test of need which would allow no variation or uncertainty in its application. Such a test had already been devised in the eighteenth century, in certain parts of the country, through a refusal to give relief except in the workhouse: those who were 'offered the house' and accepted it could then be regarded as genuinely in want. The test had been legalised by the Act of 1723 which, as already mentioned, enabled parishes to unite to provide themselves with a more adequate workhouse, but had been repealed in fact by Acts of 1782 and 1795. It had, however, been restored in 1820, and it was the experience of 12 years in certain centres which, presented in the Commission's Report, and urgently pressed by Chadwick, made the case for an important modification in general poor-law policy.

**'The 43d of Elizabeth'**    The case claimed to be based on a return to the pure principles of 1601 by setting the poor to work in accordance with what were proclaimed to be 'THE SPIRIT AND INTENTION OF THE 43d OF ELIZABETH'.[12] This ingenious attempt to exploit reverence for tradition with radical principles of utilitarianism unfortunately revealed an ignorance, or wilful ignoring, of the actual terms of the Elizabethan system, as critics were not slow to point out at the time. The Elizabethan statutes, as was shown earlier, made provision for 'houses of correction' in which 'rogues and idlers' could be compelled to work, but provided for the unemployed poor only 'a convenient stock of materials', upon which, presumably, they were to work at home. What the 1834 report did, in fact, was to confuse the house of correction with the setting of the poor to work. Its argument was that as it was not always possible, or convenient, to provide normal work, the workhouse 'appears to be the only means by which the intention of the statute of Elizabeth, that all the able-bodied should be set to work, can be carried into execution'.[13] Lest the workhouse should attract by its comfort or security, however, the principle of 'less eligibility' was to apply, and the workhouse to deter all but the most desperately needy cases by its strictness of discipline and its restraint upon liberty. Families were to be separated, workhouse clothes worn, silence preserved at meals, all visiting or visitors prohibited and smoking and beer-drinking not allowed. Adequate food and shelter were to be provided, but that was all, and adequacy was not to be interpreted liberally.

**The Test of Pauperism**   Such was to be the remedy for the lax operation of the poor law: 'the offer of relief on the principle suggested by us would be a self-acting test of the claim of the applicant'. This, indeed, was the beauty of the system—'if the claimant does not comply with the terms on which relief is given' (that is, if he refuses the 'offer of the house') 'he gets nothing; and if he does comply, the compliance proves the truth of the claim—namely, his destitution'.[14] This seemingly simple and infallible 'workhouse test', by which Chadwick set great store for the rest of his life, was to prove the most enduring provision of the 1834 report. What the report also achieved was the drawing of a clear distinction, in theory, between poverty and pauperism. The poor, who had hitherto been helped, in very many cases, by the system of allowances in supplementation of wages, were now to be left to their own devices. Only the destitute, who knew not where else to turn for support, were to receive relief, and in so doing were to become paupers. The Elizabethans had spoken simply of 'the poor'. The nineteenth century distinguished between poverty and pauperism and provided for the latter almost penal treatment. Experience was to show that even pauperism was not quite the simple issue that the hurried investigations of the Commissioners of 1832 had suggested. Not until later, however, was it realised that the fundamental problem of *poverty* remained, and that 'the course of industrial progress', looked to so confidently, was in fact neither unimpeded nor able to overcome poverty.

**The New Administration**   To ensure that the new principles were properly carried out, and to avoid the variety and laxity of the prevailing system, the Commission made proposals which, translated into law by the Poor Law Amendment Act that followed, not only created a national system of poor-law administration where previously there had been chaos, but began the shaping of English government to modern purposes. Hitherto such policy as had existed had been made, within the broad lines of the Elizabethan system, only within the individual parish, or at best in the eighteenth-century unions of parishes, and had been subject to all the vagaries of local opinion, prejudice and sentiment. The Elizabethan legislation had prescribed only the aims of policy, the means having been increasingly left to local action. Now not only the aims but the detailed means were laid down, and a central body was established to prescribe the means and ensure their being carried out. 'The bane of all pauper legislation', the Commission reported, 'has been the legislating for extreme cases. Every exception, every isolation of the general rule to meet a real case of unusual hardship, lets in a whole class of fraudulent cases, by which that rule must in time be destroyed.'[15] Legislation was not enough in itself to enforce the general rule and to ensure that the workhouse test and the principle of 'less eligibility' were strictly and consistently applied everywhere. There must be a more efficient local administration and, for the first time, central control and inspection. To provide more adequate local resources parishes were to be grouped in Poor Law Unions, with elected Boards of Guardians and paid full-time officials. At the centre was to be, not a government department but a Central Board of three Commissioners, with Assistant Commissioners to serve as inspectors. All this was purely Utilitarian in tone and reflected particularly the teaching of Bentham: it aimed at efficiency and the greatest good of the greatest number, and left no discretionary powers. As the Report argued, if the abuse of legislating for extreme cases were to be avoided such cases of extreme hardship could not be legislated for and must be left to private charity: the balance of advantage lay that way.

The significance of this system of administration lay not only in its reflecting Utilitarian principles but in the pattern it provided for a national approach to the many local problems that were now pressing for attention. Central direction of policy was combined with local control of administration by professional officials. The notion of an independent Central Board, not subject to detailed Parliamentary scrutiny and control, was introduced in the naïve hope that in this way the poor law could be kept free of party political warfare. The hope was vain, for, as Walter Bagehot wrote in his *English Constitution* (1867), Parliament would not let the Board alone, but 'poked at it'[16] (as it pokes at similar Boards today) until in 1847 the experiment was abruptly wound up and the three Commissioners were replaced by a President of the Poor Law Board sitting in Parliament like any other Minister. In the meantime, however, the pattern of a central Department, with local authorities and permanent officials, had come to be accepted, and was being applied to other branches of government. The Boards of Guardians themselves, administering the 600 Unions into which the 15,000 parishes of England and Wales were combined, endured until 1930, when their functions were absorbed, under the Local Government Act of 1929, by the Local Authorities. The Poor Law Board itself was replaced in 1871 by the Local Government Board, which in 1919 became the Ministry of Health.

'Well-regulated Workhouses'    Quite apart from the political difficulties which it encountered and the fierce opposition it aroused in the country, the Central Board of 1834 found itself far less effective, however, than the framers of the Report had hoped it would be. The Report was intended to present a reasoned case on which enlightened opinion would be prepared to act. In fact it was soon apparent that the main concern in many areas was simply with the reduction of the rates. 'Less eligibility' and the workhouse test were adopted as money-savers rather than as means for the redemption of demoralised paupers. Chadwick and others had hoped that the uniting of parishes would enable provision to be made for adequate workhouses, classified according to the needs they were intended to meet, whether those of old people and the sick, children, able-bodied men and able-bodied women. The Report presented a startling picture of the average 'general mixed workhouse' in which all categories were jumbled together in what was in effect 'a large almshouse',[17] without any discipline for the able-bodied or any training for the young which would encourage them to prepare for a more hopeful future. What was wanted, it was argued, were separate buildings where each class might receive appropriate treatment, where 'the old might enjoy their indulgences without torment from the boisterous; the children be educated, and the able-bodied subjected to such courses of labour and discipline as will repel the indolent and vicious'.[18] These, provided that the workhouse test was applied, would be 'well-regulated workhouses', more economical in administration and more effective in checking pauperism. In practice, however, this elaborate policy was found to be impracticable. Separate buildings were more costly, and if, as had been anticipated, old buildings inherited from the previous parish administration had been used, they would have proved too scattered. In the event Parliament, at the instance of rate-paying interests, refused to give the Central Board powers to compel Guardians to spend any adequate sum on workhouses, and no serious attempt was ever made at classification. For some time all classes in need of relief were pushed into the one 'general mixed workhouse', which provided the simplest answer to all problems and made for ease of supervision. What, of course, was needed was an analysis of those in distress—the able-bodied, whether unemployed, idle or vagrant, the children, the elderly and the sick in body or mind—and appropriate methods for dealing with them based on something better calculated to meet their needs than the mere workhouse test. The obsession with the able-bodied rural labourer receiving allowances in the supplementation of his wages dominated the whole enquiry, however, and the next 60 years were to be spent in making good the omissions, until, after special arrangements had been made for the children and the sick and to some extent for the elderly, in 1905 even the able-bodied without work were given help outside the poor law and in 1908 the old age pensioners. From the moment that the Act of 1834 was put into operation, in fact, information began to be gathered on its inadequacy, and the first revisions were made in the next decade: with ever-increasing knowledge and understanding of the problems involved, the process was still not completed by the reforms of 1948.

**Limitations of Reform**   However unsuitable it might be to the circumstances of the applicant, the workhouse test was gradually applied, however, after 1834, and workhouses were conducted on principles deliberately designed to deter. The simple fact was that it was not appreciated at first how many of those compelled to rely on public relief were, for various reasons of age or infirmity, even of temporary infirmity, incapable of supporting themselves. For such people, and children were included among them, if some temporary measure of out-relief would not meet the case, 'less eligibility' and the workhouse test were wholly irrelevant issues. The only point that could be made in favour of such conditions was, in the case of an elderly person, that he should have provided for himself by thrift in earlier years, and, in the case of a child, that someone should similarly have provided in advance for him. The Report took the view that it was no business of the State to interfere with 'the ordinary laws of nature' by providing 'that the children shall not suffer for the misconduct of their parents—the wife for that of the husband, or the husband for that of the wife'.[19] Where there was genuine misfortune, in the interests of the greatest good only private charity could temper the strict application of the workhouse test: better that one individual should suffer than that the laxity of the pre-1834 period should return.

The Influence of the 1834 Report    How much this attitude, not argued by the Report but laid down as axiomatic, came to dominate official thinking, even under changed conditions, was revealed in the evidence of a senior official of the Local Government Board before the next great poor-law enquiry, the Commission of 1905–9. Under examination by George Lansbury, the Assistant Secretary of the Board, J. S. Davy, afterwards Sir James Davy, expressed his regret 'that any decent man should have to go into the workhouse',[20] but added that even if such a man were in need through no fault of his own, '. . . he must stand by his accidents; he must suffer for the general good of the body politic . . . what you have to consider is, not this or that pauper, but the general good of the whole community'.[21] There spoke the authentic voice of 'the greatest good of the greatest number': Davy, Lansbury complained, was 'steeped in what he described as the eternal principles laid down by the Poor Law Commissioners of 1834'.[22] Utilitarianism was dying hard, and the Local Government Board was one of its last strongholds. Davy clearly had in mind the caution of the 1834 report against legislating for extreme cases, and the Local Government Board itself was no less clearly concerned not with the shaping of a policy which would meet social needs but with the application of principles laid down, after what proved to be inadequate consideration of the evidence, in 1834.

Poverty, Pauperism and Charity    What is remarkable and impressive, indeed, is the respect long paid to 'the principles of 1834'. 'The labours of the early reformers of Poor Law administration', wrote Thomas Mackay in 1899, 'are regarded with reverence and admiration by every thoughtful student of social history.'[23] It was widely expected in official circles that the Commission of 1905 would be compelled by the evidence to do no more than restate the 1834 principles and insist on their strict application. The success which the reforms of 1834 did meet in abolishing the wage-allowance system was regarded as tantamount to the abolition of the whole problem of extreme poverty among the able-bodied. Yet by the end of the nineteenth century it was apparent from the careful social enquiries which were being conducted by such pioneers as Charles Booth that the real problem was not pauperism but poverty, not the excessive reliance upon public relief that had been checked in 1834 but the utter inability of many people, for reasons quite beyond their control, to pull themselves up by their boot-straps as the 1834 report had assumed that all could. Many, very many, were doing this, but a considerable class was finding it impossible, and social investigators were revealing to a shocked public how large that class was and how little removed from actual destitution. For such people the Local Government Board, in its narrow and pedantic attachment to the principles of 1834, had no remedy, apart from some relaxation of rules in times of acute distress. The answer of the 1834 report to these 'extreme cases', which were so numerous as hardly to qualify as 'extreme', lay, of course, apart from personal thrift, in private charity, and the 60 years that followed the Poor Law Amendment Act of 1834 were the heyday of charitable activity, culminating in the strict principles of the Charity Organisation Society of 1869. Private charity, which could be dropped at any time, was regarded as not open to the same abuses as public relief. 'A man who does an act of charity', said J. S. Davy to the 1905 Commission, 'is doing himself good, whereas the guardian who gives relief is doing himself harm.'[24] This extreme view was reflected by Mackay: 'The burden undertaken by private benevolence may be a dead weight, but it cannot become an active centre of disease. The voluntary principle has a healing and antiseptic influence, and contains no widespread advertisement of the advantage of unsocial habits.'[25] 'Healing and antiseptic influence'; it is the authentic voice of latter-day Utilitarianism and of the genuine but narrow charity of Victorian wealth. As Dickens commented in *Our Mutual Friend*, one would 'appreciate our Poor Law more philosophically on an income of ten thousand a year'.[26]

**'Collateral Aids'**    Yet the Act of 1834 had failed to achieve much of what Chadwick and others had hoped for. True, the parish allowances were stopped, though not everywhere at once, and the total cost of poor relief, which had been just over six million pounds in 1833–4, fell by about one million pounds in the next 10 years. It continued to fluctuate between five and six millions until the late 60s, after which, however, it rose steadily to 10 millions in the 90s and 14 millions by the time that the Royal Commission of 1905 was appointed. Expenditure per head of the population was then only 7d. a year less than in 1833: the failure to prevent this increase in cost was clearly not due merely to the growth of population. Equally clearly there was no general 'repulsion from the Poor Law' such as observers at the turn of the century assumed had been the primary object of the 1834 system. In fact, however, the objects, as planned, had been more constructive than this. What Chadwick himself had hoped was that, while all but the absolutely destitute were discouraged from applying for relief, the 'repressive measures' to achieve this should be accompanied by 'collateral aids'. Among these he included attention to health and housing, the importance of which he appreciated even before the revelations of his 1842 report, education and, in order to wean working men from the drinking which was almost their only solace, 'public parks and zoos, museums and theatres'.[27] For the able-bodied, though he wished to make them fend for themselves, he wanted a modification of the settlement laws, which would encourage them to seek work outside their own parishes. All this was to come in time, but the actual system established under the Poor Law Amendment Act of 1834 did not even carry out the proposals of the Report on which it was based, and certainly gave no heed to Chadwick's collateral aids. Thirty years of pressure were needed, for instance, to break down the resistance to any change in the settlement laws, even to provide for an extension of the settlement from the parish to the Poor Law Union of which it formed part under the new system. Not until 1865 and 1876, as shown in chapter 2, were the necessary modifications made in traditional practice, vital though these were, as Chadwick realised, to the mobility of labour.

## 2 The Poor Law in Operation

The Policy in Practice    Similar resistance, as has already been mentioned, met the proposals for specialised workhouses meeting particular needs: in practice it was the 'general mixed workhouse' which was everywhere established. Nor was the Central Board able to give the firm lead for a consistent and unified policy which had been intended. Indeed it was not long before the pressure for local control and parsimony at the centre together created the situation, long to be the distinguishing mark of the Local Government Board, that instead of initiating and guiding public policy the central body devoted its energies to checking and restraining local authorities whenever they showed any tendency to stray beyond the limits of what a narrow interpretation of poor-law policy permitted. From the start, in fact, the central body lacked the power to make anyone do anything. What was remarkable was that it was able to persuade the local authorities to do so much before the first great administrative change of 1847, which finally made the central body a governing and ministerial rather than a reforming institution.

A handicap from the first was the neat principle of 'less eligibility', which had seemed on paper to promise so ready a way out of the morass of allowance-pauperism. Unfortunately, no one knew, Chadwick least of all, by what standard eligibility was to be measured. Who was the 'independent labourer' whose condition was to be superior to that of the pauper, and how were his earnings to be estimated? Even the workhouse, for all its limitations and discomforts, was a better place than many independent labourers could afford. In fact, of course, there was an almost infinite variety of standards throughout the country, and the more careful the adherence to the principle of 'less eligibility' the greater the variety of standards of relief. Hence the great differences in practice which, as time went on, marked the actual operation of the 'reformed' poor law, contrary to all the hopes and expectations of the Commissioners of 1832. Nor did the Central

Boards, in their various forms, fail to add to the variety by their own policies, which again were variously interpreted.

'Less eligibility' was an abstraction. More real, and no less subject to local variations, was the giving of relief in their own homes ('out-relief') to the elderly, the sick and even, in times of emergency, to the able-bodied. The problem of the 'impotent poor' was hardly touched on by the 1834 Report, and no attempt was made by the Act to interfere with out-relief to them. The relief given was only too often inadequate and in the interests of efficiency attempts were in time to be made to persuade Guardians to replace it with adequate in-relief in the workhouse. Here was ample scope for variety of practice, as there was also in the definition of the kind of emergency for which the able-bodied might receive out-relief. In short, by the end of the century the poor law was not only still in existence but was being applied with almost as great a range of practice as before 1834, while it was only too evident that it was leaving certain serious social problems if not untouched, certainly unsolved. Hence the Royal Commission of 1905.

**The Rural Areas**    What actually happened after 1834 was that many problems forced themselves on public attention to which the famous Report had no answer, or to which it even gave what was manifestly the wrong answer. When the Act was passed and the new Commissioners were appointed, with Chadwick, to his disappointment, only their Secretary, the first attack was launched on the easy target of the southern counties. Here success attended the Board's efforts, though mainly at the expense of the rural labourer, who found himself deprived of his accustomed allowances. It had been assumed that once the vicious system of allowances was abolished wages would rise, but this did not happen. A succession of good harvests and the alternative employment offered by the new railways eased the situation, but the lot of the agricultural labourer remained miserable enough, at least until the great changes that took place in English agriculture later in the century, when new methods and the competition of imported foodstuffs drove very many men off the land (see note, page 153).

**The Industrial Areas**    If the effect on rural wages had been miscalculated, the failure to grasp the essential problems of the industrial areas was almost disastrous. There was already in those areas the free market for labour which it was sought to establish in the south: the difficulty was through all the ups and downs of industrial growth to provide work for those only too willing to take it. The workhouse test was meaningless in circumstances where work was simply not to be had. A Bolton manufacturer wrote to Chadwick in 1841, in the middle of the years of acute depression which later gave their name to the 'hungry 40s', 'When we who live amongst it, see a thousand families brought to poverty by mere want of employment, the Poor Rates doubled, and parties asking relief or pining in want who never asked for relief before, we cannot stand silently by or stamp them all as imposters.'[28] The workhouses under these conditions could not accommodate all the able-bodied who required relief, and out-relief was the only alternative. Thus, to take only one telling example, and that not an extreme case, poor-law expenditure in Sheffield rose between 1837 and 1843 from £12,000 to £55,000, most of the increase being spent on out-relief, while almost as much again was paid by the trade unions to their unemployed members.[29] So much for the scorn poured in the 1834 Report upon anyone 'who attributed pauperism to the inability to procure employment'.

**Industrial Opposition**   It was, indeed, the attempt, begun in 1837, to apply the 1834 system to the problems of the industrial areas, of which it had shown itself to be almost entirely unaware, that came near to breaking the system before it had started and certainly caused it to be seriously modified. Wild rumours spread as to the intentions of the new Act and in many places the appointment of Boards of Guardians was forcibly prevented by great crowds. The resistance was associated with the Ten-Hours agitation, and such fervent advocates of factory-reform as Fielden, Bull and Oastler therefore took a leading part in it. Fielden prevented the application of the Act to Todmorden while Oastler held Huddersfield and in Bradford the military had to be called in to protect the new Guardians. Fielden also led the attack in the House of Commons, where he was supported by Disraeli, recently elected to the House, who pressed for the repeal of the Act as a disgrace to the country, which 'announces to the world that in England poverty is a crime'. The whole conception of the new workhouses lent credence, of course, to the view that poverty was to be treated as if it were a crime. Indeed, one official confided to Oastler that conditions in the workhouses were to be 'so severe and repulsive as to make them a terror to the poor and prevent them from entering'.[30] This was 'less eligibility' with a vengeance, but it merely rendered frantic men who despite every desire for work could not get it. Nor was the situation eased by the fact that some of the southern Guardians, now firmly applying the law in the rural areas, were arranging for the emigration of their surplus labour to the industrial areas. Inevitably this looked suspiciously like a policy aimed both at forcing down wages and at preventing, or breaking, strikes. It seemed all the more sinister when signs of industrial depression began to appear, though the policy was then suspended. One can imagine, however, the rough reception accorded to such immigrants as the Buckinghamshire labourer mentioned in the previous chapter. It was particularly this 'blackleg' policy that roused Oastler to fury and he denounced the whole system as 'an act of TREASON' in an hysterical speech afterwards reprinted as a pamphlet under the resounding title, *Damnation, eternal Damnation to the fiend-begotten, coarser-food New Poor Law*, one of the most widely known of his writings.[31] The poor law, a contemporary observed with more moderation, but no less bitterness, 'did more to sour the hearts of the labouring population than did the privations consequent on all the actual poverty of the land'.[32]

**The Lack of Alternatives**  Unfortunately the opposition had no alternative scheme to offer. Oastler pinned his hopes to the Ten-Hour Bill, but even that was no final remedy. Better hours and conditions of work and better wages could, it is true, buttress the workers' conditions against depression and the poor law, but, as was shown in the previous chapter, it was to be many years before manufacturers and economists could reconcile these aims with sound industrial progress. The prevailing view was that labour was in danger of being spoiled and must be kept in its place: 'the English labourers', a Liverpool clergyman complained, when justifying the bringing-in of Irish labour, 'have unfortunately been taught their rights till they have almost forgotten their duties'.[33] When they heard such views as these the workers could not but associate the employers' approval of the new poor law with their opposition to the Ten-Hour Bill and regard both as evidence of a plot to keep them in subjection. The prison-like conditions of the workhouses then assumed a new significance. Not until some improvement of industrial conditions had been secured, trade-union organisation had been strengthened and trade-union, friendly-society and co-operative funds had been built up, did the workers achieve some margin of protection. Meanwhile pressure for the Ten-Hour Bill was allied with agitation against the poor law and both became merged in Chartism.

**Modifications in Policy: the 'Labour Test'**  The forces of order were too strong, however, and with no practicable alternative in sight the new poor law was gradually applied throughout the industrial areas as in the agricultural. By 1839 the process was well-nigh complete, the Unions were formed and the Boards of Guardians at work. Circumstances in the industrial areas, however, caused a modification of policy in practice. Throughout the country outdoor relief was from the beginning continued to the sick and elderly and this practice was eventually given formal regularisation by the *Outdoor Relief Regulation Order* of 1852. Similar relief to the able-bodied and their families was permitted for a time, in view of the industrial depression, but when by 1844 conditions had improved, it was formally prohibited, except in cases of emergency, by the *Outdoor Relief Prohibitory Order* of that year. The exceptions were defined as cases of 'sudden or urgent necessity', a phrase which was intended to allow a good deal of flexibility in interpretation, and in the hands of humane and considerate Guardians did so. For more normal conditions, however, as it was recognised to be impossible in times of depression in industrial areas to find room in the workhouses for all who would be in need of relief, a 'labour test' had already been instituted. The *Outdoor Labour Test Order* of 1842 permitted outdoor relief to the able-bodied in return for work, work which would be both a return for the money received and a test of the applicant's need of relief. This was an ingenious combination of 'less eligibility' and the workhouse test, and was widely adopted, though experience showed, as it had done long before, that it was impossible to find reasonable work for men to do: hence the numerous stone-yards for stone-breaking up and down the country. Yet, even with a labour test, outdoor relief was better than the workhouse.

The labour test was a crude attempt to apply the principles of 1834 to the special problems of the industrial areas. Its application in practice varied a great deal and contributed to the confusion of poor-law practice which the Commission of 1905 set out to unravel. At times a strict attempt to apply it could have quite fantastic results. In his evidence to the 1905 Commission J. S. Davy cited an occasion at Blackburn when it had been difficult, owing to the number of applicants, to find enough relief-work, and recourse had been had to the crude expedient of compelling the men to attend at the workhouse and sit, without occupation, in its dining-room for some hours each day. A more degrading device it would have been difficult to find, and not surprisingly, after the first amused reaction, the numbers of men attending began to drop off. 'At the end of a week', Davy commented, 'we had found out the most effective labour test I have ever seen.'[34]

The comment is a revelation of the outlook with which the poor law was applied. Although this had not been the intention, the method adopted in 1834, and adapted in 1842, to check and prevent abuses had become a frankly-avowed deterrent.[35] What happened to the needy who refused to accept degradation was no one's concern, unless private charity took a hand. If a man refused relief on such terms as were prescribed he was regarded as not genuinely destitute, much in the same way as in the 1920s and 30s an unemployed man could be regarded as 'not genuinely seeking work'. Idlers there no doubt were, but there were also men with pride who struggled to manage without recourse to help offered on terms that shamed them. As the Mayor of Nottingham wrote in 1840, 'the poor (from *dread of the House*) sell or pawn one article of clothing or furniture after another until they have scarcely anything left'.[36] This attitude, however, the nineteenth-century poor-law system seems never to have understood. Chadwick and his colleagues had had no intention of making the acceptance of relief under conditions of genuine need a mark of disgrace, but, narrowly conceived and with the abuses of the years before 1834 in mind, this was the notion that coloured practice. In fact, there were many who looked on applicants for relief as the failures of society, regardless of the reasons for their need, saw them, indeed, as people 'whose only success is the acquisition of a character indisputably incompetent'.[37] 'In every country it is unfortunate not to be rich', commented that keen-eyed observer, Alexis de Tocqueville, soon after the establishment of the New Poor Law, 'in England it is a horrible misfortune to be poor.'[38]

**The Horror of the Workhouse**    It was this attitude to the unfortunate which, taken together with the prison-like character of the workhouses, made the poor law an object of horror to the working classes in the nineteenth century. Oastler and others concerned in political agitation fiercely denounced it and with it 'the three Bashaws' of the Board who supervised it, and a lively pamphlet war sprang up all over the country. The workhouses, as symbols of tyranny, were stigmatised as *Bastilles*. The pamphleteer G. R. W. Baxter published in 1841, under the title *The Book of the Bastiles* (*sic*), a collection of denunciatory quotations from pamphlets, through which he sought to save the country from 'the nostrums of a new-fangled philosophy' and 'the rotten remains of the jawbone of Malthus filched from his tomb'. Typical of local comment in an industrial area were the criticisms of Samuel Roberts, 'the Pauper's Advocate', in Sheffield. In a whole series of vigorous pamphlets Roberts proclaimed that 'the doom of the new Poor Law is sealed ... God is against it' and called for a return to 'the divine Poor Law of Elizabeth'. The paupers in the workhouse, reflecting what was now the widespread view, he described as 'prisoners guilty of nothing but poverty'.

It was, indeed, as prisons that the workhouses were regarded. 'Gaols without guilt' the Webbs have called them, and Lloyd George described them in 1909, in an even more striking phrase, as 'the gaol as well as the goal of poverty',[39] from which old age pensions were to deliver the elderly. The dislike and horror with which the workhouses were regarded have, of course, been preserved in contemporary literature. The workhouse of *Oliver Twist* (1837–8), for instance, with its thin gruel, so typical of 'less eligible' fare, is only too well known, and has made a phrase immortal. Dickens returned to the attack in *Our Mutual Friend* (1864–5), in which Betty Higden, with her terror of becoming 'like the poor old people that they brick up in the Unions' and her proud determination to die 'untouched by workhouse hands',[40] symbolises the working class's aversion. In *Little Dorrit* the workhouse is unfavourably compared with the debtors' prison in which William Dorrit is confined and in which he receives the aged pauper Old Nandy, of whom William says in pity, 'In the Workhouse, sir, the Union; no privacy, no visitors, no station, no respect'.[41]

Dickens was moved by the revelation, which 'Podsnappery' dismissed with its 'peculiar flourish', of poverty preferring to face starvation rather than to seek relief, and portrayed it, in highly coloured style, in the character of Betty Higden. His picture drew criticism and in the famous postscript to *Our Mutual Friend*, which includes the account of the railway accident which nearly killed him, he rounded on his critics with his denunciation of the illegality and inhumanity of poor-law administration, the worst, he maintained, 'since the days of the STUARTS'.

To the early period of the new system, because based on contemporary records, belongs also the vivid impression in Arnold Bennett's *Clayhanger* of the workhouse looming over the early years of his master-printer, Darius Clayhanger. From the workhouse Darius, as a boy, had been rescued, with his parents, by the Sunday School superintendent, Shushions. The melodramatic whisper of 'The Bastille!', with which, nearly half a century later, an ageing Darius receives the news that Shushions, now senile, is himself dying in the workhouse, and the effort he makes to prevent his actually dying there, are a telling evocation of Victorian attitudes.[42]

The workhouses were, and were long to remain, the principal target of criticism of the principles and operation of the poor law. George Lansbury's grim account, in his autobiography, of his first visit to Poplar Workhouse after his election as a Guardian in 1892 is well known: '. . . going down the narrow lane, ringing the bell, waiting while an official with a not too pleasant face looked through a grating to see who was there, and hearing his unpleasant voice . . . made it easy for me to understand why the poor dreaded and hated these places. . . . It was not necessary to write up the words "Abandon hope all ye who enter here" . . . everything possible was done to inflict mental and moral degradation . . . of goodwill, kindliness, there was none.'[43] This was after considerable improvements had been made on the original standards. The impression made on an impressionable man who was himself the essence of goodwill and kindliness explains why under Lansbury's lead the Poplar Guardians got themselves into trouble for the generous policy they adopted, so that 'Poplarism' eventually became a byword, and in 1921 the whole local Council, led by Lansbury, even found themselves for a short spell in prison. It was not only workhouse conditions that Lansbury criticised, though these were bad enough as he described them, with their whitewashed walls, the jangling keys, the huge books for recording names, the hideous coarse clothes and the complete lack of underclothes, even of sanitary equipment for women.[44] It was even more the whole attitude to the poor that disturbed him: 'decent treatment and hang the rates!' was to be his policy.[45] In the early years of the twentieth century, when the social conscience was stirring and others, too, were deploring the workhouse spirit, John Galsworthy gave literary expression to their criticism in words that echo Lansbury's protest: '. . . . you have a horror of the needy. You invite us, but when we come you treat us justly enough, but as if we were numbers, criminals, beneath contempt—as if we had inflicted a personal injury on you; and when we get out again, we are naturally degraded.'[46]

Comments such as this and protests such as Lansbury made were becoming by no means uncommon by the turn of the century.[47] They helped to prepare opinion for the changes of policy made in the 10 years before 1914 by such measures as the Unemployed Workmen Act, Old Age Pensions and Unemployment Insurance, changes which worked themselves out over some 40 years until, in the words quoted in chapter 1, a Minister could appeal to those in need not to hesitate to claim 'the rights which a Christian and civilised society gives'. No longer do the needy make their way to the forbidding workhouse to face degradation: the officials of the one-time National Assistance Board (now part of the Ministry of Social Security) will if necessary seek them out in their own homes, and the Ministry's own local offices and interviewing rooms are a far cry from the whitewashed prisons of the poor law. It is above all the dignity of the individual, even of the poorest, which has been asserted, and this was a consideration which the reformers of 1834, obsessed as they were with the degradation of the allowance system, thought of only in negative terms.

**Collateral Aids—Thrift**    That relief was, as is now accepted, a matter of right, not of charity, was the theme of the protest against the 1834 poor law made in the House of Commons by Disraeli in 1837, in support of Fielden's unsuccessful attempt to prevent the application of the law to the industrial areas. Another critic, Thomas Arnold, who, as has already been shown, was keenly alive to the distresses of the industrial workers, deplored the harshly negative approach of the new law and the failure to add to it measures 'of a wider and more positively improving tendency'. Chadwick, as we have seen, had plans for such 'collateral aids' and it was along these lines that, as the needs became manifest to all, much was gradually to be done during the rest of the nineteenth century. Much had also to be done, however, by the workers themselves. The 1834 report justified its faith in 'less eligibility' as a standard that would still satisfy human needs by drawing attention to the high level of savings in the savings banks of the country and to the number of agricultural labourers who were depositors. Personal thrift was obviously regarded as not only a necessary but a possible protection against pauperism, and it is indeed true that there was during the century a tremendous increase of friendly-society and trade-union funds.[48] 'What sent up friendly society membership by leaps and bounds?', asked an official of the Ancient Order of Foresters in 1898, when old age pensions were under discussion, and the answer was simple—'fear of the poor law',[49] an answer seemingly confirmed as early as 1836 by a comment by one of the poor quoted in the second annual report of the Poor Law Commissioners, 'we must look out for ourselves . . . now that there is no parish to look to'.[50] Arnold in 1839 exclaimed in a letter to a friend against this driving of the poor 'into economy by terror': 'Economy itself is a virtue which appears to me to imply an existing competence; it can surely have no place in the most extreme poverty; and for those who have a competence to require it of those who have not, seems to me to be something very like mockery.'[51]

Yet the assumption was that, once the indulgences of the pre-1834 period were withdrawn, prosperity, and therefore savings, could not but increase. The 'unimpeded course of industrial progress' would not only maintain the worker and his family but would enable him to save for sickness and old age. It was a comforting thought, from which it followed inevitably that not to encourage thrift and discourage improvidence was to do an ill-service to the workers. It was a commonplace of social criticism in Victorian times—and later—that the poor spent their money unwisely: to quote once again from Mackay's account of the poor law, which is almost a compendium of prevailing Victorian opinion, the need to provide for periods of disability is therefore 'a blessing in disguise'.[52] Hence the long opposition to old age pensions, on the grounds that to award pensions would discourage the young worker from saving. In the words of Nassau Senior, 'old age is so much the general lot of human nature that it would strike too much into the providential habits of the poor to make anything like a regular and systematic provision for it'.[53] What opinions such as this failed to take into account, of course, even granted adequate wages, was the difficulty of persuading a young man to make provision himself for an eventuality so remote and uncertain as old age seems in early life. Further, the poor law itself for long positively seemed to discourage thrift, since the possession of any means at all, even the result of provident habits, formally disqualified an applicant for relief.[54] Not until the years between 1894 and 1904 was it finally decided that small friendly-society payments need not disqualify, though even this concession was resisted by Local Government Board officials, one of whom argued that any relief given of right 'must tend to encourage improvidence'.[55]

What was eventually discovered when old age pensions were established in 1909 was that many old people who came forward to claim their pensions had concealed their need out of fear of the poor law, and had struggled on somehow on the verge of destitution. They were evidence, Lloyd George said in 1911, of 'a mass of poverty and destitution in the country which is too proud to wear the badge of pauperism',[56] and, as recorded in chapter 1, the same phenomenon was to be observed again in 1940 when supplementary pensions were inaugurated. Here is a searching indictment of all attempts to 'test' need, whether under the 1834 poor law or under the 'means test' regulations of the 1930s. The assumption that because people have not come forward for relief they are not in serious need has been disproved again and again. Ironically enough, society today, because of earlier discouragements and degradations, has actually to coax the needy to claim their rights.

**Friendly Societies**  The response to old age pensions in 1908 was something of a surprise, but as Lloyd George made clear in introducing his insurance scheme in 1911 it was well known that many workers, however provident they endeavoured to be, were unable to save enough, through their friendly societies or otherwise, to protect them against life's ills; this despite the growth of savings which had already impressed the commissioners of 1832–4. Friendly societies of various kinds had long been in existence as local 'societies of good fellowship', as they have officially been described, generally centred upon an inn and providing the means by which a group of men could mutually provide for sickness and the support of widows and orphans. They were first accorded statutory recognition in 1793, and a series of Acts in the nineteenth century, notably those of 1846 and 1875, gave them a legal status and a central Registry to watch over their affairs. Their great development during the century was due in part, no doubt, to 'fear of the poor law', but quite as much to the need for protection against illness and the desire to have money available in case of need among men who would normally consider themselves as safely above the reach of the poor law. Indeed, as came to be realised, it was precisely those who were most likely to need poor-law assistance at some time who, from the very inadequacy of their earnings, could make least provision for a rainy day. The friendly societies were, as Lord Beveridge has said, 'as natural a by-product of industrialization as was the smoke of the factories'.[57] With their democratic origins and organisation, their good fellowship, their fundamental seriousness of purpose, their discipline and their solemn ceremonial, a relic of earlier gild pageantry, which brought a touch of colour into many lives, they were the perfect expression of the solid worth of the more prosperous sections of Victorian working-class life. Their very development was evidence of the gradual spread of a measure of prosperity among the workers. Yet, as Lloyd George pointed out in 1911 when introducing his Insurance Bill, less than half of the working population were even moderately covered against the effects of illness, fewer than one in ten against unemployment.[58]

Despite many failures and not a little fraud, the membership and resources of the friendly societies reached impressive proportions. The first general figures became known in the 70s, when the Royal Commission on the societies (1871–4) undertook its investigations. By that time many of the local societies had expanded into such great national organisations as the *Oddfellows* and *Foresters*, both of them dating, in their modern form, from the 30s. These were, and still are, societies with branches, federal in structure, and, although originally developed out of the need for sick pay, offering many other benefits—old age pensions, funeral benefit, endowment insurance and the like. They were the 'Affiliated Orders', which through their constitutions preserved the fellowship of the local friendly societies from which they had grown. In the 70s their membership amounted to some million and a quarter, their funds to more than seven million pounds. Thirty years later, on the eve of the Liberal reforms, their membership had increased by one million, their funds by 16 million pounds. In addition there were such unitary societies as the *Hearts of Oak*, founded in 1841. In all there were in 1905 some six million members of friendly societies, with funds amounting to more than 40 million pounds.

**Funeral Insurance**    The other great motive of insurance was the avoidance of pauper burial, widely regarded with the horror and shame of which Betty Higden is the pathetic literary expression. Out of this motive came two major developments. There were, first, the 'collecting societies', which employed agents to collect small weekly premiums, the leading Societies being the Liverpool Victoria, Royal Liver and Scottish Legal, all of them founded in the 40s or early 50s. In addition there were the Industrial Assurance Companies, to which burial insurance was a business like any other. Of these the largest and wealthiest was from an early date the Prudential, which was originally founded in the bitter experience of the cholera epidemic of 1848–9, began its oddly-named 'industrial assurance' in 1854 and by the 70s had one million policy holders: when its first Secretary, Sir Henry Harben, died in 1911, its funds amounted to £77,000,000. Run as it was on strict business lines, and skilfully exploiting, almost as a State guarantee, the need, from which friendly societies were by law exempt, for a government duty stamp on its policies, the Prudential attracted enormous support at a time when many small friendly and burial societies were defaulting through bad management or downright fraud. For many years it offered burial insurance on relatives, and especially on children, which was technically illegal and manifestly open to serious abuse, but which nevertheless showed by its popularity that it met a real need. The Royal Commission on Friendly Societies of 1871–4, which paid particular attention to the Prudential, unsuccessfully urged the government to enter this field of 'industrial assurance', with its high administrative costs, its pushing methods, its numerous lapsed policies and its large profits. The administrative problem of collecting a multitude of tiny premiums was, however, in the absence of any wide scheme of national insurance, an insuperable one, while the government was in any case reluctant to undertake any activity that might interfere with the friendly societies. Though recognising that the situation was unsatisfactory, Lloyd George in 1911 was unable even to attempt to tackle the problem, and it was not until 1948 that, under the National Insurance Act of 1946, a State 'death grant' to cover funeral expenses was at last introduced. As a formidable critic wrote, with characteristic pungency, in 1937, the efforts made earlier to introduce this desirable reform were consistently resisted, in the name of 'thrift' and 'self help', 'by those who had made large fortunes out of the practice by others of these virtues'.[59] The problem of taking the profit-motive out of the practice of thrift was, however, no easy one until the institution, after the Second World War, of an all-embracing national system.

By 1911, as Lloyd George noted, there were in existence 42 million policies for funeral benefit.[60] This was the most popular form of personal thrift; inevitably so, for few among the working classes could hope, without a long period of saving, to meet the sudden heavy call of funeral expenses, particularly on the scale then demanded by convention and respect.


**Other Savings**    To these protective provisions must be added the resources of the building societies and the Post Office Savings Bank, instituted by Gladstone when Chancellor of the Exchequer in 1861 to encourage small savings. In 1870 post-office deposits amounted to 15 million pounds, in 1905 to 200 million. Building society assets increased in the same period from 18 to 60 million pounds. Building societies and post-office savings were beyond the reach of all but the better-paid sections of the working classes, but there were also the trade unions, which provided for their members much the same benefits as the friendly societies. Trade-union membership in 1905 amounted to about two million, their funds to nearly £6,000,000, and their annual benefit payments to about £2,000,000, though this was little more than a third of the total paid out every year by the friendly societies. Small wonder that it was difficult, in the light of these figures, to believe that many workers still lacked savings and insurance against sickness, unemployment and death, though this had become clear by the early years of the new century. There were in fact only too many who found it difficult to put aside regularly even the minute sums that insurance and friendly-society payments called for. The Royal Commission on the Aged Poor had recognised in 1895 that for many the setting aside of money for old age, even if it could be achieved, meant a hard struggle and deprivation: 'We do not suggest that, in exercising the thrift necessary for a provision in old age, working men should lead penurious lives or deprive themselves of reasonable comforts.'[61] The struggles and sacrifices that lay behind this revealing comment may well be imagined. Unfortunately, 'penurious lives' were precisely what low wages and fear of the poor law compelled many to lead, despite the substantial savings of so many others. In its enforced penury and denial of comforts, thrift, as Arnold Toynbee observed, 'may often brutalise a man as much as drink'.[62]

**The Temperance Movement—Samuel Smiles** One much publicised method of thrift which had a significant place in Victorian social activities was, of course, the temperance movement, the struggle against the wastefulness and physical degradation induced by 'the demon drink'. Until the changes wrought after 1914 by legislation and taxation and by new social habits based in great part on rising standards of prosperity and education, indulgence in drink was a common phenomenon among all classes, most deprecated among the poor because most obvious among them. It is difficult in these days of greater sobriety to recall the shame and squalor with which drink was associated and the hopes of moral and economic salvation that were held out to those who would 'take the pledge'. Mercifully, nowadays drunken brawls and the sight of men reeling home on a Saturday night are largely a thing of the distant past. A century ago, however, saving on drink was a favourite device of Samuel Smiles, that apostle of self-help, with his admiration for the self-made men of the Victorian pantheon. Smiles was fond of showing how much could be done with the pence saved by giving up beer: 'how much of human happiness', he wrote in *Thrift* (1875), 'depends upon the spending of the penny well'. Spending the penny well, by which he meant looking after the pence until they became pounds ('a penny saved is the seed of pounds saved'), could not only liberate the thrifty from the dread of the poor law, but could lay the foundations of a handsome fortune, with perhaps 'a Liverpool Mayor' thrown in.[63]

Smiles did not invent the creed he preached, but, as the vast sales of his books showed, he gave his period, the age of capital accumulation, the perfect expression of one of its standard virtues. What he and other advocates of universal thrift failed to recognise, however, was that the friendly-society and trade-union savings of the working classes were much less a minor form of capital investment than a mutual insurance against the ills of life. The emphasis on brotherhood, the portrayal of the Good Samaritan and other appropriate characters on certificates and processional banners, the use of such mottoes as *Bear ye one another's burdens*, all testified to the fundamental helpful fellowship of the organisations (the co-operative movement in origin was similarly inspired). To miss this feature is to miss the significance of much nineteenth-century working-class organisation, but it was a mistake which middle-class observers like Smiles commonly, if under-standably, made.

**Abandoning the 'Principles of 1834'**  From this sketch of the resources accumulated and developed by the working classes in their own defence we turn to consider the operation of the 1834 poor law and the introduction of other measures of social policy to meet needs exposed by the impact of the Industrial Revolution. When in the 1920s the Webbs came to write the account of the 1905 Poor Law Commission, of which Mrs Webb was a member, in their classic sur-vey of poor-law development, they could point to only one real achievement of that abortive Commission, the discovery of what had really been happening since 1834. So much respect was still being paid in 1905 to the 'principles of 1834', especially, as the quotations already made from the evidence of J. S. Davy to the Commis-sion have shown, in high official circles, that until the Commission reported it was not generally realised how much those sacred principles had in fact been whittled away. What the Report of 1909 revealed, the Webbs pointed out, was that the principles of 1834 'had been, almost unawares, gradually abandoned in practice', and that 'there had grown up, during the preceding half century, an array of competing public services which were aiming, not at the prevention of pauperism, but at the prevention of the various types of destitution out of which pauperism arose.'[64] The process of the prevention of destitution was far from complete, but, as has already been suggested, 1905 and the years of Liberal reform that followed marked an important stage in the process, a turning-point, in the treatment of one class of the destitute, the able-bodied, now coming to be called the 'unemployed'. It was, however, the revelation of what had happened to the principles of 1834, and the refusal, in either Majority or Minority Report, to return to them, that marked the real significance of the Commission of 1905-9 and helped to set public policy, in time, on new paths.

**The 1834 Poor Law in Operation**  The three Poor Law Commissioners, with Chadwick as their Secretary, administered the new law from 1834 to 1847, when they were replaced by the Poor Law 'Board'. Under constant pressure from the 'poking' of Parliament and from the hostile agitation in the industrial areas, they failed, much to Chadwick's disgust, to press their policy. In the 40s they both formally permitted a considerable degree of out-relief, even to the able-bodied, and relaxed their supervision of local administration. Chadwick, after a number of quarrels, increasingly turned his attention to the sanitary problems raised by his 1842 report, and from 1847 was no more concerned with poor-law matters. The immediate cause of the changes of that year was the scandalous case of the Andover workhouse, where paupers had been so ill-fed that on being set to work at grinding bones for fertiliser they had fought over such scraps of food as the half-rotten bones afforded. The case exposed the slackening of control at the centre and led to the parliamentary storm out of which the Poor Law Board emerged as a minor government department. A new Act was passed at the same time to establish an Inspectorate and to offer some improvement in workhouse conditions. One significant improvement was the granting of permission to old married couples over 60 to occupy a separate bedroom in the workhouse, though in practice few had the courage, or the knowledge of the regulations, to take advantage of the concession, which long remained, as was complained in the House of Commons, 'a dead letter'. Not until 1885, in fact, was the concession made obligatory.[65] Until then, as Flora Thompson has written in the delightful, but unromanticised, record of the conditions of her childhood in the 80s in a North Oxfordshire hamlet, *Lark Rise* (Juniper Hill), 'old couples were separated, the men going to the men's side and the women to that of the women, and the effect of this separation on some faithful old hearts can be imagined'.[66] If this concession of 1847 took 40 years to become effective, there were numerous other respects in which workhouse conditions continued spartan, not to say deterrent; not until 1868, for instance, were Guardians compelled to provide such minor comforts as backs to the benches on which old people sat or little chairs for children's sick-wards, while it was only in the 90s that toys for the children could be supplied.

**Deterrence**   In truth, workhouse conditions were for long little better than deterrent not merely to the able-bodied but to the sick, the aged and the children, the classes for whom the 1834 report had proposed special arrangements. This was an almost unavoidable result of the economy that concentrated all classes in a general mixed workhouse, but it was equally an application of 'less eligibility'. The sick, the aged and the young among the poorer but self-supporting classes were far from well off; the conditions for those who had to come into the workhouse had therefore to be still worse. Since, however, this could not be achieved by any positive action, it could be managed only by what amounted to hardly more than neglect. This inevitably led to abuse and scandals, which in time roused public opinion to demand better measures and a more positive policy. Thus, in 1849, at the height of the national cholera epidemic, there were serious outbreaks of disease at 'farm schools' at which workhouse children from London were being boarded, or 'farmed', out, and the exposure of the conditions under which they lived led to a more adequate provision of workhouse schools. Again, in the early 60s, in addition to the serious distress caused by the 'cotton famine', the result of the American Civil War, there was considerable unemployment and poverty. Many of those forced out of work preferred to risk starvation rather than face the rigours of the workhouse—a condition that Dickens had in mind in his attacks on the poor law in *Our Mutual Friend*—and the criticism that followed led to the setting-up of a parliamentary committee. Only a few years later, at the time of the cholera epidemic of 1866, there were revelations about the condition of the sick in workhouse wards that caused such an outcry that policy was abruptly reversed and from 1867 the building of proper hospitals was encouraged.

## 3  New Trends from the 1860s

**A New Policy**    The change of policy in 1867 brought to an end 20 years of comparative inactivity that had followed the establishment of the Poor Law Board, and prepared the way for the Local Government Board of 1871, with its wider responsibilities. From the 70s the policy was increasingly adopted of confining deterrence to the able-bodied and of making more adequate provision for those unable to care for themselves. The process was inevitably hastened by the reforms in both central and local government which broadened the basis of political responsibility and brought democracy nearer.

(1) *The Children*    In the case of children more was gradually done, both to provide an education which would help to fit them for an independent life and to remove them from the workhouse atmosphere, though it was not until 1915 that Guardians were at last forbidden to keep children in a workhouse with adults. As early as the 30s some workhouse schools had been started and Dr Kay and Dr Arnott had stressed in their reports the need for more. It was with his care for the education of workhouse children, indeed, that Dr Kay began the distinguished career in education that saw him in 1839 on the staff of the Education Committee of the Privy Council, the precursor of the Board (later, Ministry) of Education, and eventually Sir James Kay-Shuttleworth. There was reluctance in many areas, on the grounds of 'less eligibility', to provide for workhouse children education which was not available for other children, and, as Kay recorded, it was sometimes felt that to teach a pauper child to write was both preposterous and dangerous, 'like putting the torch of knowledge into the hands of rick-burners'. Yet, as Dickens asked pertinently in 1850, 'should pauper and outcast infants be neglected so as to become pests to Society or shall they be so trained as to escape the pauper-spirit? . . . Common sense asks, does the State desire good citizens or bad?'[67]

The problem was how best to care for the children. Few workhouses could afford an adequate school and an Act of 1844 encouraged Unions to combine to provide 'District Schools', though little advantage was for some time taken of this measure. The preference in London was for 'farming out', but after the tragic revelations of 1849 District Schools were established. Others followed in the more densely populated areas, but until the coming of a national system of elementary education in 1870 the workhouse children in most Unions were dependent on what the workhouse school could offer them. The large District Schools, 'barrack schools' as they came to be called, with anything from 500 to 2,000 children, were in any case no answer to the problem. They both cut the children off from the community ('hot-house plants' one German critic of the system called them[68]) and failed to provide anything remotely resembling a family atmosphere, while at the same time they only too often produced seriously unhealthy conditions. Their further development was prohibited in 1896. An alternative arrangement, adopted at Neath and Birmingham in the late 70s, was the Cottage Home, which broke the large institutions into smaller 'families' for living, though maintaining central school facilities. A more humane and less institutional approach, however, was that adopted in 1893 in Sheffield, where 'Scattered Homes' were provided. This system took advantage of the education provided by the public elementary schools but spread the children through the city in scattered homes so that they went to different schools and mixed with other children. This system, as the Chairman of the Sheffield Guardians told a parliamentary committee in 1896, had the great advantage of removing 'the workhouse taint' and was the most advanced of its time: it was to be widely adopted. Not until 1929, when the Boards of Guardians were abolished, however, did the education of poor-law children finally and completely become a matter for the Local Education Authorities. Meanwhile the Poor Law Commission of 1905-9, in its Majority Report, while recommending close co-operation between Guardians and their Local Education Authority Committees, paid a tribute to the *esprit de corps* of the poor-law schools which is too choice a specimen to be overlooked: '. . . . abundant evidence is to hand that those educated in these schools carry away with them a memory of happy days spent there . . . and that they find the membership of the school a bond of union of no mean strength. Results like these are the pride and glory of our great public schools, and it goes far to justify the Poor Law school system that it produces, in a smaller measure no doubt and in humbler form, results of the same kind.'[69] Here, as in one or two other places in the Majority Report, one can surely sense the touch of the aristocratic chairman, Lord George Hamilton. Yet, even if this comment claims too much, the education of pauper children, within the limits set by the times, was not without its successes. One fear, that it might produce lifelong paupers, was swept away by a special investigation in 1896, which showed that of 38,000 inmates of London workhouses only 200 had been educated in the workhouse. Its effects might better be judged, in fact, from the career of Will Crooks, whose hatred of the workhouse and District School in which he spent some time as a boy of eight in 1860 coloured his outlook when, with George Lansbury, he became a Poplar Guardian in the 90s and later a Member of Parliament.

One obvious method of care for poor-law children which was only slowly adopted was that of boarding-out. Traditionally this method had been much used in the old poor law, but it was long deprecated after 1834 on the grounds that suitable homes were difficult to find and that any payment made to working-class foster parents would be likely to be 'more eligible' than the amount they could afford to spend on their own children. From the late 60s, however, as part of the change of policy introduced in 1867, boarding-out was reluctantly permitted, and within 20 years it was being openly encouraged. From 1862 a number of children were also placed in some of the many homes run by voluntary social workers and societies, of which the most famous were the Homes started by Dr Barnardo in Stepney in 1870. It was a study of the methods used in certain of these voluntary societies that encouraged the development of cottage-homes. The voluntary societies were particularly concerned with the blind, crippled and defective children, for whom the workhouse could not yet make adequate provision, but they also offered training, especially in the training-ships which prepared boys for the Royal Navy and the Merchant Navy, one of which, the *Arethusa*, began its work in 1866 as a development from Lord Shaftesbury's 'Ragged Schools'.

(2) *The Sick*  Chadwick's revelations had shown in 1842 how much pauperism was due to illness, and, as we shall see, a beginning had been made in the provision of a public health service. Little was done by the poor law, however, until the 60s, except to allow outdoor relief in the case of illness even to the able-bodied: not until 1865 was a Medical Officer attached to the Poor Law Board. Meanwhile workhouse medical officers and district medical officers attended the paupers and in the economical early days of the revised poor law their services were even sought by public tender. In 1842, however, the doctors were put on a salaried basis: readers of Trollope will recall that Dr Crofts in *The Small House at Allington* (1864) received £100 a year 'for the medical care of all the paupers in the union'.[70] Even with allowances made for the limitations of Victorian medical knowledge the service was not extravagant: not until 1864, for instance, were Guardians allowed to supply such 'expensive medicines' as cod-liver oil and quinine. The next two years, however, saw much public agitation about the conditions of the workhouse sick, stimulated by a series of epidemics that culminated in the widespread cholera outbreak of 1866, with its death-roll of nearly 20,000. It was realised that, despite the cleaning up that had been done since 1842, a more extensive and more determined attack on disease was everywhere required: sanitation was not, after all, enough. At the same time the causation of disease was at last beginning to be understood: infection and contagion called for the isolation and improved care of patients. In 1867 the President of the Poor Law Board declared categorically in the Commons that deterrence must no longer be the aim in dealing with the workhouse sick; a new policy would be adopted.

There followed a remarkable period of reform and development in what was to prove an embryonic national hospital service. Unions everywhere were encouraged to combine to form 'Sick Asylum Districts' large enough to support hospitals to which the sick could be removed from the workhouses, and the most striking results were achieved in London, for which special arrangements were made by the Metropolitan Poor Act, 1867. A Metropolitan Common Poor Fund, pooling the resources of London Unions and parishes, was established, together with a Metropolitan Asylums Board for building and maintaining isolation hospitals for infectious cases, infirmaries for the non-infectious, asylums for the mentally-ill (the lunatics, as they were still crudely called) and dispensaries for those who did not need in-treatment: soon there were no fewer than 14 isolation hospitals. At first only paupers were admitted, but infection was no respecter of persons and in the interest of the public health the hospitals were soon thrown open to all who needed them. Isolation and other hospitals apart from the poor law had been sanctioned by the Public Health Act, 1875, and were encouraged by later Acts, but were slow to become adequate to their task. The Local Government Board formally recognised in 1878 that for many people treatment in the poor-law hospitals was 'the only mode in which their medical needs can be adequately met',[71] and five years later, in 1883, the Diseases Prevention Act legalised admission to the hospitals without any question of poor-relief. Stately 'Infirmaries' were now built up and down the country, and are still in use today. In 1885 a still more significant measure was passed. Hitherto the acceptance of any form of poor relief, even if it were only treatment at a hospital, had disqualified a man from the franchise, on the grounds that no one should have a share in the election of those who were responsible for relieving him. The disqualification had not been a serious one until 1867, when the vote was extended to working-men in towns, but it became still more serious when working-men in the rural areas became voters in 1885, particularly so in Ireland where rural poverty was rife. Quite apart from the disfranchisement of paupers, it was manifestly preposterous that men should be disfranchised merely because they, or members of their families, had taken advantage of the poor-law hospital facilities which in many cases, as the Local Government Board had acknowledged, were all that were available to them, and in 1885 the clumsily-styled Medical Relief Disqualification Removal Act was passed.[72] Henceforth medical relief alone did not disqualify a voter. It was the first step towards the complete removal of electoral disqualification from those receiving State assistance. Twenty years later the Unemployed Workmen Act and the Old Age Pensions Act removed it from those who were affected by these measures, but it was not until 1918, when the franchise was still further extended, that the disqualification was finally removed altogether.

At the time of the Poor Law Commission of 1905-9 strict poor-law officials such as J. S. Davy, who, as his evidence to the Commission showed, would even have disfranchised Civil Servants,[73] were still deploring the 1885 concession, which they rightly saw to be 'the first nail in the coffin'. As purist defenders of the principles of 1834 against demagogic indulgence they regarded the measure as the ominous beginnings of a return to earlier laxity. Yet it was in fact no more than the recognition of a real need. With the better understanding of disease had come also great advances in surgery, made possible by the use first of anaesthetics and then, from Joseph Lister's pioneering work in the 60s, itself a development from Pasteur's discoveries, of antiseptics. Hospital facilities were inadequate to meet the growing demands of a population that was itself growing apace. Hence the success of the poor-law hospitals. After 1885 they were increasingly used by non-paupers until, as the 1905 Commission recognised, they had become 'practically State hospitals'.[74] They were mainly restricted, however, to London and the other large centres of population. Elsewhere people were dependent either on workhouse sick-wards or on voluntary hospitals, which varied greatly in size and efficiency and proved unequal to the demand. By 1906, as the Poor Law Commission noted, there were almost as many beds in the London poor-law hospitals as in the voluntary hospitals of the whole of England and Wales, and they were being used by much the same classes of people.[75]

London, in fact, with its great teaching hospitals as well, was reasonably adequately served, and drew patients from other parts of the country. As a noted social worker, Mrs Helen Bosanquet, who was a member of the 1905 Commission, had commented 10 years earlier in a study of the problem of poverty, 'the poorer people of London obtain gratis medical and surgical treatment of the very first class, and such as none but the very rich can afford to pay for'.[76] What was long overlooked, of course, was that this treatment was too often given in a manner humiliating to the recipient that has left its mark even on the National Health Service of today. The doctors and surgeons, and still more the consultants, concerned, whose professional advancement depended to no small extent on their practice among those patients, were too much a professional élite, very conscious of giving their services. What the poor-law development had shown was the general need for a greater public provision of hospital services, free from any hint of charity or relief, and this point was stressed to the 1905 Commission by the doctors who gave evidence before it. What was wanted, though it was not to come until much later, was, as was insisted by one witness, the distinguished medical administrator, Dr George Newman, afterwards, as Sir George Newman, Chief Medical Officer of the Ministry of Health (1919–35), 'unification of the public medical services', with disease regarded as a 'nuisance' to be removed 'quite irrespective of poverty and destitution'.[77] This was a bold proposal, if a logical corollary of what had been happening since 1867 and 1885. That it could be put at all was evidence of the frustration felt at the attempt to handle the medical problems of the country in watertight compartments.

With the improvement of hospital services went an equally striking growth of professional nursing. One of the most telling revelations of the 60s had been the standard of workhouse nursing, usually undertaken by any woman inmate. Proper training of nurses was put in hand, though the use of paupers continued until it was expressly forbidden by the Local Government Board as late as 1897. This, as a senior poor-law official told the 1905 Commission, was 'one of the most marked revolutions in Poor Law administration',[78] though the acute shortage of trained nurses for some time prevented the regulation from being strictly enforced. The number of nurses employed, though still far from adequate, rose between 1880 and 1910 from less than 2,000 to 6,500. This increase was matched, of course, by a general development of nursing services, including the District Nurses developed from charitable activity in Liverpool in the 60s and extended throughout the country with the aid of the funds subscribed by the women of Britain to celebrate Queen Victoria's Jubilee in 1887, which were devoted by the Queen herself to this purpose.

'The Crusade Against Out-relief'   With the change in policy towards the workhouse sick, and a correspondingly more liberal treatment of poor children, there came from the late 60s, and especially after the establishment of the Local Government Board in 1871, a sterner attitude towards out-relief. If policy were relaxed towards those who manifestly could not help themselves, it could be applied more stringently to others, and there were the prevailing notions of 'social Darwinism', popularised by Herbert Spencer, to justify sterner measures. Hence what the Majority Report of 1909 called, in its survey of earlier developments, 'a crusade against out-relief'.[79]

The number of those in receipt of out-relief, which had fluctuated around 750,000 in the 50s, had been forced up by the Lancashire cotton famine and again, after the end of the American Civil War in 1865, by industrial depression, reaching 860,000 in 1868 and 880,000 in 1871. Such was the distress in London that in 1867 a Mansion House Fund of £15,000 had been raised and distributed: yet the calls on this fund were so great that the average amount given was no more than a few pence. What was revealed was the existence, not only of exceptional distress among men normally employed, but of permanent poverty, due largely, though this was not appreciated until much later, to under-employment. Hence the army of casual workers and beggars with which London swarmed and the many charitable societies that sprang up to help them. Such out-relief as was normally given by the Guardians was little enough, as it was always assumed that private charity would also be forthcoming. Two shillings or 2s. 6d. a week was regarded as sufficient, but no attempt was ever made to ascertain whether it was in fact supplemented. This condition of things, as later investigations were to show, maintained a vicious circle by keeping down wages, especially in the 'sweated' trades, against which there was in time to be such an outcry.

In his evidence to the Royal Commission on the Aged Poor of 1893 J. S. Davy complained of these meagre doles: the Guardians, he maintained, had no right to send a pauper 2s. a week and wash their hands of him.[80] The proper course of action, as he and his colleagues of the Local Government Board constantly insisted, was either to give adequate relief, if it were justified, or to 'offer the house'. Adequate relief was costly and open to abuse, while the workhouse was unpopular; it was easier and more comforting to the Guardians, therefore, to offer a dole. In the words of one witness to the 1905 Commission, many Guardians considered 'that as long as they can salve their consciences by giving out-relief of some sort they have dealt with the case'.[81] Only too often they dealt with cases in so hasty and perfunctory a manner that, as the 1893 Commission noted, an instance was known of 177 cases being settled in 71 minutes.[82]

It was against this attitude that the 'crusade' of the 70s was directed. Out-relief was not completely prohibited, but it was discouraged except in cases of emergency: in other cases, including those of the aged, the workhouse was to be offered; in the case of the able-bodied, the 'labour test'. Exceptional cases of hardship, where a point could be stretched, were to be left to private charity. This was the policy laid down in a Minute of 1869 and reinforced by a circular of the new Local Government Board in 1871. It was accompanied by a determined effort to carry out an efficient organisation of private charity, through the Charity Organisation Society, founded in 1869.[83]

**The Charity Organisation Society**    The Charity Organisation Society was much criticised in its day. George Lansbury called it 'brutal'[84] and it was undoubtedly the most unpopular of the philanthropic societies. An American historian of charitable enterprise, in a tactful but telling phrase, has regretted being unable to view the Society's long record 'with less qualified enthusiasm'.[85] Its aim was first to co-ordinate the many charitable efforts being made and prevent their overlapping and, secondly, to offer adequate help in cases of distress by investigating circumstances and trying to put people on their feet. All its intentions were admirable, but poor people disliked being investigated as much as charities disliked being co-ordinated, and the c.o.s. became little more than another voluntary charitable organisation. It was particularly disliked since, as it never achieved its real aims and was always short of funds, and as it insisted on giving either adequate relief or nothing at all, it often turned cases away. Its attitude also made it unpopular. It was criticised as unfeeling and aloof, and it could be 'infuriatingly smug',[86] while it was always inclined to look for personal failure in cases of distress. Its outlook can perhaps be summed-up in a quotation from a study of poverty by one of its most ardent workers, Mrs Bosanquet, which has already been referred to: 'character is one amongst the economic causes. . . . If you can make a man or woman more honest, sober and efficient than before, he will be more likely to find an opportunity of rendering service to the community (e.g. to find work).'[87] Unexceptionable doctrine, but of little comfort to a man out of work through no fault of his own. As one critic with experience of c.o.s. work complained, too much was made of the false antithesis of character and circumstance:[88] it was not so much 'the perverseness of individual poor people' that was at fault, but 'the nature of the social organism', which the Society, for all its zeal for enquiry, had failed to investigate.[89] Nevertheless, the Society rightly saw the need for the rehabilitation of those demoralised by poverty, and through its insistence on thorough investigations and adequate help made a significant contribution to social policy and practice, becoming the pioneer of the family case-work which it continues under its present name of the *Family Welfare Association*, adopted in 1944. It attracted much able support and was influential in official circles, contributing, for instance, a powerful contingent to the 1905 Commission on the poor law.

The c.o.s. was long opposed to all State intervention, except through relief in the workhouse, and its attitude chimed well with the crusading spirit of the Local Government Board in the 70s. What was hoped for from the 'crusade' was not so much that the numbers in the workhouses would increase, for in fact there was little spare room, but that relatives and friends would come to the assistance of those in need. If this happened, if, that is to say, there was a diminution of pauperism, it was easy to assume that no real need had existed. The ever-present fear of a recurrence of pre-1834 conditions blinded the Local Government Board and c.o.s. officials alike to the desperate poverty that would do anything rather than enter the house. This was particularly true of many of the elderly. One of the many books that pressed their problems upon the public during the 20 years of agitation that preceded the introduction of old age pensions in 1908 expressed their dilemma in these words in 1892: 'I know of no darker spot on our national honour than the struggle for existence on the part of those who, after having toiled and moiled in the heat of the day, manage to keep themselves out of the workhouse . . . and too often lay down the burden of life in the struggle.'[90] It was almost in these words that Lloyd George was to justify his Bill in 1908.

**Numbers on Out-relief**   The result of the campaign against out-relief, however, was that numbers fell from 880,000 in 1871 to 569,000 in 1878: thereafter they settled down to something over half a million, fluctuating around that figure for 30 years. The population rose in that period from 24 to 34 millions, but half a million outdoor paupers seem to have been the irreducible minimum. Indoor paupers, who numbered some 140,000 in the 70s, began to creep up in the 80s and reached nearly a quarter of a million in the early years of the new century. The increase was due partly to the rise in the population, and particularly to the increase in the number of elderly, many of whom were forced into the workhouse by the 'crusade', but it reflected also the increase in hospital facilities. What it manifestly did not reflect, however, was the fall in the amount of out-relief, and it is extraordinary that, even in such years of depression as the late 70s and the middle 80s, there was no significant increase. Improvements in wages and a great increase of friendly-society and trade-union activity probably do much to account for this fact, but that something was due also to the deterrent policy of the 'crusade' was suggested by the revealing social investigations that began with Charles Booth's work in the 80s and that were to prepare the way for the developments we shall be considering in the next chapter. The very existence of charity, a Local Government Board official once commented, 'strengthens the hands of the Poor Law administration in adherence to rule'.[91] How much actual distress was checked by private charity it is impossible to say, but, active though charity was, it was, nevertheless, like the 1867 Fund, hardly more than a drop in the bucket.

**Depression and Socialism**   How much distress could be caused by a trade depression was shown again in 1885-6. This was the occasion of a memorable Mansion House Fund, when £79,000 was raised and largely squandered. It was also the occasion of the first irruption of Socialism into British politics. The first Socialist organisation, the Social Democratic Federation, had been started by the stockbroker and convert to Marxism, H. M. Hyndman, in 1884. Early in 1886 it led an unemployed demonstration in London and the crowd for a time got out of hand. Hyndman was arrested and with him a young agitator, John Burns, who as President of the Local Government Board 20 years later was to prove a disappointment to those whose interests he claimed to represent. The demonstration did little harm, but it shocked people into fears of revolutionary violence and the Mansion House Fund leapt up almost overnight: in two days it increased from £19,000 to £72,000. The pouring out of the Fund did little good, for, although attempts were made to give the money to those who most needed it to get through the bad times, much of it went to the permanently unemployed or underemployed whose problems it did nothing to solve. It was, indeed, as William Beveridge wrote 20 years later, an 'orgie (sic) of relief'.[92]

**The Chamberlain Circular, 1886**   This was an extreme case of indiscriminate relief, but it was characteristic of the growing concern at the apparent insolubility of the problem of poverty, to which an edge was now being given by Socialism (1884 was also the year of the foundation of the Fabian Society). Casual charity sometimes had its comic side: the 1905 Commission recorded a case in which a wealthy woman, touched by a charity sermon, drove into poor streets and recklessly distributed grapes and champagne.[93] Much that was done for the poor was equally casual, and equally unhelpful. Moved by the plight of the unemployed, and perhaps by the disturbances in London, Joseph Chamberlain, when President of the Local Government Board in 1886, took a step that was intended to be more constructive and that proved the precursor of the Unemployed Workmen Act of 1905, and therefore of much else.

Birmingham had been hit by the depression in 1885 and Chamberlain, then out of office, had endeavoured to move the local Guardians to give exceptional help, though without success: the workhouse, or relief with a degrading 'labour test', was all that was offered. When, in February 1886, Chamberlain took the Presidency, which he was soon to resign over Irish Home Rule, he was struck by the failure of the statistics of poor-relief to reflect the prevailing distress, and rightly drew the conclusion that men were unwilling to turn to the Guardians for help. He therefore issued a Circular calling on Local Authorities to provide municipal work as an alternative to poor-relief. As he said in the House of Commons, 'Nothing was more wonderful or more admirable than the way in which the better class of working men in the United Kingdom shrank from any resort to the Poor Law, undergoing the greatest privations, amounting almost to actual starvation, rather than have recourse to what they believed to be degradation.'[94] Two conditions were that the men employed should be certified by the Guardians as deserving more than pauper treatment and that the wages they received should be less than those normally paid for similar work.

This new device for helping the deserving without involving them in the poor law looked unexceptionable on paper, but proved of limited help in practice. It was regularly re-adopted after 1886 in times of distress, and became, indeed, a perennial practice in places such as West Ham, where winter unemployment was normal. In practice work was given to any and all who applied, without certification or check, while the influence of the trade unions soon put a stop to the paying of lower wages. On the other hand the work offered, since it had to be both such as did not interfere with ordinary employment and such as any man could undertake, was hard to find and unattractive. It was not unknown for a Council to overcome the difficulty by shutting up their road-sweeping machine, for instance, and giving the sweeping to men in need.[95] In the main, too, it was not the men usually in steady employment, the men whom Chamberlain had had in mind, who applied for help. They naturally preferred to rely on their trade-union and friendly-society funds and their savings, and struggled along until times were better. Such were the dread and shame of the poor law and the dislike of unskilled work that few of this type came forward. Nevertheless, the theory of a helping hand during a bout of unemployment held the field and seemed to be confirmed by the increase in the number of able-bodied men in the workhouses in the years of depression in the mid-90s and, again, after 1904. Not until statistics were gathered under the Unemployed Workmen Act of 1905 was it realised that it was chiefly the underemployed and the casually employed who were benefited. Even the benefits were small, however. Usually there were so many applicants that the work had to be shared out and each man received only a few days' work and wages. Yet, as evidence to the 1905 Commission showed, there were those who regarded themselves, when normal work was slack, as regularly 'working for the Guardians', or for the local Council.[96] For them the 'labour test' stoneyard or municipal digging or road-making, or such other tasks as the Guardians or the Council could think up, was the indispensable support of a miserable livelihood.

A 'New Poor Law'?    It was not in this way that distress arising from unemployment was to be cured, but from 1886 it was at least clear that the country was seized of the problem. From this time also is to be dated a steady relaxing of the administration of poor relief. Partly it was due to a growing realisation of the extent of the poverty existing in the midst of obvious signs of plenty, partly to the removal of ignorance about social conditions by the revelations of Charles Booth, 'General' William Booth of the Salvation Army and others, partly also to the democratisation of the franchise (extended to local government in 1888), which gave opportunities of direct political activity to those who knew at first hand what those social conditions were. In 1894 the financial qualifications necessary for election as a Guardian were removed (see note, page 153); the similar qualifications for appointment as a Justice of the Peace remained until 1906. (Winston Churchill was to describe the office of J.P. as 'the citizen's Privy Councillorship'.[97]) This step brought such working-men as George Lansbury and Will Crooks on to Boards and with them a number of women, few of whom had hitherto been eligible. In 1885 there had been only 50 women Guardians in the country; in 1895 there were more than 800 and in 1909 more than 1,200.[98] (Not until 1907, however, were women admitted to local Councils and only in 1919 did they acquire the right to stand for Parliament.) Already by 1892 the economist Alfred

Marshall was arguing that the poor law was still being administered•too much *for* the working classes instead of *by* them, and that when working-class rule, 'already near at hand', finally came, great changes would follow.[99] Certainly poor-law policy could hardly be the same after the various changes of the ten years from 1884 to 1894, and the results were soon seen. In 1891 books and toys were permitted in the workhouse; in 1892 men were provided with tobacco, and two years later women received a corresponding ration of dry tea to mash for themselves. This was hardly 'less eligibility' and reflected a greater humanity.

In the case of the aged the modifications of policy were such as to cause the able but inflexible Secretary of the Charity Organisation Society, C. S. Loch, unappreciative of the significance of political change, to exclaim in 1900 that a new poor law was coming into existence.[100] Charles Booth had shown in his investigations into poverty in London in the 80s that at least a third of those who reached the age of 70 had to accept poor relief, however thrifty they had been in earlier years. Many who were allowed a pittance by the Guardians lived, as Flora Thompson has recorded of her Oxfordshire hamlet, 'in daily fear of the workhouse . . . unless they had more than usually prosperous children to help support them'.[101] Public agitation and concern were stirred as the plight of the elderly became increasingly known, and the desirability of a new policy was brought home by the adoption of old age pensions insurance in Imperial Germany in 1889. In 1891 Chamberlain came out in favour of a modest first step, and four years later the whole subject was investigated, though inconclusively, by a Royal Commission. More will be said of these developments in the next chapter in connexion with the introduction of pensions in 1908. In 1896 the President of the Local Government Board, the genial Henry Chaplin, whose character would certainly not have stood a c.o.s. investigation, suggested in a Circular that old people who had led thrifty lives need not be forced into the workhouse, and four years later followed this with the more sweeping suggestion that they should normally be kept out of it and given adequate relief in their own homes. Moreover, it was ruled by the Out-door Relief (Friendly Societies) Acts, 1894 and 1904, that, when need was assessed, payments from a friendly society were to be ignored.

All this did, indeed, look like a 'new policy' and it was accompanied by improvements in conditions and greater freedom for the aged whose circumstances compelled them to enter the workhouse. The only indulgence, indeed, at which the Local Government Board seems to have jibbed was the provision of afternoon tea for elderly men![102]

So did the 'crusade' die out, under the pressure of wider knowledge of conditions and political advance. The officials of the Board, ever conscious of their duty to the principles of 1834, were left mourning. The year 1890, J. S. Davy told the 1905 Commission, 'forms a sort of epoch in poor law administration',[103] and 1894 had brought an even greater influence to bear upon it. In truth, the concessions made to the sick and the aged, the experiments undertaken in the care of children and the efforts made to save the unemployed from the poor law, though they amounted to little enough and the sum of their influence was not yet appreciated, were already shaping a new attitude to the poor law and proving the inadequacy of the old regime. As the Majority Commission Report of 1909 said of one aspect of policy, 'the great principle of 1834 is not adequate to the new position'.[104] What the new great principle was to be was not yet clear, though it was already apparent that it would need to be something more fundamental and constructive than 'less eligibility'.

## 4  The 'Collateral Aids'

**The Preventive Services**   Despite the stirrings of conscience about the conditions of the victims of the economic order which were being felt at the beginning of the twentieth century, opinion was not prepared for any thorough-going remedy, as the Minority Report of 1909 recognised. Distress from unemployment, it noted, seemed to those better off as 'part of the natural order of things and no more to be combated than the east wind'.[105] Yet by this time a considerable measure of development of what Chadwick had called 'collateral aids' was not only accepted as natural but regarded as essential in the public interest.

The process had begun in the 40s with the first attempts at the improvement of sanitary conditions. Chadwick's famous report of 1842, which has been described earlier, was followed by a Royal Commission on the Health of Towns, which revealed the inadequate and dangerous state of drainage and water supply in most of the large towns of the kingdom, and the chaotic condition of local administration, with Improvement and other Commissioners for particular purposes but no co-ordinating authority or policy. The obstacles to reform were considerable. The correlation of dirt and disease had been established, but the transmission of disease was not understood. There was not even agreement as to the best forms of drainage: Chadwick experimented with materials for sewers and produced the first glazed earthenware pipes, which were to prove the *sine qua non* of sanitary engineering, but his advocacy of them owed as much to their cheapness as to their efficacy. Worse still than ignorance, however, were the inertia and opposition which any attempt at reform had to overcome. Chadwick had already drawn attention to the ignorance among the upper classes of the conditions of life of their poorer fellow citizens. Reforms on which public money, and especially ratepayers' money, was to be spent were widely regarded, except in times of epidemic, as needless extravagances. Worse still, they were an interference with property and if administered, or even merely stimulated, from the centre were a threat of centralisation against freedom and local responsibility. Forty years later, as the Royal Commission on Housing noted, in words which have already been quoted, any suggestion of central control was still in some parts 'condemned without trial'. Nor were the objections put only from the property-owning classes. Radical working men who were agitating for free trade and the franchise were suspicious of reforms which, in the old tradition of political jobbery, might merely create pleasant posts for 'aristocratic hangers-on',[106] and this suspicion of the motives of the reformers was widespread. Not for many years was it accepted that the sanitary and health services required the full-time attention of expert officers. Indeed in one case, admittedly an extreme one, during the cholera epidemic of 1854, a Medical Officer was appointed for three weeks and then dismissed, 'the cholera having for some days ceased in the District'.[107]

It was particularly the resistance to central control and the domination of local government by the rate-paying property owners which delayed reform. Had it been possible to spend on civic services even a part of the increment accruing to property owners and landowners from the expansion of the towns, town-planning would not have had to wait for a century and effective slum-clearance would have been begun before the 1930s. The Housing Commission of the 80s complained helplessly of the tax levied on the public for the 'development' of land the increased value of which owed nothing whatever to the landowner, but had no remedy to offer. The problems were seen in the 40s, and later, not as problems in the government of developing centres of population but as technical difficulties in the removal and prevention of nuisances. As in the case of the poor law the primary aim was to get the able-bodied pauper on his feet, so in matters of sanitary reform all would be well, it was believed, if water-supply, drains, street-paving, cemeteries and parks were attended to. Hence the slow advance of legislation, which deferred an effective Public Health Act until 1875 and adequate housing legislation still longer.

The Health of the Towns    The Commission on the Health of Towns reported in 1844-5. It recommended the establishment of a Central Board of Health, with strong local Boards throughout the country to be responsible for draining, cleansing and water-supply. These recommendations were pressed by an organisation formed to advance sanitary principles, the Health of Towns Association, which had branches throughout the country and included among its members such men as Disraeli, Dickens and Lord Ashley. Chadwick, as a public official, did not actually join the Association, but he was active in it behind the scenes. Legislation was delayed by an inevitable wrangle over the evils of centralisation, and by the political preoccupation with Ireland and free trade, but the threatened return of cholera, which struck the country disastrously in 1848-9, brought in 1846 the first Act. This was the Nuisances Removal Act, the very title of which indicates the limitation of its approach. Under this Act powers were given for the cleaning up of towns, but no special authorities were created for the purpose locally, and when the cholera did strike the task fell upon the Guardians, who, true to the principles of 1834, proved unwilling to act except when destitution was established. Some towns, forewarned by the debate over the Commission's report, and anxious to avoid central control, promoted private Bills establishing their own sanitary authorities. Outstanding among these was Liverpool, which in 1847 appointed the first Medical Officer of Health in the country, Dr William Duncan. Duncan had been working in Liverpool for some years and had done much to reveal the wastage of life there, with an infant mortality rate of 225, as against the national average of 153, and an expectation of life at birth of only 19, compared with a national average of about 40. His appointment was followed a year later by that of Dr John Simon as M.O.H. for the City of London. Simon, of French Huguenot descent, was one of the greatest and ablest of public health pioneers. After seven years in London he became the principal medical adviser to the government and in 1871 Chief Medical Officer of the newly-formed Local Government Board.

**John Simon**    Simon, a man of deep humanity, was haunted throughout his life by the thought of the terrible wastefulness of disease, and by the poverty which made disease almost unavoidable. He saw for himself the unequal incidence of illness and death to which Duncan was also drawing attention, and devoted himself to securing a better balance through improved conditions: 'The diseases which are known to prevail in different districts with such surprising degrees of inequality are eminently the diseases which can be prevented.'[108] Yet no mere sanitary improvements, he maintained, could be adequate, 'unless the importance be distinctly recognised . . . of improving the social conditions of the poor'.[109] The question was '*how far the poor can be made less poor*',[110] for poverty itself was 'among the worst of sanitary evils',[111] and still worse was the hopelessness it engendered, which led many to indulgence and crime: 'overhead is the dreariest grey, and, for horizon, death in workhouse or hospital'.[112] Improved living conditions were essential, and, for all the economic assumptions of the times, property rights could not be allowed to stand in the way: 'The factory chimney that eclipses the light . . . the melting house that nauseates an entire parish, the slaughterhouse that forms round itself a circle of dangerous diseases—these surely are not private, but public affairs . . . And as for the rights of property— they are not only pecuniary. Life, too, is a great property.'[113] What efficient medical administration could achieve he showed in only six years in London, so scouring the City with sanitary improvements and scourging the Corporation with his findings that the cholera epidemic of 1854 proved only one-quarter as deadly as that of 1848-9. If Chadwick, through the 1848 Act and the General Board of Health, had encouraged the appointment of full-time specialist Medical Officers of Health to create sanitary conditions, it was Simon who set the pattern throughout the country, and in the process made himself a figure of national importance.

Prevention could come only through knowledge and legislation, he maintained, and his greatest services lay in his encouragement of research into the causation of disease, in his creation of an effective inspectorate and administrative machine, and in his stress on the necessity for legislation, without which, 'as far forward as any present judgment would willingly speculate, the same terrible waste of adult life must continue'.[114] In matters of public health administration Simon insisted on the need for a Minister of Health, with medical advisers at the centre and in every locality bearing a full, and not merely an incidental, share of administrative responsibility. This was, however, an ideal that was not to be achieved for many years. Simon himself resigned from the Local Government Board's service in 1876 because of his inferior status in a Department dominated by poor-law practice, and it was not until 1919 that there was a Minister of Health and a Chief Medical Officer (Sir George Newman) with adequate status.

**The Public Health Acts**    The Nuisances Removal Act was followed at last in 1848 by the first Public Health Act. This made it possible to establish Local Boards of Health with powers over such necessary services as water, cleansing, draining and the paving of the streets where they did not already exist under private Acts, and there was also a central 'General Board of Health' with limited powers of supervision and control, though without any direct answerability to Parliament. Chadwick and Ashley were among the members of the Board, but there was no doctor until 1849, when Chadwick's old colleague, Southwood Smith, was added at the height of the cholera epidemic. The Board saw the country through that epidemic, and helped to set up a large number of local boards, but its powers, limited as they were, were resented, and neither Chadwick nor Ashley had any grace of address to placate opposition. As laymen they fell foul of the doctors, between whom and Chadwick there was always little love lost: in an age when many doctors had more pretensions than skill Chadwick bluntly preferred 'men selected for their special knowledge of real practical sanitary work, and . . . un-knowledge of theoretical medicine'.[115] There was also a long wrangle with the engineers over methods of drainage. Chadwick was an ardent advocate of the narrow glazed pipe, but many engineers preferred man-sized brick tunnels, and it was not until the 80s, when the Association of Sanitary Inspectors was formed and elected him its first President, that Chadwick's pioneer services were fully acknowledged.

As with so much of the early local government legislation, many of the powers under the 1848 Act were permissive and therefore widely ignored. Thus, Medical Officers of Health could be appointed, but as it was not until 1872 that their appointment became obligatory their spread was slow. Despite Liverpool's example, for instance, Manchester made no appointment until 1868, about the same time as Leeds, but Birmingham, Sheffield and Newcastle all waited until the Act of 1872. Even then part-time appointments were permitted until 1909, and in small areas until 1929.

The chief weakness of the General Board of Health was, however, its independent position, intentional though this was, and its lack of a parliamentary spokesman. It lasted until 1854, when in view of the intense opposition to it (and to Chadwick) its powers were not renewed. John Bull, *The Times* maintained in a well-known comment, was weary of the 'perpetual Saturday night' of cleanliness: Chadwick and his colleagues had come to 'make the cholera itself scarcely a more dreaded visitation than their own'.[116] Herbert Spencer undoubtedly spoke for

many in denouncing 'Over-Legislation'.[117] By this time the Board had succeeded in setting up local boards in little more than half the country, covering a
population of only some three million in a total of 18, though the next 20 years
were to show that these three million, together with such towns as Liverpool,
which were covered by private Acts, were on the whole less subject to epidemic
disease than the rest. What had been achieved, together with something of the
motives that inspired action, may be seen in such reports as those of Dr Stephen
Piper, the medical officer appointed to Darlington under the 1848 Act. The death-
rate in the worst parts of Darlington, Piper commented in 1855, had been
reduced from 69 to 23: 'By the cultivation of sanitary science, we improve not
only the health of the population, but also their social, moral and domestic
habits. Apart from the desire to promote their welfare, it is but an act of self-
defence; for the rich man who lives in a comfortable and luxurious home, must
keep in mind that his mansion cannot be safe, when the dark and filthy hovel
breeds pestilence beside it.'[118]

Yet in 1854 the Board of Health was reconstituted, on a more modest basis, as
a normal government department, like the Poor Law Board, with a ministerial
President. In the face of the prevailing prejudice in favour of local control it
lasted only a few years, however, its powers being divided in 1858–9 between the
Privy Council and the Home Office, the former assuming responsibility for general
health matters, with a Medical Committee to direct them, and the latter controlling urban sanitary affairs, under a special sub-department, the Local Government Act Office. (Ironically enough, the changes were debated during the
memorable 'great stink' of 1858, when owing to drought the Thames revealed
itself as the open sewer it then was.[119]) Simon, who had been with the Board of
Health since 1855, was appointed Medical Officer to the Privy Council Committee,
and there began the most influential part of his career.

Whatever the deference paid to the principle of local control, it was clear
within a few years that it was not effective. Special returns prepared by the
Registrar-General at Simon's request showed no general improvement in mortality from sickness, and demonstrated only too clearly that unequal incidence of
disease which had struck Simon at the outset of his career. Then in the mid-60s
came a fresh visitation of the cholera, and it was symptomatic of the failure to improve conditions substantially that among the first victims was one of the medical
officers of health appointed, albeit on an economical part-time basis, under the
1848 Act.[120] Stronger measures were obviously needed. A more effective Sanitary Act was therefore passed in 1866, *requiring* local authorities to take action,
and Simon rejoiced that 'the grammar of common sanitary legislation' had at last
acquired 'the novel virtue of an imperative mood':[121] he saw himself henceforth
as the nation's 'Superintendent-General for Health'.[122] Ever since his attachment to the Privy Council he had been undertaking detailed investigations throughout the country into the nature, problems and incidence of disease, assisted by a
team of brilliant young men, all of whom were to make their mark on medical

history (and eight to follow Simon himself as F.R.S.[123]). More knowledge was therefore available, even if the biology of infection was still imperfectly understood. Moreover, the doctors were at last being properly organised. Their professional association, the British Medical Association, was becoming more active, and in 1858 the General Medical Council and the Medical Register had been established, while three years later, as a result of Florence Nightingale's famous labours, the training of nurses was begun. There was also a Social Science Association, founded in 1857, to stir and lead opinion. The problem, Simon saw, was to direct to every part of the country the improved services now available, and to rationalise and strengthen the central administration. 'A parquetry unsafe to walk upon' was his characterisation of the confused situation at the centre,[124] under which not only the Privy Council and the Home Office (the latter both directly for factories and burial grounds and, through the Local Government Act Office, for urban sanitation), but the Poor Law Board (through the Guardians) and the Board of Trade (for water supplies and industrial effluent) had, by virtue of various pieces of legislation, been given public health responsibilities, which at times actually brought some of them into conflict. The situation was such, as Simon complained, that there was, in effect, one authority for every privy in the country, and one for every pigsty; one authority to prevent nuisances, and another to abate them,[125] while resistance to any open suggestion of central control was so intense that even an attempt to formalise well-established administrative practice could be denounced as 'centralisation'.[126] Yet confusion and weakness at the centre were matched by local inertia and indifference, which, indeed, they tended to foster. Hence, for instance, the complaint of the *Pall Mall Gazette* in 1866 that, for all the praise lavished on English local government, the leaders it threw up resembled nothing less than village Hampdens and embryo statesmen: 'they need a strong hand over them'.[127]

Under these circumstances, with Simon agitating inside the government and the British Medical Association and the Social Science Association active outside, the reform of central and local government for public health purposes was at last taken in hand. In 1868 Disraeli's Government appointed the Royal Sanitary Commission to investigate the situation and, though its hand was hardly as forceful as the *Pall Mall Gazette*, or Simon himself, would have wished, its Report, when it appeared in 1871, brought significant changes. A central Local Government Board was set up, and Public Health Acts followed in 1872 and 1875, the need for two bites at the cherry being due in part to public indifference and preoccupation with such more exciting political issues as the Ballot Act of 1872 and the settlement in the same year of the 10 years' old dispute with the United States over the Confederate cruiser *Alabama*.[128] The second Act was the work of Disraeli's second administration, though, despite common opinion, it owed nothing to him personally.[129]

The great Act of 1875, with its 343 clauses, in the shaping of which Simon had played a considerable part, had nothing that was original in it, but consolidated and systematised existing legislation, and rounded off some 30 years of confused and controversial development. 'The fact that Preventive Medicine has now been fully adopted into the service of the State', Simon wrote some years later, 'is indeed the *end* of a great argument',[130] and so it proved. The Act provided, in fact, the basis for all later developments, and, although the twenty-ninth public health measure in as many years,[131] it was so thoroughly conceived that it was to endure unchanged for more than half a century.

Under the Act a uniform service of sanitary authorities was established throughout the whole country, in towns the municipal authorities, in country areas, since there were no other administrative bodies until the establishment of County Councils in 1889, the poor-law Unions. In every locality medical officers of health and sanitary inspectors were to be appointed. At the centre was a government department, the Local Government Board, responsible for both public health and the poor law, with a Chief Medical Officer to advise: in the words of the Royal Commission, 'local administration under central superintendence' was the guiding principle. In practice the superintendence did not amount to as much as Simon, for instance, had hoped. The uniting of the Privy Council's health responsibilities with the poor-law administration placed the control of policy in the hands of the cautious bureaucrats of the poor law: the public health and the medical advisers who were to supervise it took a second place. Hence Simon's disgusted retirement. Yet, as has well been said of the 1875 Act, 'all the cities and towns in this country have become places fit to live in under provisions contained somewhere in this Public Health Act'[132]: it ranks, indeed, as one of the great statutes of the nineteenth century, and thus, belatedly, were Chadwick's aims achieved, though the achievement was mainly Simon's.

The cholera epidemic of 1866 was therefore as great a stimulus to the public health in general as to the care of the sick poor. Medical Officers of Health were now everywhere in existence and their knowledge of the incidence of disease was increased by the Registration Act of 1874, which required that doctors should sign certificates of the causes of death, and by the compulsory notification of infectious disease, begun with cholera under the 1875 Act and continued by the Notification of Diseases Act of 1889. Medical officers themselves had to undergo special training: the first diploma in public health was offered in 1870, and in 1888 such diplomas were made obligatory for the public health service. In the 80s and 90s came at long last the great discoveries of the bacteriologists, which rendered intelligible the efforts of the sanitarians for the control of disease and prepared the way for inoculation and immunisation.

**Smallpox and Vaccination**   One of the great scourges of the past, which had already been brought to a considerable extent under control during the nineteenth century, was smallpox. Dr Jenner's discovery of vaccination had been made in 1798, and in 1840, in an attempt to check the disease, vaccination was provided free for children by the Guardians. Smallpox was particularly a disease of children in overcrowded housing conditions and its incidence in the crowded hovels of the industrial centres appalled observers. If not checked, a doctor reported from Manchester in 1842, it will 'not only entail a heavy burden upon the poor-rates but, what is of still more serious import, will prove most disastrous to the moral as well as the physical welfare of the community'. The tremendous significance attached to the prevention of the disease through 'the immortal discovery of Jenner', at a time when few other diseases could be prevented, is illustrated by many references in medical and poor-law literature. It loomed so large as even to justify mention on a memorial to a successful doctor. In the grounds of the Sheffield Infirmary, for instance, is a memorial to Dr Robert Ernest, house surgeon for 44 years, who died in 1841: it bears the inscription, 'Upwards of eighty eight thousand Patients passed under the care of Dr Ernest besides forty eight thousand Children whom he vaccinated'.

In 1853, in an effort to stamp out the disease, compulsory vaccination was introduced by a private member's bill, though lack of the means for compulsion limited its effectiveness after the first impact. Other Acts, with increasing powers of compulsion, followed in 1861, 1867 and 1871, largely inspired by Simon, who was at the same time carrying out investigations into the disease and establishing efficient administrative machinery for vaccination throughout the country. A great epidemic in the early 70s, the worst known in Britain, which cost 44,000 lives, made the final Act of 1871 acceptable, and gave the country the most thorough and effective system of vaccination anywhere in the world, without even, until 1898, any concessions to the conscientious scruples which some people felt. Thus was created what has been called 'a Victorian National Health Service',[133] a remarkable invasion of private liberty in the name of personal and public health, which was justified in the event by the steady reduction in mortality from smallpox from the 70s, until by the end of the century cases were comparatively rare. Compulsory vaccination was not formally abandoned until 1948, however, though by then it had become largely a dead letter.

**Food and Drugs**  To these measures for the public health must be added the legislation for the protection of the public against fraud in foodstuffs and medicines. The adulteration of food, especially of bread and confectionery to improve their colour, had reached such proportions by the middle of the century as to alarm medical opinion, which from 1850 began to press for government action. Tennyson, the mirror of so many of the hopes and doubts of the age, reflected the general concern in *Maud* (1855):

> *And chalk and alum and plaster are sold to the poor for bread,*
> *And the spirit of murder works in the very means of life,*

while *Punch* in 1851 denounced the confectioner selling highly-coloured cakes to children as one who 'plays HEROD among the innocents'. A parliamentary enquiry was held in 1855, and there followed the Adulteration of Food Act, 1860, which forbade the adulteration of food and the addition to it of injurious ingredients. Something more than a mere ban was needed, however. The Sale of Food and Drugs Act, 1875, gave powers for the appointment of public analysts, but it was not until such appointments were made compulsory by a further Act in 1879 that effective action could be taken. The grosser forms of carelessness and deceit in the preparation and sale of food, from which the working classes were the worst sufferers, were then checked, though it was not until later that any national standards of purity and hygiene were established. Meanwhile the first measure for the control of the conditions under which bread was baked was passed in 1863.

In the case of one important foodstuff, milk, the full significance of Dr Robert Koch's discovery of the tubercle bacillus in 1882 had to be appreciated before the supply could be safeguarded by pasteurisation. This was a development of the twentieth century, though the value of the process in keeping milk fresh was recognised as early as 1890. During the nineteenth century working-class children at least drank little milk, which was as well, since an uncontaminated supply would have been a matter of chance.

**Other Measures**    Among other measures aimed at improving conditions of life and work, most of them due, at least in the first place, to the efforts of private members of Parliament, may be cited Acts for the encouragement of museums (1845), public libraries (1850), baths and washhouses (1846), parks (1847), playgrounds (1852), and the enclosure of commons (1876), and for the checking of atmospheric and water pollution (Alkali Act, 1863; Rivers Pollution Act, 1876), all of them at first, however, cautious and limited in their effect.

**The Completion of the Environmental Services**    Altogether, by the end of the nineteenth century England had become a healthier and safer place to live in. From about the time of the Public Health Act of 1875 onwards the death-rate began to fall. In the 50s it had been around 22 per 1,000, and by the end of the century it had dropped to 17. In the same period the average expectation of life at birth increased by about ten years. The improvement did not, however, affect very young children, whose death-rate remained at about 150 for each 1,000 live births throughout the nineteenth century, and did not begin to fall until after 1910. Here was an indication of the limitations of the sanitary measures advocated so long since by Chadwick, Simon and others, and at last brought into effective operation. The mere improvement of environment, however successfully that was done, clearly left many problems untouched. The welfare of children and mothers, in particular, called for more personal services, and it is significant that until they began to be developed the infant mortality hardly improved at all.

It was also in the more personal approach to health problems that a real check to the greatest of all human scourges, tuberculosis, was to be found. Tuberculosis during the nineteenth century was, as it had long been, one of the most serious killing diseases, accounting for about one death in six and flourishing in the over-crowded conditions and among the underfed, overworked masses of the Victorian towns. By the end of the century the death-rate from the dread disease had been reduced by one half. Improvements in housing and working conditions, better food, higher standards of personal cleanliness and the reduction of infection through the increasing use of hospitals for treatment, had all contributed to the reduction, but deaths still numbered more than 60,000 a year, while, because of the length of the illness, even when recovery took place there was great poverty and distress among sufferers and their families. Tuberculosis had, indeed, become, as evidence to the 1905 Commission showed, what cholera and typhoid had been 60 years earlier, 'the most pauperising of all diseases', while because of its high incidence and its tenacity it accounted, it was estimated, for not less than one-seventh of the total cost of poor relief.[134] Moreover, dislike of the poor law, even of pauper medical aid, kept many sufferers from seeking the early attention which the disease called for, and condemned them, at best, to a long illness, which in overcrowded homes exposed their families to serious risk of infection. Hence Lloyd George's concern with this 'terrible scourge of consumption' in his plans for National Health Insurance in 1911. Until the more dramatic successes of the new drugs of recent years the steady improvement in the control of the disease came from a combination of personal health services with the environmental, together with a programme of public education that began with the establish-ment of the National Association for the Prevention of Tuberculosis, under the aegis of the Prince of Wales (afterwards King Edward VII), in 1898.

By the beginning of the present century, therefore, new needs, or old needs long masked by grosser evils, had come to light, and it was clear that despite the confident hopes of earlier years controllable disease was still causing poverty and suffering. Industrial society could no longer be surveyed in the mass and cleansed of its ills; it had to be broken into its individual components and their needs and difficulties examined more narrowly. From 1875, it has well been said, 'the sani-tary idea began to be overhauled by the concept of the individual Mr Harris or Mrs Stevens, or of the Jones children.'[135] But this part of the story belongs to later chapters.

**Housing** The improvement of sanitary conditions was but one aspect of the environmental services; from the first investigations in the 30s, as has already been shown, the concern for decent housing was no less keen, though, in loyalty to the tradition of *laissez-faire*, far more was left in this connexion to private enterprise. Filth could be removed and water supplies purified, but to tackle housing was another problem. However shoddy, a house was a substantial struc-ture, in itself an article of commercial value occupying land which had a value at a time when land was still regarded as the basis of all values. How was defective housing to be improved? If it were so bad as to cry out for destruction, should its owner be compensated, and if so at what valuation? Large landlords could be

obstructive enough, though not all were so and many took pride in seeing adequate housing erected on their property, but the bane of housing reform was often
the small 'slum landlord' who depended upon his rents for his livelihood (like
Mrs Codleyn who gave Arnold Bennett's Denry Machin his start in the world[136])
and lacked the means to effect improvements. It was long before it was realised
that the community must interest itself in the matter.

The housing problem was a double one. The first and most obvious need, in the
interests of public health, order and morality, was the destruction of the filthy,
crumbling, overcrowded rookeries of the slums and the laying-down of minimum
standards for new housing. The second need, which came only slowly to be
appreciated, was to ensure the provision of decent sanitary accommodation for
those who lacked the means to provide it for themselves: this called for legal powers
to local authorities, but little was done until the Treasury itself offered financial
inducements.

Throughout the nineteenth century the demand for houses far exceeded the
supply. Even in the last decade of the century, a period of exceptional building
activity, the growth of population still outstripped the provision. It was this backlog, intensified by the check to building that occurred even before the war of 1914
(and that owed something at least to the threat of the 1909 budget to land values),
which presented the nation with the vast housing problem of the 1920s.
The worst result of the steady pressure of population was, of course, in overcrowding. The 1891 census, for instance, showed that throughout the country
as a whole over one-tenth of the population lived more than two to a room,
while the average concealed proportions as high as one-fifth in London, Bradford
and Huddersfield, one-quarter in Plymouth and one-third on the north-east
coast. The Royal Commission on Housing of 1885 recorded cases in which, as
in one London borough, 11 families lived in 11 rooms and, as in Newcastle, 140
families occupied only 34 houses.[137] In some parts of the country, it commented
grimly, overcrowding was not increasing simply because houses were already so
full that no more people could be crowded into them. The effects on health were
serious. Sheer exhaustion from overcrowding led to loss of work, and disease
was only too easily spread. Under these conditions it was difficult for people to
live in decency and avoid pauperism or charity. Twenty years later the Royal
Commission on the Poor Laws returned to the evil effects: 'The same poverty
that helps so largely to cause the overcrowding helps also to diminish the vitality
and power of resistance to the communication of the disease which overcrowding
facilitates . . . the broad conclusion appears to be incontestable that bad housing
conditions largely contribute to pauperism.'[138]

From the 80s improvements in transport and the coming of workmen's
fares, introduced by the Cheap Trains Act, 1883, made it possible for towns to
spread: men no longer had to live on top of their work, though vast numbers still
did. In the first decade of the twentieth century, with electric trams in general use,
the electrification of London's Underground in hand and motor-buses coming in,

building spread and overcrowding did to some extent diminish. Much still remained, however, and the efforts of private enterprise to improve it left a legacy of dull, mean houses to dominate the scene in so many industrial areas. It was not much that the Victorian workman could afford and whether he rented his house, or could rise to the struggle to buy it through a building society, his needs were usually met in the numerous 'estates', with their long rows of orderly houses of dull brick and grey slate, innocent of all but the more elementary sanitary arrangements, which cast a gloom upon the spirit today and necessitate State assistance (under the Housing Acts of 1958–9) to make them habitable by modern standards.

Earlier in the century the clamant demands for additional housing were only too often met by crowding dwellings into odd spaces left by previous building. Houses were squeezed in with scant regard for light and air, and where the needs were greatest, and the means the least, the very name given to the buildings erected of somebody's 'rents' disclosed the indifference of the builder to human needs; 'not houses, nor dwellings, nor cottages, nor buildings', as Charles Booth noted in sorrow, 'but just "rents"'.[139] Gustave Doré's grim drawings of overcrowded slums in London in the early 70s are well known. 'Rents spread with rags', wrote the journalist companion of his *London Pilgrimage*, Blanchard Jerrold, 'swarming with the children of mothers for ever greasing the walls with their shoulders; where there is an angry helplessness and carelessness painted upon the face of every man and woman.'[140]

From the time of the exposure of insanitary conditions in the 40s many efforts were made to provide decent housing for the poorer working-men on terms that they could afford. Housing Associations of various kinds were formed and found, much to the satisfaction of philanthropists, that they could let homes at a modest return on their money. The most famous of these organisations was the Peabody Trust, founded in 1862 by an American business man settled in London, George Peabody, who gave and bequeathed in all half a million pounds for the purpose, and whose 'Buildings' still function (see note, page 153). There were numerous other societies and associations, but they were largely confined to London and, despite all their efforts, their contribution to the housing of the rapidly expanding population of the metropolis was small. By the early years of the twentieth century they were providing accommodation in London for rather less than 150,000 people, the Peabody Trust itself having by then constructed some 5,000 flats. London's population had then increased in a generation by one million and a quarter, in the last decade of the nineteenth century alone by 300,000, and the census of 1901 showed that nearly 750,000 people were living in overcrowded conditions.

Beatrice Webb has given, in the account of her early social work in the 80s, a description of a typical block of 'buildings' of the cheaper kind, with its severely economical decoration and fittings and its communal sanitary arrangements, which could do little to encourage pride of person or home.[141] 'Block dwellings of the style known as the *Later Desolate*', one contemporary critic, the Liberal politician C. F. G. Masterman, was to call these austere attempts at philanthropy in housing.[142] 'To treat one's neighbour as oneself', complained another notable social worker, Samuel Barnett, in words quoted with approval by Beatrice Webb, 'is not to decorate one's own house with the art of the world, and to leave one's neighbour's house with nothing but the drain-pipes to relieve the bareness of its walls.'[143]

Little though these blocks of buildings could offer in the way of amenities, they were better than the housing they replaced. Yet they were still beyond the means of many workers and they even had the perverse result of intensifying over-crowding, for by replacing cramped accommodation with roomier and more expensive homes they drove the really poor to huddle closer in what was left. The same result, as the 1885 Commission noted, followed from the extension of the railways in London and the building of the great termini: the Midland Railway, for instance, pulled down 500 houses in the 60s to make room for St Pancras and its marshalling yards.[144]

**Octavia Hill** Beatrice Webb began her career in 1885 as a volunteer rent-collector at Katherine Buildings, near St Katherine's Docks in East London, a block built on a site cleared of slums and catering for what she called 'the aborigines of the East End',[145] people poorer and less regularly employed than those in what the 1885 Commission styled 'Peabody Town'. The erection of the Buildings was a social experiment inspired by the example of the pioneer of housing management, Octavia Hill, a grand-daughter of Dr Southwood Smith, who was a stalwart of the Charity Organisation Society and later, like Mrs Webb, a member of the Poor Law Commission. Octavia Hill had inherited her grand-father's interest in social problems and in the 60s began, with Ruskin's help, to concern herself with the housing of the very poor, buying dilapidated houses, repairing them, letting them and managing them herself in such a way as to encourage the independence and pride of the tenants while keeping the property in good condition. 'You cannot deal with people and their houses separately'[146] was the case she argued. The conditions from which she rescued her tenants are sufficiently indicated by her story of one slum landlord, an undertaker, who confessed that it was not the rents 'but the deaths I get out of the houses' that were worth having.[147] Equally revealing were the difficulties also encountered among the tenants themselves in the destruction and theft of pipes and fittings which she had installed. Among her disciples was Emma Cons, who took over a disreputable music-hall and made of it the *Old Vic*; among her other interests, the campaign for the preservation of open spaces and the countryside, which led in 1895 to the foundation of the National Trust.

Octavia Hill's work was not charitable, for she saw to it that her tenants paid their way, if it was a way that they could never have followed unaided. It was, however, a method that could operate only on a limited scale and that could do little without statutory assistance to improve substantially the condition and surroundings of a building. 'Who among us', she asked in 1874, citing cramped courts and houses she knew well, 'could ever move back that great wall which overshadowed the little houses . . . and let a free current of air sweep through the closed court?' No one could unaided, for 'owners had no interest in awarding a larger share of light and air to the dwellers in the court'.[148] It was her insistence on the need for powers to impose minimum standards that was in part responsible for the Artizans' Dwellings Act of 1875.

**Housing Legislation**    Statutory concern with housing began, though ineffectually, in 1851. There was much interest at the time in the provision of decent housing for the working classes, an interest symbolised in the Prince Consort's model houses, shown at the Great Exhibition of 1851. There was, too, much concern at the nature of a great deal of the lodging accommodation available, and in this same year Lord Shaftesbury, as a member of the General Board of Health, introduced legislation to permit local authorities not only to inspect lodging houses but to erect and operate them. His concern was to rescue the working man not only from squalor but from the casual night-shelter which was all that some had to rely on and in which they would find themselves cheek-by-jowl with tramps and even less desirable company. The night-shelters and refuges catered for much of the rootless population and there were, especially in London, many maintained by charitable bodies. Blanchard Jerrold complained of some that they offered their inmates scripture-readings instead of 'a practical labour-agency' to help them to find work.[149] All were overcrowded and the conditions provided in some were painfully primitive. Those established by the poor law, principally for vagrants, offered no more than a common sleeping-platform, divided into pens by pieces of board, and it was in the provision of casual accommodation of this kind, without the motive of deterrence but with considerable emphasis on salvation, that such organisations as the Salvation Army and the Church Army were later to find much scope.

The 1851 Act was the first of 27 housing measures passed by Parliament during the second half of the nineteenth century, and was largely a dead-letter from the beginning. As with public health before the creation of sanitary authorities in 1872, the lack of properly constituted bodies responsible for the execution of the law made action dependent upon local zeal, and therefore stultified the law's intentions. Experience was to show, indeed, that in this field of public policy, in view of the interference with private property which was involved, local authorities were for long particularly slow to act. Property owners, as substantial ratepayers, were well represented on councils and cases were known in which, when sanitary inspectors were appointed, slack officials proved to be relatives of councillors. It is not without significance that the first really effective Housing Act came in 1890, after the broadening of the franchise and the reconstruction of local government. As with the administration of the poor law, the advance of democracy made great changes possible. Even then, however, authorities were reluctant to undertake more than a minimum of building: it was still assumed that private construction could meet almost all of the need. 'In the last resort', commented a Birmingham Housing Committee in 1914, 'if private enterprise fails, the Corporation must step in, but they feel very strongly that the public money can be used to much greater advantage than building houses.'[150]

Treasury loans to local authorities for housing became possible as early as 1866, but in the 20 years before the Royal Commission on Housing reported only one loan was actually made (though such private organisations as the Peabody Trust made use of the facility) (see note, page 153). The first significant Housing Act was that of 1868, which tackled the problem of insanitary housing and laid down the principle that the owner of a house must keep it in good repair. If this were not done the local authority could take action to see that the house was repaired, or, if necessary, rebuilt. The Act represented an important step forward, particularly in the recognition of the State's duty to interfere, in the interests of public health, with the sacred rights of property: Parliament, in the words used by Joe Chamberlain a few years later, 'recognised something higher than property'. The powers given were until 1890 merely permissive, however, and therefore little used. Seven years later, in 1875, Disraeli's Home Secretary, R. A. Cross, encouraged by an investigation carried out by the Charity Organization Society in which Octavia Hill took a leading part, carried a broader measure, the Artizans' Dwellings Act, which dealt not with single insanitary houses but with insanitary areas which needed clearing and reconstructing. Local authorities were given powers, though still only permissive powers, to acquire and clear whole areas. As, however, compensation was to be paid at a valuation and the people dispossessed were to be re-housed on or very near the site, the burden placed upon authorities was a heavy one, and only limited use was made in practice of this Act (see note, page 153). The problem of compensation, indeed, long bedevilled the whole issue, and the duty to re-house checked many authorities until Treasury grants became available in 1919. Inevitably compensation was seriously over-estimated. In London, for instance, a loss of £1,500,000 was sustained through the clearance of 59 acres under the 1868 and 1875 Acts, and Glasgow spent an even larger sum: as a London official complained wryly of one scheme, it would have been cheaper to give 'every man, woman and child £100 or £150 to start them in life somewhere else'.[151]

Already some authorities had acquired by private Acts special powers for controlling bad housing. Manchester prohibited the building of back-to-back houses as early as 1844,[152] though it took 60 years to clear existing ones. Liverpool, with 100,000 slum dwellers, in 1864 gained private powers to clear insanitary property: in 40 years rather more than 6,000 houses were demolished. Most of the new building needed was left to the private builder, though certain minimum standards were required of him by bylaws passed under the Public Health Act, 1875, and these guaranteed improved, if not ideal, conditions.

**Chamberlain and the Cross Act**   Liverpool undertook a modest re-housing project, in tenements, under the Artizans' Dwellings Act, but the Act's most spectacular results were seen in Birmingham. There a great 'improvement scheme', planned and carried by Joseph Chamberlain during his mayoralty, cleared a noisome slum area and gave the city its proudly-named Corporation Street. Chamberlain had long been alive to the problem of squalor, and in a Sanitary Conference at Birmingham early in 1875 criticised those who could think only of stern punishment 'when the people whom we have suffered to grow up like beasts behave like brutes': 'What folly it is to talk about the moral and intellectual elevation of the masses when the conditions of life are such as to render elevation impossible! We find bad air, polluted water, crowded and filthy homes and ill-ventilated courts prevailing in the midst of our boasted wealth.'[153] Chamberlain was appalled at the conditions in the worst slums of the city, which had a death-rate twice that of other quarters and were murderous to children. He welcomed the introduction of Cross's Bill, on which, indeed, his advice was sought, and when the Bill was passed he opened to the Corporation his improvement scheme of 'sagacious audacity', comparing it in magnitude and significance to Disraeli's recent *coup* over the Suez Canal shares. More than 40 acres of closely-built squalor were bought (at a cost of £1,500,000) and were cleared, a great new road was driven through and the surrounding areas were laid out for building. Within five years the death-rate had been more than halved. As elsewhere, however, new building was left to private enterprise, though it was to prove incapable of meeting the growing need. Not until 1890 was any municipal housing undertaken, but even with assistance from the rates the rents then charged, 5s. 6d. a week, were more than the poorer workers displaced by slum clearance could afford. A special Housing Committee of the Corporation was set up in 1901, but progress was slow. On the eve of the war of 1914 an investigation by a committee under a rapidly-rising Councillor, Joseph Chamberlain's son Neville, disclosed that 200,000 citizens of 'the second city in the Empire', nearly one-quarter of the total population, were still living in back-to-back houses.[154] Ambitious schemes were then prepared under the Housing and Town Planning Act of 1909, but like other plans in other places had immediately to be deferred. When Neville Chamberlain succeeded to his father's office and became Lord Mayor in 1915 Birmingham and the country were intent on other needs.

**The Bitter Cry**  The two housing acts of 1868 and 1875 were amended and strengthened in 1879 and 1882, but with little effect on the general situation. Public opinion was stirring, however, and the economic distress of the 80s produced a long series of grim revelations in the Press under such titles as *Horrible London* and *Squalid Liverpool*. 'The smouldering question has become a brightly burning one', wrote the journalist G. R. Sims in the first of his *Horrible London* articles in the *Daily News*. Sims saw the slums, with their poverty and wretchedness, for himself and marvelled that people could survive in them: 'How these people live is a mystery. It is a wonder that they are not found dead in their wretched dens.'[155] He saw to his horror how slum clearance under Cross's Act seemed to be but clearing space for 'a cemetery for cats and a last resting place for worn-out boots and kettles', while the dispossessed inhabitants crowded closer together into dens with thieves and prostitutes. 'The ultimate result', he feared, 'must be pestilence or revolution', and there were some, indeed, to whom the unemployed troubles of 1886 and the onset of Socialism seemed unpleasantly like the march to Versailles of an English revolution. This was seeing things in too lurid a light, but it is a measure of a widespread fear and bewilderment.

Still more influential than Sims's revelations was the famous penny pamphlet of 1883, *The Bitter Cry of Outcast London*, which, appealing as it did to Christian compassion and missionary enterprise (the proceeds of its sale went to advance 'the aggressive (*sic*) work of the London Congregational Union'), penetrated throughout society, even to the Queen herself. Housing conditions in East London, wrote the anonymous author (Rev. A. Mearns), only too often resembled a slave ship in the middle passage: the Artizans' Dwellings Act had in many places made matters worse, and the State's active intervention was needed to 'secure for the poorest the rights of citizenship; the right to live in something better than fever dens'.

**The Royal Commission, 1884-5**  The Royal Commission on the Housing of the Working Classes, appointed in 1884, was the response of a disturbed Parliament to the prevailing concern. The Commission was an influential one, among its members being the Prince of Wales, who had maintained his father's interest in working-class housing, Cardinal Manning and Cross, now Sir Richard: its Chairman was the able Radical, Sir Charles Dilke, close friend of both the Prince and Chamberlain. Among the many witnesses called were Edwin Chadwick and Lord Shaftesbury, both now in their eighties, and Octavia Hill. The Commission's Report, to which several references have already been made, appeared in 1885, and the first really effective Housing Act, the basis of future housing legislation as the Public Health Act of 1875 was the basis of future health legislation, followed in 1890.

The Royal Commission recognised the prevalence of the evils of bad housing, the overcrowding and insanitary conditions which caused disease, the intemperance which was often all that could make squalor bearable, the low wages and lack of transport facilities that compelled many to crowd together near their work, the frantic search for accommodation in already overcrowded areas that led to the dividing-up of large houses and the packing of families into single rooms, with rents, in London, of 4s.–5s. a room; the excessive cost of land bought under Cross's Act, sometimes more than 100 times the rateable value, the unwillingness even of many of the larger and wealthier local authorities to bestir themselves to improve matters and the inability of others through inadequate resources, the lack of interest among the more comfortable classes which allowed one London M.O.H., for instance, to live miles away from the poor district which he was supposed to serve. It saw, too, the curse of jerry-building: 'The old houses are rotten from age and neglect. The new houses often commence where the old ones leave off, and are rotten from the first.'[156] Yet it realised that the tenements which such organisations as the Peabody Trust were erecting hardly touched the problem of the really needy who could not rise to the modest rents asked: 'model dwellings do not reach the class whose need is greatest'.[157]

For the future the Commission could only urge local authorities to be more ready to take advantage of the powers they already possessed (an appeal which the young Sidney Webb, too, was now beginning to make) and recommend the extension of the facilities for by-laws in respect of new housing provided by the Public Health Act. To encourage the spreading of towns and to ease the pressure on existing housing it advised the development of workmen's fares and it argued that the railways, when they demolished houses, should be obliged to re-house the occupants, and not leave them to fend for themselves. As an essential condition of sanitary improvement it recommended the taking over of water supply by local authorities. While, however, deprecating the profiteering in land-development it offered no solution to the problem and it equally failed to suggest how the poorer victims of bad housing could be helped to meet the cost of new housing. A subsidy was the logical (and ultimate) answer, as some authorities were already discovering, but this was unacceptable doctrine. Octavia Hill, indeed, in her evidence dismissed the idea as equivalent to the rate in aid of wages that had been paid in the bad old days before 1834. Higher wages, she argued, were the solution,[158] but on this vexed issue the Commission was understandably silent.

**The Housing Act, 1890**    The Commission's Report was followed by an Act of 1885, which amended existing legislation, and five years later by the Housing of the Working Classes Act of 1890, a consolidating Act which brought together the jumble of earlier legislation and to a certain extent developed it. Authorities were encouraged to adopt improvement schemes such as Birmingham's, and their powers to demolish single insanitary houses and to engage in house building were strengthened. The confusion caused by the 1851 Act, which had seemed to confine municipal building to lodging-houses, was cleared up by the clause explicitly permitting the erection of single houses. Much was left untouched by this Act; in particular it suggested no conception of the overall planning of towns, which was to receive its first tentative legislative attention only years later, in the Housing and Town Planning Act of 1909. Much, too, was dependent on the willingness of authorities to act, and this many of them were still reluctant to do on any adequate scale: the actual achievement of the Act in improvement schemes, a close student of its working noted in 1907, had until then been 'ludicrously small',[159] and an amending Act was needed in 1900 to encourage new building by municipalities. Nevertheless, the standards laid down were among the best in the world and played their part in the improvement of the national health. The new houses now built under bylaws, if plain to the point of ugliness, were at least sanitary, even if it was not until 1909 that further back-to-back housing was at last prohibited throughout the country. Most of the new building was done by private enterprise, but in municipal building a serious start was made by some of the larger authorities, which even began to create housing estates beyond the bare needs of dispossessed slum dwellers: London, for instance, acquired its first 'new' housing estate at Tooting in 1900. It was to be long, however, before the backlog of downright bad and still more of inferior building was everywhere seriously tackled. Meanwhile the rapidly expanding industrial towns were growing regardless of the higher amenities. 'Our manufacturing towns and villages are masses of ugliness', wrote one critic in the 60s, in a plea for better conditions, 'rows of houses with no architectural feature to please the eye; the only glimpse of nature being the narrow strip of murky sky overhead.'[160] As one historian, himself active in social work before 1914, has commented bitterly, these towns were 'among the meanest, ugliest and most higgledy-piggledy in Europe',[161] and they were, alas, long to remain so. If sanitary standards were becoming adequate, planning, aesthetics and pride in citizenship of 'no mean city' were sadly in arrears, save in such pockets of venturesome (and private-enterprise) idealism as Bournville (1879), Port Sunlight (1888) and Letchworth Garden City (1903).

'We Must Educate Our Masters' Better sanitary conditions and better homes, though they might keep people in health and off the poor-rates, would not alone ensure the progressive improvement of the working classes. From the first reformers wished to see education encouraged. 'The most important duty of the Legislature', ran the significant wording of the final sentence of the 1834 report, 'is to take measures to promote the religious and moral education of the labouring classes.' Religious and moral the education was to be, to teach the poor their duty and their place, but there was nothing sinister in the design; after the revelations made by the Poor Law Commission it seemed essential to the betterment of the poor themselves that moral principles should be inculcated. This had been done by the Sunday Schools since the 1780s and there had been over the years much discussion of the advantages of literacy. Many were prepared to approve the teaching of reading, which would help workers to understand their duties, but discouraged writing as, in the words quoted by Kay-Shuttleworth, 'like putting the torch of knowledge into the hands of rick-burners'. Experience showed, however, as it was to show in other countries as industrialisation developed, that even a minimum of education produced better and more responsible workmen, though the driving force in much educational work was missionary zeal.

In the early years of the nineteenth century were founded the two voluntary societies, the National Society and the British and Foreign School Society, which were the pioneers of elementary education. The first government grant for education, a mere £20,000, was made to the societies in 1833 for school-building and when in 1838 the grant was increased a special committee of the privy council was set up to supervise it: of this committee Dr Kay (Kay-Shuttleworth) became the first secretary. The Factory Act of 1833 required children working in factories to attend school for two hours a day, and ten years later an attempt to increase the amount of schooling was foiled by bitter disagreement between Anglicans and Nonconformists over the State-endowment of Church schools, an issue which was to bedevil educational advance for more than 60 years. Education amounted at this time to little more than elementary religious instruction and the bare essentials of literacy. To teach anything more was regarded as extravagance, though Kay was firmly of the opinion that the working man needed more than mere literacy to enrich his life, and there was much voluntary activity in Mechanics' Institutes and People's Colleges. The days of State-aided higher education were still distant, however, and even Kay's hopes for a State system of elementary education were not to be realised until 1870.

The method used in schools in these early days was at first the monitorial, developed in the 40s into the use of 'pupil teachers'. Kay introduced inspectors and teacher training, and by the 50s State grants to schools were providing half a million pounds a year. In the 60s grants were made on the basis of examinations and 'payment by results', a method which may have raised and evened out standards but which imposed a constricting hand on curriculum and methods alike. By this time rather less than half of the children of the country were receiving schooling of some kind. The number of illiterates was considerably lower than this proportion would suggest, but it had become apparent that the voluntary societies were hopelessly unequal to their task. The triumph of the German educational system in the 60s with the victories of the well-schooled Prussian soldiers, and the similar triumph of the better-educated Federal troops of the United States over the Confederates, pointed the moral, and the idea of a national provision took root. Manufacturers saw the challenge of German and American trade competition and therefore found themselves at one with the trade unions and other working-class organisations which had long been pressing for compulsory education. The final incentive came with the widening of the franchise in 1867. 'We must educate our masters'—though the original reference was, more properly, to 'our future masters'—became the watch-word of the age, and the need for secular, compulsory education as an essential basis for radical political advance was stressed by the National Education League, founded by Chamberlain and others in Birmingham in 1869. In 1870 was passed the first Education Act: schools were everywhere provided, to fill the gaps left by the religious schools, schools financed by local rates and conducted by specially elected School Boards. Grants were continued to the voluntary schools, but the main financial responsibility for education now rested with local authorities, albeit, until 1902, with special authorities possessing no other duties. Education, it has well been said, 'was no longer a charity but a right'.[162]

**School Boards and Board Schools** The School Boards, like the earlier Boards of Guardians and Boards of Health, were the simple and somewhat *ad hoc* answer to the problem of finding a local responsible administrative organisation before there was any regular pattern of local government. Being subject to no control from any other body concerned with local expenditure, they were inevitably accused of extravagance, and their supersession in 1902 by the local councils created by the local government reforms of 1888 was in part an attempt to curb 'extravagant' expenditure. In fact, of course, the Act of 1902, the second great Education Act, again increased expenditure: the English seem consistently to have been shocked at the cost of educational developments they deemed desirable, and the same startled reactions were provoked by rising costs under the Acts of 1918 and 1944 as under the earlier measures.

Whatever the objections on grounds of cost, the 2,568 School Boards established under the Act of 1870 provided in their 30 years of existence some two and a half million school places in new buildings, while there were also more than 14,000 voluntary schools receiving grants. The London School Board alone built over 400 schools and under the aegis of local Boards elsewhere were erected the 'Board Schools' which can today be seen, most of them still in use, in all parts of the country. 'Austere and forbidding' C. F. G. Masterman was later to call these schools, and those who have attended them can testify to their lack of grace and dignity, their drab finish and their prison-like corridors and staircases. For all their limitations, however, Charles Booth rightly saw them, in the 80s, as 'each one "like a tall sentinel at his post", keeping watch and ward over the interests of the generation that is to replace our own', and this was the impression of another contemporary observer, Conan Doyle, who with skilful touches of authentic social comment made all the more credible his famous stories of detection. The conversation between Sherlock Holmes and Dr Watson as they looked over the London rooftops while running into Waterloo after their first visit to Woking in the case of the *Naval Treaty* is worth recalling: 'Look at those big, isolated clumps of buildings rising up above the slates, like brick islands in a lead-coloured sea.' 'The Board Schools.' 'Lighthouses, my boy! Beacons of the future! Capsules, with hundreds of bright little seeds in each, out of which will spring the wiser, better England of the future.' This was the great detective in unusually contemplative mood. 'Bright little seeds' is hardly what many teachers would have called all their charges, though, with the first generation already through the schools, manners and conditions were improving by the 90s when Holmes and Watson made their journey. It is difficult now to conceive how rough and unpromising the early pupils must in many cases have been in the poorer areas. High hopes were set on the abolition of illiteracy, but no startling miracles were accomplished. The curriculum was too narrow, the methods were too rigid, the classes too large and many children lacked the health and nourishment to benefit fully, while in any case schooling ended early and few parents would have had it otherwise when a child's earnings mattered to the meagre family budget. Attendance was made compulsory up to a minimum age of 10 in 1876 and the age was raised to 11 in 1893 and to 12 in 1899, but not generally to 14 until 1918, though from 1900 14 was possible by bylaw. There was no great enthusiasm for 'book-learning' and little enough was carried away, while for very many years there were to be complaints that the schools were out of touch with the demands of adult life. Nevertheless, the proportion of adults who had been efficiently schooled by contemporary standards rose rapidly from one-quarter in the 90s to three-quarters in 1910, and modest though the instruction was it provided the indispensable foundation of literacy and encouraged habits of punctuality, discipline and cleanliness without which the general raising of standards would hardly have been possible. 'Our Elementary Schools are now turning out a class who have tasted of the tree of knowledge', a Northumberland miner commented somewhat optimistically in the early 80s, 'this class will one day have control of the funds of our Trade and Co-operative Societies, and I have full confidence in the result.'[163] Charles Booth a few years later in his great survey of the *Life and Labour of the People in London* made a realistic assessment of what had been achieved: 'popular education has been far from wasted even in the case of those who may seem to have learnt but very little. Obedience to discipline and rules of proper behaviour have been inculcated; habits of order and cleanliness have been acquired; and from these habits self-respect arises.'[164] Forty years later the *New Survey of London Life and Labour*, carrying Booth's investigations forward into a new age, saw the turn of the century as marking a realisation among the working classes of the vital importance of hygiene and added the comment: '. . . it is impossible to doubt the connection between this change and the growth of the educated element of the adult population and especially of the parents of school children'.[165]

'Education is being spread very thin', complained Lady Florence Bell in 1907, in a study of the dismal conditions of the shipyards of the north-east coast, 'and is made to bear the burden of many unrealised, if not unrealisable, projects'.[166] Yet the organisation of the educational system, an even greater task than sanitation or health or poor-law provision in the face of the ever-increasing demand, could not but mark with a new character not only the millions concerned but the very notion of the State. How it struck the Webbs, with their passion for well-ordered administration, is revealed in a striking passage from the Minority Report of 1909, which almost reached the heights—for its authors—of poetic eloquence: 'Could there have been anything more "Utopian" in 1860 than a picture of what today we take as a matter of course, the 7,000,000 children emerging every morning, washed and brushed, from 5,000,000 or 6,000,000 homes in every part of the Kingdom, traversing street and road and lonely woodland, going o'er fell and moor, to present themselves at a given hour at their 30,000 schools, where each of the 7,000,000 finds his or her own individual place, with books and blackboard and teacher provided?'[167]

Education was not free until 1891, and although fees were low, and could be remitted in cases of serious need, for many parents the finding of the small sums regularly required was no light matter, as G. R. Sims pointed out to his readers:

'Twopence or a penny a week for each of four children is not much, you may say; but where the difference between the weekly income and the rent is only a couple of shillings or so, I assure you the coppers represent so many meals.'[168]

To make attendance possible after it had become compulsory School Boards had often to arrange in poorer areas for cheap school meals, and this was being done for 20 years before it was given statutory recognition in 1906. Medical inspection had also to be arranged in many cases, together with the distribution of clothing presented by the charitable. Compulsory schooling, indeed, in addition to its direct advantages to the young had the result of bringing to the attention of the public the conditions under which many children had to live, with their poverty, ill-health and under-nourishment, more openly and consistently than could be explained away by sweeping charges of neglect against parents. Many were the teachers who complained that their pupils could not learn for hunger, and in the days of 'payment by results', which did not end until 1895, there were occasions when children were fed in order that they might be better prepared for inspection. 'This is not charity, but far-sighted self-interest', was a remark from a village school quoted in a House of Commons debate on school meals in 1905, 'we feed them for the purpose of getting more money out of the Government'.[169]

**Elementary and Secondary Education**    'Elementary' education suggested the existence of higher grades to which pupils could aspire, but it was not until the 90s that 'higher grade' schools began to be provided by school boards, and they were ruled illegal under existing powers by the famous 'Cockerton judgment' of 1899. By this time the County Councils created in 1888 were allowed, by an Act of 1889, to provide technical and evening and other advanced classes, and it was to them that the Government was to look for the further development of 'secondary' education when the Act of 1902 was framed. The School Boards, many of which were too small to be efficient or popular, were then abolished, and education, both elementary and secondary, joined health among the growing responsibilities of the local Councils: for the first time, also, the voluntary elementary schools were fitted into the local organisation and received rate-aid, though this raised a political storm over Church schools which lasted for some years and in which a rising Nonconformist politician, David Lloyd George, made his mark. The new 'Local Education Authorities' were allowed both to create their own secondary schools, charging modest fees but with scholarships from the elementary schools, and to integrate into their own provision the old endowed grammar schools, which were now given a new lease of life. This process of integration was eased by an increase of 'free places' from elementary schools in 1907. The secondary schools, however, whether endowed or newly created, were from the first, and for a long period, the preserve mainly of the middle classes, and only a small proportion of elementary school children, hardly more than one in 20, were able to enter them. For those that remained the elementary school was not the first stage on an educational ladder but the only schooling they received, unless later they made the heroic efforts necessary to advance themselves by means of evening classes. Elementary schools, a distinguished educationalist of a later period has said, were no part of any educational ladder; 'they were as much "finishing" schools for manual workers as Miss Pinkerton's academy was a finishing school for young ladies'.[170] This shrewd comment is a pointer to a serious failing of the educational system that England was developing by the opening years of the present century, its essential class character, the reflection of the lack of social unity in the country and of the prestige enjoyed by the endowed grammar schools and, at a remove from the national system but not without influence upon it, the reformed 'public schools' of the nineteenth century, set on their feet by such notable headmasters as Arnold and Thring. Given the social conditions of the time and the narrow views of education that were current, the Act of 1902 could hardly have gone further, but it was resentment at this educational splintering of the nation that was to inspire, 40 years later, the new approach attempted by the Act of 1944, an approach still far from realised.

Despite the hopes maintained since 1870 and reflected in the Northumberland miner's comment that has already been quoted, the 'finishing school' education of the Elementary Schools did not provide an adequate preparation for the leaders of the working-class movement who, with their increasing responsibilities in trade-union and Labour party work, were so much in need of a broader understanding of the issues with which they had to contend. It was to meet their needs that the Universities interested themselves in adult education from the 70s and that the most successful voluntary organisation in this field, the Workers' Educational Association, was founded in 1903 by Albert Mansbridge. The Association's work, and especially the remarkable educational device of the tutorial class, which it conducted with the Universities, received State assistance under the regulations for grant-aid to higher education, but though it was influential it touched only the fringe of the needs of those whose schooling never went beyond the elementary level. For many other elementary schoolchildren the 1902 Act provided a way of escape into the middle class which their parents often anxiously favoured, even as middle-class parents did all they could to help their children retain their particular position on the social ladder. Sir George Kekewich, once the senior official of the central administration of education, some years after the changes of 1902, which he had wished to see take other forms, complained that the new system was turning out 'a nation of clerks'. Given the social background, the low esteem in which manual labour, and even technical skills, were held and all the uncertainties to which the working man was liable, this could hardly be avoided: education was a form of insurance, even as it was for many of the privileged who went to the Universities. 'We are all Socialists now', Sir William Harcourt had said as far back as 1889. Increasingly from 1902 this famous apophthegm might have been adapted to 'We are all middle class now'—as, indeed, today we are.

**Robert Morant**    Already before the passing of the Act of 1902 the central administration of education had been revised and a 'Board' of Education, which like other similar Boards never met, established under a President who was in fact a less respectably named Minister. The actual drafting of the Act and the vital early stages of its administration were the responsibility of a powerful and able figure, Rober Morant, who in 1902 succeeded Kekewich as Permanent Secretary of the Board. Morant had had a romantic career at the Court of Siam and since his return to England in 1894 at the age of 31 had risen rapidly in educational service. He was one of the most remarkable men and most able civil servants of his day, closely resembling Chadwick and Kay-Shuttleworth in the power of his personality, the breadth of his grasp, his immense application, the controversy he roused and the personal difficulties he caused himself by his inability to suffer fools—or any critics—gladly. He had pushed Kekewich aside and controversy pushed him in turn out of education in 1911, though just in time to direct the administration of Lloyd George's national insurance scheme. Eight years later, in 1919, he had the task, as permanent Secretary, of launching the newly established Ministry of Health, his third pioneer assignment in the social services at a time of rapid and significant expansion. Whatever his later achievements, however, the creation after 1902 of an integrated national educational service under the local authorities was a major contribution to social development.

**Education at the Turn of the Century**    With this new service advancing and secondary education at last provided, even if still inadequately, England had come far, though slowly, since the first grants had been made for education in 1833. She still lagged seriously behind such industrial rivals as Germany and the United States, however, nowhere more seriously than in University education, for which little State assistance was yet given, but hardly less so in the great field of technical education, now of increasing importance with the rapid development of engineering, electricity and the internal combustion engine. With the threat of German naval power, firmly based on a high degree of technical education, beginning to loom over the North Sea, Michael Sadler was to maintain that the British Empire depended equally on 'sea power and school power',[171] but the country was reluctant, now as later, to spend its resources on developing its school power to the fullest extent: although much was done, another half century was to pass before any sense of urgency was allowed to affect technical and University education. When in 1908 old age pensions were introduced Masterman noted the middle-class reaction to this provision for the old age of the working classes, now added to the arrangements for the education of their children: the middle-class parent, struggling to pay for his own children, 'wonders where it is all going to stop'.[172] Yet in the 1905 parliamentary debate on school meals, which has already been referred to, a speaker could argue thus: 'The future of the Empire, the triumph of social progress and the freedom of the British race depend not so much upon the strengthening of the Army as upon fortifying the children of the State for the battle of life.'[173] This was a far cry from the principles of 1834. A new conception of society and of the functions of the State was clearly emerging. Social progress had begun with the revelations of the 30s and 40s. Its greatest advances were yet to come, but the way was being prepared by the continued revelation of needs, deficiencies and defects, and by the challenges presented in the opening years of the new century.

The nineteenth century, at least in its earlier phases, is usually thought of as the age of *laissez-faire*, but whatever the interpretation placed on the great explosion of British industrial and commercial activity, and whatever the resistance to legislative interference, there clearly never was any length of time in which society was left to itself. *Laissez-faire*, it has well been said, 'is quite literally the only untried utopia'.[174] The tendency to collectivism, which gradually gathered pace during the century against the will and without the realisation of so many, can be traced back to Bentham, but took shape from the practical grappling with social ills that marked so much of the period. Problems of public health, in particular, so often provided the initial prompting, as this chapter has shown and that arch-critic of collectivism, A. V. Dicey, would seem to have grasped about the turn of the century.[175] Yet little could have been done without the resources which industrialisation was building up. Walter Rostow has seen the whole conception of the welfare state as a manifestation of technical maturity in a society,[176] and his interpretation of the process which has been described in this chapter as a decorous exploration of objectives beyond the margin of technological virtuosity may be recalled at its conclusion.[177] The next chapter is concerned with explorations which, if at the margin, certainly proceeded at a rate that was more than merely decorous.

*Note to page 104.* For a thorough study of the application of the new policy and of reactions to it, based on hitherto little used contemporary material, see N. C. Edsall: *The Anti-Poor Law Movement, 1834–44* (1971).

*Note to page 126.* These qualifications had already been removed in the case of boroughs in the Municipal Corporations Act, 1882.

*Note to page 139.* See J. N. Tarn, 'The Peabody Donation Fund. The Role of a Housing Society in the Nineteenth Century', *Victorian Studies*, 1966.

*Note to page 142, line 8.* This loan was raised by the Corporation of Liverpool, which borrowed £13,000, though only very reluctantly, to build what became the first municipal housing in the country (St. Martin's Cottages). (For this and the following reference see J. N. Tarn, 'Housing in Liverpool and Glasgow. The Growth of Civic Responsibility', *Town Planning Review*, January 1969.)

*Note to page 142, line 25.* It was assumed that, once sites were cleared, private enterprise could build houses, and Authorities were in fact discouraged from building themselves. In practice, however, private builders could not build working-class homes cheaply enough, as Liverpool found when after ten years of debate it was reluctantly compelled to construct Victoria Buildings itself.

# 5 | The Turning Point: Social Reform 1905-14

## 1 *The Contrasts of Edwardian England*

When in the new post-war world of the 1920s Lord George Hamilton, Chairman of the Poor Law Commission in the far-off Edwardian days of 1905-9 (that 'experienced politician and attractive *grand seigneur*', as Beatrice Webb called him[1]), came to write the record of his 40 years of public life, the Commission stood out in his memory as at once the most arduous and the most significant of the many tasks which had fallen to his lot. Considered in the context of all that had led up to it and all that had happened since it reported, the Commission, for all its immediate ineffectiveness, could be seen as marking a decisive turn in social policy. 'The object and incitement of the nineteenth century was to accumulate wealth, whilst the duty of the twentieth century is the far more difficult task of securing its better distribution',[2] this was to Hamilton the fundamental lesson of the mass of evidence which the Commission had acquired during its investigations. He himself was surprised, as he admitted, at the evidence of the unequal distribution of the wealth that industrialisation had brought to Britain and the smallness of the share that certain classes had received[3]: as Beatrice Webb commented, in words that recall Chadwick,[4] on the conditions of life enjoyed by Lord George and his like, 'their lives are so rounded off by culture and charm, comfort and power, that the misery of the destitute is as far off as the savagery of central Africa'.[5] Even allowing for the great social and economic differences that existed in society, differences which, like most people of his time, he accepted as part of the natural order of things, Hamilton could not but acknowledge that many workers had never received a fair share of the growing national wealth. Remedial and preventive services were doing little enough to redress the balance: they left untouched the real needs of many people, a whole class, in the closing words of the Majority Report, 'whose conditions and environment are a discredit, and a peril to the whole community'.[6]

Strong though these words were for an official report, they represented, in fact, no sudden revelation. Investigators of various kinds had been saying as much for 20 years, and patiently marshalling the facts and figures that proved the point. To most of the population, however, the facts and figures were often no more than a nine days' wonder, quickly forgotten in the press of life. To many others, themselves but little removed from the poverty line, they were something not to be acknowledged, something from which the fearful gaze had to be averted. Just before the 1914 war Mrs Pember Reeves, wife of the brilliant New Zealander who was Director of the Webbs' pet creation, the London School of Economics, sympathetically recorded the conditions of those Londoners whose wages were, in the phrase of her title, *Round about a Pound a Week*, and noted how, in their fragile security, they shrank from contact with those whose financial status was even lower: 'The poorest people are anxiously ignored by those respectable persons whose work is permanent, as permanency goes.'[7] Among those enjoying greater security, as Chadwick had observed long since, there was no greater degree of understanding or contact. There was in all sections of society, in fact, as the Majority Report acknowledged, 'unconsciousness of and unconcern in the wants, the failings and the sufferings of those outside their immediate circle'.[8] It was the removal of some at least of this unconsciousness, the stimulation, through the sheer weight of evidence, of some degree of concern, that made of the first decade of the twentieth century a turning point in social policy. In this process the Poor Law Commission played its part, presenting, much to the chagrin of those who had most desired its appointment, both in the Majority Report and, still more, in the Minority, the case for a wholly new approach.

The irony of the situation, as many had realised, was that, while social improvement at home came so slowly and left so many islands of neglect, Britain's exuberant imperialism had been assuming greater responsibilities overseas. As far back as 1889 G. R. Sims, moved by the incongruity of a forward policy in Africa against the sordid background of *Horrible London*, had posed the issue: 'Is it too much to ask that in the intervals of civilising the Zulu and improving the conditions of the Egyptian fellah the Government should turn its attention to the poor of London and see if it cannot remedy this terrible state of things?'[9] Yet, as far as official policy was concerned, the process of imperial expansion was hardly less a matter of 'unconsciousness and unconcern' than social problems. In both Egypt and South Africa Britain found herself saddled with duties which she had never intended to undertake. The pressure of events, and the need to forestall moves by others, created situations in which, for instance, it was the anti-imperialist Gladstone who had to move in Egypt. At home there was no such compulsion. There was no danger of revolution to speed reforms, for those who were worst off were the least able of any to take violent action: despite such scares as the unemployed demonstrations of 1886, the danger, as C. F. G. Masterman, for instance, pointed out in Edwardian days, was not of revolt but of despair.[10] Meanwhile, for many people conditions were improving, if slowly, with the rise of wages, while, as Mrs Pember Reeves and many others found, there was as yet little enough fellow feeling for those lower in the scale. In truth there was a 'white man's burden' in Britain no less than in Africa, as the very title of 'General' Booth's *Darkest England* was intended to suggest. But there was a confident, and by no means hypocritical, expectation, disputed but not as yet disproved, that economic growth would cure all ills, even as it would civilise Africa through trade: the weight of poverty at home was simply not appreciated. There was in any case the fundamental distinction between domestic and imperial policy that to tackle social problems at home meant interference with property, whereas the establishment of order and peaceful development overseas was essential for its protection. Moreover, domestic and overseas needs competed for Britain's growing supplies of capital: it has been shown, for instance, that building flourished best at home when overseas demands for capital were slack. Overseas investment, greater though its risks were, offered higher returns and drew emigrant British labour after it: the housing conditions of the people of Britain therefore depended to some extent on developments at the ends of the earth. Imperial entanglements also delayed social reform. Had it not been for the South African War of 1899–1902 old age pensions might well have been introduced earlier, if not in the form they eventually took, though at the same time it was the revelation of the poor physique of many would-be recruits that led to the appointment of the Physical Deterioration Committee of 1903 and so to school meals and medical services in 1906–7.

The desperate poverty of the neglected classes among an imperial people struck the signatories of the Majority Report of 1909 as it had struck Sims 20 years earlier, and their concern coloured the peroration with which they rounded off their recommendations. It opened on a high note with a reference to the sentiments which the noble music of Elgar had turned into the anthem of Edwardian imperialism: '"Land of Hope and Glory" is a popular and patriotic lyric sung each year with rapture by thousands of voices. The enthusiasm is partly evoked by the beauty of the idea itself, but more by the belief that Great Britain does, above other countries, merit this eulogium.'[11] But these fine sentiments, like Kipling's *Recessional* of the Jubilee Year of 1897, were matched by other, more disturbing, considerations: 'To certain classes of the community into whose moral and material condition it has been our duty to enquire, these words are a mockery and a falsehood. To many of them . . . there is in this life but little hope, and to many more "glory" or its realisation is an unknown ideal.'[12] There followed the reference, already quoted, to the conditions which were 'a discredit and a peril' to the nation, and the report ended on the sombre note which reflected the deep impression which the investigations and revelations of four years had made upon the Commission: 'No country, however rich, can permanently hold its own in the field of international competition, if hampered by an increasing load of this dead weight; or can successfully perform the role of sovereignty beyond the seas, if a portion of its own folk at home are sinking below the civilisation and aspirations of its subject races abroad.'[13]

The contrast was all the greater because of the high degree of affluence enjoyed by so many and the luxury flaunted by the really wealthy. With comfort and richness in the home on a scale never before imagined, crowds of servants, enormous meals, extravagant attire, rapid means of locomotion and luxurious holiday resorts, the wealthy Edwardians were the supreme hedonists of British history, and for many others the age was one of solid comfort. The national income had risen to some 2,000 million pounds and overseas investments to nearly double this amount: 'we might have expected to find', commented the Majority Report, 'that by this time industrial poverty at least was disappearing'.[14] True it was that for many wage-earners there was at least some margin for modest comfort, and for aping, at a remove, the indulgences of those better off. A Sheffield witness, giving evidence to the Poor Law Commission in 1906, spared no classes in his denunciation of the pleasure-seeking habits of 'gambling, drinking and unproductive sports' that were spreading so rapidly, egged on by the incitements of the Press 'to go pleasuring weekends',[15] and the Majority Report gravely deplored the example set the poor by the 'rich and ostentatious': 'Witness after witness has noted the extravagance in dress, the restless craving for amusement, the increasing time spent in watching sports or games—in a word, the subordination of the more serious duties of life to the frivolity and amusements of the moment.'[16]

This was to speak as if vast sums were being wasted, as if watching football were the equivalent of a Roman orgy—or of such a typical Edwardian country-house weekend as Lord George Hamilton often enjoyed—yet there were no vast sums to waste, even in the aggregate. Of the swollen national income not much more than half went to the 19 million people (with as many dependants) whose income was below £160 a year, the point at which liability for income-tax (at 1s. in the £) began, and the dividing line, as Lloyd George said in his budget speech of 1909, between sufficiency and gentility.[17] The other half of the national income, or something less, went to the fewer than five million of the population who remained, £152,000,000 of it to people with incomes of more than £5,000 a year. Of the vast number below the £160 income level, there were some 15 million wage-earners, nearly one-third of whom, investigations had shown, received wages inadequate for the proper support of their families. For them, indeed, life had little to offer but the dreary round of ill-paid or only occasional employment, inadequate food and housing and constant wearying care, leading to indifference or worse. 'If the poor were not improvident', Mrs Pember Reeves argued against the sweeping accusations of unthriftiness and extravagance heaped upon such unfortunates, 'they would hardly dare to live their lives at all.'[18] Masterman, watching the spread of the holiday resorts with their stately hotels (most of them still standing half a century later as relics of a more flamboyant era, if often put now to other uses), pictured in 1909 his contrasting impressions of *The Condition of England*: 'While the white hotels rise on all the shores of England, and the apparatus of pleasure is developing into ever new and ingenious forms of entertainment, continues through the nights and days the grey struggle of the Abyss.'[19] Another contemporary, Arnold Bennett, luxuriating at the 'Royal York' at Brighton in 1910, saw the contrast still more pointedly: 'I am obsessed by the thought that all this comfort, luxury, ostentation, snobbishness and correctness, is founded on a vast injustice to the artisan-class.'[20]

In general, conditions were deteriorating for wage-earners in these Edwardian years. Since the serious depression of 1886 rises in wage-rates and a fall in the cost of living had raised real wages, for those regularly employed, to half as much again as they had been in 1880 (the average for *all* employed was nearer one-third) and to three-quarters above the level of 1850. Yet they were still low enough and were not to rise again for a decade, while the cost of living was to take a sharp turn upwards. Not many workers received much more than 30s. a week, even without periods of sickness, slackness or unemployment, and the average was nearer £1. 'The results of the system', said a pioneer of economic statistics of the period before 1914, 'have not produced a satisfactory livelihood to the bulk of the population', and their position was not improving.[21] The abyss, too, was near enough, as Lady Florence Bell realised from her study of conditions in ship-building in 1907: 'We are apt to believe that once employment is secured all must be well, so long as the workman is steady and knows how to manage his money. But we forget how terribly near the margin of disaster the man, even the thrifty man, walks, who has, in ordinary normal conditions, but just enough to keep himself on.'[22] We need to find a means to make the poor less poor, Dr (Sir) John Simon had said in 1890, reviewing, after a lifetime in the public health service, the limited progress that had been made.[23] He had in mind the lowest wage-earners, but the investigations of Charles Booth and Seebohm Rowntree had shown just how poor, and how numerous, the poor were.

## 2 *Social Thought and Social Conscience*

**Individualism and Collectivism**  There were as yet few thoroughgoing Socialists who demanded a radical reshaping of the economic organisation of the country to provide a fairer share of its resources for the under-privileged majority. The improvement in wages had been achieved by the trade unions which had been patiently building up their strength within the prevailing system and merely demanding for their members a larger share of the larger output and profits that were being produced. Yet the very growth of the unions, protected as they were by the Acts of 1871 and '75, had been one aspect of the slowly changing attitude of the State that has been sketched in the previous chapter. In 1885 the Fabian Society had set out, as Bernard Shaw explained in his Preface to the 1908 reprint of the first *Fabian Essays in Socialism* of 1889, 'to make it as easy and matter-of-fact for the ordinary respectable Englishman to be a Socialist as to be a Liberal or a Conservative'.[24] In those first essays Sidney Webb had drawn attention to the way in which thinkers and practical men alike had been moving in the direction of collective action for the relief of the less favoured members of society: 'In the teeth of the current Political Economy, and in spite of all the efforts of the mill-owning Liberals, England was compelled to put forth her hand to succour and protect her weaker members. Any number of Local Improvement Acts, Drainage Acts, Truck Acts, Mines Regulation Acts, Factory Acts, Public Health Acts, Adulteration Acts, were passing into law.'[25] 'Little by little and year by year', the orthodox *Economist* commented in 1895, 'the fabric of State expenditure and State responsibility is built up like a coral island, cell on cell.'[26] What was emerging, Sidney Webb suggested, was the 'unconscious Socialism' of a 'house-keeping State', and the Fabian inevitability of this gradual, pragmatic approach to a largely unsuspected collectivism was the theme of a notable work of the turn of the century, A. V. Dicey's *The Relation between Law and Public Opinion in England during the Nineteenth Century*, first delivered as lectures at Harvard in 1898 and published in 1905. Dicey's, again, was a more orthodox view. He deplored the tendency of collectivism to set up the opinion of an expert against the individual's judgment of what was to his best advantage and, somewhat equivocally, cited the laws against the adulteration of food as a typical example. The selection of this illustration revealed both his penetration and its limitations. He saw the process, as few others did, and grasped its significance, but he failed to understand its motive force: hence, for instance, his dismissal of old age pensions, in his second edition of 1914, as 'in essence nothing but a new form of out-relief for the poor'.[27] To say 'nothing but' was, as we shall see, to miss the whole point of the case for old age pensions, but the combination in so percipient an observer (as he said himself, 'few indeed have been the men who have been able to seize with clearness the causes or tendencies of the events passing around them'[28]) of a grasp of contemporary processes with only a limited realisation of their inner significance is in itself a comment on the confused social thinking of the time. What was happening, in fact, was that the State was intervening, not to restrict the liberty of the individual but to enlarge the liberty of those who without its aid could not protect themselves.

It was a logical and yet at the same time a strange reversal of the individualist doctrines by which the nineteenth century had been guided. If, in the true spirit of Benthamism, archaic restrictions had been removed and the individual set free to pursue his own interests, it was hardly 'the greatest good of the greatest number' that had followed. The legislature had been compelled, however reluctantly, to intervene to secure to all at least minimum standards. Health, housing and factory conditions, education, the prevention of the adulteration of food and the legal protection of trade unions had all been the subject of legislative action, not in the first place in deference to any doctrine but simply to safeguard society as a whole, lest worse befall—in short, for the greatest good of the greatest number, measured, however, not solely by the individual's estimate of that good, but by the collective opinion of society. Health and housing legislation, though it interfered to no small extent with the liberty of the individual, could be regarded as benefiting society even more than the individuals it protected, since it checked the disease and squalor which bred epidemics from which all might suffer. Education was necessary to establish the informed electorate without which democracy might become anarchy, and to train the workman in the skills of advancing industry. J. S. Mill had argued in his famous essay *On Liberty* (1859) that the only justification for interference by the community with the liberty of an individual was to prevent harm to others: 'his own good, either physical or moral, is not a sufficient warrant'. Yet inevitably this narrow view had been displaced: protective legislation had gathered its own momentum and the individual's own judgment of what was to his benefit had been in a number of directions superseded. In some cases, as with the laws protecting foodstuffs, the general interest had been the guide, though, as Dicey pointed out, the matter was one which the individual, albeit with a good deal of trouble and expense, could have seen to for himself.[29] In other cases, as with factory legislation, it was a particular class which benefited; in yet others, as in the case of education, the benefit was to some at the direct expense of the rest. The Utilitarian view might demand, as Mill had claimed, 'the subjection of individual spontaneity to external control, only in respect to those actions of each, which concern the interest of other people', but by the end of the nineteenth century the process had gone further than this and, though as yet only to a modest extent, the conception of welfare had begun to replace that of utility. A 'nineteenth-century revolution in government' had, in fact, taken place.[30] The social conscience was being stirred by the conditions of the less fortunate members of society and legislation was beginning to be shaped to improve those conditions, not merely to secure what seemed best for society as a whole. Some restriction of the complete liberty of certain people—employers, landlords, parents in respect of their children's need of education—was seen to be necessary in order to secure the real conditions of liberty for others to whom, as the Majority Report acknowledged in 1909, the true enjoyment of liberty was but 'a mockery and a falsehood'. It was beginning to be realised that, as a modern commentator on Dicey has said, in words already noted, 'there is much that the State can do which is not only consistent with liberty but essential to it'.[31] Thus did a new conception of society begin to take shape. It was an unconscious process, a step towards the collective control of the nation's resources, though not Socialist, for all the arguments of the Fabians, since it implied no change in the ownership of those resources.

Nor did it imply any acceptance of an inevitable approach of Socialism, as the Fabians believed. Each new instance of collective concern with social problems was swallowed, but was not seen as part of a process which would lead in time to a Socialist State. The 'ordinary respectable Englishman' of the middle classes did not become a Socialist: looking at his tax and rate demands he asked rather, in words quoted earlier, 'where it is all going to stop'.[32] It was certain sections of the working classes, with a few middle-class allies, that in 1900 founded what was to become a *Labour* Party, with, in 1906, a small but solid group of M.P.s of its own and at length, in 1918, a Socialist programme. A Socialist party drawn from all classes was a later creation. The Fabians, in fact, proved to be little more than the

'Micawber club' which one derisive critic had styled them.[33] Nor were other propagandists more fortunate. When in 1894 the Royal Commission on Labour, which had been in session since 1891, finally reported, its soothing sentiments, vague recommendations and easy acceptance of the chances of industrial peace angered its trade-union members, among whom were Tom Mann and the famous 'Mabon' (William Abraham) of the South Wales miners, into presenting their own minority report, in which they put the case for a more active social policy: 'We think it high time that the whole strength and influence of the collective organisation of the community should be deliberately, patiently and persistently used to raise the standard of life of its weaker and most oppressed members.'[34] This, however desirable, was but beating the air in 1894, as ineffective as the confident expectations of the Fabians themselves.

**Working-class Movements**   Had the working classes, with all the voting strength that they had possessed since the political reforms of 1867 and 1884, accepted the Marxist interpretations of their class-interest and moved as one, they could, no doubt, have achieved much. 'The difficulty in England', the Fabians complained in 1896, 'is not to secure more political power for the people, but to persuade them to make any sensible use of the power they already have.'[35] Even had unity and united action been feasible, however, there was little desire for independent action. Most working men were Liberals, but there were many Conservatives, and a few Conservative working men, especially in Lancashire, sat in Parliament. Socialists were rare and the trade unions mainly concerned with limited practical aims, while industrial organisation was still on a comparatively narrow basis. Figures for trade-union membership were uncertain until after 1886, when A. J. Mundella, as President of the Board of Trade, inaugurated a Bureau for the collection and publication of statistics which, when in Office again in 1892, he converted into a Department of Labour, with its own *Gazette*. Total membership was probably about one million in the 80s, and although it had doubled by 1900 it did not reach 2,500,000 until 1910, after which, however, there was a spectacular advance to more than four million by 1913. Until 1910 membership was still principally in the more skilled and concentrated trades, coal, engineering, shipbuilding, cotton, and though some unions, especially in the mining areas, were able to secure the return of their own members to Parliament, it was not until about 1900 that the trade unions, faced with the hardening of opinion against them that was to culminate in the Taff Vale Judgment of 1901, were prepared to support a specifically 'Labour' approach to politics, and thus open the way for the formation of a Labour Party. Politics was still thought of by most people as an occupation for the wealthy and leisured, and, although the removal of financial qualifications for local councillors had made it possible for working men to stand in local elections, there was no State payment to M.P.s until 1911. After 1867 and 1884 the working classes were wooed by the existing parties, but they did not take over. Not until 1945 were the Fabian hopes of a

conversion realised: the men who started an independent Labour political movement in 1900 certainly saw themselves as for the present nothing but a pressure
group.

**Facts and Philosophy**    Yet the collectivist tendency, from which the Fabians
had hoped so much, did continue. Dicey was one of the few other contemporary
observers who could see the underlying pattern in what was happening, and because of his more orthodox approach his interpretation was more acceptable. He
was typical of his age, however, in failing either to analyse the reasons for the
process or to draw the conclusions as to future developments which to the Fabians
were so obvious. Beyond noting the preoccupation of the wealthy with the condition of the poor which had been so marked a feature of the period since about
1850, he had no explanation to offer.[36] He had the clue, however, in his hands.
Discussing in his second edition the introduction of National Health Insurance,
he made the pregnant observation: 'Before 1908 the question whether a man, rich
or poor, should insure his health, was a matter left entirely to the free discretion or
indiscretion of each individual. His conduct no more concerned the State than
the question whether he should wear a black coat or a brown coat.'[37] What concerned, and perturbed, Dicey in health insurance was the great increase in
collective control that resulted from it. What he did not explain was why the
legislation was introduced. It was not done from any philosophical addiction to
collective control, as Sidney Webb would have had it done, but simply because of
the revelations of the inadequacy, for certain classes of the community, of any
provision they could make for themselves. It was, in short, the facts of the situation which were calling for urgent consideration, facts which the widening scope
and efficiency of government, its improved sources of information, its greater
responsiveness as the result of democratic advances in local and central elections,
together with a growing social consciousness and conscience in the face of the
revelations of neglect and of the inadequacy of existing legislation, were increasingly forcing upon public attention. 'Legislative opinion', Dicey said himself in the closing passages of his book, 'is itself more often the result of facts than
of philosophical speculations.'[38] This might well be taken as the keynote of the
rise of the Welfare State.

**Social Pity and the Liberal Landslide**    Lloyd George, when he introduced
his National Health Insurance scheme to the House of Commons in 1911, saw
it as the outcome of 20 years of thought and teaching which had profoundly
influenced public opinion. He had had the good fortune, he said, to be 'carried
forward on a tide of social pity that was only waiting for a chance of expression'.[39]
To make his case he drew upon the statistics of the trade unions and friendly
societies, the pioneers of health insurance, on other statistics which, as in the
1840s, revealed the connexion between illness and pauperism, and on such recent

revelations as the unexpectedly large demand for old age pensions, which had shown a largely unsuspecting country how much there was of poverty and destitution, which, in Lloyd George's words, 'is too proud to wear the badge of pauperism (and) would rather suffer from deprivation'.[40] Others in these years were quoting freely from the reports of Charles Booth and Rowntree, which, as *Hansard* shows, offered a mine of argument for parliamentary debates. There were, too, the findings of the Physical Deterioration Committee, on which Lloyd George, as an ardent 'pro-Boer', had commented acidly during the election of 1906: 'The country that spent two hundred and fifty millions to avenge an insult levelled at her pride by an old Dutch farmer is not ashamed to see her children walking the streets hungry and in rags.'[41]

How far opinion had come in little more than a decade from the hopeless demand for State intervention put forward in the 1894 Minority Report of the Labour Commission, which was quoted earlier, is suggested in Lloyd George's own vigorous assertion of the State's responsibility, as in a speech at Swansea, before a congenial Welsh audience, in 1908: 'In so far as poverty is due to circumstances over which the man has no control, then the State should step in to the very utmost limit of its resources.'[42] 'Very utmost limit' could hardly have been intended to be taken too literally, but that it could be said at all was evidence of a change in spirit and emphasis, a change of which the 'Liberal landslide' of 1906, which gave the Liberals a majority of 346, was a forceful expression. Lloyd George hailed it as a constitutional revolution: 'I believe there is a new order coming from the people of this country. It is a quiet, but certain, revolution, as revolutions come in a constitutional country.'[43]

A revolution, even a constitutional one, the Liberal success hardly was, except as an expression of reaction against nearly 20 years of Conservative rule, and although social reform was to prove a major preoccupation of the Liberal Government it had not been an election issue. Indeed, the discredited Conservative leader, A. J. Balfour, was to complain that the election had been won on no policy at all. Nevertheless, he himself saw in his party's defeat signs of a change that was something more than the swing of the pendulum. 'We are face to face (no doubt in milder form)', he said, 'with the Socialistic difficulties which loom so large on the Continent. Unless I am greatly mistaken the election of 1906 inaugurates a new era.'[44] A new era it assuredly was, if less fundamental and sweeping in its changes than Lloyd George and such colleagues as Winston Churchill— or Conservative critics—believed, and the new group of 29 Independent Labour M.P.s was a portent, as Balfour realised. Their very presence was to heighten awareness of social problems and the sense of urgency. As another contemporary observed in 1910, Socialism, which in 1905 had been no more than 'a thing of the air', had already come to be regarded as 'a great force',[45] and it was the growing Liberal preoccupation with reform, no less than the steady clamour of the Labour group, which brought the new force and the new era to public consciousness. The ground had, however, already been prepared by the trend to collectivism and such recent legislation as the Unemployed Workmen Act, no less than by the exposure of conditions which had stimulated concern.

**Stirrings from the 1880s**   The previous chapters have shown that the pre-occupation with social conditions began with the 1834 changes in the poor law, and developed as it became clear that economic advance would not of itself remove anomalies and create a secure prosperity for all. It was from the 80s that the preoccupation became general and that organised working-class pressure began to make itself felt, the 80s that marked, in Beatrice Webb's phrase, the 'no man's land' between the passing of the old doctrines and the acceptance of new ones.[46] The 80s saw, on the part of the government, the extension of the demo-cratic franchise to the countryside, the reform of local government, the in-auguration of a statistical service for economic affairs, a series of investigations including the Royal Commission on Housing, the spread of the public health services and the cautious approach to free elementary education and to higher education. Private investigations produced such disturbing, if lurid, accounts of poverty and squalor as Sims's *Horrible London*, Mearns's *Outcast London* and the Salvationist 'General' William Booth's *Darkest England*. Economic depression shook complacent confidence in progress, produced the Mansion House Fund and the Chamberlain Circular, and stimulated Socialist agitation and the creation of the first Socialist organisation. At the end of the decade came the Dockers' Strike, symbol and stimulus of the 'new Unionism' of unskilled workers, organised, unlike the older 'craft' unions, by industries.

**University Settlements and Social Investigation**   With all this came, too, a widespread stirring of social conscience, 'a new consciousness of sin',[47] as Beatrice Webb called it, of the moral obligation of the rich to the poor. 'Whilst we have been dreaming that the millennium was coming', wrote Mearns in *The Bitter Cry of Outcast London*, 'the gulf has been daily widening which separates the lowest classes from all decency and civilization.' Among the more fortunate it was especially at Oxford that the new spirit was felt. There it was that, mainly under the inspiration of the teaching of T. H. Green from the 70s until his early death in 1882, there developed the Idealist school of English philosophy, which was to influence many of the politicians and social reformers of later years.[48] Green himself was well informed on the social issues of the day, 'full', one observer commented, 'of the "condition of the people" question',[49] and though not the collectivist that Dicey thought him, aware of the need for government action to improve conditions. To the nineteenth-century Liberal tradition of the removal of restraints he opposed a more positive conception of action by the State to enable its citizens to grow in freedom, 'freedom in the positive sense . . . the liberation of the powers of all men equally for contributions to a common good'.[50] This idealistic conception, already somewhat dimmed by Green's disillusionment at the action of the newly-enfranchised working men in helping to return Disraeli at the election of 1874, nevertheless caught the imagination of many young men at Oxford. Asquith, Herbert Samuel, Ernest Barker, A. D. Lindsay were among many who came under Green's spell, and through them his influence has extended into our own day. Close to him was the brilliant young Arnold Toynbee, ardent social reformer and pioneer historian of the industrial revolution, who died, at the age of only 31, a year after Green himself. Their work and teaching gave an impetus to social thought and activity that has still not faded: the philosopher Henry Sidgwick wrote in 1884 of the situation they had left, 'The world is in a rather sternly philanthropic frame of mind, rather social-istic, rather inclined to find culture frivolous and to busy itself with the poverty in the East End of London.'[51]

In the East End of London, at St Jude's, Whitechapel, was Samuel Barnett, devotedly combining parochial with social work. One of the great social pioneers of the day, he had been a friend and admirer of Arnold Toynbee, whose work he decided to commemorate in 1884 by founding an institution which should bring university men to the people in need. 'Toynbee Hall' was established in that year and with it one of the most striking practical manifestations of the new frame of mind, the University Settlement movement, which brought earnest young men to live among the poor in the hope of understanding and helping them, and which was to spread not only throughout the country but into many parts of the world. Barnett was Warden for 12 years and stamped the whole movement with his devotion. His aim was the laudable one of bridging the gulf between rich and poor, of doing something 'to weld Classes into Society'.[52] Whether so ambitious and difficult an object was ever achieved may be doubted, but what the Settlement movement did achieve was to provide local centres for social work and adult education and almost unrivalled opportunities for able young men to learn something about the problems of society which would stand them in good stead in their later careers. Toynbee Hall, a nearby observer at Poplar, George Lansbury, complained later, had little permanent social influence, but its young men got good posts in government and municipal service![53] As the young men included two, Lord Beveridge and R. H. Tawney, who made their mark in their several ways and amply repaid any debt they owed to Whitechapel, after careers not particularly rich in official plums, Lansbury's remark may be taken as the suspicious reaction of East London to philanthropic patronage. It was at Toynbee Hall that Beveridge, as Sub-Warden from 1903 to 1905, made the first investigations into the problem of unemployment which were to have such far-reaching consequences. Among many other residents at various times were several who were later to be the chief architects of the new social services of 1909–12, R. L. Morant and W. J. Braithwaite, who helped to establish National Health Insur-ance, H. Llewellyn Smith, who, as Permanent Secretary of the Board of Trade, was responsible for the inauguration of both Labour Exchanges and National Insurance, and E. H. Aves, Chairman of the first Trade Boards. Yet another of those connected with the Settlement who were later to achieve distinction was C. R. Attlee, Secretary in 1910–11. It was social work in East London that made a Socialist politician of the Conservative barrister that Attlee had been.

**Charles Booth**   Canon Barnett, it may be noted, having started his career as a supporter of the Charity Organisation Society, under the influence of his environment in Whitechapel came to be an advocate of such alternatives to poor relief as the old age pensions and school meals which the C.O.S. steadfastly resisted. Another who learnt from practical social work in London the inadequacy of the C.O.S. prescription was Basil Kirkman Gray, author of a scholarly *History of English Philanthropy*, published in 1905, which revealed what Gray called the 'exhaustion' of private charity in the face of widespread poverty.[54] What near acquaintance with conditions did for these two was done for many others by the revelations of Charles Booth's *Life and Labour of the People in London*, begun in 1886 and only completed, 17 years and 17 volumes later, in 1903. This, the greatest social enquiry ever undertaken in England, could justly be styled 'epoch-making', and though many others, including Beatrice Webb and some inmates of Toybnee Hall, took part in it, it was essentially one man's achievement.

Charles Booth was a wealthy Liverpool shipowner, with a profound interest in social problems and a flair for investigation. He had settled in London in the 70s and under the influence of the social ferment of the times had determined to get at the facts of poverty. He first studied, in the census returns of 1841 to 1881, the distribution of employment, but in 1886, realising the need for more actuality and more detail, he set on foot a far more ambitious project. This was a detailed survey of conditions in London aimed at bringing out not only the varied employment but the degree of affluence and poverty of its people, with all the social influences that told upon them. Booth was moved by the prevailing distress of the depression years, but the immediate occasion of his project was the undertaking by the newly established Social Democratic Federation, under the leadership of the famous Marxist stockbroker, H. M. Hyndman, of a close survey of working-class wages, which showed that no fewer than a quarter of them were inadequate to keep men in health. Like many others Booth rejected these findings out of hand as sensational and 'incendiary', but characteristically he sought out Hyndman and informed him that he proposed to check and counter them. His object was to get at the facts behind the economic distress of the 80s, and in the event he found himself actually confirming the S.D.F.'s conclusions.[55] The East End and Central London were examined and patiently recorded in detail, house by house, but the task proving impossibly long the rest of London was surveyed as to social conditions only, street by street. The whole colossal venture, covering more than a million families, was Booth's own conception and responsibility. It contributed much to the advancement of the scientific study of society, and brought to Booth himself recognition and acknowledgment in his appointment as a Fellow of the Royal Society and Privy Councillor.

In the gathering of his evidence Booth used the census returns of 1881 and

1891, but for the precise and detailed information which he required, acting on a hint from Joe Chamberlain, who had used the same method when preparing for slum clearance in Birmingham, he drew upon the intimate local knowledge of the school attendance officers, who for many hours submitted to the questioning of himself and his staff of assistants. In this way did the official statistics and the officers of a State service, all of them manifestations of the growing collectivism, contribute to the better understanding of society. Without statistical information and a corps of officials the services instituted by Parliament could not have been carried out. Booth showed to what further ends both could be put, though, 'born field worker' that he was,[56] he added much of personal experience and observation.

The survey attempted no explanation and offered few remedies. It was, as Booth himself declared from the first, not intended to be more than a vast 'instantaneous picture' (the phrase used at this time in photography for what later came to be called a 'snap'), providing the accurate and detailed evidence on which alone policy could be based: as such it proved, sometimes to his disgust, a mine of information for partisans of all schools including even some who thought that it would 'tend to foster discontent among the poor'.[57] What it showed, with a wealth of detail that only Booth's resources and patience could have produced, was that while about half of the population could be ranked as comfortably-off working class, no less than one-third, amounting in all to over a million people, was on or below the poverty line, which he set at about a pound a week. About one-third of the population, too, lived in conditions of overcrowding and squalor, with an average of two to three persons to a room, while the death-rate varied from 11 to 25 per 1,000, and varied almost exactly with the incidence of poverty. All this was startling and revealing enough: it was more valuable, the *Morning Post* commented, in a hit at some other recent publications, than 'an ocean of sensational writing',[58] and in Beatrice Webb's words it 'reverberated in the world of politics and philanthropy'.[59] It struck the philanthropists with particular force, for what Booth was able to demonstrate was that charity was largely irrelevant. Where it had been practised most thoroughly and systematically over the years, in the manner prescribed by the C.O.S., 'the people are no less poor . . . there are fewer paupers, but not any fewer who rely on charity'.[60] In fact, charity was doing little more than relieve the rates: it left poverty unsolved, a conclusion which Kirkman Gray was also reaching at this time.[61]

Booth's particular concern, as his survey piled up the evidence of poverty, overcrowding, ill-health, child neglect and moral decay, was with the problem of the rather fewer than 10 per cent of the 'very poor', amounting in all to some 300,000 people, who were for various reasons, and especially through irregularity of employment, incapable of supporting themselves and their families. Like Sir John Simon he wanted to see the poor less poor, and with a prophetic anticipation of the basis of future welfare provision he argued that the community, in its own interest, should 'take charge of the lives of those who are incapable of independent existence up to the required standard'.[62] If this were done he thought that the rest of the community could safely be left to look after itself. Among the incapable he particularly counted the elderly, and he was among the earliest advocates of old age pensions. An article of Sidney Webb's first drew his attention to the relation between old age and poverty, and he soon proved the connection for himself both from his London survey and from detailed studies he made of poor law and census returns. 'The official figures show beyond dispute', he wrote in 1894, 'that nearly one-third of the old in England and Wales receive parish relief . . . old age stands out plainly as the prevailing cause of pauperism after 65.'[63] The figures showed, indeed, that the proportion of paupers among the elderly, one-quarter at age 65, rose rapidly as age advanced to two-thirds at 75 and three-quarters at 80.[64] With the revelation of the sheer amount of dire poverty, this was one of the most startling and significant of Booth's discoveries, though the facts and figures had long been there, in official returns, for all to see. Another point which he was one of the first to bring to public attention was the incidence of intermittent and casual employment and its serious consequences as a cause of poverty. He showed, as later observers, and especially Beveridge, were to confirm, that, although unemployment through cycles of depression was a serious problem, under-employment as a consistent feature of the economic scene was still more serious. In the East End of London, which he investigated so thoroughly, and especially in the docks, too many men were competing for work: 'they are not unemployed', Booth maintained, 'they are badly employed'.[65] It was a case which within 20 years Beveridge and the Poor Law Commission were to drive home and which was to prepare the way for labour exchanges, trade boards and unemployment insurance.

**Seebohm Rowntree**   Booth's findings contributed much to the general unease about conditions and particularly to concern at the plight of the elderly. From the beginning of the 90s, indeed, until the passing of the Old Age Pensions Act in 1908 the problem of poverty in old age was a major concern in politics and social work alike. But for the South African War, as has already been suggested, something might have been done earlier. Before considering the steps that eventually led to old age pensions, however, a further enquiry into poverty, which was inspired by Booth's work and strikingly confirmed his conclusions, must be mentioned. This was Benjamin Seebohm Rowntree's *Poverty : A Study of Town Life*, a survey of conditions in York in 1899, published in 1901, before Booth's final volume had appeared. Rowntree was the son of the Quaker cocoa manufacturer, philanthropist and pioneer of industrial welfare, Joseph Rowntree. He early followed his father's interests and a long life enabled him to supplement the original study of 1899 with similar surveys in 1936 (*Poverty and Progress*, 1941) and 1950 (*Poverty and the Welfare State*, 1951), reviewing conditions under the changing circumstances of welfare provision.

The 1899 study was undertaken to see how conditions in a country town compared with those of London. Much to his surprise Rowntree found an almost exact correspondence. By a careful examination of needs and costs he established a minimum standard of income necessary for the bare maintenance of physical health, and his survey showed that 28 per cent of the population lived below this standard, a proportion only slightly smaller than Booth's figure for London. In York, as in London, moreover, the statistics revealed the greater incidence of ill-health and the higher death-rate among the poor, the death-rate being double that among people better off. Booth had deplored the condition of many children, but Rowntree endeavoured to test it by comparing heights and weights for different income-levels, and found, for instance, that at 13, the age for leaving school and starting work, boys from the poorest homes were on the average 11 lb. lighter and $3\frac{1}{2}$ inches shorter than others from better homes even of the working class. When the book appeared in 1901 the first figures for recruitment for the South African War, of which so much was to be made later, had just appeared, and Rowntree was able to show the correspondence between the low physical standards of many recruits and those of the schoolchildren he had been investigating. This, even if the physical and mental suffering inevitably involved could be overlooked, was a serious matter in itself at a time of keen international rivalry, when Britain was conscious of the passing of her old industrial supremacy and the South African War was revealing the opposition and envy of other Powers. 'That in this land of abounding wealth', Rowntree concluded, 'probably more than one-fourth of the population are living in poverty, is a fact which may well cause great searchings of heart.'[66] This was a theme which Liberal ministers, especially Lloyd George and Churchill, were to embroider in many speeches in the years ahead. *Poverty* made a deep impression on Churchill when he read it, at Morley's prompting, soon after its publication, and with his recent experiences in South Africa in mind he was struck, as Sims had been in the 80s, by the incongruous combination of ascendant imperialism abroad and desperate poverty at home: 'I see little glory in an Empire which can rule the waves and is unable to flush its own sewers'. 'The social condition of the British people in the early years of the twentieth century', he was to say at Leicester in 1909, in words that recall Rowntree's, 'cannot be contemplated without deep anxiety.'[67] This serious concern was to be the driving force of the Liberal reform.

**The Liberal Government**    The Liberals brought no challenging political philosophy to the task they assumed in 1905, and in the general election of 1906, which sweepingly endorsed the change of government, no programme of social reform was proposed, though the Prime Minister, Campbell-Bannerman, had hinted at poor law reform and mitigation of 'the evils of non-employment'.[68] The Ministry was, indeed, a mixed team, divided not long since over the South African War, and united only in devotion to free-trade and such unsettled issues of Gladstonian Liberalism as Ireland and the House of Lords. Only on the radical wing was there any active concern with social problems, though political necessity and the presence of the powerful Labour contingent in the Commons were soon to turn Liberalism into new courses. Campbell-Bannerman was an elderly man who had yet to show the stuff of which he was made, but who was to have only two short years of life in which to do it. Next in succession was the brilliant lawyer and House of Commons man, Asquith, a moderate unemotional figure well fitted by nature to lead a lively team, but no creative innovator, though as a one-time student of T. H. Green alive to some social issues. Closely associated with him was the intellectual Haldane, who probably understood better than most of his colleagues what government was about, but whose task was to bring order and economy into the War Office. At the Local Government Board, and therefore in a key position, was the tame demagogue John Burns, whose zeal for reform had burnt out since the days in the 80s when he had led the unemployed demonstrators and the striking dockers. Burns had by this time lost touch with the working classes, but his vanity and stubbornness and his claim to be the authentic voice of the people were to stand in the way of any substantial reforms affecting the Local Government Board and were effectively to block any action on the poor-law reports of 1909.

**David Lloyd George**    The bright sparks of the Ministry were the two who, as rivals in well-doing, were to make the most substantial contributions to social progress, David Lloyd George and Winston S. Churchill. Lloyd George had in his time so many careers that it is difficult now to recapture the hopeful radical of these early years, still only in his middle 40s but long since an acknowledged power in the Commons. An emotional reformer such as only Wales can produce, with the ardour and eloquence of the preacher that in another day and age he would have been, he had grown up in an atmosphere of opposition to the Anglican landed establishment in Wales and had determined, from early youth, with all the passion and ambition of an ardent nature, to devote himself to social reform. 'Incalculable wealth and indescribable poverty dwell side by side', he said in one of his earliest public speeches as a Member of Parliament,[69] and nearly 20 years later, during the political crisis stirred up by his 'People's Budget' of 1909, he spoke to a great audience in Caernarvon of the boyhood days when he had gathered sticks after a storm, and drew the parallel: 'After this storm has passed there will be plenty of firewood to warm the hearths of old people and to brighten the lives of the poor.'[70] In these two speeches, one as an unknown Welshman, the other as a controversial Minister of the Crown, is to be seen the faith that moved him, subtle politician and charmer and ruthless manager of men that he was. His principles he had learned as a boy in Llanystumdwy, under the influence of his uncle Richard Lloyd, to whom, significantly, he sent in 1910 a copy of the Finance Act which the People's Budget had at last become, inscribed to 'the real author of this budget'.[71] From these early days he carried with him that opposition to the Anglican Church that made him one of the leaders of non-conformist revolt against the rate-aided grants to Church schools introduced by the Education Act of 1902. From these days, too, came the dislike, typical of the nineteenth-century radical, of the landowning interest, which he always contemptuously referred to as 'the Dukes'. It is doubtful whether at this time he understood the industrial society in which he played his part, but as President of the Board of Trade from 1905 to 1908 he showed his supreme skill as a negotiator in the settlement of industrial disputes and his ability to overcome the stubbornness of men and events. It was said of him later that he could charm a bird out of a tree, but, as the battle over the 1909 budget was to show, he was also a fierce and resourceful fighter. He read little, but knew how to get what he wanted from others: few but Franklin D. Roosevelt, indeed, have ever been his equal as a manager—and user—of men. The 'Old Liberals', he said at Swansea in 1908, had won a better status for the people politically; it was for the 'New Liberals' to remove the immediate economic causes of discontent in poverty, insecurity and bad conditions.[72] This was as far as his political philosophy went, if his emotional reaction to poverty and distress can be dignified with such a term, but if the reaction was emotional the emotion was deep and sincere, mercurial though its expression might be: as J. L. Garvin told him, he 'followed the gleam'.[73] His creed was but a halfway house on the road to the complete control of the national resources in the general interest which was now being advocated by the Labour allies of the Liberal party in Parliament, and he never went further. The attitude of mind which he shared with his colleagues was succinctly expressed by the most brilliant of them, Winston Churchill, in the phrase 'Socialism attacks Capital, Liberalism attacks monopoly'.[74] To him when Chancellor of the Exchequer fell first the long-delayed plans for old age pensions which Asquith had prepared, and then, heralded by the revolutionary trumpetings of the budget of 1909, the great insurance schemes for sickness and unemployment.

**Winston Churchill**  Lloyd George was 42 when he first took office, Churchill only 33 when he succeeded him as President of the Board of Trade. Churchill, too, was to have many careers, and the path which took the cornet of horse of 1895 to the Premiership at a time of even greater crisis than Lloyd George had known was as full of strange turns as that which had earlier brought the boy from Llanystumdwy to the same terrible responsibility. Churchill had entered politics as a Conservative in 1901, after his adventures in South Africa, but, as he has said, he 'drifted steadily to the left'[75] and eventually parted with the Conservatives on the issue of tariffs. His own views and a pious regard for the principles for which his father, Lord Randolph, had sacrificed his career led him to Liberalism, and his rise, with all the social influence that he commanded, was rapid. Perennially youthful, confident and challenging, with the gift for sparkling and trenchant phrases that in later years was to be one of the inspiring features of his finest hour, and possessing, like Lloyd George, a flair for catching the spirit of the times in which he moved, he expressed in resounding speeches the moderate aims of the Liberals and made them sound like trumpet blasts against the Jericho walls of Conservatism and industrial neglect. 'The cause of

Liberalism', he proclaimed in 1906, 'is the cause of the left-out millions',[76] and it was a phrase of which in the next few years he was to make much. He was, perhaps, hardly the man for the humdrum round of ministerial duties, for he loved too much the excitement of politics. Now, as later, however, given a great idea to which to devote his exuberance and his political adroitness, he was a master of the field, even if, as a pawky comment on him later had it, he seemed never to realise that there was no Victoria Cross in politics.[77] The cause of the left-out millions gave him just the battle-cry he needed, for was there not wastage of human resources and had not his father sacrificed his career for economy in the State? He was, too, still young enough to learn from men he could respect, and Lloyd George taught him much, as he later acknowledged. Labour Exchanges, Trade Boards and unemployment insurance were to be his contribution to social policy, and they, with the health insurance that Lloyd George introduced, were to prove, under conditions of depression not yet suspected, the bases of a new attempt to moderate the rigours of industrial society.

**The Liberal Programme**   The concern of the Liberal programme as it eventually took shape was with the prevention of the poverty that Booth and others had so glaringly revealed, poverty due not to drink or moral inferiority, as many in the nineteenth century had unthinkingly believed, but, as Lloyd George pointed out, in the speech with which he introduced the 'People's Budget', to old age, sickness, the death of a bread-winner or unemployment.[78] It did not seem that any extreme measures were called for to remedy these ills. The traditional Liberal respect for the freedom of the individual could accept a limited degree of collective control in order to protect those who had been shown to be unable to protect themselves, and the necessary steps could be taken without any violent upheaval. 'It is through the agency of Liberalism', said Churchill in the election speech in which he coined the apt phrase quoted above, 'that society will be able in the course of time to slide forward, almost painlessly—for the world is changing very fast—on to a more even and a more equal foundation.'[79] It was not a matter of controlling or sharing wealth but of ensuring to all an adequate minimum, so that whatever the extremes of affluence none should be in actual want: 'we want to draw a line below which we will not allow persons to live and labour'.[80] This was Liberalism echoing the doctrines of the Webbs, whom by this time Churchill knew, but it was far removed from Socialism: it aimed at dulling the edge of monopoly, no less the monopoly of the State than of the capitalist. Economic competition was to continue, but, as Churchill hopefully proclaimed only above the line, not below it, and the State was to interfere, where necessary, not to guarantee work and maintenance, for that would be too gross an interference with freedom, but as 'the reserve employer of labour'. This was the Liberal compromise, and, apart from the special problems of old age pensions, insurance provided the ideal means for its achievement, insurance which was essentially a personal matter, but which was to be encouraged, enforced and extended by the State to ensure its adequacy.

The statistics of friendly societies and trade unions showed that only a minority of the working population was in fact able to make private provision for protection, and Booth had long since revealed how large a proportion of old people was compelled to turn to poor relief as the only defence against starvation. The problem of the elderly had in fact been before the public for nearly 20 years before it was finally tackled, though awareness of the true nature of the problems of unemployment was a more recent development. It is to the campaign for old age pensions, culminating in the Act of 1908, that we now turn, and this will be followed by consideration of the treatment of unemployment, first in the Unemployed Workmen Act of 1905, passed in the last stages of the Conservative administration, and then in the Liberal legislation, with Labour Exchanges, the 1909 budget, with its implications for social policy, and the insurance scheme of 1911, which dealt not only with unemployment but with the perennial problem of distress through sickness. There are, too, other aspects of social policy, especially in the care of children, to be considered, and one major feature of these years, the Poor Law Commission of 1905-9, to which so many references have already been made, calls for examination and assessment. The Commission was one of the great disappointments of the period, but despite its ineffectiveness the material it gathered, and the various proposals it offered, supplemented the fertile activity of other agencies and contributed therefore to the developments which made of this period a great turning point in social policy.

## 3 The Liberal Reforms: (1) Old Age Pensions

It took nearly 20 years, a Royal Commission, several parliamentary committees, some abortive bills and numerous private endeavours to get old age pensions carried.[81] There were many reasons for the delay, but it was nevertheless, as one of the pioneers of National Insurance, W. J. Braithwaite, commented in his diary, 'a political scandal'.[82] The greatest difficulty was with finance. Booth had revealed the size and seriousness of the problem, but its cost, variously estimated at from eight to 24 million pounds a year according to the size of the pension and the age at which it was to be paid, caused dismay, and in the end only a budget surplus overcame the problem. Furthermore, there were many to argue that as the pensions were but out-relief under another name the Guardians could do all that was necessary in cases where personal thrift or charity could provide no solution. This was particularly the argument of the Charity Organisation Society and the Friendly Societies, all of them obsessed with the moral advantages of private rather than State action and fearful lest action by the State should prejudice voluntary effort. The C.O.S. had operated a modest pension scheme of its own for some years, but always found it difficult to raise sufficient money for it,

while the friendly societies, opposed though they were to government intervention, could offer little help to their older members, whose claims upon them, as the
proportion of elderly in the community increased, were proving, indeed, an em-
barrassing burden. If the societies did not provide pensions the claims of their
older members for sick pay, inevitably larger in old age than earlier in life, represented an equivalent, and what the societies, in their suspicion of any government proposals, failed to realise was that pensions would relieve the strain of
these claims upon their funds. Even if the principle of pensions could have been
accepted, however, there remained the vexed question of the financial basis.
Should the pensions be contributory or paid for solely out of taxation? Argument on this point went backwards and forwards for many years. Understandably, the friendly societies were doubly opposed to contributory pensions, which
could hardly fail to affect their incomes: few working-men could have afforded
a double scale of contributions. Yet it was not until 1902 that the societies accepted the idea of non-contributory pensions, and even then on the grudging
condition that the pensions should go only to the 'thrifty and deserving'.[83] Well
might one enthusiast for pensions complain that in their attitude to the needs of
the aged the societies were more conservative than the Conservative Primrose
League itself.[84] Through their close contact with the most self-sufficient sections
of the working class, however, the societies represented a powerful political
interest, as even Lloyd George was compelled to acknowledge: their influence
could not be discounted.

The first Minister to concern himself with the problem of the aged was Joseph
Chamberlain. Imperial Germany had introduced pensions in 1889, as part of the
system of social insurance which Bismarck had been building up since 1883 as a
counter to Socialist agitation, and Chamberlain was quick to take note of the
German example. Until his attention was diverted by the South African War and,
later, by 'tariff reform' he took a leading part in pressing for a pension scheme.
In the early 90s, after his breach with Gladstone, he was in the political wilder-
ness, as a 'Liberal-Unionist', until in 1895 he took office with the Conservatives
as Colonial Secretary, and in 1891 he advocated a modest scheme of State encouragement for voluntary savings for old age. This cautious move did at least
open the subject politically and in 1893 the Royal Commission on the Aged Poor
was appointed to look into it. From the first the Commission recognised the
gravity of the problem: 'We cannot but regard it as an unsatisfactory and deplorable fact that so large a proportion of the working classes are in old age in receipt
of poor relief.'[85] Chamberlain and Booth were among the members of the Commission, but, as they complained in a Minority Report in 1895, the witnesses
were too carefully selected: too many represented traditional opinion and few
advocates of change were called. Hence the 'meagre suggestions' of the Majority
Report of 1895,[86] which recommended no major changes. It asked that outdoor
relief should be adequate and that conditions in workhouses should be improved,
but left future provision on the one hand to the discretion of the Guardians and on

the other to the friendly societies. The Commission did its best, however, to disprove the suspicion that the aged poor were harshly treated. Since 1885, it pointed out, workhouse couples over the age of 60 had been allowed to live together (though Charles Booth, for one, doubted whether many knew of this concession or ventured to claim it[87]). Workhouse life, it was admitted, was dull, but tea, tobacco and newspapers were now provided, while visiting was allowed at intervals of a few weeks and the kind of work required, mostly oakum picking and wood chopping, was not heavy. It was a dismal record, and this was implicitly recognised in the suggestion that the atmosphere of workhouses could be still further lightened. The main result of the Commission, however, apart from the sigh of relief from the friendly societies, was the Local Government Board circular of 1896, referred to in the previous chapter, which discouraged the forcing of thrifty old people into the workhouse, together with the further circular of 1900 which required them normally to be relieved in their own homes. At the same time it was decided that claims for relief should no longer be prejudiced by the possession of small friendly society payments, a significant, if obviously desirable, reform.

The Royal Commission's findings were vitiated by its traditional approach. It took the view, as recorded earlier, that 'pauperism is becoming a constantly diminishing evil, ultimately to disappear before the continuous progress of thrift and social well-being',[88] and failed to recognise that if pauperism, in the sense of the 1834 reforms, was indeed disappearing, poverty remained. It was easy to insist that if there were any problem of poverty in old age the poor law could take care of it until such time as the poor law itself withered away. This was the 1834 spirit, but applied, not, as the reformers of 1834 had intended, to the able-bodied, but to some of those whom the men of 1834 themselves had recognised—nay, taken for granted—as proper objects of poor-law concern, even outside the workhouse. The problem, in short, was a physical one of poverty, not a moral one of pauperism, such as had so deeply concerned the earlier reformers, and the contrast was stressed by at least one notable contemporary thinker, the economist Alfred Marshall, in his evidence to the Commission. The moral fear of pauperism was so great, however, that to the last many resisted the notion of payment to old people who were not actually absolutely destitute and compelled to seek aid. Thrift in early life, it was insisted, was the true solution, and when savings were exhausted the poor law could step in. Whether, in fact, at prevailing rates of wages everyone could save was never investigated, though the C.O.S. perversely maintained that the fact that working-men could manage on less when on strike proved that they could save more from their wages.[89] At the same time the fear and dislike of the poor law which was so common and kept so many in want from applying for help was conveniently disregarded: a pension, as Charles Booth argued, 'would lift from very many old hearts the fear of the workhouse at the last'.[90] Yet such was the failure to understand the attitude of the poorer classes that even in 1908 it was still being argued that pensions would be recognised by the aged themselves as merely poor relief under another name. It was not understood that the other name, and the fact that all below a certain income level were equally entitled to the pension without the shame of confessing themselves destitute or the fear of the house, made at the receiving end all the difference in the world.

Bismarck himself had justified the payment of old age pensions with an argument of which much was to be heard during the English controversy: it was unfair, he claimed, to pension soldiers while allowing 'the veterans of industry to die in misery'. This was the kind of case which, as an earlier quotation has shown, Crabbe had been arguing nearly a century before, and it was an obvious one to press. 'We are all servants of the nation', commented a study of 1892, which was inspired in part by Booth's work, 'and the labourer on the land serves the State every bit as much as the civil servant and the officer in the army and navy, who *get* their pensions.'[91] 'It is rather hard', urged Lloyd George in his turn, justifying the pensions in his Limehouse speech of 1909, 'that an old workman should have to find his way to the gates of the tomb, bleeding and footsore, through the brambles and thorns of poverty.'[92] In the 90s, however, this kind of argument made little impression. The faith was still strong that economic progress would before long remedy poverty, and it took the revelations of the Poor Law Commission of 1905–9 to disabuse many minds.

The disappointment of 1895 did not for long restrain the advocates of pensions. The return of the Conservatives to power, with Chamberlain in office, led to the appointment in 1896 of a Treasury committee under Lord Rothschild, but as it was precluded from considering any but contributory pensions and two of its members were leading officials of the friendly societies, the resultant report of 1898 was a foregone conclusion. In the following year, however, a new stimulus appeared with the adoption by New Zealand of a non-contributory pension scheme, and public agitation began in England under the leadership of Booth, the Rev. Francis Stead, warden of a Settlement in East London, and Frederick Rogers, an influential trade-unionist who was first chairman of the Labour Representation Committee, forerunner of the Labour Party. The T.U.C. lent its support, passing resolutions in favour of pensions at every annual conference until they were established, and the Co-operative movement also joined in the campaign. There followed the setting up of a Select Committee of the House of Commons, introduced by Chamberlain and with Lloyd George among its members. The Committee, stirred to activity by the general concern, reported in only three months, coming down in favour of a scheme for non-contributory pensions for certain classes in need at 65, paid through the Post Office but closely linked with the poor law and hedged by conditions as to past 'industry and reasonable providence' which the Guardians were to attest. It amounted to little more, however, than a device for providing outdoor relief on somewhat less unfavourable terms, and though it went further than many Conservatives were prepared to approve it aroused little interest. The annual cost, it was estimated, would be some 10 million pounds a year, rising to over 12 million by 1911. This last was a revealing estimate, for in fact it was little less than the amount actually required in 1911-12 for pensions at 70. As Lloyd George was to confess, when pensions were at last granted, the number in want claiming them proved even larger than had been anticipated.

The proposal to make pensions non-contributory was a significant one, for while Denmark and New Zealand had introduced similar schemes the German pensions were based on contributions from the employee, the employer and the State, as National Insurance was to be in Britain from its introduction in 1911. There was, however, a world of difference between old age pensions and insurance against sickness and unemployment. For a man in the prime of life, as Churchill argued in 1909, old age was far off and provision for it therefore seemed unnecessary, whereas unemployment, sickness and accidents might come at any time: 'those vultures are always hovering around us'.[93] Moreover, if pensions were to be paid out of contributions it would be many years before any could be received: the present generation of old people, known to be seriously in want, would gain nothing. Hence the decision to pay pensions out of general taxation, which was adhered to in 1908, and not altered until 1925, when the whole pension scheme was overhauled and extended.

When the 1899 committee reported, Chamberlain had for four years been a minister in a Conservative government, and his activities, together with various other ministerial pronouncements and election promises, seemed to many to pledge the Conservatives morally to some measure of aid to the aged. Their failure to act was legitimately held against them by the Liberals. Chamberlain, however, had aroused hopes which he could not satisfy. His own attitude to pensions was always cautious and equivocal. He wished to use them to supplement and encourage private saving among the 'deserving poor' and through the friendly societies (the 'undeserving' being left to the poor law), and was opposed to all universal schemes. Yet even in this he was far ahead of many of his political colleagues. Moreover, he was unwilling to finance any scheme through taxation. Ever since he had taken over the Colonial Office his mind had turned increasingly to tariffs as a means of strengthening the economic links of the Empire while at the same time serving as a method of indirect taxation for raising money for social purposes at home. For him the South African War, the climax of his administration, proved to be the parting of the ways. In the 90s, though increasingly caught up in imperial affairs, he had still been active in social policy. His interest in old age pensions had been matched by the perseverance with which he pressed through the Workmen's Compensation Act of 1897, a measure which, building on the slender foundations of the Employers' Liability Act of 1880, at last recognised the duty of industry to pay compensation for death or injury to its workers regardless of legal quibbles about negligence. This was very much a personal success for Chamberlain, even if, as mentioned earlier, it did but carry out a proposal made nearly half a century before by Chadwick. Industry could and did insure itself against compensation claims, as Chadwick had urged, but the raising of the money for old age pensions was another matter, and the outbreak of war in 1899 put the proposals of that year into cold storage. By the time government expenditure was returning to normal in 1903 Chamberlain was off on another tack. He had been stirred by the war, the imperial conference of 1902 and his own tour in South Africa to a wider conception of imperial unity, and had quarrelled with the Treasury over 'imperial preference' and plunged into the campaign for 'tariff reform' which was to dominate his last years of political activity. Tariffs were intended not only to unite the Empire, but in the face of Victorian conceptions of economy at the Treasury, to provide the money for social reform at home. To many, even in the Conservative party, however, they were anathema, and in 1906 the Conservatives, torn by this new issue and enfeebled by too long a period of rule, at last went down to defeat.

By this time many more proposals for old age pensions had been put forward and in 1906 Asquith, as Chancellor of the Exchequer in the new Liberal government, promised to introduce them as soon as he had a budget surplus. The pressure continued, and in 1907 a notable private member's bill was promoted, though unsuccessfully, by the soap-manufacturer and philanthropist W. H. Lever (afterwards Lord Leverhulme), then M.P. for Wirral. The budget surplus came at last in the following year, and Asquith took advantage of it to make provision for pensions. He succeeded Campbell-Bannerman as Prime Minister in April 1908, but presented the budget which he had framed, leaving the introduction of the necessary bill to the new Chancellor of the Exchequer, Lloyd George, who now took in hand the first of the decisive measures of social reform which he was to carry.

Asquith had been working on pension schemes since 1906, but the case for them had been given added point by the growing electoral strength of Labour, especially after its capture of 'Old Liberal' seats in the by-elections of 1907.[94] Lloyd George's interest in pensions, like Asquith's, was not merely an electoral manoeuvre,[95] but he acknowledged that 'it is time we did something that appealed straight to the people',[96] and rejoiced that taking over the pension bill 'leaves the coast clear for me to initiate my own schemes' (see note, page 227).[97] His mind was already turning to other and wider projects, and within a few months he was to pay the visit to Germany, to study German social insurance on the spot, that was to have such significant consequences.

For all the long delay in its presentation and the slow preparation of opinion over 20 years, the Old Age Pensions Bill introduced a new principle into social policy. Hitherto relief had been provided, as an act of grace, for all the needy from *local* funds and only after a test of destitution. Now for the first time payments were to be made, as of right, from *national* funds to a section of the needy, the elderly, within strict limitations of age and means, but with no test of actual destitution. Once the idea of pensions was accepted only national provision, as Asquith himself pointed out, was possible, for otherwise there would be the local variations and the difficulties about settlement which had plagued the administration of the poor law. The very ease with which the measure passed was, in fact, an indication of the general recognition of the inadequacy of the poor law and of the need for a new approach: as some stern critics complained, the pass was sold without a fight.

The pensions were to be paid to people over the age of 70 whose incomes did not exceed £31 a year, the amount being 5s. a week for those with a maximum income of £21, and less, by weekly units of 1s., for those with incomes between £21 and £31. (A joint pension of only 7s. 6d. had been proposed for married couples, but an outcry in the Commons prevented this ungenerous economy from being pressed.) There were no means of ascertaining the total cost, but Asquith had estimated it at six million pounds, and it was felt that this was as much as the national finances would stand. The proposals were assailed as inadequate from both sides of the House: Philip Snowden, indeed, now at the beginning of his parliamentary career, maliciously suggested that the Government had had the psalmist's 'three-score years and ten' in mind and hoped that few would live to enjoy their pension![98] The Government agreed that the pensions did not provide enough, but maintained that they were not intended to be more than a helping hand to the needy and that they went as far as the financial position would permit. 'We have not pretended to carry the toiler on to dry land', said Churchill in a public speech, 'what we have done is to strap a lifebelt around him'[99]: five shillings is not much, he was to say later, 'unless you have not got it'.[100] As it was, there was considerable opposition in the House of Lords, where, until they were muzzled by the Parliament Act of 1911, Conservative peers, smarting under the defeat of 1906, were playing the part of watchdogs of traditionalism. They denounced the pensions as 'a vast measure of thinly disguised outdoor relief', the results of which would be 'profoundly demoralising', and there were even comparisons with the 'policy of doles which had been fatal to Rome'.[101] These views echoed the lingering resistance of the Charity Organization Society. The pensions, C. S. Loch wrote in an article on 'Charity and Charities' in the eleventh edition of *Encyclopaedia Britannica* (1910), were 'a huge charity started on the credit of the state', which would ultimately entail vast expense and, 'history has proved', general demoralisation.[102] A large majority carried the measure in the Commons, however, the Conservatives recognising its justice and being disinclined in any case to risk the responsibility of opposing it. The total cost in the first full year, 1909–10, proved to be not six million pounds but more than eight million, and the increase was a revelation of the amount of unsuspected poverty among the aged. It had been calculated, though without any claim to accuracy, that rather more than half a million people would apply for pensions in 1909. In fact the number proved to be 650,000 and it rose rapidly to 930,000 in 1912 and to 970,000 in 1914. The cost, which Asquith had so hopefully underestimated, rose equally rapidly to more than 12 million pounds by 1913. So was England launched upon a new course.

It might have been expected that the payment of old age pensions would have been matched by a decline in the cost of poor relief, but in fact the immediate effect was small (see note, page 227). Lloyd George was right in pointing out that the pensions had shown that there was 'a mass of poverty and destitution in the country which is too proud to wear the badge of pauperism', and Churchill graphically described their humane effects in a speech at Nottingham in 1909: 'Nearly eight millions of money are being sent circulating through unusual channels, long frozen by poverty, circulating in the homes of the poor, flowing through the little shops that cater to their needs, cementing again family unions which harsh fate was tearing asunder, uniting the wife to the husband and the parent to the children.'[103]

What the pensions actually meant to the recipients can be seen from a telling passage in Flora Thompson's *Lark Rise*, in which the lot of old village people struggling to keep themselves out of the workhouse is described: 'When the Old Age Pensions began, life was transformed for such aged cottagers. They were relieved of anxiety. They were suddenly rich. Independent for life! At first when they went to the Post Office to draw it, tears of gratitude would run down the cheeks of some, and they would say as they picked up their money, "God bless that Lord George! (for they could not believe one so powerful and munificent could be a plain "Mr") and God bless *you*, miss!", and there were flowers from their gardens and apples from their trees for the girl who merely handed them the money.'[104] This was hardly the demoralisation of 'thinly disguised outdoor relief', such as some stern critics, champions of the waning principles of 1834, had anticipated. Ironically, in view of the tribute paid by the *Lark Rise* pensioners, it was in the Lords that these stern critics were most vociferous.

Yet, although the pensions were widely regarded as a serious breach in the sacred principles on which the poor law had so long been conducted, the dangers of moral harm to the community were not overlooked in the regulations governing them. Thus, pensions were denied to any old person who accepted poor relief between 1 January 1908 and 31 December 1909 (by which time, it was expected, the poor law would have been revised), or who had been in prison within 10 years (later reduced to two years), or who had 'habitually failed to work according to his ability, opportunity or need, for the maintenance or benefit of himself and those legally dependent upon him', unless—saving clause—for 10 years before reaching the age of 60 he had insured himself through a friendly society or trade union. This last condition, morally irreproachable as it was, was yet most difficult of application, and was repealed in 1919. It reflected the lingering notion that it was the weaklings, the feckless, who got into difficulties, that there were work and wages for all who cared to have them: the pensions were to be only for the deserving poor, the others must rest content with the poor law. As has already been mentioned, however, acceptance of a pension did not affect voting rights as did poor relief: where a pension could properly be paid, it was paid as of right, not of grace, and created no second-class citizens. It was unequivocally recognised, therefore, that men could fall into want through no fault of their own and that it was the duty of the community to relieve them without imputing blame or imposing shame. The moral obloquy so long attaching to poverty was at last beginning to give way to social concern.

At the same time, however, it was *poverty* that was relieved: the 'lifebelt' was offered to the poor, not merely to the destitute. The 'means test' (to use a later expression) that was applied was narrowly conceived: the possession of only 12s. a week disqualified for pension and the full amount was given only to those with 8s. a week or less. Yet to help those with means, even within these narrow limits, was a new principle, even if a logical extension of the concession already made under the poor law to old people in receipt of friendly society allowances. For the elderly, at least, *destitution* was no longer to be a prerequisite of aid.

Old Age Pensions were the first national social service and no offices existed to administer them: even Labour Exchanges and National Insurance offices lay still in the future. The administrative problem was overcome by the establishment, through the Local Authorities, of local committees, which were assisted in their necessary investigations by the only government department which possessed the network of local offices and the experienced investigators which were needed, the Board of Customs and Excise. Although when *contributory* pensions were introduced in 1925 responsibility for them went to the Ministry of Health, the non-contributory pensions of 1908-25 remained, somewhat inconsequentially and with some modifications from 1943, with the Customs and Excise until 1947, when the whole system was at last overhauled. Such was the practical logic of English government. The actual payment of pensions was committed to the only government department with the local facilities for making payments, the Post Office: hence the direct knowledge of Flora Thompson, herself for some years a Post Office assistant, of the appreciation expressed by pensioners to 'that Lord George' and, in practical fashion, to the girls who served them.

## The Liberal Reforms : (2) Unemployment

Old age pensions opened a new chapter in the history of the community's care for its less fortunate members, but the actual turning-point in social policy had already come, not in 1908 but, as has earlier been suggested (and as Lloyd George himself realised at the time), in 1905, with the Unemployed Workman Act, the first attempt to tackle unemployment as a national problem. Unemployment was recognised in these years, as Churchill said in a speech at Dundee in 1908, as 'the problem of the hour'.[105] Distressing as was the condition of so many among the aged, unemployment was a cause of distress still greater, because of its effect on homes and families and the mysteries of its causation. The nineteenth century, secure in its faith in expanding industry and commerce and the readjustments of the market, could largely ignore unemployment as a phenomenon, but from the 80s onwards the problem forced itself upon public attention. The worst days lay far in the future, in the unhappy 20s and 30s of the twentieth century, but already it was realised that with the coming of a world-wide economy industrial prosperity and regularity of employment were dependent upon what happened in distant parts of the earth. Events 'as independent of our control as the phases of the moon' and 'as unpredictable as an Indian famine', said Churchill at Dundee, could affect the well-being of thousands, and the government therefore had responsibility towards unfortunate men caught up in difficulties which they could neither understand nor avert.[106] 'We know it will come', said Lloyd George of unemployment in 1911, when introducing his insurance scheme, 'and that distress will come with it.'[107]

**Joseph Chamberlain and the Unemployed**    As early as 1886, as has already been shown, the plight of the unemployed had moved Chamberlain, when President of the Local Government Board, to introduce special measures to provide work without the stigma of the poor law. This was the first recognition of social responsibility and was based on a theory of 'tiding-over', which bore little relation to the actual situation. It was supposed that worthy men, out of work through no fault of their own and unwilling to endure the shame of poor relief, needed help to tide them over until they were again employed. Municipal relief work was arranged to help them, and the experiment was repeated in the depression of the early 90s and again ten years later, when the South African war boom had collapsed. In some areas, indeed, relief work became a regular service in winter-time when employment was slack: as the Majority Report of 1909 pointed out, the very evils of relief in aid of wages which the 1834 reforms were intended to check were returning in another form: 'If casual labourers are supported year after year at certain seasons at the cost of the rates, their yearly wage is just as effectively subsidised by the community in 1905 as their weekly wage was subsidised by the community in 1832.'[108] In fact, though the point was not yet understood, there were various forms of unemployment. Chamberlain had intended to help men affected by what was later to be called a depression, but the help provided went largely to men who as seasonal or casual labourers knew nothing of regular employment. 'It is not the business of the community', said Balfour in 1909, in unconscious imitation of the strictures of 1834, 'to pay during the winter months to keep the labour going which certain manufacturers want to use only in the summer.' In truth, however, it was precisely this which was to a certain extent being done. The notion of 'tiding over' men normally in work was an emotional reaction to distress, based on no statistical investigation: few such men applied for special relief, which too closely resembled poor-law assistance. Those who did apply were the men on the fringes of industry, men who were part of a reserve of labour occasioned either by fluctuations in the size of the labour force required or by seasonal variations. Whatever its origins the reserve force was always larger than was in fact required: large numbers of men were therefore chronically underemployed, working only spasmodically. They were not strictly *un*employed, or did not regard themselves as such. They did not therefore necessarily seek poor relief, which would in some areas have led to their being 'offered the house': in 1906, for instance, 111,000 of them applied for help, but only 13,000 went on poor relief. There was always the hope that their turn for work would come, as, indeed, it occasionally did. 'The man who does not succeed today', wrote Beveridge in his pioneer study of unemployment in 1908, 'may succeed tomorrow; meanwhile he lives on hope and charity and his wife's and children's earnings.'[109] It was to these men that municipal relief work particularly appealed: they formed the great majority of its recipients.

Yet this was neither what Chamberlain had intended nor a solution of the problem of unemployment, even if it did relieve the feelings of those who clung to the theory of 'tiding over' and were puzzled at the continuing need for help. Distress, as Beveridge was to insist, was not occasional and temporary but a chronic evil of *under*-employment, to which at times actual *un*employment added its tragic quota. Relief works solved nothing, for the normally employed man shunned them and they merely kept the under-employed, as Balfour complained, ready at hand when his services might again be required by an employer. Moreover, they were extravagant and wasteful. It had long been recognised that this was true of work done as a condition of outdoor relief under the poor law: stone-breaking, for instance, could produce, in one notable, but not exceptional, instance during the severe winter of 1895, broken stone of a value of 4*s.* per ton at a cost of as much as £7.[110] The disproportion was not so great in municipal relief work, but was serious enough, varying as it generally did from one-third to two-thirds. If the will to work was present, which was usually far from being the case under poor-law conditions, skill and strength and healthy physique were usually lacking for unaccustomed labour. In the case of municipal work there were usually other bars to efficiency as well. The majority of men employed, Booth noted in his London survey, 'were quite willing to work, but were hopeless, many of them demoralised by years of casual employment'.

**The Lack of Information**    In truth the labour market was badly organised, or, rather, not organised at all, and, as the Majority Report claimed with some justice, poor relief, indiscriminate charity and municipal relief works all alike tended to maintain the situation by checking the free movement of labour: even as between the different areas of London, for instance, there was no means of finding where work was scarce, where plentiful, and of bringing labour and work together. None knew where work was to be obtained, or had the heart to go on seeking it over the years of bitter disappointment, or the skill to seek alternative jobs. Some trade unions provided an information service about vacancies for their own members, and even the means to travel in search of work, but this covered only the more skilled. It was no one's business to enquire whether there was enough work to go round, and employers were satisfied only if there were available at all times all the labour they might be likely to need. Hence, for instance, the redundant labour-force and gross under-employment at the docks, which Booth revealed in all its misery. Hence, too, Beveridge's insistence that unemployment was a problem, not of the individual but of *industry*, not of individual failure but of industrial maladjustment and disorganisation. Hence, again, the first independent measure pressed on Parliament by the newly-arrived Labour group after 1906, the Right to Work Bill of 1908, which, though thrown out on second reading, underlined, even as Beveridge's *Unemployment* did in the same year, the necessity for a new and more understanding approach.

Little enough was in fact known of the scale and incidence of unemployment. That there was a problem was recognised from the 80s, but the 67 volumes of the Royal Commission on Labour of 1891–4 had no remedy to offer and could only point to the dangers of seeking a remedy in public employment. The hard winter of 1895 produced the *Select Committee on Distress from Want of Employment*, the very title of which revealed the unfamiliarity of the name, if not the conception, of *unemployment*, which in fact appears in the Committee's report in quotation marks. The Committee's report recognised the unwillingness of the 'respectable unemployed'[111] to apply to the Guardians, but could suggest no more than that the Local Government Board should have the power in times of widespread distress to declare 'distressed districts' (an anticipation of the 'Distressed Areas' of a later period) in which 'deserving persons' could get assistance without recourse to the poor law.[112] The problem was still seen, in short, as an occasional one, calling for methods of 'tiding over'.

**The Incidence of Unemployment**   The mid-90s were years of increased unemployment, though the position had improved by the end of the decade. Such trade-union statistics as existed were from 1886 collected by Mundella's Labour Bureau (from 1892, Department of Labour) at the Board of Trade and showed that, while unemployment had stood as high as ten per cent among registered trade-union members in 1885, the percentage had dropped to two by 1890, only to rise to six by 1895. It fell back to less than three at the turn of the century, but again stood at six in 1904 and was four in 1906. The fluctuations lent support to the tiding-over theory, but in fact the published figures referred to only a minority of workers, and those the more skilled. Of 2,544 unemployed recorded in Sheffield in the winter of 1905–6, for instance, only 54 were members of a union,[113] while in Paddington in the same period the proportion was much lower, only one in 328,[114] and these were but typical instances of the smallness of the percentages of workers in any way protected by trade-union organisation and funds.

Moreover, as Beveridge was the first to point out, the percentages represented, not a certain proportion of union members out of work throughout the year, but a much higher proportion—on a long-term average about seven times the number—of members unemployed at some time or other during the year.[115] Hence his insistence that, taking into account also the vast numbers of the casually employed who were not members of a union, 'distress through want of employment is not a temporary but a chronic evil'.[116]

**Remedies—Tariff Reform and Farm Colonies**  Beveridge's book did not appear until 1909, however, and by then much more light had already been thrown on the problem, though it was still not clear to most other observers what was being illuminated. After reasonably good conditions of employment during the years of the South African War, the economic situation deteriorated during 1902 and 1903 and by 1904 was causing anxiety. Unemployment was rising rapidly and with it the amount of pauperism, which until 1901-2 had been falling steadily for 30 years. British trade seemed to be stagnating in the face of growing competition and there were genuine fears for the future. These fears Chamberlain sought to exorcise by his vigorous campaign for 'tariff reform', a campaign which the Liberals resisted with no less vigour and rather more success. Tariffs, Chamberlain maintained, were to be the panacea for social ills, guaranteeing industrial activity and employment and providing the means for the payment of old age pensions, in preference to what an ardent tariff reformer (in a sly dig at a slip of the tongue by Lloyd George during a Commons debate on the pensions[117]) was to characterise as the Liberal policy of 'looking for hen-roosts to rob'.[118] Towards the end of the year in which this attractive thesis was first advanced the intensification of East London's endemic distress caused Canon Barnett and others to propose a new approach, the establishment of 'farm colonies' in the country, to which unemployed men might be sent for work until conditions improved, while their families were supported at home in London. 'Back to the land' seemed an obvious remedy for urban unemployment at a time when the rapid decline of English agriculture in the 70s was still a living memory, and was in any case in the line of the radical utopian tradition that stretched through Chartist and Owenite experiments in the nineteenth century to the seventeenth-century 'diggers'. Now there were many who hoped to train the unwanted townsmen for farm work either in England or in the Colonies, to which, and especially to Canada, a steady stream of emigrants was already moving. The Salvation Army had for some years supported a 'farm colony', and an enthusiast for land settlement, the wealthy soap manufacturer Joseph Fels, had recently bought an estate in Suffolk, Hollesley Bay, for use by the unemployed. Conditions deteriorated further in 1904 and in the autumn of that year Walter Long, as President of the Local Government Board, unsuspectingly took the first step towards the tackling of the unemployment problem by the State. A conference that he then summoned, to consider the general relief of unemployment in London, though concerned with voluntary and charitable measures, was to prove the precursor of the significant, if inadequate, Act of 1905 and therefore of the further measures that were to flow from it.

**Remedies—Walter Long and the Unemployed Workmen Act**  Walter Long was a country squire, a true-blue Conservative, limited and paternalistic in his outlook, as became a representative of the Tory landed interest, but a worthy member of his order and a conscientious politician, though with no claim to brilliance or penetrating understanding. He had held junior office in Lord Salisbury's last Cabinet and since 1900 had presided over the Local Government Board, and his solid worth was to make him in 1911 the favoured candidate of old-fashioned Conservatives for the leadership of their party in succession to Balfour. Despite his limitations he was a man of warm sympathies, to some extent free from the narrow influences of Local Government Board tradition and alive to the stresses of the times. Above all he was anxious, as he saw unemployment increasing, to provide more suitable help than the poor law afforded, to preserve from what he recognised as the degradation of the poor law 'decent respectable men' out of work through no failure of their own. 'Many a man has told me', he said in the House of Commons, in justification of his concern, 'that when he entered on his career of destitution the fact that he had been put to polish the same brass knob, or to clean the same window which half a dozen had cleaned before, degraded him.'[119] It was a sign of the changing opinion of the times that Long realised that this sense of helpless degradation existed, that the problem was no longer the mere relief but the *prevention* of destitution. He saw, as many others were beginning to see, that the normal processes of economic readjustment to which the nineteenth century had pinned its faith, were manifestly inadequate, that the community must in some way offer its protection and assistance to men whom these processes had temporarily cast aside. 'We were making paupers', he was to say later, 'of men who were willing and anxious to be self-supporting citizens'[120], and in his evidence to the Poor Law Commission in 1907 he spoke with feeling of the distinction between these and the weak and idle for whom the poor law was intended: 'But for the other class—the men who want work and can't get it and have nobody to turn to for guidance—that these people should be manufactured into paupers seems to me to be a national crime.'[121] He felt, too, as an earlier quotation has shown, the force of the appeal of Socialism to those for whom society was doing so little, and in this also he was reflecting changing opinion: the very existence and agitation of an embryo Labour Party was sharpening appreciation of Labour's needs. Keir Hardie, as one of the few Labour Members of Parliament before the election of 1906, was constantly pressing for consideration of the problem of unemployment, and early in 1905 a new, and to some observers disturbing, phenomenon began to appear, the first of a series of descents upon London by unemployed men that came to be known, then and later, as 'Hunger Marches' (the expression was coined by one of the principal organisers, the fervent idealist Stewart Gray). The summer of 1905 was also to see the first great unemployed demonstration in Hyde Park, while there were many deputations, including one from the East End which its leader, George Lansbury, later claimed as the real inspiration of the Unemployed Workmen Act.[122]

It was against this background that Long, with naïve sincerity and but little understanding of the true nature of the problem, sought some means by which help could be given to those who deserved better than the workhouse, without at the same time doing any violence to the economic order. As he told the Poor Law

Commission, 'I am confident that some *via media* must be discovered between the extreme school who say that the Poor Law is sufficient . . . and the other extreme school who say that the State must employ everybody whether good or bad.'[123] This might be regarded as a simple definition of Liberal policy in the years after 1906, no less than a statement of Long's own aims. Whatever improvements the Liberals might strive to make, they were at one with the Conservatives in resisting any fundamental change in the economic system. The difference between them lay in the greater willingness of the Liberals to use the power and resources of the State to relieve poverty and distress, and it first showed itself over the very measures which Long introduced in 1904 for checking distress through unemployment.

Long's plan accepted Chamberlain's earlier view of the need for by-passing the poor law in the case of men genuinely unemployed, but went further in recognising that, especially in so great an area as London, the unco-ordinated efforts of local authorities and charitable societies were inadequate in times of special distress. Joint committees of local authorities, boards of guardians and charitable organisations were to be formed, not to provide relief or employment but to investigate cases and hand on those who could properly be assisted outside the poor law, either to local authorities or to a Central Committee which alone would have funds for the provision of work. In addition, and the innovation was an important one, the joint committees were to act as employment bureaux, putting employers and workmen into touch with each other: in practice, little enough was done in this direction, but the idea was much in the air and was soon to develop into the State provision of Labour Exchanges.

The Central Committee was to find work for men who could not be employed locally, raising funds for labour colonies on the land or for special local authority projects. The funds were to be mainly voluntary, for although Long was willing to permit local authorities to make grants, though only for administration, he was firmly opposed to any Treasury assistance, and in practice hardly any ratepayers' money was used. The Committees were active in the winter of 1904–5, but although some 46,000 men applied for help and 26,000 were recognised as eligible it is doubtful whether more than 5,000 were actually given work, though three times as many more were employed, if only for a few days, by local authorities under the arrangements inaugurated in 1886. As was constantly realised later, *ad hoc* schemes for the useful employment of large numbers of men could not be thought up at short notice: far more consistency of economic and social policy was required, and this was not to be achieved until much later, after the tragically depressed years of the 30s. Moreover, it soon became apparent that, even with Walter Long's encouragement to co-ordination, local authorities and farm colonies could not provide enough extra employment: government action was essential, as Beveridge was to insist.

The first modest measure of government activity came, indeed, in 1905 with the Unemployed Workmen Act. Long himself left the Local Government Board in March of that year, being succeeded by the Prime Minister's brother, Gerald Balfour, but he had already prepared for the next step and the Bill was carried during the summer of 1905. Unemployment and distress were still rife, and the experiment of 1904 had achieved no permanent results. Indeed, it was only too easily shown that men who had been given temporary help to 'tide them over' had in most cases failed to find regular work. It was obvious that more permanent machinery was required and that if such machinery were to be developed throughout the country legislation was needed. The Unemployed Workmen Bill made it possible to extend the 1904 scheme to most authorities and empowered them to add to the voluntary resources available for the relief of unemployment the product of a halfpenny rate (or, with the Local Government Board's consent, a penny rate). 'Distress Committees' were to be formed for the investigation of need and could provide work, establish labour exchanges and arrange, in suitable cases, for emigration. Their funds were to be partly voluntary and partly raised from the rates, and the basis of their activities was, in fact, a special charitable fund, the Queen's Fund, amounting to £153,000, which was raised in response to a public appeal by Queen Alexandra. Whether private charity was equal to the demands to be placed upon it was not considered in the anxiety to avoid a Treasury commitment, though fortunately the Government's Liberal successors were to prove less unwilling to pledge financial support.

Gerald Balfour admitted in introducing the measure that 'the government do not disguise from themselves the importance of the new departure they are making',[124] but argued that public feeling was such that if nothing were to be done for the unemployed more extreme measures might later on be adopted. It was, indeed, a new departure, a tacit admission of State responsibility, which, however limited its intention and effect, could never be reversed. Most of the opposition to the Bill came, as Herbert Samuel jocularly pointed out to the House, from the Government's own benches,[125] for strict Tories resented the proposal to draw on the rates: the Bill was, in fact, carried only with Opposition support. Those who resisted it and those who approved it alike realised that it was only a first step, and, indeed, one of the first measures of the new Liberal government in 1906 was to renew the Act and provide Treasury funds for its operation. Though most of the Queen's Fund had by then been spent, unemployment continued and it was manifestly impossible to repeat the special appeal: £200,000 was therefore voted from the Treasury. From that moment unemployment was fairly and firmly a national responsibility.

The Act: a Turning Point    Beveridge, when he gave evidence before the Poor Law Commission, described the Act as the final effort to grapple with unemployment by means of temporary relief works.[126] Experience since 1886 had indeed shown that no solution lay in this direction. Yet the Act should not be underestimated: in its acceptance of a measure of national responsibility it marked a decisive turning-point in national policy, even if it preceded old age pensions only because it made, at first, no demands on national funds. Keir Hardie, in a shrewd thrust at the Tories, claimed that it did no more than carry out the true intentions of the Elizabethan poor law, in setting the poor on work,[127] but it was Lloyd George who realised most clearly what had happened. Though he voted for the Bill he criticised it for its inadequacy, describing it, in topical metaphor, as 'like a motor-car without petrol or only such petrol as it could beg on the road'.[128] More petrol was to be provided by the Treasury in 1906, but for all his criticism Lloyd George had already seen that the Bill contained 'the germs of a revolution',[129] for it recognised the right of a man to expect work, even if it did nothing to provide it. The Act, he wrote to his brother William, in words already quoted in part, 'is one of the most revolutionary departures of modern times. The Tories don't realise what they have let themselves in for.'[130] It did, indeed, do something to prepare opinion for the far more radical measures which Lloyd George and his colleagues were to introduce, but above all it had made of unemployment, as public opinion had already made of old age pensions, matter for national, not local, concern, to be treated apart from the poor law as a problem of undeserved poverty, not of destitution through moral failure. Hence, for instance, the provision that the acceptance of help under the Act should not disenfranchise a man, as poor relief did. This provision, soon to be extended to the old age pension scheme, was in itself a formal recognition that the unemployed, though dependent on society for help, had done nothing to justify forfeiture of their civil rights.

In its operation the Act threw much badly-needed light on the nature and incidence of unemployment, reinforcing the lessons which Beveridge was to preach in his book of 1909. The men who took advantage of the help it offered were, in the main, not the normally employed, temporarily out of work, for whom the scheme was devised, but the ubiquitous under-employed and irregularly employed, who had been for 20 years the principal beneficiaries of all special schemes. Few skilled men applied, for they had their trade unions and friendly societies to fall back on and hoped thereby to weather the storms of unemployment. A skilled man, a notable newly-elected M.P., James Ramsay MacDonald, told the Commons in 1906, would not go to a distress committee 'until he had abandoned all hope of being able to see the inside of a factory within a tolerably short space of time'.[131] Of the 111,000 applicants for assistance in the Act's first year, in fact, more than half were general labourers and a further 20 per cent building workers: all of these, with another 10 per cent of men in engineering and shipbuilding, were in notoriously irregular occupations.

In short, the Act failed in its purpose simply because it was based on the continued fallacy of 'tiding over'. It gave a good deal of help where help was sadly needed, but the aid was only temporary and did nothing to solve the real problems, except, perhaps, in the few thousand cases of assisted emigration. With the decline of unemployment from 1909 the number of applications to the Distress Committees fell from 196,000 to 24,000 in 1913-14, and the Act itself lapsed during the war, though it was not finally repealed until 1929.[132] Whatever its limitations it had at least revealed the immense scale of under-employment, with its accompanying poverty and insecurity, and the need for the statistical information without which social problems could not even begin to be understood. How little immediate understanding there was even of the phenomena produced by the Act itself was revealed, for instance, by the conflicting impressions of its working in Sheffield given to the Poor Law Commission by the President of the Trades Council and the Deputy Lord Mayor of the City. The latter argued that so few deserving men had come forward that the 'fallacy' of continuous unemployment among men really willing to work had been exploded,[133] the former that skilled men would not take advantage of the Act, which in any case offered no work that could not have been provided in other ways.[134] More evidence on unemployment and its impact was clearly needed, and this within a few years Beveridge and the Poor Law Commission itself were to provide.

**Remedies—Beveridge, *Unemployment* and Labour Exchanges**   William Beveridge, the son of an Indian Civil Service official of advanced views, came to a career in social investigation and reform through Toynbee Hall. As Sub-Warden there in 1903-4 he took part in Canon Barnett's attempts to relieve unemployment by providing work in the country, and it was concern at the poor results of these efforts that turned him to the study of the phenomenon of underemployment. 'I remember asking myself', he has said in his autobiography, 'what had gone wrong with economic laws in East London; if there was no demand for these men why did not they either go away or starve and die? What kept them just alive where they were?'[135] In 1905 he became Secretary of a Committee on Unskilled Labour formed by the Charity Organisation Society and a member of the Central Unemployed Body for London established under the Unemployed Workmen Act. Towards the end of that year he left Toynbee Hall for the *Morning Post*, for which he was to write leaders on social problems until 1908, when Winston Churchill drew him into the Board of Trade to organise Labour Exchanges, and set him on the path that was to lead, long years after, to the Report of 1942. *Unemployment. A Problem of Industry*, completed before the Board of Trade appointment, was published early in 1909.

Labour Exchanges were Beveridge's 'King Charles's head'[136] in these early years. Exchanges had been established in a number of countries, notably in Germany as supplements to Bismarck's scheme of social insurance, but, while a few had also been set up in Britain, their functions had been limited almost entirely to relief. Walter Long's measures of 1904-5 encouraged their development but, again , as part of the functions of the Distress Committees. Beveridge, as a member of the Central Unemployed Body, insisted on them as an essential part of its machinery, but he realised, especially after the visit he paid to Germany in 1907, that they were indispensable to the broader handling of unemployment as a problem of industrial organisation rather than of individual relief. This was the case that he pressed in turn upon the *Morning Post*, the Webbs, the Poor Law Commission and, on a decisive occasion at dinner at the Webbs' in 1908, upon Winston Churchill. It was the case that secured his appointment to the Board of Trade and that made Labour Exchanges the first direct reform of the industrial order by the State.

Beveridge's case, as he argued it in *Unemployment*, was a simple one. The twin evils were under-employment and unemployment, but whereas unemployment was a variable, if recurrent, phenomenon, under-employment was a permanent feature of the industrial scene. Men normally in regular work needed protection against the bad times which the experience of 50 years showed occurred with ominous regularity every seven to ten years. Such protection they could not adequately provide for themselves alone, but it could be provided collectively, and was in fact provided by certain trade unions for their members, though the number covered was only about one-third of the minority of workers actually organised in unions. Such collective cover could also be provided, and provided more widely, by the State, and there was, in fact, as Beveridge found, much discussion in Germany of the feasibility of extending the Imperial system of sickness and accident insurance to cover unemployment, though it was to be many years before this development actually came. The indispensable counterpart to unemployment insurance was the Labour Exchange, where employers and workers alike could register their needs and where unemployed men could be required to 'sign on' each day, as they were required to do by some unions, as proof of need until work was found. Without Exchanges the fact that a man was unemployed could not be known, nor could the man himself know of openings available to him: the Exchange was therefore an effective test both of need and of willingness to work. As Beveridge wrote in *Unemployment*: 'The Labour Exchange thus opens a way of "dispauperisation" more humane, less costly and more effective than that of the "workhouse test"—the way of making the finding of work easy instead of merely making relief hard.'[137] Nor was the Exchange less effective as a means of combating under-employment. The real evil of casual and irregular work, as Booth had long since recognised, was that to ensure an adequate labour force many employers, especially in unskilled occupations, liked to have as many men waiting for work as they could hope to employ at their busiest times. If, however, the men could be registered at Exchanges, instead of waiting at employers' gates, their number would be reduced, and the surplus found other work elsewhere, trained for some other occupation or helped to emigrate. Labour Exchanges could not alone cure the evils of unorganised industry, but they were an indispensable part of any cure. Hence Beveridge's enthusiasm for them, which, as he has recorded in his autobiography, made the abolition of want seem, when he went to the Board of Trade, 'only just round the corner'. Such was the generous hopefulness of these years, the hopefulness that characterised the Liberal legislators, confident, as Churchill was when he instituted Labour Exchanges in 1909, that economic conditions could be improved without the violence to existing institutions that the Socialists demanded.

While Beveridge was completing *Unemployment* in 1908, the Poor Law Commission was in the throes of recording its findings, to which, on the subject of unemployment, Beveridge himself had contributed much. The book and the two Reports of the Commission eventually appeared in the same month of February 1909. Majority and Minority Reports alike came out strongly, if on different lines, in favour of Labour Exchanges and unemployment insurance with State assistance. That the Minority Report, as the work of the Webbs, should take such a line was to be expected. What was of particular interest was the case argued by the Majority, which showed how the pressure of evidence, gathered not only from Beveridge but from the Commission's own 'special investigators', brought the signatories to the realisation that, for the treatment of unemployment, the poor law, Chamberlain's relief measures and the Unemployed Workmen Act were all alike irrelevant. It was recognised not only that economic fluctuations brought unemployment to men normally fully employed but that there was, in the phrase of the heading of the relevant section of the report, THE NEW PROBLEM: CHRONIC UNDER-EMPLOYMENT.[138] Under these circumstances, the report admitted, 'the great principle of 1834 is not adequate to the new position' and new measures had to be sought. Labour Exchanges and unemployment insurance were essential and the Commissioners were also at one with Beveridge in recommending the spread of public works and, a point on which Beveridge himself had laid great stress, a serious and sustained attempt, including the raising of the school-leaving age to 15, to train young people for industrial life and deflect them from mere 'blind-alley' jobs.[139]

**Churchill and the Labour Exchanges**   Churchill's immediate adoption of Labour Exchanges was a notable example of the attitude of the Liberal legislators to reform. Once it was accepted that something had to be done, ideas were borrowed freely. Although the Poor Law Reports did not appear until 1909, Churchill had some six months' notice of their proposals. Even before this, however, he had been in touch with the Webbs, had heard Beveridge's views and had secured him for his Department, where another distinguished public servant, Hubert Llewellyn Smith, was already installed as Permanent Secretary. It was a time when politicians of all parties, sensitive, whatever their own predilections, to the 'tide of social pity', were, as Beatrice Webb confided to her diary, 'mendicants for practicable proposals'.[140] With no social services yet developed, and few Civil Servants therefore qualified to advise, it was in the sense of the dichotomy of Beveridge's autobiographical study of nearly half a century later, *Power and Influence*, the heyday of the influence of the informed outsider upon political power. That the informed were to overestimate their influence and in time to find themselves ignored was but to be expected, if not by themselves. The Webbs, impatient to impose their views, soon suffered this fate, and Beveridge was to find in 1942 that he could not repeat his earlier success with his old chief, now an elevated and redoubtable political hand. For the present of 1908, however,

Churchill was as anxious to learn as others to teach. The diagnosis of distress was apparent in unemployment and insecurity, the remedies were ready to hand, while from Lloyd George, whose 'lieutenant'[141] he was proud, then and later, to call himself, Churchill the wealthy young aristocrat had learnt something of the desperate conditions of poverty and insecurity amid which so many millions lived. A notable speech in 1908 at Dundee, where, after defeat in Manchester, he had to seek the customary re-election upon taking office, launched the new President of the Board of Trade upon his career as a social reformer: 'In this famous land of ours . . . we have not yet succeeded in providing that necessary apparatus of insurance and security, without which our industrial system is not merely incomplete, but actually inhumane.'[142] The characteristic touch of the first words, which was to stir a later generation to enthusiasm, was expressive of the fusion of traditionalist and reformer which was Churchill at this time, but the whole speech was redolent of the advice and opinions which his mentors were now presenting to him. Thus, the distinction drawn between unemployment and under-employment obviously owed much to Beveridge, as did the insistence upon casual labour as 'the creation of industry', not of personal failure. Still more notable was the origin of a phrase that was in time to acquire historic significance. To the plea for Labour Exchanges Beveridge was adding, in the case he was now preparing for publication, suggestions for the relief of the unemployment which even Labour Exchanges could not cure. Working hours could be made elastic, public-works schemes could be planned to come into effect in times of unemployment, and insurance could bring about 'an averaging of earnings between good and bad times'. When *Unemployment* appeared its penultimate chapter bore the sub-title 'The Averaging of Work and Earnings', and this phrase Churchill was to make particularly his own. At Dundee he spoke of the need for 'averaging machinery',[143] and with his own incomparable touch he later developed the phrase, during the discussions on National Insurance in 1911, into 'bringing in the magic of averages to the aid of the millions',[144] a happy gloss upon the reference to the 'left out millions' which he had coined in 1906, and a phrase which was to acquire new currency with Beveridge's proposals of 1942 for the extension of social insurance.

Churchill became President of the Board of Trade when Asquith succeeded Campbell-Bannerman as Prime Minister in April 1908. By July he had Beveridge in the Department preparing the case for Labour Exchanges and during the autumn he secured the Cabinet's agreement. The necessary Bill was carried in the following summer and the first 83 Exchanges were opened on 1 February 1910. Beveridge was appointed Director of the new service and had the task of establishing it throughout the country: he remained at the Board of Trade until war drew him into the Ministries of Munitions and Food. The Labour Exchanges themselves, renamed Employment Exchanges in 1916, passed to the Ministry of Labour on its establishment at the end of that year.

From the first, as Beveridge had desired, the Exchanges were intended as part of a wider scheme based on insurance. Problems of national defence, and especially of naval defence against Germany, were much in the air in 1909, and Churchill, like his father, Lord Randolph, an advocate of efficient economy in defence, turned the prevailing disquiet to good purpose by presenting his Labour Exchanges Bill as part of a policy of social improvement which would protect the country from dangers 'against which fleets and armies are of no avail'. One hundred Exchanges, he is said to have declared in a moment of enthusiasm, would be less costly and more valuable than one new battleship,[145] a remark that was in fact to be prophetic of the part the Exchanges were soon to play (and were to play again in 1939-45) with the coming of a war that was to make greater demands upon the manpower of the nation than any previous conflict. The dangers that Churchill had in mind in 1909, however, were those of social waste through unemployment, and against these, with national defence in mind, he held out a safeguard: 'If I had to sum up the immediate future of democratic politics in a single word I should say "Insurance"—Insurance against dangers from abroad, Insurance against dangers scarcely less grave and much more near and constant which threaten us here at home.'[146] Bismarck, the advocate of Reinsurance in foreign policy and the originator of German social insurance, would have approved both sentiments.

Labour Exchanges were to prepare the way for insurance, which was to be operated through them: only in this way could all types of workers, skilled as well as unskilled, be attracted to them. They were, however, to be voluntary (against the advice of the Webbs) in the hope that their effectiveness would ensure their use, and their appeal was to be increased by facilities for the unemployed for washing, clothes-mending and the provision of refreshments (strictly non-alcoholic, for these were the days of the 'glorious beer' controversy). Meanwhile, preparations were to be made for the introduction of insurance, though at first, since there were few precedents for the experiment, only in a limited number of trades. It was a bold and imaginative programme that Churchill flung in May, 1909, at a thin and largely unprepared House,[147] and Labour Members received it with enthusiasm. 'A good Labour night' was the comment of D. J. Shackleton, then President of the T.U.C.,[148] and Arthur Henderson rejoiced that Labour's 'Right to Work' Bill of the previous year was being adopted, if only 'in penny numbers'.[149]

Labour Exchanges were in several respects an innovation. For the first time a government department existed merely to be of service to the citizen, not to collect money from him or even to sell things to him. Once established they became 'almost as obvious a public institution as the Post Office',[150] and their utility was soon to be put to severe tests, so much so that Beveridge, in the new edition of *Unemployment* which he produced in 1930, complained that they had never been able to tackle their real task of organising the labour market, having been diverted, first to the mobilisation of man-power in war and then to the distribution of relief in the catastrophe of long-term unemployment that followed.[151]

To ensure their adaptability to local conditions their administration was de-centralised in 11 regions, each with a local advisory committee representative of both employers and employed. They had at first much suspicion to wear down, particularly in view of the connexion of earlier models with the distribution of relief. Employers suspected that they were the haunt of the workshy, workers that they were intended for the recruitment of cheap labour and blacklegs. Though the number of engagements made through them increased to some 3,000 a day by 1914, this represented only one-third of the vacancies in the few trades which were covered by insurance and for which, therefore, there were statistics available. They were used chiefly by skilled men, and, as Beveridge had anticipated, could do little unaided for the unskilled. Attempts made, by Beveridge and others, to bring order into the desperate disorder of dock labour, for instance, were a total failure and were to continue so, except in wartime, until 1946. A Committee on Government Contracts was set up in 1914 to consider the use of public-works contracts as an offset to unemployment, but war intervened. Churchill, taking his cue from Beveridge, had hoped for a system of 'reserve industries' which could be applied in times of depression 'like organ stops',[152] but this foreshadowing of the Full Employment policies of the Second World War was pushed into limbo by the First (see note, page 227).

Nevertheless, though there was still no grappling with the fundamental problems of economic insecurity and fluctuation which brought about unemployment, Britain at least possessed from 1910 the framework of a national system of information and assistance such as had not existed before. When the first payments were made to insured unemployed men in January 1913, Beveridge, after a visit to a London Exchange, could comment to his mother, with justifiable pride in the new machinery: 'Seeing the men lining up in a perfectly orderly way to get paid ... and realising that the same was happening at 1,400 other places ... and had never happened anywhere before, was quite impressive to my vanity.'[153]

**Other Measures—The Miners' Eight Hours' Day**  Before National Insurance is considered two other significant measures of 1908–9 must be mentioned. The first concerned the miner's working day. Protecting the worker against unemployment was one thing, endeavouring to control his conditions of work quite another. In 1908, however, after nearly 20 years of Parliamentary pressure, the miners, who now had 16 representatives, including Keir Hardie, in Parliament, at last got the Eight Hours' Day which they had originally claimed as far back as the 60s. Although the working hours of women and young people, as has been shown earlier, had been controlled since 1844, this was the first statutory regulation of the hours of men (apart from some limitation of railway hours imposed to check accidents). It was justifiable, even under *laissez-faire* conditions, and in the face of prophecies of ruin from the coal-owners, because of the exceptional difficulties and dangers of work underground, but it was directly attributable to the strength of the organised working-class vote in Parliament, which had already brought a strengthening of the position of the Trade Unions by the Trade Disputes Act of 1906. A similar attempt to limit the hours of the notoriously overworked shop assistants failed, though the Shops Act of 1911 granted 'early closing' and the weekly half-holiday. The miners followed up their victory with a claim for greater security of wages, enforced in 1912, when wages were lagging behind industrial recovery, by a six weeks' strike. Government intervention then brought a Minimum Wages Act, though the details were left for district settlement. Behind the miners at this time were pressing the railwaymen, and the last years before the war were indeed a period of increasing industrial tension, with the more militant elements, disappointed at the slow progress of reform since 1906, spoiling for direct action.

**Other Measures—Churchill and Trade Boards**    At the other extreme from the miners, helpless and exploited, were the workers in the 'sweated' trades, many of them women in dressmaking, for instance, who toiled long hours for the most miserable of returns. Their conditions had been studied by Beatrice Webb in the 80s and by a House of Lords Committee in 1888-91, but in the face of governmental reluctance to interfere in matters of wages it was not until 1908, after the *Daily News* had organised two revealing exhibitions, that the problem was tackled. It was Churchill who took the matter up, and the Trade Boards Act which he carried set up representative Boards for the settlement of minimum wages in certain trades, the first being those concerned with tailoring and the making of paper boxes, lace and chains. Again a new principle had been admitted, and though it was not carried far before 1914 a second Act greatly expanded its operation in 1918. Already in 1906 Churchill had defined the Government's social policy as drawing a line 'below which we will not allow persons to live and labour',[154] a phrase and aim obviously inspired by the Webbs' campaign for 'a national minimum of civilised life' and by the revelations of Booth and Rowntree. Pensions for those most in want through old age, Trade Boards for the protection of the worst exploited and least organised among the workers and Insurance against unemployment, these were practical measures towards a minimum, even if they offered little and there was no attempt made to decide what the minimum should be, or, indeed, whether explicitly there should be one at all.

**Remedies—Churchill and Unemployment Insurance**    Unemployment Insurance appeared as Part II of the great project which was the culmination of social reform in these years, the National Insurance Act of 1911, the first part of which established Health Insurance. Since it was in the Board of Trade that the unemployment insurance scheme was drafted, by Churchill, Llewellyn Smith and Beveridge, and from the Board of Trade, until it passed to the Ministry of Labour, that it was administered, it will be convenient to consider here Part II of the Act, leaving the more elaborate and controversial Part I for examination with the rest of Lloyd George's achievement as Chancellor of the Exchequer. The connexion between the two parts was in any case fortuitous: they were planned separately and given quite different administrative machinery. Eventually new Ministries, Labour (1916) and Health (1919), were created around the two services, and it was not until 1945, when one Ministry of National Insurance was established, that the two at last came together.

Health Insurance was essentially Lloyd George's contribution: he was not greatly interested in unemployment insurance (or, indeed, in Labour Exchanges until he saw their practical value in wartime), though the original suggestion that Churchill should take it up may have come from him.[155] In unemployment insurance the compelling influence was undoubtedly Churchill's; 'a signal instance', Beveridge was to write later, 'of how much the personality of a single Minister in a few critical months may change the course of social legislation'.[156] Churchill, it is true, left the Board of Trade in February 1910, to become Home Secretary, and was succeeded by Sydney Buxton, but he retained his interest and spoke strongly for Part II when it was introduced in the summer of 1911: 'There is no proposal in the field of politics that I care more about than this great insurance scheme.'[157] Already, when introducing Labour Exchanges in 1909, he had described his proposals for unemployment insurance and it was these that were shaped into Part II. The case for insurance lay in the 'magic of averages'; in the way in which by small payments, with government assistance, a man could protect himself against the risks of unemployment. 'By sacrifices which are inconceivably small', Churchill argued, 'families can be secured against catastrophes which otherwise would smash them up for ever.'[158] Such sacrifices, however, few were able to make unprompted or unaided, most men preferring to run the risk and to insure, when they could, against the greater certainties of death and sickness. As Lloyd George showed, when presenting his over-all scheme in 1911, though there were in being 42 million death policies, only six million workers, less than half of the total, made any insurance provision against illness, and only one and a half million, fewer than one-tenth, any against unemployment.[159] Yet of trade-union funds paid out every year more than a quarter went to members out of work, a considerably higher proportion than was paid to those who were off-work through accident or injury.

Trade unionists were still only a small proportion of the working population and it was concern at the total inadequacy of insurance protection for the unskilled, in particular, that caused the Majority Report of the Poor Law Commission to recommend a scheme of insurance for them assisted by State funds and administered through trade unions. The Minority Report preferred a voluntary system for all, with payments shared between the State and the unions. Beveridge had recorded, however, that German investigations suggested that a State system of compulsory insurance was possible, once a workable test of unemployment had been devised, and it was such a system that Churchill adopted. Labour Exchanges made it possible to apply a test, and the practice of trade unions in requiring unemployed members to 'sign on' was taken over. It was in this way, as Beatrice Webb observed, that the Exchanges proved to be 'the thin end of the wedge' which, a quarter of a century later, took the unemployed out of the poor law.[160] From Germany came the method of registering contributions by sticking stamps in an 'unemployment book' (later to be more simply known as 'cards'), kept by the employer.

The advantage of a compulsory scheme was that, applying as it would to all, it would not be in danger of being swamped by bad risks, but if the scheme were to be effective it called for higher contributions than the individual workman could afford and for recognition by employers that they also stood to gain, while State supplementation was required, in Churchill's words, 'to make it just worth while for the superior workman to pool his luck with his comrades'.[161] Hence the triple weekly levy, again on the German model, with employer and employed contributing $2\frac{1}{2}d$. each and the State a further third of the total. In return for his contribution the workman would be guaranteed 7s. a week during unemployment, qualifying for one week of benefit for each five contributions paid, subject to a maximum limit of 15 weeks in any year. The actuarial basis was of a somewhat dubious nature, as Beveridge acknowledged in his autobiography,[162] but proved to be sound. The scheme started in its two stages, of contribution and benefit, in July 1912 and January 1913, against a fortunate background of rising employment, and by August 1914, when war upset all calculations, a surplus of more than three million pounds had been collected. It was, literally, 'a risky adventure into the unknown',[163] which succeeded, without any precedents to guide it, thanks to careful work in the Board of Trade and to ready acceptance and co-operation outside.

In view of its experimental nature the scheme was restricted to a small group of trades which paid low wages and were known to be subject to serious fluctuations —building, shipbuilding, mechanical engineering, ironfounding, vehicle construction and saw-milling—covering in all some 2,250,000 men, though the exact number was unknown until the scheme started. To encourage steady employment in these trades there were refunds to employers who kept men regularly at work and to workmen who by the age of 60 had drawn less in benefit than they had paid in contributions. There were also arrangements, to which some importance was attached, for supplementing existing voluntary schemes and encouraging new ones. These 'fancy clauses' (the expression is Beveridge's) proved unnecessary or unworkable and were later withdrawn, but they are evidence of a necessarily cautious approach to the latest of the attempts made since 1886 to grapple with unemployment outside the poor law.

The benefits offered in 1911 were deliberately set low to discourage malingering, but, like old age pensions, were in any case not intended to provide more than a 'lifebelt' to supplement other savings. There was no question of a 'national minimum' or even of family allowances: 'dependants' benefits' were introduced only in the quite different conditions of heavy unemployment after the war. Unemployment insurance was intended to do no more than, in Beveridge's phrase, to average a man's earnings between good and bad times, or, as Churchill put it, to pool his luck with that of his fellow-workers. It was, in fact, essentially *insurance*, socially organised and socially supplemented to give the citizen some protection against the miseries of depression and the proved inadequacies of *ad hoc* relief. In 1916 the scheme was extended to munition workers, but attempts to widen its scope still further, in preparation for the stresses of resettlement after the war, were resisted by workers and employers alike. The coming of peace, however, brought the difficulties that Beveridge and others had anticipated. Various temporary measures had to be adopted, including the 'donation' scheme, which entangled insurance with the ominous name and notion of 'the dole'. A new Act in 1920 extended unemployment insurance to all manual workers, except those in agriculture and domestic service (who were not brought in until 1936-7), and to the lower-paid non-manual workers. It was, however, already too late. Eleven million workers were now covered, but the post-war depression put two million of them out of work in 1921, and the number was not to fall below one million before the Second World War (in the 30s it almost reached three million and did not fall below two million until 1937). In 1920 there was a reserve of £22,000,000 in the Unemployment Fund, but this disappeared in six months and as part of the new scheme power had to be given to borrow from the Treasury to cover those whose right to benefit had been exhausted. Insurance was swamped by relief, and, as was shown by an investigation in 1926, insurance contributions from that part of the insured population that had never suffered unemployment, almost one half, were in effect a tax levied for the relief of the other half. Hence in the end, though not until 1934, the decision to separate assistance to the long-term unemployed from the insurance scheme, and the setting-up of the Unemployment Assistance Board.

**The Significance of Insurance**   This sketch of later developments, which we shall have to consider in more detail in the next chapter, has been inserted to draw attention to the limitations of the 1911 scheme. Insurance, like Labour Exchanges, was not intended, either by Beveridge or by the members of the Poor Law Commission, to provide a full answer to the problem of unemployment. Such other suggestions as they made would have been of little service under the appalling conditions of post-war depression, but they had at least shown the need for an attack on unemployment on a wide front, with plans prepared in advance to meet the onset of depression. The two Acts of 1909 and 1911 covered only part of the ground, and a third of a century was to pass before Full Employment became a practical consideration, but they were bold innovations in their time, and without the experience of their working later developments would hardly have been possible. As the Blanesburgh Committee reported in 1927, 'an unemployment insurance scheme must now be regarded as a permanent feature of our code of social legislation',[164] and to this Beveridge added in his 1942 report the confident assertion that 'benefit in return for contributions, rather than free allowances from the State, is what the people of Britain desire'.[165] It was the decisions of Lloyd George and Churchill in 1909-11, based as they were on the long-standing practice of trade unions and friendly societies, that set this pattern. One of these at least had his doubts, however, about the future. A note from Lloyd George to his private secretary in 1911 reveals that he was thinking of insurance as 'necessarily [a] temporary expedient': 'Hope State will acknowledge a full responsibility . . . for sickness, breakdown and unemployment. It really does so now, through Poor Law; but conditions . . . have been so harsh and humiliating that working-class pride revolts . . .. Gradually the obligation of the State to find labour or sustenance will be realised. Insurance will then be unnecessary.'[166] 'The obligation of the State', be it noted: this was revolutionary doctrine in 1911, and Lloyd George was well advised to keep it to a confidant. Nevertheless, it may be wondered now whether Lloyd George was not in fact right, whether insurance rather than State assistance based on graduated taxation, or the curious assortment of the two that has been evolved, is necessarily the most desirable answer to social problems. The Webbs certainly objected to the whole conception of compulsory insurance with Treasury backing, though they realised, with characteristically lofty recognition of human frailty, that 'public opinion has got firmly into its silly head that insurance has some mystical moral quality, which even covers the heinous sin of expenditure from public funds'.[167]

This, however, has to be acknowledged, that insurance dispelled the poor-law taint from which working-class pride revolted: it was, in fact, from this that its popularity stemmed. Flat-rate contributions for flat-rate benefits was a principle that none could impugn. It was, moreover, thoroughly respectable in the eyes both of the insured and of those who were above the need for insurance of this kind. Making the working-man pay for himself, even if he paid only part, was highly acceptable to those who had been opposed to 'free' old age pensions, and placated many critics.

## The Liberal Reforms : (3) The Poor Law Commission, 1905-9

Much has already been said of the Poor Law Commission of 1905-9, and the influence of both the Majority and Minority Reports upon the introduction of Labour Exchanges and Unemployment Insurance has been shown. Before proceeding to a consideration of the other great insurance scheme, Part I of the Act of 1911, and of the 'People's Budget' that preceded it, the Commission must now be described. It was a grand inquest of the state of the nation in matters of poverty, and, though its direct effects were limited, it marked the end of nineteenth-century attitudes and opened the way for a new approach to social problems.

The Commission was appointed by Balfour on the very day in December 1905, that saw his government resign. It was appointed, he acknowledged later, because he realised that the poor-law system was 'antiquated and utterly worn out' (see note, page 227). The immediate decision was that of his brother Gerald, who earlier in the year had succeeded Walter Long at the Local Government Board, but it reflected the growing concern at the way the policy of relief was moving; there were even suggestions that the pre-1834 conditions were returning.[168] The last few years had seen an increase in industrial depression and distress and Long had already shown his concern for the unemployed. Public opinion, though inevitably more concerned with symptoms than with causes, was becoming more alive to the issues involved, and the general concern was reflected in the parliamentary debates, in which it was given point by the pressure of the few Labour members. Inside the Local Government Board it was realised that the principles of 1834 had been much whittled down in practice. As was shown in the last chapter, relaxations of policy in the last decade or so of the nineteenth century made 1890 seem in retrospect a turning point in poor-law history, so that that stern critic, C. S. Loch of the C.O.S., could complain in 1900 that a new poor law was coming into existence. In 1905 a devoted adherent of strict principles, J. S. Davy, became Assistant Secretary of the Poor Law Division of the Local Government Board and it was to his lamentations at the backsliding that had taken place, lamentations which, as already shown, he repeated forcefully to the Poor Law Commission, that the Commission's appointment was in no small part due. Davy's desire was to expose what had happened and to reassert the principles of 1834. As his evidence revealed, he had little understanding of the conditions of his time and of the inapplicability of the old principles to them. Those principles, hastily thrown together in the 1830s on inadequate evidence and less understanding, had assumed the force and value of revelation: to Davy they were sacrosanct, In this, however, he was but typical of the Local Government Board as a whole. There are many stories of the department's narrow interpretation of its functions, but one will suffice. Over many years permission to build a maternity hospital had been withheld from a local authority on the grounds that, although the Public Health Act of 1875 had authorised the building of hospitals for the sick, childbirth was not sickness 'within the meaning of the Act', and it was not until 1914 that the prohibition was withdrawn.[169] By such methods the Board had gained over 30 years the reputation of sending its inspectors, in the words of the famous *Punch* cartoon, to 'see what Johnny is doing and tell him he mustn't', and Davy did not disguise his disapproval of what Ministers and Parliament, as well as local Guardians, had done to the principles which the Board existed to cherish. As he told Beatrice Webb, though he had some administrative reforms in mind, he wanted the Commission to recommend a strict return to the principles of 1834, 'to stem the tide of philanthropic impulse that was sweeping away the old embankment of deterrent tests.'[170]

Once the decision to appoint a Commission was taken the selection of members was shrewdly done, even if its purpose was in the end frustrated. It was in the main a conservative, not to say Conservative, body, as was to be expected, but one with much experience of poor relief or social work. Among the 18 members, in addition to four senior officials of poor law administration, were such stalwarts of the c.o.s. as C. S. Loch, Mrs Bosanquet and Octavia Hill, together with Charles Booth, George Lansbury and, significant choice, Mrs Sidney Webb, whose membership made the Minority Report possible. (Samuel Barnett, now a canon of Westminster, was sounded, but declined a place on the Commission.) As Chairman of this motley band was named Lord George Hamilton, an old political hand of 60, who had held office under Lord Salisbury and Balfour, and had resigned with Chamberlain over tariff reform. Mrs Webb's description of Lord George as a *grand seigneur* has already been quoted, and in her diary she pays tribute to the tact and charm with which, though without much understanding of what was afoot, he kept his team together. He himself found the task a heavy one, 'very tiring and at times impossible', as he comments in his autobiography, because of the obduracy of the preconceived notions of his colleagues.[171] He wondered, indeed, why he had been chosen, and apart from the fact that another obvious choice, C. T. Ritchie, Chancellor of the Exchequer until his resignation over Tariff Reform, had recently died, the reason is probably to be found in his character and reputation. When invited to become Chairman of the London School Board in 1894 he had consulted Salisbury, who had advised acceptance, because, he records in his autobiography, 'I had an inherent wet-blanket element within me which would damp down the heat of the more violent of the protagonists'.[172] This wet-blanket element was to be much tested during the long months of the Commission's existence, from December 1905 to February 1909, when its reports at last appeared.

**The Majority Report**    The Commission was instructed to enquire not only into the working of the poor law, but also—and the addition was a significant one in view of what we have already described of its findings—into the means adopted outside the poor law 'for meeting distress arising from want of employment, particularly during periods of severe industrial depression'. Of its working we know something from the publication of the lively partisan diaries of Mrs Webb, but we cannot here do more than note the principal recommendations of the two Reports. In all, the Commission produced 47 volumes of evidence, and to some few parts of this, as to portions of the Reports, passing reference has already been made. There were undoubtedly those, among them Davy and the c.o.s. members of the Commission, who had hoped that a return to the strict application of the principles of 1834 would be recommended. The weight of evidence, however, was so much against simple deterrence and a return to stricter administration as remedies for the complex problems of poverty that the Commission was at one in recommending the frank acknowledgement of the modifications that had already been made and the adoption of others. As the evidence came in, Beatrice Webb noted with satisfaction that it all pointed 'away from bad administration as *the* cause of pauperism and towards bad conditions among large classes of the population as the overwhelmingly important fact'.[173] The result was a surprising degree of unanimity on the Commission for a considerable reshaping of the poor law, and even for some not inconsiderable modifications in principle.[174] There was general agreement that the Guardians should go and be replaced by the Local Authorities, that deterrence and 'less eligibility' should be abandoned, that more should be done to give positive help to those in need, especially old people, children and the unemployed, and that in particular the school-leaving age should be raised to 15, Labour Exchanges established and unemployment and invalidity insurance encouraged, while the disfranchisement of those in receipt of relief should at least be limited. There, however, agreement ended. The Minority Report wanted the immediate 'break-up of the poor law', and would settle for nothing less, whereas the Majority wished to keep the poor law in being, whatever modifications were made in practice. The Majority recognised the 'associations of harshness, and still more of hopelessness',[175] gathered round the poor law, and therefore proposed to rename it 'Public Assistance' (the name that was finally adopted in 1929) and similarly to call applicants for Assistance the 'necessitous' rather than the 'destitute', but their approach still had lingering elements of the old moral attitude that saw those in need as the failures of society. 'The causes of distress', they maintained in their Report, 'are not only economic and industrial; in their origin and character they are largely moral',[176] and in considering the disfranchisement of those receiving Assistance they argued that 'those who . . . have failed to manage their own affairs successfully ought not by law to have power to interfere in the management of the affairs of others'.[177] Yet they saw the need for different methods of handling the different categories of the necessitous, and, in particular, for a special approach to the problems of unemployment, though, notwithstanding all the preventive services that had been built up, they wished still to deal with the necessitous as a class apart from the rest of the community (even school meals were to be transferred from the education authorities to public assistance). The rigours of administration were to be softened, it is true, and not merely by a change of name. The ubiquitous 'general mixed workhouse', condemned in 1834, was again denounced and was to be broken up, outdoor relief was to be renamed 'Home Assistance' and more adequately provided, medical relief was to be better organised, and children and the aged were to be better cared for. All this, however, was to be done as a service apart. It was no longer to be administered by the Guardians, for the Unions had proved themselves unsuitable and inadequate units. Instead, it was to be the concern of the larger local authorities that had come into existence less than 20 years earlier, the County and County Borough Councils, which had already absorbed those other *ad hoc* authorities, the School Boards. Scope was still to be left for private charity, however. The Local Authorities would work through Public Assistance Committees, with which would be associated 'Voluntary Aid Committees' to organise charity and supplement public assistance, with private personal service and supervision, Voluntary Aid being 'more sympathetic and more elastic than official assistance can be'.[178] In time, it was hoped, all applications for public assistance would 'pass through the sieve of Voluntary Aid',[179] and to encourage this in the case of unemployment Home Assistance, in a curious echo of 'less eligibility', should be 'in some way less agreeable'[180] than Voluntary Aid, though how this was to be achieved was not explained.

The poor law and private charity were therefore to be alike retained, if in new forms, and all their proposals, the Majority Report made clear, were intended to introduce not changes of principle but improvements in machinery.[181] In fact, of course, the improvements were such as to introduce the cautious, though no doubt unconscious, beginnings of new principles. If not revolutionary in intention they were at least revolutionary in embryo:[182] 'in their sober way they also mark the end of 1834'.[183] Typical was the proposal not to disfranchise those who were on relief for less than three months in a year, which was put forward as an improvement but implied a change of principle that must in time have been extended. Voluntary Aid, it has been suggested, would similarly have declined as Public Assistance developed.[184] In the special case of unemployment the improvements proposed introduced new principles of prevention, in the form of insurance against unemployment and invalidity (though through voluntary organisation, not the State), with Labour Exchanges, public works in times of depression, changes in the school curriculum to fit children better for industry and a higher school-leaving age to check blind alley jobs.

The proposal to introduce invalidity insurance was a significant move, as, like the recommendations of unemployment insurance, it helped to prepare opinion for the more ambitious National Insurance scheme of 1911. It was intended to cover men forced out of work by ill health, and although no detailed scheme was prepared it was suggested that the need might be met by weekly contributions of rather less than 4d., which was the amount actually fixed in 1911.

The Majority's proposals for the medical care of the necessitous were less ambitious. The previous chapter has said something of the development of the poor-law medical services and especially of the growth of poor-law hospitals, which, as the Commission was compelled to recognise, had in some places become in effect State hospitals. Doctors, however, and in particular the increasingly important Medical Officers of Health, were restive under conditions which made preventive medicine almost an impossibility. In no other field of poor-law administration were the 'harshness and hopelessness' which the Commission had diagnosed so much in evidence to deter the needy from seeking help when they most needed it. The results were serious for the community as a whole, no less than for the individual, and told most tragically in the case of tuberculosis, which accounted, it was calculated, for one-seventh of all poor relief. 'Disease much oftener causes poverty than poverty disease' was the comment in 1907 of a distinguished medical administrator, Dr (afterwards Sir) Arthur Newsholme,[185] then M.O.H. for Brighton and from 1908 to 1919 Principal Medical Officer to the Local Government Board. Like his colleague Dr George Newman, who was to succeed him in 1919 as the first Chief Medical Officer of the Ministry of Health, Newsholme pressed on the Commission, when he gave evidence before it, the need for the unification of all public medical services and for treatment, in the public interest, regardless of pauper or other status. This, indeed, was the burden of the medical evidence that the Commission took. Nowhere more than in matters of health was there urgent need for preventive work rather than mere relief, but the poor-law authorities were in no position to provide it. Yet the evidence of the medical witnesses, the Webbs wrote, 'transformed the outlook of the Commission'.[186] Davy had insisted that medical relief was usually the first step to pauperism, and his view was endorsed by poor law witnesses with such frequency as 'might almost entitle it to rank as a Poor Law axiom'.[187] The full weight of evidence showed clearly enough, however, that this was 'only another way of saying that sickness is a cause of pauperism': 'it is not the medical relief, but the sickness and its disabilities, which cause the persons to come upon the rates for maintenance'.[188] The case put by the medical witnesses for a more constructive approach was thus driven home.

The evidence did not altogether convince the Majority,[189] however, and its recommendations provided for no more than a muddled Medical Assistance Committee under the Public Assistance Authority, with contributory 'Provident Dispensaries' (and 'choice of doctor') for all below a certain wage level. 'The specialist', said the Report, in a criticism of the Minority's proposals which was aimed in part at their plans for separate treatment of health problems, 'is too apt to see only what interests him . . . . and to disregard wider issues.' In fact, of course, this is precisely what the Majority themselves did: their proposals were an administrative patchwork, meeting certain recognised needs but not proposing any fundamental changes, except by implication, or lighting on any guiding principle such as had obsessed their predecessors of 1834.

The proposals showed, too, as has well been said, 'an unimaginative lack of fundamental resentment' at the conditions of life of so many people,[190] which revealed, for instance, how far removed the Majority were from Lloyd George's 'tide of social pity'. Yet they had come far, if not yet far enough, and if the influence of the c.o.s. was, inevitably, strong upon them, a clue to their attitude is to be found in the Society's *Review* for 1905: 'The provision by every man for the immediate and contingent requisites of himself and those dependent on him . . . is a social duty. . . . The problem . . . is to discover . . . at what point this provision for self may be said to have broken down without reproach to the individual.'[191]

By 1909 the Majority was clearly prepared to investigate this point, and to recognise that not every individual in need necessarily deserved reproach. Their desire to respect and maintain private charity was, in the circumstances of the time, understandable, and had its justification in the concern of the c.o.s. for personal service and casework at a time when professional social workers were rare: 'There is in personal sympathy and devotion . . . an anti-septic property which wards off . . . the dangers due to an attractive legal provision for the poor.'[192] The phrase is reminiscent of one quoted earlier,[193] and was probably penned by the same hand, but the dilemma of people accustomed to regard as altogether undesirable the giving of help, unless it were, in the words of their Report, 'preventive, curative and restorative', and intended 'to foster the instincts of independence and self-maintenance amongst those assisted',[194] was clear enough. What was at least recognised was that the problems of the necessitous were national, not local, and called both for more efficient local administration and for greater control and assistance from the central government. Hence not only the proposals for the reorganisation of public assistance under the local Councils but the suggestion in the Report that the President of the Local Government Board should become a Secretary of State and that government grants to the Councils for public assistance work should be greatly increased. The upgrading of the Presidency, which increased John Burns's salary from £2,000 to £5,000, was, in fact, the one immediate result of the Report's appearance which had not already been to some extent anticipated. The Presidency of the Board of Trade was similarly elevated at the same time.

**The Minority Report**   With the Majority Report appeared the challenging document signed by the four members of the dissentient Minority, Mrs Webb, Lansbury, the Rev H. Russell Wakefield, afterwards Dean of Norwich and Bishop of Birmingham, and the trade union representative on the Commission, Francis Chandler. Here there was no disregarding of wider issues. The report was largely the work of the Webbs and led to the strenuous campaign in which, with a lively band of supporters, they preached its doctrines up and down the country, forfeiting in the process much of the sympathetic interest of the Liberal Ministers whom, thanks to Mrs Webb's comfortable private income, they had been able to dine at their hospitable, if austere, table. Though the Majority Report stole the headlines at first, rather to the Webbs' chagrin,[195] the Minority Report made a great impression, and sold some 500 more copies: the popular demand for Blue Books may be said, in fact, to date from its appearance in octavo form. It had the great advantage over its rival document that it was based on a simple principle and a fresh approach. It insisted that destitution, not pauperism, was the problem, that the conditions of life for so many people were such that they could not unaided escape extreme poverty and that the remedy lay not in relief but in prevention. This was disturbing doctrine to a public now uneasy but brought up to believe that dependence on relief was a sign of moral failure. The Webbs also believed that it indicated moral failure, but they argued that the failure was the community's at least as much as the individual's. What was needed was such a mobilisation of the community's resources as would *prevent* anyone, at any age, from falling into destitution, unless he had criminal propensities. Children were to be properly cared for and educated, adults to be protected against sickness, disablement and unemployment, the elderly to be assured a modest income. There was, in short, to be a recognised 'national minimum' below which no-one was to be allowed to fall, 'the provision, for the citizens, of whatever was called for in the public interest'.[196] Already much had been done by way of legislation on health, housing, factory conditions and education since 1834 to prevent destitution, and the revelation of how much had in fact been done was one of the 'discoveries' of the Commission. What was now sought was the logical sequel, the completion of the process, which would lead to the 'break-up of the poor law', its abolition as a special service, and the handing of social problems to other agencies. The competent authorities would be the local Councils, which would set up special committees to care for the children, the sick and the elderly, and there would be a unified medical service, while a local government officer 'of high *status*', to be called the Registrar of Public Assistance, would have the task of co-ordinating all forms of help given.[197] The poor law being now 'intellectually bankrupt'[198] in its handling of the unemployed, a national authority, the Ministry of Labour, would be established, to prevent or minimise unemployment. The Ministry would provide Labour Exchanges, together with training centres for those unable to find work. Industrial training and longer school courses would be provided for the young, and a 10 years' programme of public works would be planned, to be put into operation in times of depression. Insurance would be voluntary and conducted by the trade unions, though with State subventions. Detention colonies would take care of the idle and wastrels, and retraining would be a condition of maintenance for those unable to find work through a Labour Exchange,

This last was a condition by which the Webbs set considerable store. They were opposed to unconditional help, which, Mrs Webb observed in her diary, seemed to them 'under the present conditions of human will, sheer madness'[199] (though with the pious qualification, 'whatever it may be in good times to come'). Hence their opposition to Churchill's insurance scheme: 'The *unconditionality* of all payments under insurance schemes constitutes a grave defect. The state gets nothing for its money in the way of conduct'.[200] (This argument, it may be noted, Churchill was brushing aside, as 'mixing up moralities and mathematics', when it was presented to him by Llewellyn Smith[201] at about the very time that Beatrice Webb recorded it in her diary.)

The Webbs shared this view of insurance, though Mrs Webb was, as always, the more uncompromising of the two. Masterman earlier had been horrified at her 'zeal for disciplining people', and had 'prayed that he might never fall into her hands as an unemployed'.[202] Sidney Webb, for all his opposition, was more restrained, and more willing to see whether Churchill's scheme could be modified in practice. How their own plans, as set out in the Minority Report, would have fared, especially when faced with the widespread long-term unemployment that was to come in the 20s, it is not difficult to imagine. The Labour reaction to them at the time was one of amused scepticism.[203]

The Minority proposals were, therefore, not without their moral content, and however much they may have shocked some there was nothing revolutionary about them. In fact, as Beatrice Webb was later to point out, they implied a belief that society could be improved without being overturned: 'Rightly or wrongly, we believed in "the inevitability of gradualness". We were content to leave the future to take care of itself.'[204] The only revolution that was called for was one in the hearts of men: as the Webbs told Churchill over dinner one night, 'We want to *really change* the mind of the people with regard to the facts of destitution'.[205]

The Minority Report seems now less startling than it did when it first appeared, and in the context of more than half a century of development the common ground it shared with its Majority counterpart is more apparent. To many contemporaries, however, the differences loomed large: 'differing so much, agreeing in so little' was Churchill's verdict on the two reports.[206] It was unfortunate, no doubt, that separate reports should have appeared: a single unanimous set of proposals, could it have been agreed, might have achieved something. As Samuel Barnett commented regretfully, unanimity would have been 'invincible'.[207] Yet if the failure to agree is deplored, as it often has been, and the responsibility is largely laid upon the Webbs who, as Beatrice's diary makes clear, were determined to press their case, the significance of their insistence upon making a clean break with the past and demolishing the poor law must not be overlooked. The failure of their campaign showed them to be bad tacticians, but in view of what was to happen later some at least of their long-term strategy was sound. If the Minority's recommendations were not to be carried out, the very existence of the report, with its case for a fresh start on sound principles, was an inspiration, and an influence on opinion. Indeed, by the time that the Maclean Committee looked into the matter again in 1917, as part of the work of the Ministry of Reconstruction, Lord George Hamilton himself had become a convert.

Apologists for the Majority Report have often criticised the Minority for proposing a break-up of the poor law on the grounds that, apart from the unconvincing device of the Registrar of Public Assistance, it would have entailed the disintegration of any social casework service for the family as a whole,[208] though one suspects that it was rather more the preservation of the poor law than of the family that was uppermost in the Majority's minds. There is much to be said on both sides, but the question is one beyond the scope of this study. It is, however, difficult to see how, despite the considerable areas of agreement, a reconciliation of the two viewpoints within one report could have been achieved. The measure of agreement had at least the effect that there was astonishingly little protest at the abandonment of the deterrent poor law. As Beatrice Webb observed at the time, 'that the principles of 1834 should die so easily is certainly a thoroughgoing surprise'.[209] Public opinion on the poor law could never be quite the same again, though whether the Webbs' campaign throughout the country achieved much may be doubted: one recent apologist for the Majority Report is unsparing in his criticism of them—'Their achievement was to alienate the government, bore the country and postpone reform.'[210]

**The Local Government Board and the Report**   Many there were, however, who hailed the Minority Report with enthusiasm, or were converted by it, though to others the sweeping nature of the scheme and the calm assurance of its authors in the obvious rightness of their conclusions were goads to fury. Burns, in particular, coached by his permanent officials, refused to consider either report, stood by the Guardians and insisted that he could do anything that was necessary to improve conditions: 'Social Reform, that's me' was the claim put into his mouth by a jibe.[211] 'The Poor Law', he argued in the Commons, 'is in a new atmosphere . . . not now the hard unsympathetic attitude it used to be, but it is sympathetic, progressive, reasonable, and adaptable to any sensible demand that may be made upon it.'[212] (The target at which 'sensible' was aimed was obvious enough.) Even the striking concurrence of the two reports in recommending that the poor-law services should be taken over by the local authorities, though confirmed by the Maclean Committee in 1917, was of no avail for 20 years to come. As Asquith said when a bill based on the Minority Report was debated in the Commons, the Guardians would die hard.[213] With the Local Government Board unshaken and no agreed report to unite opinion in favour of change, the Poor Law Commission, from which so much had been hoped, petered out in awarding John Burns a wage increase.

Some changes were, however, made under Burns's direction. In particular, the special needs of children, which had been increasingly recognised in practice over the past 30 years, were now acknowledged. The maintenance of children in workhouses was discouraged and eventually, in 1915, prohibited, and it was laid down that, when families received outdoor relief, care should be taken to see that the children benefited. In the matter of outdoor relief there was a relaxing of conditions. Where relief was given it was to be adequate to ensure that the recipients were 'sufficiently fed, clothed and lodged', a definition open to varying interpretations, but implying something more than the barest minimum. Moreover, cases were to be followed up. Improvements were made in workhouse practice, especially in the supply of nurses, still far from adequate, and the ill-omened name of 'workhouse' was itself abandoned: henceforth there were to be only poor-law 'institutions'. In the case of able-bodied men, when relief was offered in return for labour it should be rather to keep them occupied than to serve as a deterrent 'test', and in any event Guardians were left the right in special circumstances to waive restrictions. Both of these last points were to acquire unexpected significance through the great increase of distress from unemployment after the war, and to add to the unhappy confusion of policy in the post-war years.

These changes of detail, though not unimportant, served but to underline the immediate failure of the Poor Law Commission to recast the poor law. The failure was not, however, purely one-sided. The Local Government Board ran true to form, but there were also other Departments whose Ministers had schemes afoot which stole some of the thunder of the two reports. Old age pensions were introduced before they appeared, and even if this was not the case with labour exchanges and unemployment insurance the reports did no more than confirm decisions already made, while it is known that Lloyd George's preparations for the National Insurance Act of 1911 were well advanced before he even looked at the Majority Report, with its plans for invalidity insurance.[214] It was certainly simpler, and politically more rewarding, to pick out some choice plums than to attempt to remake part of the machinery of State. In any case only Asquith could have moved Burns to action, and Asquith, 'an old-fashioned individual', as he described himself,[215] was not interested in poor law reforms, feeling that pensions and insurance would do much of what was required.[216] Moreover, the reports appeared at an awkward moment, shortly before the budget of 1909 burst upon a startled country, while the very nature of the budget itself suggested that it would achieve by other means what the Poor Law Commission had set out to do. By the time that the budget storm was over the Constitution had been in danger and there had been two General Elections in a single year. After the second there was the great National Insurance scheme, followed by the Home Rule Bill and, before long, war. Given the need to mobilise and unite opinion and overcome prejudice there was little enough time between 1909 and 1914. Had John Burns been another man the issue might well have been different, though it is difficult to conceive of Lloyd George and Churchill being content with the position of lions under the throne. As things were, the problems were tackled piecemeal, in typical, empirical English style, and nothing more was to be heard of a national minimum, of 'a line below which we will not allow persons to live and labour', until Beveridge took up the Webbs' cases in 1942. Probably, had war not intervened, something would have been done after the reforms of pensions, exchanges and insurance had had time to make themselves felt. Burns was moved from the Local Government Board to the Board of Trade in February 1914, and replaced by Herbert Samuel, while Lloyd George had plans for the association of National Health Insurance with the Local Government Board, plans which were to take shape after the war in the setting-up of the Ministry of Health. The coming of the war cut across further developments, and when, later, reconstruction was studied the poor law was not a first priority. However, for all its inconclusiveness the Commission had brought to a point the unease at social conditions which was the reverse side of the gaiety and opulence of the Edwardian era. Canon Barnett saw in it 'an answer to disbelievers in progress'.[217] It certainly marked an awareness of social problems greater than he would have believed possible in East London in the 80s.

## The Liberal Reforms: (4) The People's Budget, 1909

The Budget of 1909, which provided the finance for the social reforms of these years, seems now a modest measure, but it stunned Parliament when it was presented and brought howls of protest from those it affected. The key to Liberal policy had long been the breaking or restraining of privilege, and the budget was devised as another stage in this process. During the past half century political power had been spread, the majority of men enfranchised, the ballot made secret, education provided, the State service opened to competition and influence in many ways diminished. There remained, however, the influence of inherited property and especially of property in land, at one time the only basis of political power. Land by the end of the nineteenth century was no longer what it had been, as Oscar Wilde's Lady Bracknell testified in a famous scene, but it was indispensable to the expansion of the country's new source of wealth in industry and to the growth of the towns in which the industrial population had to live. Landowners, as the Royal Commission on Housing had complained in the 80s, profited by development to which they had contributed nothing at all, and there were many elements in the Liberal party set on restraining both the economic advantages derived from land and the political influence its owners possessed, especially in the House of Lords. 'We shall stand or fall by the land', was a Liberal declaration in 1906,[218] and Lloyd George three years later denounced the 'selfish and stupid monopoly' of land ownership.[219] He himself as a boy in Wales had grown up in an atmosphere of resentment against the local landowners and was spoiling for a fight. The Lords obliged by giving him one.

The defeated Conservatives had made it clear that they would use their great majority in the House of Lords to check Liberal legislation, and although a trade-union bill had been allowed to pass they had blocked measures concerned with education, plural voting and the licensing of public-houses. The watch-dog of the constitution had become, in Lloyd George's happy phrase, 'Mr Balfour's poodle', and the Liberals were looking for an issue on which to go to the country for a mandate to restrain the poodle's veto on their legislation. Lloyd George presented the issue in the budget of 1909 and the Lords fell into the trap by opposing it: the result was the Parliament Act of 1911, which transformed the veto into a delaying power. As Lloyd George wrote gleefully to his brother, 'never has there been such a delivery of our enemies into our hands since the Syrian Army was stricken with blindness'.[220] The budget was devised not only to raise money for the social services which were being planned, but also to control the development of the land in the interests of all, and it was this second aspect that roused such bitter opposition. Lloyd George's task as Chancellor was no easy one in those early days of modest taxation. The naval rivalry with Germany was beginning to make heavy expenditure on the Fleet necessary, old age pensions had to be provided, on a scale greater than had been anticipated, and, with Churchill, Lloyd George had already decided to introduce a national insurance scheme. The natural corollary to this was such employment on public works as could be devised and there was urgent need for expenditure on the roads, on afforestation and on rural development. To meet these needs would entail the acquisition of land and Lloyd George insisted that the landowners who through development and the exploitation of minerals were gaining so much from the country's industrial expansion should contribute substantially to the relief of poverty and insecurity. Asquith had already in 1907 introduced important changes of policy, making graduations of tax possible by distinguishing between 'earned' and 'unearned' income and imposing a 'supertax' on high levels of estate duty. Lloyd George now extended supertax to the upper income levels and further graduated income-tax, lowering it to 9*d.* for smaller incomes and raising it to 1*s.* 2*d.* for the larger. He also introduced a principle of considerable social significance by bringing in child allowances for small incomes, the allowance being £10, which was increased in 1914 to £20. His aim was not only to meet current needs but to provide a flexible instrument of taxation, fair in its incidence, which could be used to raise larger sums as the needs of defence and social policy increased. Thus, there were also increased taxes on beer and spirits, tobacco, cars and petrol, all of which were to prove capable of expansion in the difficult years ahead on a scale almost unthinkable in 1909. Lastly there were the 'land value duties'. A proportion of the unearned increment on land was to be levied as a duty every time land was sold or leased, and even undeveloped land was to make a contribution. Worse still from the point of view of the landowner, a survey and valuation of the whole country was to be made, a necessary basis for further development of taxation of this kind. The budget was, as Lloyd George said, a war budget, a means of raising money 'to wage implacable warfare against poverty and squalidness',[221] taxing 'the pleasures of the few in order to spare the sorrows of the myriad'.[222] Its immediate effect, however, was to rouse implacable warfare in the country, with a Budget Protest League to organise opposition, and Lloyd George on a glorious stump that began with the famous Limehouse speech of July 1909, in which he denounced the landlords who had sold for housing what were for them 'golden swamps'.[223] From among his opponents he selected for special attention, both as landowners and as members of the House of Lords, the dukes, whom he held up to ridicule: 'Oh these dukes, how they harass us . . . a fully equipped duke costs as much to keep up as two Dreadnoughts and they are just as great a terror and they last longer.'[224] Churchill was not far behind him in idealism or in scorn. The House of Lords he brushed aside as 'an institution absolutely foreign to the spirit of the age . . . a picturesque and fitfully lingering memory',[225] while he explained the purpose of the budget as 'to buttress and fortify the homes of the people'[226]: 'We ought to be able to set up . . . an unbroken bridge or causeway, as it were, along which the whole body of the people may move with . . . security and safety against hazards and misfortunes.'[227]

Despite the opposition, the budget was eventually carried, and the issue of principle between the two Houses of Parliament settled by the Parliament Act. The way was now clear for Lloyd George's most ambitious project, the National Insurance Bill. Of the budget plans all but the land duties established themselves and the war clinched them as part of the country's financial apparatus. The land survey proved a failure, however, and was in the end abandoned. It failed to produce the expanding amount that had been hoped for, and cost almost as much in valuation as it produced: it was eventually abolished in 1920. One unfortunate result it had was a discouragement of house-building: it was one of the elements in the check to housing before 1914. Lloyd George himself, however, never lost his concern for the best development of the land. He had plans in 1914 which were interrupted by the war and in the 20s organised a great Land Campaign to relieve unemployment.

As an instrument of social reform the budget of 1909 was soon to be obliterated by the enormous demands made on the national resources by the war, but except in the matter of the land the principles it established were to provide the spring-board for development, as he had intended. With the yield of income-tax rising from £32 million to £47 million it increased the revenue from some £150 million to nearly £200 million, and made easily possible, therefore, the payments for the new social services, which, beginning with £8,500,000 for old age pensions in 1909-10, were almost £20 million in 1913-14.

## The Liberal Reforms : (5) National Health Insurance

**The German Example**   When introducing the budget Lloyd George had spoken with enthusiasm of the German system of social insurance. Feeling be-tween the two countries was rising and the heavy naval estimates which the bud-get had to cover were dictated by the concern for Britain's security at sea which had produced the costly *Dreadnought*. There were, nevertheless, other aspects of policy in which, Lloyd George insisted, 'we must put ourselves on a level with Germany': 'I hope our competition with Germany will not be in armaments alone'.[228] This was also Churchill's view. 'Thrust a big slice of Bismarckianism over the whole underside of our industrial system', he had urged on Asquith a few months earlier, 'the Minister who will apply to this country the successful ex-periences of Germany in Social Organisation . . . will at least have left a memorial which time will not deface.'[229]

The great insurance scheme of 1911, which the 1909 budget made possible, was, apart from the unique British institution of unemployment insurance, directly in-spired by the German model. As has already been mentioned, Lloyd George was not aware of the insurance proposals of the Majority Report of the Poor Law Commission until his own plans were well advanced. In the summer of 1908, however, he had spent some time in Germany seeing for himself the working of the German insurance system, and his mind had in any case been turned towards insurance as a result of his experience in steering old age pensions through the Commons. The amendments proposed there would have cost, he estimated, some 60 million pounds. How, then, were any further schemes to be financed? 'The aged we have dealt with', he said in a speech at Swansea soon after his re-turn from Germany, 'we are still confronted with the more gigantic task of dealing with the rest—the sick, the infirm, the unemployed, the widows and orphans.'[230] Pensions needed to be supplemented, in particular, by some provision for those

who became ill or incapacitated before pension-age and for the widows and orphans left by those who died prematurely. Yet the cost would be too great to be
borne directly by the State: some contributory scheme had to be devised. Hence
the appeal of German social insurance. Lloyd George returned from Germany, as
he acknowledged, 'tremendously impressed' by what he had seen, especially by
the great improvements that had been effected in the conditions of the people at
small cost to the State. Here was a model for what he wished to do in Britain, and
he sent officials to study it in more detail.

### The Insurance Example—Friendly Societies and Industrial Assurance

There was a model, too, though an inadequate one, in the provision already made
by many people in Britain through trade unions and friendly societies, which has
been mentioned in the previous chapter. The principle of insurance was established and accepted, though it did not go far enough. More than six million people
were covered, it is true, and there were more still involved in the activities of the
collecting societies and in industrial assurance, but if others, again, were improvident or unwilling there were many who were genuinely unable to afford any
regular premiums larger than the few pence required to ensure decent burial. The
friendly societies alone had a quarter of a million lapses every year, and there were
other organisations that frankly covered their benefits from lapsed policies.
Moreover, the friendly societies were not always financially sound and in a position to meet their commitments, while in times of depression the smaller ones
tended to disappear. The societies, Lloyd George said in 1909, had achieved
wonders, but more was needed: 'the community must lend its powerful aid'.[231]
Only half of the working population was insured for sickness benefit, and not all
of these had even the inadequate medical attention that was arranged by societies
on a contract basis. A wide scheme was called for, but as Lloyd George assured the
group of friendly-society representatives whom he consulted after his German
visit, he intended to work through them and merely to develop and extend their
existing service.

### The Impact of Tuberculosis

One particular disease, with serious social
implications, of which Lloyd George made much in presenting his plans, was
tuberculosis, 'the terrible scourge of consumption'[232] from which his father had
died, with its 75,000 deaths a year at this time, one-third of them in the prime of
working life. This dread disease, though, as shown earlier, its incidence had
diminished considerably during the nineteenth century, was a heavy burden on
voluntary insurance: the average length of illness in one great friendly society
for instance, was more than a year. Only some 13,000 beds were available
in the whole country for the institutional treatment that was required and more
were urgently needed. Lloyd George had been impressed by the sanatoria he had
seen in Germany and one of the most valuable, and least controversial, of the

provisions of the Insurance Act was the contribution of £1,500,000 for sanatoria for the use of the whole population, not merely insured persons.

**The Position of the Doctors**     Tuberculosis, however, was not only significant as, in the words used by the Poor Law Commission, 'the most pauperising of all diseases': it was a disease of environment which at the same time called for a long period of skilled attention for the patient. Its treatment therefore linked the nineteenth-century conception of the 'health of towns', which had created the environmental services organised in the Public Health Authorities (themselves largely completed by the Housing and Town Planning Act of 1909), with the twentieth-century conception of personal health services embodied in the medical practitioner with his attendant services of consultant and hospital. Interest was shifting in the first decade of the century from the sanitary official to the G.P. and the shift was revealed by the rise of the medical profession in status and esteem, with a corresponding increase in the influence and authority of the British Medical Association. Already in 1905 the B.M.A. had expressed its concern at the inadequacy of the typical 'contract service' under which so much of the country's doctoring was done for friendly societies, provident associations and sick clubs, and had proposed a Public Medical Service organised by the profession. The Webbs, in the special report on the medical services which they prepared for the Poor Law Commission (and afterwards published as *The State and the Doctor*) similarly deplored the 'scandalously inadequate' return which many doctors received for their 'labours of Sisyphus', and urged the better organisation of medical care, with a unified service. Even before Lloyd George's proposals were known the *British Medical Journal* was suggesting State assistance,[233] and the uneasy debate that was going on in professional circles must be seen against the background of the fact that the total return to the doctors was some 14 millions a year, while no less than three millions more were being spent by the public on 'patent' medicines alone.

**Lloyd George and the Doctors**     Lloyd George seems to have taken no account of the profession's own discussions, and his proposals when they appeared were challenged and seemed likely to be delayed by furious medical opposition, though in the end the 'doctors' revolt' produced such favourable terms that the 1911 Act has been called the general practitioner's Act. Nor did he make any attempt to link the services he was creating with the existing public health services under the Local Government Board. Dislike and distrust of Burns and of the officials he relied on probably played a considerable part in this decision, though within a few years Lloyd George himself was regretting it. The letting slip of an opportunity to create a unified health service, such as the Webbs and the leading Medical Officers advocated, difficult though that would have been, was unfortunate. The social services as they have developed have suffered too much from fragmentation.

**Pressure Groups and 'Approved Societies'**    Lloyd George had to yield much to the doctors, but the most powerful influence he had to contend with came from the business interests in insurance, the collecting societies and industrial insurance companies: he complained cynically himself that everyone seemed to have been at him but the undertakers![234] The work of the American scholar, B. B. Gilbert, who has made the first detailed investigation into the voluminous records of the time, has indeed shown that, whatever its original inspiration, in its final form National Health Insurance was essentially the outcome of pressure-group activity, bearing little resemblance to Lloyd George's first thoughts.[235] This was to some extent unavoidable, for so little was known of the needs and possibilities, of the scale of the interests involved and of the machinery likely to be required. In his determination to achieve something viable Lloyd George had to be prepared both to improvise and to compromise. What eventually emerged was a vast improvisation, shored up by a scheme that represented a compromise between his own determined adaptability, the entrenched strength of the commercial insurance interests, the desperate struggle of the friendly societies to keep going and the unreasoning opposition of the medical profession, all of them exploited by the Conservative Opposition through their angry frustration over the 'People's Budget' and the Parliament Act.

The key problem was that of widows' and orphans' pensions, regarded by both friendly societies and commercial insurance interests as a threat to their death benefit policies. Whether Lloyd George ever seriously considered the payment of a *funeral* benefit, such as he was certainly to favour later,[236] is doubtful, though he was concerned at the vast profits made by the insurance companies out of the provision made by the working class to avoid a pauper funeral.[237] From the point of view of friendly societies and insurance companies, however, any payment on death was unacceptable, whether in a lump sum or by way of a widow's or orphan's pension, and Lloyd George had to yield over pensions. He had not, in fact, realised what was at stake. From the first he had intended to use the friendly societies for the administration of his scheme, and especially for the distribution of insurance benefits, but the pressure of the commercial interests, with their 30 million policies and 80,000 door-to-door collectors, was too great for them to be denied a place. Many of the collectors had their own 'books' on which their livelihood depended, and through their unusually direct contact with their clients, on their very doorsteps, their influence was a political asset of no mean order, or a potential threat. Lloyd George thought at first that 'a few tens of thousands' would buy them out, but discovered to his consternation that many millions would be required. At the moment when serious efforts were being made behind the scenes to overcome the constitutional crisis over the House of Lords he even toyed with the idea of a coalition government to overwhelm the collectors: 'They visit every house, they are indefatigable, they are often very intelligent, and a government which attempted to take over their work without first securing the co-operation of the other Party would inevitably fail.'[238] Without such political defences pensions were impracticable. 'If a scheme of national insurance is taken in hand by any Party Government', Lloyd George was forced to admit, 'it must be confined to invalidity.'[239] So it was that pensions, the original object, disappeared, and national insurance became a matter of sickness benefit. Having won the first round, however, the insurance interests were determined to protect themselves against any possible revival of death benefits of any kind. Sickness benefit could be administered through the friendly societies, as Lloyd George intended, but they also had death benefit interests, which might prejudice the position of the insurance companies, who therefore decided to join in. 'It is our intention to step forward and work this sick business', ran one authoritative statement, 'and a paramount reason for doing so is that thereby we shall most effectually conserve our existing business.'[240]

The man who did most to persuade the insurance interests to this course was their leading advocate, Howard Kingsley Wood, an able insurance solicitor who now first appeared on the political scene and was destined to become a notable figure in the post-war years. 'Slim . . . and innocent-seeming (not being)', was the impression of Kingsley Wood formed by a civil servant deeply involved in the complex negotiations.[241] Lloyd George, to whom this description might also have been applied, consoled himself with the reflection that the companies had to be 'squared' to prepare the way for death benefits later.[242] Kingsley Wood knew better, however: 'We have got L.G. there' (putting his thumb on the desk) 'and shall get our own terms.'[243] The result was the artificial creation of the 'Approved Society', a device destined to last until 1946. Lloyd George seems genuinely to have hoped that the encouragement to the principle of voluntary association would give the friendly societies a new lease of life, and provide in addition most of the administration of national insurance, but the whole scheme rapidly became bureaucratic and mechanical, with the added disadvantage of differences of benefit through different societies. The chief gainers were the insurance interests, which were able to use their position as 'approved societies' for the encouragement of their regular business.

**Planning and Carrying the Act**   The planning and carrying of Part I of the 1911 Act, a measure for which there were no precedents, was a prodigious feat, a triumph for a remarkable band of men, who did not spare themselves in the task —among politicians, Lloyd George himself, Rufus Isaacs (later, Lord Reading; then Attorney-General), C. F. G. Masterman, Under Secretary of State at the Home Office, and Dr C. Addison; among Civil Servants and other advisers, John Anderson, W. J. Braithwaite, J. S. Bradbury, R. Chalmers, Warren Fisher, Arthur Salter, G. M. Young, W. A. Greene and, in the final stages of administrative organisation, R. L. Morant, to name only the principal figures, all of them destined to great things. 'A very exciting time . . . with something of the feeling that one was taking part in a sort of Charge of the Light Brigade' was the apt description of one young enthusiast from the Inland Revenue Department who was called in to help.[244] Nothing quite so vast, so controversial and of such significance had been tackled before. The Conservative publicist J. L. Garvin called it in the *Observer* 'the greatest scheme of social reconstruction ever yet attempted'.[245] The whole project was a triumph for Lloyd George, a classic masterpiece of political management and manœuvre, with 'the Goat', as his officials called him (reasonably enough, in view of certain aspects of his private life), bounding with zest from difficulty to difficulty, and pushing the whole thing through by sheer exuberance and endurance. The demands made on the officials were stupendous, but he was well served, for he had no monopoly of idealism or zeal.

With Part II the Act established new habits of thought and conduct for the country, creating such commonplace institutions of everyday life as the doctor's panel and the insurance stamp. It provided, in the words of its title, 'Insurance against Loss of Health and for the Prevention and Cure of Sickness'. Insurance was covered by the collection of contributions—4*d*. a week from employees, 3*d*. from employers and 2*d*. from the Treasury (Lloyd George's 'ninepence for fourpence')— from all wage-earners (not merely from certain groups as in the case of unemployment insurance) in return for which, with certain variations, 10*s*. a week was paid, together with such items as 30*s*. 'maternity benefit', while medical attention, with medicine, was provided on a 'panel' system (a weekly benefit of 10*s*., rather than the 5*s*. originally intended, had been made possible by the dropping of pensions). The payment of benefit, with such supplements as they could afford, was entrusted to the approved societies. Medical care, after protests from the doctors, who with their memories of contract service refused to be controlled by the societies and wanted free choice of doctor, was put under the supervision of local Insurance Committees, with medical representatives. At the centre were the four Insurance Commissions, one for each part of the kingdom, and a National Health Insurance Joint Committee with Masterman as its first chairman.

In practice the scheme meant little enough in the way of prevention: in fact, despite its title, it proved to be rather a scheme for sickness insurance than one for health, though without a unified health service little more could have been expected. Yet one important innovation, in addition to the grants for sanatoria, was the penny per insured head allowed for research, which made possible the Medical Research Council. No provision was made for consultant or hospital services, however, though Lloyd George was soon planning developments in these directions.

Until a late stage in the preparation of the Bill Lloyd George was undecided as to its fundamental financial structure between the building up of a reserve fund on an actuarially sound basis (which he called 'being virtuous') and the immediate paying out of larger benefits, on the lines of the 'dividing' friendly societies, with their annual adjustments. Eventually he decided on financial respectability and the decision—'the Victorian business man's belated answer to the breakdown of the

Victorian Poor Law', it has ingeniously been called[246]—was decisive for future developments. Such developments Lloyd George himself already saw as necessary—medical treatment for the whole family instead of merely for the wage-earner, increased sickness benefit, pensions at 65 and widows' and orphans' pensions—and all were to come in time, though the first, and most desirable, not until 1946. To him, as has already been suggested, insurance was a necessary but temporary expedient. 'A great social experiment: I never put it higher than that' he said in 1914,[247] and but for the war the following year would have seen a critical enquiry into its working. By many contemporaries insurance was thought of as 'dishing the Webbs'[248] (the phrase was John Burns's), creating an acceptable alternative to their 'national minimum', and Burns even temporarily overcame his dislike of Lloyd George to assure him that National Health Insurance rendered both the Majority and Minority reports unnecessary.[249] Lloyd George himself saw more clearly, as a famous speech at Birmingham testified: 'I have joined the Red Cross. I am in the Ambulance Corps. I am engaged to drive a wagon through the twistings and turnings and ruts of the Parliamentary road.'[250] What might have followed when the ambulance had arrived was suggested in the note to his private secretary quoted earlier, a more thoroughgoing State scheme without the limitations of insurance. The 'ambulance wagon' idea stuck, however, for it chimed well with the prevailing notion of relief for the few rather than organised social assistance for the many. Many years later Ernest Bevin, who had no time for such palliatives, was to dismiss the Beveridge Plan as this 'Social Ambulance Scheme'.[251]

Of twistings and turnings and parliamentary ruts there were many in the months between the Bill's introduction in May 1911 and the Royal Assent in December. The worst opposition, however, came from outside. The Webbs continued to oppose the whole insurance scheme, both for its compulsory nature and because it did nothing to *prevent* sickness or unemployment, while the trade unions objected to any contributions being levied at all. The employers of domestic servants, stimulated by a bitter campaign on the part of the Harmsworth newspapers, were up in arms, and there were frenzied scenes when fashionable ladies voiced their protest at being made to lick stamps. The doctors, disgusted by Lloyd George's scales of remuneration and by his refusal to limit the 'panel' system to the lowest income groups, and ever-suspicious of any threat of lay control, were the most serious objectors and it looked at times as if they would delay the scheme's coming into operation: the country could manage without Lloyd George, but not without them, some of the more extreme boasted. Morant, who as a disciple of the Webbs did not in any case think highly of the scheme, despaired almost to the last. In fact, however, and particularly in the matter of professional freedom, Lloyd George very largely met the doctors' claims, if somewhat belatedly, though there was almost as much suspicion and dislike of him as of another Welshman 35 years later: after a meeting with the B.M.A. he commented wryly that there had been nothing like it since Daniel entered the lions' den. He had paid too little attention to professional susceptibilities, but there was much disunity among doctors and once he had made his concessions he divided and wore down the opposition, winning over from the recalcitrant B.M.A. many who saw the advantages of the scheme for their patients and themselves. One important stroke on Lloyd George's part was the freeing of doctors from friendly society control by placing medical benefit under the local insurance committees, another the separation of those he called the 'swell Doctors' from their humbler colleagues, while in the background he wielded the threat of a rival salaried medical service. The medical part of the scheme duly came into effect on the appointed day in January 1913, and the doctors were actually some of its chief beneficiaries. For many of them there was an immediate doubling of income and their prestige and position in the community were greatly enhanced. Contract service continued, it is true, but in a more acceptable form and without lay control, while the possibilities of private practice actually widened. It was 10 years, however, before the B.M.A. recovered its strength.[252]

'The Grand Achievement'—and After    So began social insurance in Britain, the triumph of the man who made the nation lick stamps, and the first beginnings of a new sense and conception of social organisation and responsibility. It had needed an enormous effort to get it started, but started it was, and Winston Churchill, with all the denunciations and disagreements in mind, hailed it with justifiable satisfaction: 'Beginnings are usually hard . . . but ten years hence all these bickerings will have been forgotten. . . . We shall wonder how we ever could have got on without it, and a younger generation, taking their places in a healthier, happier and more wisely organised society, will thank us for the grand achievement.'[253] Perhaps this was expecting too much, but it expresses the hopeful idealism of the times. The Liberal Government, as Churchill had hoped, had left a memorial that time would not deface. 'Most people', he was to say many years later, 'are unconscious of how much their lives have been shaped by the laws for which Lloyd George was responsible.'[254] Nevertheless, the scheme had been hurried through, and much more remained to be done. Morant, true to the Webb inspiration, was soon considering a consolidation and unification of health services, with more pay for better qualified G.P.s,[255] and Lloyd George made plans for the first improvements in his 1914 budget. War intervened, however, and for several years plans had to be set aside. How much had been hoped for from the new projects is clear in a comment by Christopher Addison, the medical academic, now an M.P., who in 1919 was to take over the new Ministry of Health: 'When one thinks of all our schemes of social reform just set agoing and of those for which plans had been made in this year's Budget, we could weep.'[256] It is well to remember that the inheritance to which the Ministry of Health succeeded was not necessarily what Lloyd George would have created by 1919 had he not been diverted to other and sterner tasks.

*The Liberal Reforms : (6) The Beginnings of the Welfare Services*

**The Problem of the Birth-rate**   Whatever might be said in Part I of the
National Insurance Act of the prevention of illness, and whatever might be hoped
from Part II for the prevention of unemployment, the Act was essentially concerned with relief, or with prevention only in so far as it meant preventing the
individual from being brought to destitution by poor health or industrial depression. In matters of health the preventive services were those of the Medical
Officers of Health, and, as has been seen, National Health Insurance was created
independently of them. Yet there was in these years much concern at the inadequacy of the preventive services and increasing recognition that the nineteenth-
century reforms had left much still to be done. This showed itself particularly in
problems of child health, but was driven home by the unexpected phenomenon
of a steadily falling birth-rate, which seemed to contradict all that Malthus had
taught a century before. The birth-rate had reached its maximum in the 70s at
35 per thousand, but by the end of the century had fallen below 30. In 1905 it
stood at 26, by 1910 at 25. It was a development which in view of imperial
responsibilities, especially the unspectacular but steady emigration to the
Dominions, and of the increase of military power on the Continent, was regarded
with some alarm. In social policy the prospect of fewer children and an ageing
population now began to loom up for the first time. As one M.P. said in a debate in
1905, care for the children was 'good economy and good Imperialism'.

**Infant Mortality**   A particularly disquieting element in the fall of the birth-rate
was the continuance of a high infant mortality. The death-rate as a whole had
fallen from 22 in the 60s to less than 17 by the turn of the century, but the rate
among children in their first year was as high, at over 150, as it had been in the 50s
and had actually risen in recent years: in 1899 it reached 163, the highest recorded
in Britain. The average, of course, concealed wide variations in different parts of
the country. Thus, in 1905, when an improvement had begun to be noticeable,
the variations still ranged from 111 to 212, and Rowntree in his investigations in
York in 1898 had found that even within a single city the variation was from 94
among the better-off to 246 among the very poor.

Conditions were little better among the survivors in the poorer districts. Rowntree showed that a large family was second only to low wages as a cause of extreme
poverty, and the results of poverty and bad conditions were seen in the poor
physique and stamina of many children and young people. Now that all children
were attending school it was possible to see how many lacked adequate food and
clothing, and there were numerous cases of children too enfeebled to study. When
the test of war came in 1899, 40 per cent of the recruits offering themselves
had to be rejected on physical grounds. A few years later, in 1906, the first conference on infant mortality was held in London, and John Burns in addressing it

contrasted the soldiers and policemen of London, most of them countrymen, with the weedy youngsters who stood about idly watching them, 'anaemic, saucy, vulgar, ignorant, cigarette-smoking hooligans'.[257] Yet it was with such as these that the future in part rested. Hence a growing concern in these years with the upbringing of children and conditions in the home which was producing significant results well before 1914. Already children had been withdrawn from factories and forced into schools: it had been tacitly accepted that they were to this extent a responsibility of the whole community and not merely of their parents. Now, however, it was particularly the younger children who were considered, and the older ones in so far as the parents, for whatever reason, failed in their physical care.

**Maternity and Child Welfare**   Care for infants had begun in 1872 with the Infant Life Protection Act, passed to check the dreadful traffic of 'baby-farming': in 1897 it was extended to cover children up to the age of five. 1889 had seen the first Act for the prevention of cruelty to children, stimulated by the formation of the N.S.P.C.C., and the concern for the legal protection of children culminated in the Children Act of 1908, the 'children's charter'. In the 90s the rising infant mortality caused serious alarm, but it was observed by Medical Officers of Health that a high proportion of the deaths was due to diarrhoea in hot weather. The failure was not one of ordinary sanitation, but of personal hygiene in the home and especially of food conditions aggravated by the flies that fed on horse-manure (now no longer a feature of our streets). Sir Arthur Newsholme, who as Chief Medical Officer of Brighton and later at the Local Government Board did much pioneer work in child health, records in his autobiography the significant fact that nearly three-quarters of the cases in Brighton occurred in homes that were not such as to demand action by the sanitary authorities.[258] Clearly the nineteenth century's passion for clean water and surroundings was not enough: the problem was to ensure clean food for babies and intelligence and training in the mothers to use it. It was, that is to say, a social problem, not a task for sanitary inspection. It was from the realisation of this that there developed the Maternity and Child Welfare movement, which owed little to legislative encouragement but began in the concern and enthusiasm of voluntary societies and individual Medical Officers of Health, and was pressed by Newsholme after he had joined the Local Government Board in 1908. Characteristically, it was not until 1914 that any grants in aid of the work were forthcoming from the Board: until then amounts spent from the rates were regularly disallowed by the auditors but passed on appeal, a typical L.G.B. administrative device.

France, faced earlier with a falling birth-rate, had already introduced the provision of clean milk for babies who could not be breast-fed, and her example was much studied in England. The first milk depôt in this country was opened by the local authority at St Helens in 1899. Liverpool followed in 1901 and Battersea, John Burns's home and constituency, in 1902, while Rowntree founded a depôt at York, with the aid of a voluntary society, in 1903. The mere provision of milk, it was soon realised, was not enough: on a subject so bound up with tradition and superstition advice and assistance were needed by the mother. There followed, therefore, the institution of Health Visitors. Such Visitors, organised by a voluntary society, had been active in Manchester since the 60s, but now began to be appointed generally by authorities to advise on infant care. One difficulty was that although the registration of births had long been compulsory there was no method of reporting to the Medical Officer of Health so that he could offer timely help. Huddersfield, which had one of the best organised services of milk depôts and health visiting, overcame the difficulty in 1906 by promoting a Private Act for compulsory notification of births within the borough. This was so successful that in the following year Burns carried through Parliament the Notification of Births Act, giving authorities that desired them similar powers: a further Act in 1915 made notification compulsory throughout the country. The chief advantage of these measures was that it made possible the development of health visiting, but there was no statutory recognition of the developing services until the tardy passage of the Maternity and Child Welfare Act in 1918, by which time the number of Health Visitors in the employment of local authorities amounted to some 3,000.

At the 1906 conference on infant mortality Burns made an eloquent appeal for special care for mothers: 'Concentrate on the mother. What the mother is the children are. Let us glorify, dignify and purify motherhood by every means in our power.'[259] Already, in 1902, a Midwives Act, which became fully operative in 1910, had been passed to improve the standards of midwifery, though it was not until 1914, when Burns had left it, that the Local Government Board was at last prepared to authorise the erection of maternity hospitals by authorities. After 1906, with the growing recognition of the need, came free and cheap meals for poor mothers and 'schools for mothers', later to be known as infant welfare centres, established with the aid of grants from the Board of Education, though not without grumblings from the Local Government Board. In 1911, as part of the Health Insurance scheme, came 'maternity benefits', based on friendly society practice, inadequate though these were to meet the many serious needs of childbirth.

The result of all this activity was a fall in the infant death-rate from 163 per 1,000 in 1899 and 151 in 1901 to 128 in 1905 and 95 in 1912: it has since declined to less than 20, only one-eighth of its level at the beginning of the century. (The rate in industrial areas was inevitably higher than the national average, and the fall there has been all the more striking. In Sheffield, for instance, a peak rate of 202 was reached in 1901: the rate is now around the national average, a significant point in itself.) Maternal mortality also fell, though not so spectacularly until the introduction of the sulphonamides, and is now also only a fraction of what it was in 1900.

**Child Welfare—School Meals**    For older children the decisive event was the presentation in 1904 of the report of the Interdepartmental Committee on Physical

Deterioration. The Committee had been appointed as a result of concern at the statistics on recruiting for the South African War, and its title was evidence of a widespread belief that the race was deteriorating. H. M. Hyndman, in a letter to the *Morning Post* in 1900, however, drew attention to the real reason for the poor physique of many would-be recruits: 'Lack of good food, good clothes and good air in children is the main reason why some 50 per cent of our urban working-class population is unfit to bear arms. Even from the new "Imperialist" point of view this is a serious matter.'[260] The committee found little evidence on earlier conditions to justify the preconceived notion of deterioration, but uncovered enough on the existing unsatisfactory standards of health and physique of many school-children. Its recommendations, though not all were immediately acted on, were pointers to many future developments, and included the more general appointment of Medical Officers of Health, the improvement of standards in food and drink, the regulation of overcrowding and air pollution, attention to infant welfare, the training of schoolgirls in cookery and hygiene, and, of greatest immediate importance, the provision of meals for underfed children and the medical inspection of all children, with special attention to eyes, ears and teeth.

School meals were already being provided in many places, mainly through charitable organisations, but the government refused to give statutory authority, though in the Commons' debate on the report it had shrewdly been argued that feeding hungry children 'was not sham Socialism but real patriotism and general Imperialism'. The Poor Law Committee had not yet been appointed, and it was still possible to argue that if children starved it was only because they were neglected, and that if meals were provided it would be an invitation to employers to keep wages down and to parents to waste their money on drink. The government preferred to rely on charitable provision, but a special committee appointed in 1905 showed how much authorities were in fact co-operating with charitable societies, and when the Liberals took office the Education (Provision of Meals) Act, 1906, was one of their first measures, though forced upon them by pressure inside and outside Parliament.[261] The Act was a cautious one. Authorities were empowered either to make use of voluntary organisation, contributing only for administration, or to provide meals themselves at the cost of a halfpenny rate, with the cost recovered from parents wherever possible. By 1910, when the first report appeared, 96 authorities were levying rates for school meals and the number of meals provided had risen from less than three million to more than nine million: more needy children were being fed in London by the education committee than by the poor law. Voluntary societies, which could hardly cope with the need on this scale, were tending to leave the task to the authorities, and the development was such that in 1914 Lloyd George made provision for meeting half the cost from the Treasury. By this time more than 14 million meals were being provided for 158,000 children, and Lloyd George insisted that Saturdays and holiday periods should be covered, as well as school-days. The Act had required the setting up of 'Children's Care Committees' to look into the circumstances of children needing feeding: in many cases, it was realised, the trouble was not so much lack of food as lack of suitable food, and it was hoped that advice might be given. Taken all in all, the innovation was a hopeful one, a modest preparation for the school meals and school milk of a later period.

**Medical Inspection**   Medical inspections followed in 1907, under the Education (Administrative Provisions) Act of that year. In the early 90s some authorities had appointed school medical advisers, though with limited functions, and the special arrangements authorised for blind and deaf children (1893) and defectives and epileptics (1899) gave them further responsibilities. Now under the stimulus of the Physical Deterioration report the medical inspection of all elementary schoolchildren was arranged. It was infrequent and it was inadequate, treatment being left to the parents, but as the first personal health service to be established by Act of Parliament it marked a great advance, from which there could only be further progress. Within a few years, indeed, it was realised that advice to poor parents to take their children to a doctor was—inevitably—only too often ignored, and in 1912 the Board of Education instituted grants to local education authorities to make treatment possible. This was the real beginning of a school medical service in a full sense, and a revolution had soon occurred in the care and attention given to children.

**Juvenile Employment**   Society was at last recognising its responsibilities to those who were its future and who were as yet incapable of caring for themselves. A natural development from the care of children at school was assistance to them in seeking work on leaving school. Beveridge and both of the Reports of the Poor Law Commission had recognised the evils of the 'blind alley' occupations in which young people were exploited by employers at low wages and dismissed, with no training to assist them, when they were old enough to claim adult wages. When Labour Exchanges were instituted Juvenile Advisory Committees were attached to them, but it was realised that the task was primarily one for the education authorities, and the Choice of Employment Act, 1910, empowered authorities to set up their own Juvenile Employment Bureaux. The two services developed side by side, according to local preference, and when unemployment insurance was introduced some education authorities administered the scheme for insured young people in their area.

**The Children Act, 1908**   To round off the special legislation on behalf of children there came in 1908 the Children Act, a consolidation and development of the existing law that Home Office officials and such interested organisations as the N.S.P.C.C. had been urging for some time. Its champion was Herbert Samuel, now Under-Secretary at the Home Office, who skilfully steered the lengthy Bill, which repealed no fewer than 39 earlier measures, through the Commons. In the previous year, with the Home Secretary, Herbert Gladstone, Samuel had been responsible for the introduction of Borstals, which he himself had named, in preference to the original title of 'Juvenile-Adult Reformatories', after the Kent village where an experimental institution of the kind had been established.[262] At the same time he instituted, on an American model, the Probation service. The Children Act was no less far-reaching and constructive. The scattered earlier legislation concerning infant life protection and cruelty to children was embodied in it and was extended to cover negligence, and it became an offence to allow children to beg or to smoke. For child offenders there were significant innovations. Imprisonment was abolished, remand homes were set up to keep them out of prison while awaiting trial, and, most important of all, they were to be tried in special Juvenile Courts. The emphasis, in fact, was no longer on punishment but on treatment, and care was taken to see that parents were associated with both trial and treatment. The Act was equally a recognition and an embodiment of a new attitude to children that had already been seen in the innovations of 1906 and 1907. Children were now properly regarded as the wards of the community and it was recognised that the community, through its control of the conditions under which they were brought up, was itself to no small extent responsible for what they were—and would be. The Act was a great step forward and was to stand until replaced in its turn by the Children and Young Persons Act of 1933.

## 4 *Contemporary Comment—The Webbs and Churchill*

Here our survey of the great developments of the Edwardian era may well stop. Social provision had come far since 1834. Instead of a concern merely for the destitute, gradually there had grown up a recognition of the need for wider, specialised services for all. The great advances in the material conditions of life made possible by the industrial revolution had not affected all equally, or equally beneficially. To most people, in one way or another, organised society could ensure the advantages of modern civilised living more effectively than the individual could secure them for himself—though this qualification hardly applied, perhaps, to Lloyd George's Dukes. Many, however, could not hope to enjoy the smallest advantages without society's active aid. A society limited to preserving the peace and preventing destitution was now an anachronism. So much more could be done by organisation, and in these early years of the twentieth century was beginning to be done. How much was in fact done and how effective it was in the face of still unsuspected ills we must consider in the next chapter. For the present we may conclude with two quotations, both of them from familiar sources. The first is from the Minority Report of the Poor Law Commission: 'Fifty years hence we shall be looking back with amazement at the helpless and ignorant acquiescence of the governing classes of the United Kingdom, at the opening of the twentieth century, in the constant debasement of character and *physique*, not to mention the perpetual draining away of the nation's wealth that idleness combined with starvation plainly causes.'[263]

Against this stark indictment of Edwardian social conditions, written in 1908, we may set the hopes, the too optimistic, perhaps too easily persuaded hopes, of the reforming section of the governing classes, as expressed by Winston Churchill —in tones that were, nearly 40 years later, to become so familiar to Britons throughout the world—in his election address at Dundee in the same year: 'Humanity will not be cast down. We are going on—swinging bravely forward along the grand high road—and already behind the distant mountains is the promise of the sun.'[264] If this was, indeed, an over-optimistic view of a coming dawn the achievement of the Liberals—that is, in the main of Churchill and Lloyd George themselves—was, as one recent commentator has justly said, 'stupendous'. 'They took the British State into an entirely new field of activity, and although by no means solving the problem of the condition of the people, they settled the lines upon which the eventual solution would be found.'[265] Britain has gone far since 1908 along Churchill's 'grand high road'.

*Note to page 178.* Rising unemployment at this time was also a cause of greater concern in social policy.

*Note to page 180.* Not until 1911 was the full benefit of the new pensions felt, as until then anyone who had recently received poor relief was ineligible. By 1912, however, the number on *outdoor* relief, the most obvious beneficiaries of the pensions, had fallen by 130,000 though as by then the number of pensions being paid had reached 930,000 Lloyd George's comment was more than justified. On the other hand, as might have been expected, the decline among *indoor* paupers, that is, those resident in workhouses and infirmaries, was much less, from something over 60,000 to rather less than 50,000.

*Note to page 195.* The Development and Road Improvement Funds Act, 1909, made funds available for agricultural improvements and road development, with particular regard to 'the general state and prospects of employment', but the requirement seems to have been little regarded, and the principal eventual outcome of the Act was the Road Fund of 1920.

*Note to page 200.* For a valuable examination of the scanty material on the origins of the Poor Law Commission of 1905 see articles in *The Bulletin of the Institute of Historical Research*, November 1969 and November 1971. The evidence for the part played by Walter Long is of particular interest.

# 6 | Between the Wars

## 1 *The Post-War Scene*

When towards the end of 1918 the nation emerged from what Lloyd George in his *War Memoirs* graphically and justly called 'our bloodstained stagger to victory', it was into a new world that it came. It was a new world externally, a world of revolution, of the collapse of traditional systems, a world that looked hopefully towards a new order of international co-operation which would prevent any recurrence of the dreadful disaster of war on a big scale, but that was for the present in a state of economic chaos and, in many places, of social disintegration. It was also a new world internally. The fundamental unity of the British people had stood the unprecedented strain of a conflict for which they had been in every sense unprepared, but social, political and economic conditions had been stirred and shaken as never before, and with them the ideas that underlay them. The country that had begun the war with the inept cry from some of 'business as usual', with a refusal to believe that there could be money enough to carry on the battle for more than a few months, had ended with the first sketch of a totalitarian control of men and resources. Conscription, so long the basis of Continental military power, had at last been imposed, after much fierce political controversy, in 1916, though only for the Services, and had raised the volunteer enrolment of more than four and a half million men to more than seven million. Two and a half million others had laboured at the preparation of war materials: most significant of all, perhaps, three-quarters of a million women had worked among them or in the Services. The coal industry, shipping and the railways had been placed under national control 'for the duration', raw materials had been allocated and food at first controlled and then, in the last nine months, rationed. Vast sums had been borrowed, both at home and abroad, and almost equally vast sums raised by taxation: the budget of 1918 stood at £1,000,000,000, five times the budget of 1914. Yet by contrast with the still greater efforts of 1939–45 all this had been done without forethought, had been forced on the country by the sheer pressure of the demands of the all-out struggle. Thus, for instance, the greater reliance in war finance on loans rather than on the taxation that implied a conscription of wealth; a decision that imposed a heavy strain on the post-war economy and that in the light of the earlier experience was reversed in the Second World War. Lloyd

George's triumph as Prime Minister from 1916 lay simply in the fact that by intuition, backed by native resolution and uninhibited by any concern for the traditional rules and restraints, he had mastered the situation and carried the country through by a whole series of magnificent improvisations. Hence the 'stagger to victory'. It was not totalitarianism as the world was later to know it, but it came as near the total mobilisation of resources as the struggle demanded. Henceforth it would not be possible to maintain that the country could not 'afford' anything it put its mind to. The great debate of the post-war years, with this experience in mind, was to be over the issue whether or not to employ the full resources of the State to grapple with the less bloodstained but hardly less bitter, and certainly more enduring, problems of peace. The break with the past seemed final.

In 1918, though signs of rift began to appear in the previous year, after the first Russian revolution, the nation was still outwardly united as it had never been before, but already by 1919 bitter divisions had appeared and these, widened and deepened by the handling of unemployment, were to set the pattern of the next 20 years. As soon as the war was over there was a demand for the removal of controls. Soldiers wished to return to 'civvy street' no less than manufacturers and traders wanted 'business as usual'. The result was the speeding up of demobilisation and the abolition of all controls during 1919 and 1920. In 1921 the mines and the railways were decontrolled and the Ministries with purely war-time functions wound up. As if to celebrate with bitter irony the return to what Warren Harding in America at this time was calling 'normalcy', employment fell off rapidly during the year. In the early months the number of unemployed rose to more than a million and by the summer it had reached two million: it was not to fall below one million again until full employment was imposed by the war crisis of 1940.

The problems of readjustment to peacetime conditions had been masked by the reconstruction boom of 1919, which had thrust aside the government's careful preparations. Prices rose rapidly to March 1920, when they were nearly three times their pre-war level, and then as rapidly fell when the boom collapsed. Wages followed the same curve, and it was estimated in 1922 that workers had already lost three-quarters of the wage increases they had gained during the war.[1] For those regularly in work real wages thereafter rose slowly, but the economy was not again to be at full stretch or more than nine-tenths of the labour force to be employed. Britain was faced, though few realised it yet, with the problem of the long-term readjustment of her economy to changing international conditions aggravated and accentuated by the strain of war. It seemed impossible, however, that recovery should not come and the expansiveness of the boom years immediately preceding the war be restored. With the shadow of war lifted it was assumed that life in all its aspects could be picked up where the thread had been broken in 1914. Lord Halifax, who had been in his middle 30s during the war, expressed the common attitude of his class and generation in a notable speech at Oxford in

1940, when, looking back at the earlier struggle, he contrasted the spirit of high adventure in which it had been faced with the disillusioned 'set determination' of 1939: 'We in 1914 had been born and grown up in an atmosphere of peace . . . in a world that we then thought was stable and secure. That security was rudely shaken in 1914, but not sufficiently shaken for us to have any serious doubt that it would soon be put right or to think that when the war was over the old life would not return.'[2]

The calm assumption that after all that had happened a return to the old ways was possible was not necessarily evidence of wilful blindness. It reflected a sturdy refusal to see the war as more than a tragic interruption of normal life, especially for those whose recollection after the years of endurance was of a peaceful and comfortable Edwardian world. Once the German menace was out of the way and the immediate stresses of resettlement had been overcome, life could resume its calm progress, with no thought of the further horrors that lay in wait. Hence, for instance, in the field of economics the decision already taken in 1918 to restore the gold standard as soon as practicable, a decision which, given statutory form by the five-year term of the Gold Export Embargo Act of 1920, made further political action necessary no later than 1925. What was not appreciated was not the strain imposed on the domestic economy by the war, which was obvious enough, but the economic changes that had taken place during the war, when foreign customers, for instance, had had to find other sources of supply, and the still greater changes in Britain's export markets that had been taking place for half a century. Realisation of these movements against Britain's international economic standing came only slowly, as a solid residue of permanent unemployment appeared in the industries that had long relied on exports for their prosperity. It came all the more slowly because of the wild optimism of the long-dammed flood of orders of the 1919 boom, which caused resources to be sunk in industrial development that were to prove a heavy burden when, so soon, the slump followed. Its full import was still further delayed, too, by the controversy over war debts and reparations, which was not settled until 1924 and which not only prolonged the uncertainties of the international economic situation but maintained the hopeful fiction that Germany could be made to 'pay for the war'. It was easier to blame the war, and by implication Germany, for the immediate post-war difficulties than to accept the unwelcome fact that Britain's international position was undergoing drastic readjustment, the first signs of which had long been apparent: between 1880 and 1913, for instance, her share of the international export of manufacturers had already fallen from 38 to 27 per cent and by the time that world trade was re-establishing itself in the 20s her share of the total was more than a fifth below what it had been in the pre-war years.[3] Of the old staple industries on which Britain's international economic position had been built up, cotton exports by the late 20s had diminished by nearly one half, wool and coal by nearly one-third and iron and steel by one-tenth.

Moreover, quite apart from long-term readjustments the immediate recovery of most countries was slow. Not until 1925 did the world economy again reach the level of 1913, and by that time irreparable harm had been done in situations rendered unstable by the war. The failure to organise adequate and timely help for those worst hit was an indication of the general belief in a return to normalcy, but with other conditions making for instability it was to have desperate consequences. Particularly unfortunate, as was soon to be acknowledged, was the failure to match the new political barriers created in Europe with the economic adjustments necessary to prevent their acting as obstacles to prosperous development. This background of instability and slow recovery again had its effect on a Britain to which international markets were so important.

The efforts made to remove restrictions and controls, to return to the conditions of 1913, had, therefore, to be pressed harder than had been anticipated, and though they achieved some success they were to be finally frustrated by the great depression that began in 1929. Thereafter governments had to intervene more and more actively: the totalitarian era, foreshadowed by the war, had arrived. In the 20s it had been possible to hope: the 30s as we look back seem a long glissade to catastrophe, though the 40s were to show that some at least of the lessons of post-war reconstruction had been learnt.

National Divisions—the Rise of Labour  For Britain the break with the past did not finally come until 1945. The sense of national unity in 1914–18 was strong, but not complete. The part of all classes in the war effort was recognised, the trade unions were accepted as an essential element in the mobilisation of resources, and six Labour representatives, Arthur Henderson, G. N. Barnes, W. Brace, J. R. Clynes, G. H. Roberts and S. Walsh, became Ministers, the first two being successively in the Cabinet. It was, however, hardly more than solidarity in the face of the enemy. There was not the deep sense of common purpose, the determination this time to see it through to the end, that marked the more profound unity of 1940–5. The division of opinion that remained beneath the surface was revealed only too clearly by reactions to the Russian revolution of March 1917, which took Henderson out of the Cabinet, and was soon to be enlarged and embittered. To the desire to return to pre-war conditions Labour was to oppose a programme of peace and social reform. The Labour party itself was reorganised by Henderson after his breach with Lloyd George, and was reconstituted as a national party, explicitly pledged, for the first time, to Socialism. Only through 'the common ownership of the means of production and the best obtainable system of popular administration and control of each industry and service', it was hopefully, if not altogether lucidly, proclaimed, could 'the full fruits of their industry and the most equitable distribution thereof that may be possible' be assured to 'the producers by hand and brain'. The party's programme, set out in *Labour and the New Social Order*, had been drafted by Sidney Webb and included his 'national minimum' among its aims. With the Liberals deeply divided by the breach between Lloyd George and Asquith, from which their party was never to recover, Labour now stood forward as an alternative government, with a programme in broad outline to inspire and unite the faithful and, for all its actual moderation, to strike consternation in the hearts of opponents. It was a far cry from the days of the Right to Work Bill ten years earlier, but the war had played into Labour's hands, both by its revelation of the power of collective organisation of the nation's resources for a common purpose and through the passing prosperity it had brought to industrial workers. From these, too, sprang the rapid expansion of trade union membership, which rose from some four million in 1914 to six in 1918 and more than eight in 1920, though the depression that followed was to pull it down by nearly half. Behind Labour agitation now lay not merely aspiration but the first realisation of what might be achieved with workers in demand and wages high. The sight of increased earnings, commented a sympathetic observer, 'simply encouraged a hope that after the war, when industry had settled down again, the workers might be able to maintain better homes, and get better meals, and better clothes and better furniture. The broad result of the whole experience was not so much an improvement in the standard of living as the hope of it, and the determination to secure it, after the war.'⁴ Soldiers were less well off but they too had their allowances and pensions: never before had so much money been distributed. Here is a clue to much of the furious striving of the industrial areas in the 20s. Working men had been tantalised by the brief vision of what full employment could achieve and were naturally impatient of arguments against the possibility of its being realised under conditions of peace. Technical progress was to be speeded up in the next 20 years and the comforts and graces of life to be increased and made far more generally available. Yet so many in poverty were to be denied full participation in the world's abundance:

> Can't we give a decent living,
> Don't we see that dangers lurk,
> If we hide the world's abundance
> From those people out of work.

Such were the lines of a young unemployed man of four years' standing in the late 30s.⁵ Others there were at that time, long unemployed, who asked bitterly whether it were only in war that they were wanted, and saw in its approach their only hope of escape from poverty. Twenty years earlier, with the experience of the war years behind them, it was a new order that the supporters of Labour sought in 1918, the new order which Lloyd George had prophesied in 1906 but which the Liberal reforms had not yet carried far enough.

Behind the new Labour party, and distorting most political judgments on all sides in these early years was the shadow of Russia. The second, Bolshevik, revolution in the autumn of 1917 and the formation in the following year of the Russian Socialist Federated Soviet Republic (converted and enlarged in 1923 into the U.S.S.R.) were tremendous events, the true significance of which eluded most contemporaries, enthusiasts and critics alike. The Labour supporter, who had been uneasy at Britain's wartime alliance with Russia, rejoiced in the downfall of Tsarist tyranny and in the democratic aims of the revolution: the more conservative saw rather the new tyranny and the ruthless terror of the Reds. A new element had been introduced into politics, one that threatened a recurrence of the fears and counter-fears stirred by the French Revolution more than a century before. Henceforth proposals for social reform (and much else that was innocuous, including, on occasion, support of the League of Nations[6]) could only too easily be stigmatised as Bolshevik or Communist. The extremists of the Left in Britain were comparatively few, if vociferous, and the Labour party soon saw through the tergiversations of home-grown Communism, but the Soviet experiment and experience were to colour political controversy in the inter-war years and to prove a barrier to the united approach to economic and social problems that might have eased distress and misery.

There was, however, no danger of reaction. Quite apart from the moderation of Conservatism (suitably embodied in the person of its leaders, Andrew Bonar Law and Stanley Baldwin) and the active concern of Conservatives with social policy, the organised strength of the Labour movement was now too great for its claims to be ignored. The Fourth Reform Act, the Representation of the People Act of 1918, had at last established manhood suffrage and given the vote to women, if only at the age of 30. (The Sex Disqualification Removal Act of the following year admitted women to Parliament, and their voting age was lowered to 21 in 1928.) The Act also limited, though it did not abolish, plural voting and thereby brought a little nearer achievement the old radical idea of 'one man, one vote', which was finally realised in 1948: it did, however, abolish the disqualification of voters in receipt of poor relief. The Act increased the electorate from rather more than eight million to over 20 million, and the first election under it was hastily arranged as soon as the war ended. This was the 'coupon election' of December 1918, so called because of the endorsement ('coupon') which was given to those candidates who had uncritically supported Lloyd George and his Conservative allies but was denied to Asquithian Liberals and all but a few Labour M.P.S. Labour was handicapped in the election by its pacifist elements (including Ramsay MacDonald and Snowden) and its Russian sympathies, of which much play was made by opponents, and the moment was in any case hardly one for sober reflection. Lloyd George wanted a mandate and got it. He himself promised 'a country fit for heroes to live in', a pledge on which there was to be much bitter comment in the years ahead, and there was wild talk of hanging the Kaiser and squeezing Germany to recover the cost of the war. As a contemporary recorded sorrowfully, Lloyd George won the election, but lost the world.[7] Like Churchill in 1945, too, he lost his position in the country, though that was not to be clear for two more years. In the event, with his supporters he was returned with five million votes and 484 seats. Labour, which had held 42 seats in the last election, in 1910, gained 59 seats and increased its poll by nearly two million, while the rump of the Liberal party gathered a million and a quarter votes and 26 seats. Henceforth Labour was the official opposition: the new party had arrived and having arrived had to be heard.

**Industrial Disputes** If Russian developments threatened to prejudice Labour's position, no less difficulty was caused in the early post-war years by the long series of industrial disputes, which did not work themselves out until the unhappy episode of the General Strike of 1926, and in the process gave Labour's opponents a good handle against the party. The psychology of strikes is an intriguing study, whether pursued among the strikers or among the general public, and the Labour party was often held responsible, especially in these early days, for disputes the origins of which were deep in the complexities of industrial organisation and development. In fact the war itself had put a stop to a series of strikes which, beginning in 1910, led in 1911 to a widespread railway strike, involved a million and a half men in 1912 and produced 1,500 disputes in 1913 and more than half that number in the seven months of 1914 before war brought industrial peace. This outburst of industrial action before the war was a measure of disappointment at the meagre success of Labour representation in Parliament and of frustration at the Osborne judgment of 1909, which prevented the use of trade-union funds for political activities and was not reversed by Parliament until 1913. But for the war the disputes would probably have reached even more serious proportions, and tension continued throughout the war years, especially on Clydeside. With the return of peace it burst out afresh, with an added edge of Communist emulation. Thus, more than 85 million days were lost in 1921, and there was wild talk of a general strike to impose workers' control, in various forms, on industry, which was countered by the Government's proclamation of a 'state of emergency'. The movement largely died out in 1922, however, discouraged by the onset of depression but to a still larger extent diverted back into political channels by Labour's striking success in the general election of 1922, which gave it more than four million votes and 142 seats. A Labour government seemed only a matter of time and constitutional methods therefore bade fair to achieve democracy also in industry. Yet the 12 years of agitation had left in the minds of many outside the trade-union movement a legacy of suspicion and distrust of industrial action which the half-hearted general strike of 1926 seemed to justify and which was a handicap to the unprejudiced consideration of social problems. Among Labour supporters, too, and especially among the miners, faced as they were with a slump in the demand for coal, these years left a tragic sense of frustration which added to social tension and bitterness and deepened the rift in the country.

**The Two Englands** Rifts there were in the country, not only the obvious rifts of political opposition, as between Conservative and Labour or among the competing sections of the Liberals, but the unhappier divisions caused by ignorance and misunderstanding. Unemployment was the outstanding social problem of the years between the wars, but even at its worst, from 1931 to 1933, unemployment was far from affecting the whole country equally. For those in work, in fact, the 20s and 30s saw steady improvements in conditions. On the average real wages were nine per cent higher in 1929 than they had been in 1913, and if this did not amount to very much the next decade saw a further increase of ten per cent. Prices in 1920 were about three times those of 1913, but they fell throughout the 20s to one-third above 1913 in 1929. The cost of living had then been falling since 1924: it was six per cent down by 1929 and as much as 16 even in 1936, when it was beginning to rise again. In the middle 30s, in fact, real wages were one-fifth higher than they had been in 1924. Part of the explanation of these developments is to be found, especially in the 30s, in the fall of agricultural prices throughout the world, which considerably benefited Britain as a heavy importer of food-stuffs, but there was also a marked increase in the output of industrial workers, due to improvements in manufacturing processes. Over a longer period there had been some improvement in wage-rates, accompanied by shorter working hours, which further contributed to the improvement of living standards. Thus, the *New Survey of London Life and Labour*, undertaken in 1928 by the London School of Economics as a sequel to Charles Booth's great study, estimated an increase in real wages of one-third since the 1880s, despite a shortening of the working day by one hour, and Seebohm Rowntree, in his second survey of York (*Poverty and Progress*) in 1936, found that a similar increase had taken place since his first enquiries in 1899. The number of the insured employed rose from 11 million in 1921–2 to 13 million in 1935–6 and the census of 1931 showed that even in the depths of the depression, with nearly three million unemployed, there were in all occupations, including, of course, those not covered by insurance, only half a million fewer at work than in 1921.

These overall figures covered a multitude of variations, but a true picture of Britain between the wars must show a slowly advancing prosperity as well as grim unemployment and continuing poverty. Keen concern with unemployment in-evitably suggested that it was the one test of national well-being and the touch-stone of every government's success. Hence the warning of a distinguished economist to a former pupil who had become a Minister in the second Labour government of 1929 that if he did not get rid of the regular publication of unem-ployment statistics the statistics themselves would get rid of the government.[8] In truth there were two Englands, divided, apart from the worst years of de-pression in the early 30s, by the fact of hopeful advance as against decline and decay. The one England was that of growing population and new industries, mainly in the Midlands and South-East, the other that of declining industries and decaying communities, largely in the original areas of industrial development in the North and in Wales. The one had all the elements of prosperity, expanding its factories, its housing and its facilities for comfort and enjoyment, and carrying with it a considerable class of those who still lacked their full share of the world's abundance but were easier in their circumstances than ever before. The other covered the areas of heavy and lasting unemployment and the squalid regions of general poverty. The two were symbolised in the ribbons of new housing that stretched out of London in the 30s, contrasted with the grey relics of early industrialisation and the continuing degradation of the slums. Much was said and written in the 30s of the poverty and distress of the other England, but as in the early years of the century, as the Poor Law Commission had noted, active concern was matched by much ignorance and indifference. It was the revelations of evacuation in 1939 and the profound stirrings of national unity in the crisis of 1940 that finally brought the two Englands together and caused even the least discerning to appreciate the worst of which social neglect was capable.

Between the two censuses of 1921 and 1931 the population of England and Wales increased by two million, from almost 38 million to almost 40 million, and an increase of a further million and a half was estimated in 1939. Expansion was, however, unequal. The population of the South-East, for instance, gained more than 600,000 by 1931 and a further million in the 30s, while the North and Wales declined by nearly a million. Unemployment also varied. In 1929 the over-all rate of 10 per cent concealed differences as great as eight per cent between the South-East and North-East and nearly 14 per cent between the South-East and Wales. In 1936, with unemployment at last diminishing, the differences were even greater, nine and 22 per cent.[9] Still more revealing were the variations in the incidence of long-term unemployment, which in 1936 ranged from a half of one per cent in the South-East to more than five per cent in the North-East and 12 in Wales.[10]

**Industrial Change**  The variations in population and employment reflected considerable industrial changes. A whole group of basic industries, on which Britain's position in the international economy had been largely built up, were in decline, and others barely held their own, despite the growth of the industrial population, while there were others which were rapidly expanding. The first category covered a number of industries which, though through the loss of international markets they had had to dispense with a considerable percentage of their labour force between 1924 and the middle 30s, still had a proportion of unemployed above the national average. Among these were coal, the worst hit, with one-third of its men gone, shipbuilding, tin, wool and cotton. Steel, with 10 per cent of unemployment in 1937 as against nearly 50 per cent at the depth of the depression in 1932, was only just holding its own before rearmament began, and chemicals and engineering were expanding only slowly. On the other hand, building, with its labour force increased by half, was booming, as were the new industries, notably electrical equipment and motor engineering.[11] A new industrial pattern, in fact, was taking shape.

Here, in brief, is the evidence for the existence of the two Englands, no longer quite the simple antithesis of Disraeli's 'two nations': in fact it could almost be said, with Ernest Bevin, that there was now a 'third nation' of the unemployed.[12] To the contrast between wealth and poverty was added not only the long-standing dichotomy of skilled and unskilled among the workers themselves but a division among those of comparable standing between different sections of industry and different parts of the country. There was also a political division, for only about a third of the 'producers by hand and by brain', with their families, were supporters of the Labour party. At its best, in the general election of 1929, the Labour party, though it gained a majority in Parliament, polled 8,360,000 votes to the 8,660,000 of the Conservatives and the 5,300,000 of the Liberals. After the débâcle of 1931 the position was almost restored at the next election, in 1935, but it was to be another ten years—with many desperate developments intervening—before there came the substantial break with the past that Lloyd George had anticipated.

The Influence of Labour   The story of the years between the wars is the story of the conversion of the country, not to Socialism, though by 1945 there were more Socialist voters, nearly 12 million, than there had ever been before, but to the general acceptance of a considerable measure of collectivism, tinged with Socialism. The war of 1939–45, and the revelations in its early stages of the continued inadequacy of social provision, clinched the matter, but the 20s and 30s, with their constant preoccupation with social problems, were an enforced education. The 30s, in fact, saw as anxious a search for remedies as the Edwardian years. And in the two decades, even if the Labour party could not have, or hold, national political control, it made itself felt in local government, where, within the limits of what was statutorily possible, much of the most significant practical social work was done. The Labour movement's ideas and practice therefore came to be recognised, if not accepted, and on the Council floor, for all the pleasantries of party strife, political opponents learnt that their rivals were not always as diabolical as they had been painted. Before the end of the 1930s, 60 local authorities were under Labour control and it was in 1934 that, under Herbert Morrison's leadership, the party won its greatest success, with the control of the London County Council. Already, however, in the 20s Labour councillors were forcing the pace in local administration, whether on councils or, until they were abolished in 1929, on boards of guardians. 'One of the brightest results of the growth of the Labour movement', said John Wheatley, who had been Minister of Health in the first Labour government, in the debates on the 1925 Pensions Bill, 'is that the control of the poor has passed into the hands of popular boards of guardians.'[13] Labour councillors had no monopoly of social concern, but in general they were more willing than others to press their legal powers to the limit and less concerned about the cost to the rates. This attitude, from its exemplar in George Lansbury's Poplar, was known as Poplarism, though Wheatley brightly suggested that 'Popularism' would be a more appropriate term.[14] Poplarism was resented by many for its 'extravagance', but there were plenty of non-Labour guardians and councillors up and down the country who were alive to social ills, though they may have been spurred on by Labour colleagues where they were not put off by Labour's limited concern for the rates. What was significant about the practical working of social policy, a notable Labour writer has said, was that it was 'accomplished by consent, and through co-operation'.[15] Co-operation and consent were not always easily achieved, but, if their operation was slow, with the continued need for reform it served to swing opinion in the country in preparation for more ambitious measures.

**Poverty and Plenty**   The tragedy of distress was all the greater because of the abundance of resources which the advance of science and technology and the power of organisation put at the disposal of society. John Burns had once complained of the poverty of the working class's desires, but the desires of all classes became more varied after 1918. Better and more hygienic clothing, better housing, with more water and sanitation, better transport, both private and public, more varied food, electricity in the home, the ubiquitous cinema and radio, all contributed to the ease and comfort of life. Some of these penetrated slowly enough to the areas most in need, but it is difficult to conceive of the dull emptiness of long-term unemployment without the alleviation of radio and cinema: 'Twenty million people are underfed but literally everyone in England has access to a radio,' wrote one observer, 'What we have lost in food we have gained in electricity. Whole sections of the working-class who have been plundered of all they really need are being compensated, in part, by cheap luxuries which mitigate the surface of life.'[16] It was a common complaint that money was spent on more costly luxuries that might have gone to those in need. F. W. Jowett ('Jowett of Bradford') in his address as Chairman of the Labour Party Conference in 1922, complained of the spending of 200 millions every year on 'pleasure motoring,' enough in three years to build the million houses that were needed,[17] but even before the 20s were out a car was a commonplace indulgence for the more secure of the working class. So soon, through technical advance, did scientific wonders seep throughout society. Yet that so much was within reach was an added smart to those in want. J. M. Keynes, feeling his way in 1924 towards the clarification of his views on the social functions of money, deplored the 50 millions invested abroad in the previous six months: 'Surely they cannot maintain that England is a finished job, and that there is nothing in it worth doing on a 5 per cent basis.'[18] One of his remedies was the mass production of houses, with Treasury assistance—a preview of the 'prefabs' of 20 years after—but his own views were not yet fully formed, his influence was not yet felt and the worst of the crisis had not yet come to shake the traditional shibboleths of financial power. In the 30s the Treasury did move cautiously towards a policy of pump-priming, but the experience of the Second World War was needed to drive the lesson home. As Beveridge wrote in 1944, in his study of *Full Employ-*

*ment,* 'the only sovereign remedy yet discovered by democracies for unemployment is total war'.[19] Investment in peace-time was therefore left to go its own way, and it was still an article of faith that money left to the taxpayer would provide employment more readily than if it were diverted, by way of taxation, to the Treasury. Lloyd George showed himself well aware of the limitations imposed by prevalent opinion in his contribution to the Second Reading debate on the Pensions Bill in 1925: 'You have to educate people very gradually up to their taxable capacity... when you are taxing the community you have first of all to carry its conscience and its commonsense with you.'[20]

Conscience and common sense were hardly sufficiently alive in 1925 to the seriousness of the issues involved, and conscience, as Lloyd George neatly observed, 'requires a lot of training where a tax is concerned'. Labour's appeal to conscience and common sense was regarded as confiscatory, not altogether justly, though the wild men of the party had a good deal to answer for, and Lloyd George's own plans, backed though they were by Keynes and other economists, were also suspect. 'Safety First' was the watchword, as in the election of 1929, at least until the convulsions of the 30s and the enormous demands of total war brought conscience and common sense together in the realisation that poverty, even poverty mitigated by social welfare, was intolerable in the midst of plenty.

## 2 *The Post-War Settlement : (1) Unemployment Policy*

To survey at all adequately the working of social policy between the wars would need all the resources of time, money, patience and self-dedication that the Webbs put into the many volumes of their study of English Local Government. Much of the story is in the records of government departments, and published in their annual reports, which provide a wealth of material that simply was not available before 1914 on any comparable scale. Much more is in the records of local government, whence the Webbs drew so much of their knowledge of the actual working of local administration. The balance, however, was shifting in the inter-war years: there was more, and more effective, central administration, there were more Ministries to co-ordinate and control policy. A national pattern began to take shape as it was increasingly realised that only a national policy, even if it were administered with local variations, could grapple with the problems which industrial society had created and revealed. No longer could unemployment and other ills be dismissed as passing strains; the figures were there for all to see, a temperature chart of society's inadequacy and a constant reminder of the need for further effort.

Hitherto our concern has been with the development, out of three centuries of community concern with poverty and under the impact of industrial civilisation, of the beginnings of the social services that together have made up the Welfare State. When the First World War ended, the country was better prepared than ever before to tackle its social problems, but the services which the Liberals had created were still only in their early stages. They provided in any case no *system* of relief or aid, having been developed to meet particular needs and to provide a margin of protection against ills of which the country had in the main been aware for some time. All called for extension and development, as Lloyd George for one was well aware, and all needed equally a long period of steady working to test their efficacy. It had been expected, of course, that a period of readjustment would be needed before normal conditions were restored after the war. What had not been anticipated was that unemployment insurance and the poor law together would face, as the years went by and economic stability did not return, a test of exceptional severity, quite beyond the range of pre-war experience. In the end a fresh approach had to be made in the 30s, an approach that was in fact a pointer to the great reorganisation of the middle 40s. At the same time it came to be appreciated how much of avoidable poverty the services created were still leaving untouched. However much was done it was still inadequate for the need, and the Webbs' case for a national minimum of civilised living was driven home. Beveridge in 1942 took up the lessons that had been learnt and gave them immediate relevance, even as the Liberal legislators 30 years earlier had been moved by the tide of social pity and understanding of need.

The first essential in 1919, apart from the problems of resettlement, was to bring the finances of the existing services into line with the increased cost of living, now double that of 1914. This was done for old age pensions and health insurance in 1919. Unemployment insurance, however, had greater difficulties to face in the change-over from war to peace. As early as 1915 it had been realised that the return of millions of men to normal civilian employment could not be achieved without at least temporary financial help, and a special grant, the 'out of work donation', had therefore been devised, to cover any period of immediate unemployment during resettlement. The original intention had been to confine this to ex-Service men, but in view of the narrow range of unemployment insurance, only slightly enlarged in 1916, it was decided in 1918 to extend the 'donation' to all workers covered by health insurance. Moreover, on the analogy of Service allowances the donation was to include grants for dependants. These were decisive developments. The next step was obviously to broaden the scope of unemployment insurance and, the precedent having been established, to incorporate dependants' allowances in benefit. 1920 therefore saw the creation of a new unemployment insurance scheme, covering all workers except those on the land or in domestic service or the civil service. Dependants' allowances followed in 1921, creating an anomalous situation since they were not at the same time added to sickness benefit under health insurance (nor, despite many criticisms and recommendations, was this done until the whole system was overhauled in 1946).

The enlargement of the scope of unemployment insurance was undertaken at the height of the post-war boom, when economic conditions seemed set fair, but, unfortunately, by the time that it came into operation its whole basis was already being undermined by the rapid increase in unemployment. There had been no time to build up reserves such as might have been created if insurance had been widely extended in 1916, as Beveridge and others had wished, or even in 1918, in place of the costly 'donations'. To preserve the unemployed from the poor law—and the poor law from the heavy strain of unemployment in particularly hard-hit localities—recourse was had to the device of 'uncovenanted' 'extended benefits' (in contrast with 'standard benefits' secured by adequate contributions), which came to be commonly known as 'the dole', a name of ill omen for all who lived through these years. 'Extended benefits' were in fact outdoor relief in a new and slightly less humiliating form. It was hoped, of course—indeed, at first confidently expected—that the uncovenanted aid would in time, as conditions improved, be recovered through renewed insurance contributions. This, however, was in only too many cases not to happen and the temporary extensions of benefit had themselves from time to time to be extended: between 1920 and 1927 a harassed Parliament passed no fewer than a dozen Unemployment Acts (by 1934 the number had risen to 28). After the Blanesburgh Committee of 1925–7 had examined the whole situation, a new Act, based on its recommendations, abolished the distinction between 'standard' and 'extended' benefits and abandoned the pious fiction that 'unconvenanted' payments could be recovered when the recipient was again in work. To meet the needs of those whose claims to benefit based on insurance were now exiguous, it introduced a new, and temporary, 'transitional benefit', but the hope that it would be temporary disappeared in 1930 in the onset of a still greater depression, and with it went equally the hope, anxiously clung to since 1921, that all the needs of unemployment could be met by the principle of insurance. It was this 'transitional benefit' which brought down the second Labour Government in 1931 and which, modified towards the end of that year into 'transitional payments' made by the Public Assistance authorities from Treasury grants with the aid of a 'means test', became, by another Act of 1934, the basis of Unemployment Assistance and therefore of the National Assistance of 1948. From November 1931 'uncovenanted' unemployment benefit, to use the original title, was a direct charge upon national taxation: it was at last recognised that unemployment due to fundamental economic adjustments was not an insurable personal risk, but a national responsibility.

Such were the straits to which unemployment insurance, cautiously inaugurated in 1912 to meet a limited problem of fluctuating employment, was brought by a flood of unfluctuating unemployment such as had never before been experienced. The post-war plans, devised in the light of pre-war experience, had been based on the expectation of no more than four per cent of unemployment, but in fact the over-all rate never fell below ten per cent between 1920 and 1940. Society, unprepared for such a disaster, unorganised to meet it and nervously resisting the demands of the Labour party for a fresh approach, had no remedy to offer until war again took up the slack. Unemployment therefore became the most serious of all social ills, and its dismaying shadow has stretched for many years beyond its virtual abolition. Given the conditions of the times, policy between the wars would probably have gone, in any case, much the way it did, but its lines were laid down between 1918 and 1920, in the out-of-work donation and the system of extended benefits. Ironically enough, the mere fact of the enlargement of unemployment insurance, with the addition of extended benefits, served to maintain wages among the employed and therefore contributed to the division of the country. But for unemployment benefit in all its forms wages must have been forced down. The policies of 1918–20 were, therefore, doubly decisive.

## The Post-War Settlement : (2) Industrial Councils

The Ministry of Labour, to which all the problems of unemployment fell, was a wartime creation, established at the end of 1916 in recognition of the urgent need for the full co-operation of organised labour and in hopeful expectation of improved industrial conditions after the war. To these ends were also devised in 1917 the 'Whitley Councils', joint industrial councils for the regulation of industry, named after J. H. Whitley, Deputy Speaker of the House of Commons, who was responsible for the idea. 1917 was a year of industrial tension. The great wave of pre-war strikes had not been forgotten, and there were, inevitably, many serious difficulties over conditions of wartime employment. A lively movement for workers' control, or at least for the joint control of industry, had been active in the trade unions since before the war and with its spearhead of shop stewards was gaining ground. The outbreak of the Russian Revolution was a further stimulus to agitation. Under these circumstances Whitley devised the 'joint industrial councils', which, though far from becoming as successful or as universal as had been hoped, have not been without their successes, especially in the government service, as pioneer organs of joint consultation. The councils were an expression of confidence in the future of industrial relations and were followed in 1919 by the arrangement of a large National Industrial Conference of employers and workers, but this ambitious development of Whitley's idea faded out in 1921 under the combined influence of suspicion and depression.

## The Post-War Settlement : (3) The Ministry of Health

The immediate post-war years were no less decisive for the health services than for unemployment policy. Before the war began there had already been eager discussions about their development, and Morant, in particular, had hoped to extend medical provision to the families of insured workers and to improve general practice and the hospitals. The Local Government Board, with its preoccupation with the poor law and the sanitary precautions of the local authorities, was recognised to be beyond remedy, and as the war went on opinion grew in favour of the creation of a single Ministry of Health. It was realised that demobilisation would bring many health problems and, as in the South African War, though on a much greater scale, recruiting had thrown a revealing light on the standards of health in the country. 'The combing of the country's manhood', Lloyd George wrote bluntly in his *War Memoirs*, 'had shown up the deplorable physical quality of much of the population.'[21] How much was deplorable was in fact revealed by the records of the examination of conscripts in 1917–18, which were published in 1920 and gave an average of only three men in nine perfectly fit and healthy, with four others in every nine 'almost physical wrecks'. From 1916 a number of 'reconstruction committees' were at work and in the following year a Ministry of Reconstruction was created, with Dr Christopher Addison as Minister. Owing to the hasty abandonment of controls after the war, and the imposition of economy measures, far less came of the Ministry's work than had been hoped, but with Whitley Councils the establishment of a Ministry of Health was one of its firmest interests. Aided by Morant and other enthusiasts Addison struggled to create the new Ministry and eventually, in 1919, it came into existence, with Addison himself as first Minister and Morant as Permanent Secretary. The final stages were speeded by the great influenza epidemic of 1918–19, which underlined the need for a concerted approach to health problems.

The Ministry of Health absorbed the Local Government Board and the Insurance Commissions, kept rigidly apart since 1911, and thus brought together National Health Insurance, the public health work of local authorities, including housing, now, with the return of millions to civilian life, a matter of urgency, and the whole of the poor-law administration, including hospitals and infirmaries. The mixture was an incongruous one and, as a distinguished medical specialist pointed out at the time, called for a superman to direct it, but it was to endure until 1951. Addison had found the Approved Societies opposed to incorporation in the same Ministry as the poor law and it would indeed have been preferable if health could have been handled separately. Yet, given the public health responsibilities of the local authorities and the extensive provision of poor law infirmaries, many of them rendering excellent service by no means only to paupers, as the Commission of 1905–9 had shown, it was not possible to effect a speedy disentanglement. Inevitably, however, the constructive work for health, which needed imaginative handling, tended to suffer, especially after Morant's sudden death, at the age of only 56, in 1920: housing alone, as Morant discovered in his last months, was to prove a serious preoccupation for some years.

**The Maclean Report**   There were hopes, when the Ministry was established, of an early settlement of the issue of poor-law reform which had been left over from the investigations and arguments of pre-war days. Both the reports of 1909 had recognised that the poor law had been seriously modified by the development of preventive services, and the process had gone still further since then. One of the sub-committees of the Ministry of Reconstruction, which, under the chairman-ship of Sir Donald Maclean, a distinguished Asquithian Liberal, included among its members Lord George Hamilton and Beatrice Webb, sought in 1917 to recon-cile the Majority and Minority Reports. Lord George himself had by this time become a convert to the Minority Report[22] and the Maclean Committee's recom-mendations, when they were made known in 1918, were close to it. The poor law was to be abolished and its functions to be handed over to the local authorities to be administered by specialised committees as the Webbs had wanted in 1909, with, however, and the contribution was an original one, special committees for the care of the able-bodied poor. The immediate preoccupations were too great, however, for these recommendations to be put into effect. The new Ministry of Health had first to be established and the urgent tasks of housing and the revision of health insurance given attention. Moreover, in a matter affecting so many interests a period of settled government was essential, and it was some time after the end of the war before that was achieved: in five years there were, in fact, six Ministers of Health. Not until the end of 1924, when Neville Chamberlain took over the Ministry in the second Baldwin administration, was the problem tackled. Early in the following year the House of Commons approved a resolu-tion in favour of the Maclean recommendations. Changes in the poor law and in local government were in any case part of the programme which Chamberlain had set himself, and in 1929, by the Local Government Act, the poor law, not yet abolished though largely broken up among other services, at last passed to the care of the local authorities.

## The Post-War Settlement : (4) National Health Insurance

Despite Morant's hopes health insurance between the wars was to undergo no more modification than was rendered necessary by circumstances. The scheme had originally included all manual workers and such non-manual workers as earned less than £160 a year. The increases in wages and the cost of living caused this limit to be raised to £250 in 1919, and rates of contribution and benefit were also increased. Later, with the persistence of unemployment, special arrangements had to be made so that those unable to maintain their contributions could receive medical attention, and eventually, in 1935, an Unemployment Arrears Fund was created. In 1937 young workers of 14–16 were also brought into the scheme for medical benefits. These were the principal developments of the period, and they left untouched the broad lines of the arrangements made in 1911. At the height of the economy campaign of 1922, and again in 1926, the State's contribution to the insurance fund was reduced until it represented about one-sixth of the cost of benefits and administration, a less generous proportion than in the case of unemployment insurance and pensions. The number covered by health in-surance increased from rather more than 13 million in 1914 to some 20 million, over half of the population above the age of 14, in 1939, but nearly as many dependants were left unprotected and much avoidable illness and distress therefore remained, especially, for instance, among the mothers of young families, who lacked the means to pay readily for medical attention. The scheme was an impressive piece of organisation, but it was organisation for sickness insurance rather than for the positive encouragement of health: in a more statistically-minded age it now seems extraordinary, for instance, that no attempt was ever made to evaluate the sickness returns and draw conclusions on health policy. No improvement was possible, indeed, without a drastic revision of the machinery, and by 1919 this machinery, with its paraphernalia of Approved Societies and its implicit division of the population into 'panel' and 'private' patients of the medical profession, was building up its own vested interests. The Approved Society device, adopted by Lloyd George, with characteristic adroitness, as a means of overcoming opposition to his plans, was neither providing a wholly satisfying system of benefits nor proving the instrument of democratic control which it had been intended to be. There was much criticism, and much grumbling resentment at the suspected inferiority of 'panel' service, neatly hit off by Arnold Bennett's favourite creation, the doctor's maid Elsie, in *Elsie and the Child* (1924): 'you had two voices, one for "them" and their friends and the private patients, and the other for Joe and the tradesmen and the panel patients'. Nevertheless, there was never at any time during the 20 years of peace any case for revision sufficiently drastic or sufficiently well supported in political circles or public opinion to make a change possible. Until the upheaval of the Second World War the pattern laid down in 1911 was therefore to endure, with a kind of *vis inertiae*, sustained by the undoubted, if limited, benefits it conferred, and in part, it may be conjectured, by the public's awe of the medical profession and its almost unquenchable thirst for bottles of medicine. A Royal Commission examined the whole system in 1924–6, and, although unable to produce a unanimous report, gave expression to the general concern at the inadequacies of the service, the lack of specialist, nursing and hospital treatment, the extraordinary anomaly that excluded an insured person's dependants from medical attention and (unlike unemployment insurance) made no allowance for them when granting sickness benefit, and the lack of control of the Approved Societies by their members, which the Minority Report stigmatised as a 'scandal'. The Minority would have swept away the Societies and transferred their functions to the local authorities, while extending benefits to dependants and increasing, with Treasury assistance, the range of medical services.[23] The Majority was more cautious in its approach and recommended no increase of expenditure, feeling that in the existing economic situation 'the State may justifiably turn from searching its conscience to exploring its purse'.[24] It did, however, urge that as soon as financial circumstances made it possible the medical services should be extended and sickness benefit increased to cover dependants. It also looked further ahead to the extension of medical attention to dependants and to the reorganisation of the medical service as part of the public health provision, but regarded both developments as outside the scope of an insurance scheme. Here, of course, it was anticipating the National Health Service of 20 years later. Both Reports stressed the need for a greater co-ordination of the health services, and this, too, was in time to be brought about by the N.H.S.

## The Post-War Settlement : (5) Old Age Pensions

To health insurance, though only as a matter of convenience, was attached in 1925 the contributory scheme for widows', orphans' and old age pensions, introduced by Chamberlain with the support—and, to Chamberlain's irritation, something more than support—of Winston Churchill as Chancellor of the Exchequer. This was an important extension of the existing schemes of national insurance that owed much to second thoughts about old age pensions.

Like health and unemployment insurance payments, pensions had needed in 1919 to be brought into line with the cost of living. A small increase, to 7s. 6d., had been made during the war, but like all others dependent on fixed incomes pensioners had been hard hit and this was generally recognised in the election promises of 1918. A committee was appointed to look into the matter and after it had reported a special Bill was rushed through Parliament in only one day in December 1919. The majority of the committee had recommended an immediate increase of pensions to 10s. without any means test, but although the increase was accepted the Government refused, in view of the financial situation, to do more than slightly adjust the limit on means qualifying for pensions. It did, however, remove the disqualification for receipt of poor-law relief, which had been part of the 1908 Act, and thereby made it possible for the meagre pensions to be augmented in necessitous cases.

**Contributory Pensions**   Lloyd George welcomed the opportunity of providing 'some cheer for poor old people',[25] and, although the increase did no more at the moment than meet the rise in the cost of living, as that fell the new pensions did represent a slight absolute gain. There remained, however, justifiable criticism of the penalising of thrift through the test of means, and in 1924 Philip Snowden, as Chancellor of the Exchequer in the first Labour Government, raised the limit on means other than earnings which were to be taken into account. This was the last modification of the provision for non-contributory pensions. The number involved, already well over 900,000 in 1914, was rising above the million and the cost had risen, with the recent increases, from £14 million in 1914 to more than £25 million. Moreover, it could not fail to go on rising. The percentage of the elderly in the community had increased since 1901 from six to almost eight, while in 30 years, as Churchill was concerned to point out when introducing the 1925 budget, the number of people approaching old age had very nearly doubled. Ominously enough, in the aftermath of a destructive war, the census of 1921 had shown the first fall in the number of those under 15 in the country, which seemed to be faced with the gloomy spectacle of an ageing population supported by a diminishing number of young people. The obsession with the problem of old age, 'the most important, and in some ways the most difficult, of all the problems of social security',[26] as the Beveridge report of 1942 called it, had made its appearance. The result was a change of policy, from non-contributory to contributory pensions, which, with the arguments with which it was supported, was to set the pattern of social security finance even more firmly than had been done in 1911 and to influence decisively the thinking of later periods.

**The Insurance Principle** By 1925 the insurance principle, at first regarded by the Treasury with reserve, had become respectable and accepted. In introducing the new pensions Chamberlain expressed the hope that by providing a substantial basis of security they would encourage people to lay aside more and thereby cultivate 'those virtues of thrift which have done so much for the country in the past'.[27] Security, he said towards the end of his speech, in the lofty tone appropriate to a peroration, would be welcomed by working men all the more 'as won by their efforts and self-sacrifice'.[28] This was very fine, and probably had in it rather more truth than most perorations (one of Lloyd George's brightest comments on politicians as a class was that they should be made to live up to the level of their perorations), but there were sound financial reasons for developing the social services on insurance lines. Social insurance, to quote from the later Beveridge Report, 'implies a pooling of risk.... The term "social insurance" to describe this institution implies both that it is compulsory and that men stand together with their fellows.'[29] Compulsory insurance guaranteed benefit to all who needed the protection which pooling could provide, but which could not be adequately provided without the State's power to compel all those who could benefit to join in and pool their resources and risks to achieve what Churchill hailed as 'the miracles ... of nation-wide insurance'.[30] At the same time, however, it considerably reduced the actual and potential risk to the country's finances from distress. The comparative smallness of the Treasury contribution to health insurance has already been mentioned, and the position in unemployment insurance was similar. Between 1912 and 1923, for instance, the Treasury contributed £31 million to the Unemployment Fund as against £92 million from employers and employees: in the difficult years from 1920 to 1927 the amounts were £83 million and £221 million, respectively. Even 'extended benefit', often thought of as drawn from taxation (hence, in part, the scornful connotations of 'the dole'), was, in fact, largely covered by employers' and employees' contributions, and the total of £31 million in unemployment benefit reached by 1923 compared very favourably with the sum of more than £220 million paid in old age pensions between 1912 and 1923. Here was a strong case for incorporating insurance in any development of social provision.

Lloyd George had always hoped that, as many had demanded in 1908, old age pensions would eventually be paid from the age of 65, not 70. Whatever the case for lowering the age, however, there was still a better one for providing for widows and orphans. Hitherto the accidents of working life—injury, sickness and unemployment—had been dealt with, and there were pensions for old age. There was no help but the poor law, however, when the breadwinner of a family died. 'That is the greatest evil and the greatest need of the present time', said Churchill in presenting the budget of 1925, 'inconceivable waste, degenerating into havoc, takes place whenever a lamentable catastrophe falls upon the otherwise happy, free and prosperous workman's home. Most painful of all is the position of the widow with several young children, left with a few pounds and a few belongings.'[31]

## 3 The Baldwin Government, 1924–9 : Churchill and Chamberlain

**Churchill's Policy**   The need for protection was all the greater since with their dependants the working population numbered no less than 70 per cent of the population. For this great majority Churchill now hoped to provide 'security against exceptional misfortune' as part of the reconsolidation of a stable British economy which seemed possible in 1925 with the return to the gold standard which was announced in the same budget speech. This security would be labour's share in economic stabilisation. The employer would receive his in the form of tax reliefs to encourage him in enterprise.

Such was Churchill's programme for the return to 'normal' conditions and the resumption of pre-war social developments. The attempt to put the clock back to 1914, which was symbolised by the return to gold and the determination to 'look the dollar in the face', was not undertaken (despite Churchill's later view that he was misled) without full knowledge of the difficulties it might entail. Yet it certainly overestimated Britain's ability to adjust her economy to the new conditions, even as it underestimated the deflationary effect on wages and employment. 'You have got to go back', was the view of one of Churchill's advisers, 'but it will be hell', and hell it was immediately for the already strained coal industry. The tragedy was that no precautions were taken to ease the shock to the exporting industries: it was a political blunder that told heavily against Baldwin and Churchill, though of a piece with the decision to return to those 'normal' conditions which had, in fact, ceased many years since to be possible. The long and bitter coal strike that followed, with the interlude of the abortive General Strike, made things no easier, and before the possibilities of readjustment, if they existed at all, could be properly tested the great crash of 1929 had occurred, and Churchill's experiment in reconstruction had failed.[32]

**Baldwin and Reconciliation**   If such was Churchill's programme, such also as expressed in the new pension proposals was the modest social idealism of the administration which Baldwin had formed late in 1924 with the declared object of reconciling the bitter differences in the country and restoring orderly progress. For all his limitations, and however imperfectly it was realised, Baldwin's aim, in his own later phrase, was 'the healing of the nation'. 'Give peace in our time, O Lord' were the closing words of a speech in the Commons in March 1925, in which he appealed to his party, victorious in the election of 1924, not to press their advantage too hard.[33] (The King had made the same point to him on his appointment in November.[34]) It was a speech that made a great impression at the time, 'the speech of his life', Leopold Amery, then Colonial Secretary, has called it in his memoirs,[35] though its effect was soon to be lost in the bitter memories of 1926. A few weeks earlier Baldwin had set his purpose before his constituents in Worcestershire: 'There is only one thing which I feel is worth giving one's whole strength to, and that is the binding together of all classes of our people in an effort to make life in this country better in every sense of the word. That is the main end and object of my life in politics.'[36] He undoubtedly hoped by moderation and the encouragement of social reform to quell the zeal of the Labour party for stronger measures. His outlook, however, was too narrowly political: he does not seem to have grasped that the driving force of Labour policy was less in the parliamentary battle or revolutionary doctrine than in economic distress and discontent. Hence his failure to follow up sufficiently magnanimously the defeat of the General Strike or to grapple more determinedly with unemployment. He was, however, far ahead of many of his followers in the appreciation of the Labour party's position, and he realised that it must eventually take office again, with more strength than in 1924.

**Neville Chamberlain**  Neville Chamberlain, in many respects a far more able man, had a narrower vision, and was entirely lacking in the gift for simple but felicitous expression which betrayed the sensitivity behind Baldwin's bucolic exterior. In manner 'glacial rather than genial',[37] giving the impression, one political opponent, Henry Snell, suggested, that he had been 'weaned on a pickle',[38] Chamberlain brought to politics a practical business-like approach, which yet aimed at an organisation and consolidation of social care and administration which would 'set on an unshakeable foundation a triple partnership between the State, the employer and the worker, to ensure against all the giant ills that flesh is heir to.'[39] This was a vision more substantial, if less alluring, than any Baldwin could adumbrate, despite his claims to the Labour Opposition in earlier days, 'There are men on this side of the Houses as well . . . who dream dreams and hope to see their dreams take practical shape'.[40] Unfortunately Chamberlain's idealism was locked up in himself: as one historian has said of him, in a characteristically trenchant phrase, 'Chamberlain sounded mean, even when he was conferring benefits'.[41] A great administrator, he lacked the sensitive, inspired touch and shrank from anything spectacular which might grip the imagination: hence, for instance, his cool reception of a plan of Churchill's for a grandiose campaign for housing,[42] and his later firmness in keeping him at arm's length when his services were more than ever required. Further, Chamberlain relied too much, as he showed disastrously at the end of his career, on narrow personal ties. It had indeed long been said of him that he confused the direction of a Department of State with the efficient running of a civic administration by a mayor and a town clerk,[43] and Lloyd George, whose dislike of him was of long standing, scathingly dismissed him as 'a retail mind in a wholesale business'.[44] Chamberlain himself frankly acknowledged a preference for administration over 'the game of politics'.[45] This attitude stood him in bad stead in the House of Commons and it is extraordinary that a man so devoted abroad to appeasement (in the earlier, non-pejorative, sense of the word) should, unlike Baldwin, have made so little effort to appease the political opposition in Britain. 'Sloppy sentimentality' was his phrase for any such attempt,[46] and with characteristic candour he recorded a rebuke from Baldwin for his attitude in the Commons: 'Stanley begged me to remember that I was addressing a meeting of gentlemen. I always gave him the impression, he said . . . that I looked on the Labour party as dirt.'[47]

**Contributory Pensions** When he took office in 1924 Chamberlain had planned an ambitious programme of legislation touching the poor law, local government, pensions, public health, housing, health insurance, food and drugs and smoke abatement. The possibility of lowering the pension age to 65 and extending the scheme to cover widows and orphans had been explored in official circles since 1923, and there was constant pressure to do something, at long last, about the poor law. Necessary changes in local government were tied up with the idea of relief to the poorer authorities through a modest system of block grants. The other matters were largely consolidations or tidyings of existing law. It was a stiff programme, 25 measures, of which 21 were actually carried, an achievement which, as Harold Macmillan, then a young M.P., has recorded, the troubles of later years should not be allowed to obscure.[48] One reform which he advocated (and which was endorsed by the Royal Commission on National Health Insurance), the abolition of the local Insurance Committees and the absorption of their functions by the local authorities, a first step in the rationalisation of the health services, was, however, not to be achieved.

The new pension scheme was tackled first. Churchill was anxious to reduce taxation to relieve industry, and pensions would 'balance the benefits by doing something for the working classes'.[49] The budget of 1925 duly lowered taxes to encourage enterprise, though at the same time, and quite logically, it increased the death duties on the results of past enterprise, and it made provision for the financing of the contributory pension scheme, which, since it was to come into operation at once, before any reserves had been built up, required an annual subsidy from the Treasury. For some time there had been in Parliament a campaign for a single insurance scheme, linking health and unemployment insurance and developing them. Chamberlain was unable to go so far, owing to the impracticability of combining the employment exchanges which administered unemployment insurance with the approved societies in health insurance[50] (a problem which was to disappear with the societies themselves in the very different circumstances of 1948), but he linked the new pension scheme with health insurance. Everyone covered by health insurance was immediately qualified for full benefits under the new scheme, and to the health contribution was now to be added, on the same card, 9d. a week for men and 4½d. for women, shared equally between employer and employed, in return for which there would be coverage for widows' pensions at 10s., orphans' pensions at 7s. 6d. and old age pensions at 10s. between the ages of 65 and 70 with no test of means or reduction for existing income. Beyond the age of 70 the same pension would continue, on the same terms, but technically under the old, non-contributory, scheme. To spare the Treasury at the beginning, old age pensions would not start until 1928, but the other benefits would be available in 1926. Chamberlain did not claim that the benefits were adequate, but argued that they were as large as the national finances would stand, and that they provided a reasonable basis for personal saving and industrial pension schemes. All who became contributors from the beginning at the age of 16 would eventually contribute enough to cover their own benefits, with the exception of their pensions after 70, for which they would pay only one-fifth of the cost. After 1956, however, new entrants would cover all their own benefits. In the meantime the State would have to meet the cost of benefits for those who hitherto had paid only health insurance contributions and the cost would increase as the number retiring increased: it would, in fact, amount eventually to £20 million a year and would be spread out as a permanent charge. To help to meet this rising cost weekly contributions would be increased by 2d. in 1936, 1946 and 1956. (The increase was made in 1936, but by 1946, of course, other developments had supervened.)

Such was the Chamberlain–Churchill rounding off of the great insurance plan of 1911. It completed, Chamberlain claimed, 'the circle of security for the worker',[51] and though it excluded people of limited means who were outside the scope of health and unemployment insurance he hoped in time to bring them in as 'voluntary contributors': this was in fact done in 1937, when the 'Black-coated Workers' Act', as it was popularly called, was passed. On the face of it the new scheme was a generous one, but its cost to the Treasury was not large. Churchill tried to sell it by going one better than Lloyd George's '9d. for 4d.': for 4d., he claimed, a contributor aged 20 would get benefits worth, actuarially, more than 1s.,[52] though he did not, and could not, claim that the difference necessarily came from the Treasury. They were, however, better terms than any private insurance scheme could provide and represented, as we shall see, some degree of transfer of wealth. A rising young Labour economist, Hugh Dalton, pointed out, however, that if taxation had not been reduced the pensions could have been doubled without any increase in contributions,[53] and Labour criticism fastened on the small contribution that taxation would make to benefits, especially in the long run. George Lansbury even argued that Chamberlain had gone back on the

Elizabethan poor law by shifting the burden, through insurance, from the community to the individual.[54] Lloyd George was more encouraging. He welcomed the provision for widows and orphans as an addition to his own scheme of 1911, which only the scale and unfamiliarity of the proposals for health and unemployment insurance had prevented his including then,[55] and though he deprecated the failure to go yet further and include another much-needed aspect of insurance, benefit for funeral expenses, he congratulated Churchill on his share in the plans as the product of 'an ingenious, resourceful and exceedingly audacious mind'.[56]

A Transfer of Wealth?   By 1937, immediately before voluntary contributors were admitted, more than 20 million people were insured under the Act of 1925, and more than three million were receiving benefit, nearly two million of them being old age pensioners of 65 and upwards. Contributions amounted to £32 million, expenditure to £72 million (old age pension 65-70, £20 million; over 70, £27 million; widows' and orphans' pensions, £23 million, the rest of the cost being accounted for by administration) together with £16 million for the original non-contributory old age pensions, which were now, with natural wastage through death, diminishing every year. At the same time contributions for unemployment insurance amounted to some £41 million and benefits to £35 million, while £37 million were paid in addition in unemployment assistance and £25 million in public assistance (as the poor law had been named since 1930). How much all this, with such other services as education, reflected a redistribution of resources through taxation is not easily estimated, as much depends on the income groups and services included. In 1937 all those with incomes below £250 paid £14 million in direct taxation, £407 million in indirect and £57 million in social insurance contributions, and it has been calculated, in a well-known estimate, that there was a transference of wealth to them in services of the order of £200–250 million.[57] This, while considerable, represented no more, for instance, than the amount by which the total national income could have been increased had unemployment been reduced by half.[58] Put another way, in 1913 the working classes contributed in taxation more than the cost of the services from which they directly benefited, in 1925 86 per cent of the cost, in 1935 79 per cent.[59]

Effective though the services were, within their limits, by the middle 30s, there was still, as we shall see later, much distress and want in the country, if no more, as the Beveridge Report later suggested, than could have been overcome by a redistribution of income within the working classes themselves.[60] It had, however, been shown that a more direct and constructive policy of social welfare was required. The great projects of 1911 and 1925, ambitious though they were in their scope, had not provided the full 'circle of security' of Chamberlain's phrase. Moreover, although they had resulted in some redistribution of income, that had not been done by deliberate policy, but was an incidental result of the development of the social services, due very largely to the carefully constructed system of progressive taxation of the country.[61]

**Insurance and Social Policy**   There was more in the 1925 pension scheme, however, than an incidental redistribution of income. By putting the increasing cost of old age pensions on a contributory basis it materially reduced the pressure on taxation for the future and set the pattern for the financing of social policy. The Beveridge Report, in its discussion of 'the problem of age', laid such stress on the increasing cost that it proposed a 20-year period of transition before full pensions were paid, on the grounds that 'it is dangerous to be in any way lavish to old age, until adequate provision has been assured for all other vital needs'.[62] This proposal was a considerable enlargement of the short delay of three years imposed in 1925 before the payment of contributory old age pensions began, and was not, in fact, accepted after 1942. Beveridge, however, regarded it as axiomatic that insurance contributions should be paid for a minimum pension, to which the contributor could add, as Chamberlain had intended, from his own savings or through a professional or industrial pension scheme. The question inevitably arises whether insurance is appropriate for old age, which is the common fate and not a personal accident or risk like unemployment or illness or bereavement.[63] A man if he lives will draw his pension, but he may go all through his life without receiving unemployment or sickness benefit. Old age, therefore, is hardly a risk to be 'pooled', and there is much to be said for putting the provision for it, like children's allowances since 1945, on to general taxation, as was done in 1908, leaving any supplementation to individual choice through insurance. The community responsibility was, in fact, recognised when 'supplementary pensions' were introduced in 1940 and continues to be recognised to the extent that the Ministry of Social Security supplements pensions. Since 1945, with the passing of the spectre of unemployment, provision for old age has certainly dominated the social welfare scene, as the increasing number and range of private pension schemes and the new public provision since 1959 bear witness, as well as the agitation inspired by the revelation of the inadequacy of existing pensions.

There is a further point that has to be made about the significant developments of 1925. By putting the emphasis on the flat-rate contribution, which, whatever its moral value, is a regressive form of tax, Chamberlain and Churchill cut across the progressive nature of British taxation. The results have been seen in recent years in the burden of insurance contributions upon the lower-paid worker and in the discouragement to work and the evasions of insurance, especially to be found among part-time women workers. The National Insurance Act of 1959, with its graduated contributions, represented an attempt at a new approach. In 1925 it was estimated that 30 years hence, when the insurance scheme should enter the stage which would end in its paying for itself, the Treasury would contribute £75 million to its working. In fact, the excess cost to the Treasury in 1956 of the much wider scheme then in existence was £30 million,[64] equivalent at 1925 prices to some £14 million. Such were the ultimate effects of the contributory principle.

## The Baldwin Government, 1924-9 : Unemployment and Relief

The extension of pensions, however desirable, had little relevance to the outstanding problem of the period, unemployment. Not until 1928 was the hopelessness of the situation formally recognised. In that year the Industrial Transference Board, appointed to help men to move out of the worst-hit areas, reported that it must 'quite unflinchingly' be recognised that conditions in some industries, and particularly in coal, would never again be what they were before the war. Long before this, however, the pressure of unemployment upon the Insurance Fund—and upon the poor law in the case of men with heavy family responsibilities or men whose claims even to 'extended benefit' had failed—was causing concern. Before the war the number of able-bodied men applying for relief had fallen and the very phrase 'able-bodied' had disappeared from the poor-law regulations. The total number of people on relief in 1914 was something over half a million. It fell during the war, but only to rise again, with the unemployment figures, in 1921 to a million and a half, and it remained over the million throughout the 20s, with a temporary increase to two and a half million during the General Strike in 1926. The total cost of poor relief during these years was some £150 million, but the burden was not evenly spread, only some 34 of the 631 Poor Law Unions in England and Wales being seriously affected. These were Unions in the areas of coal, heavy industry and textiles which were suffering from the loss of export markets. They contained three-quarters of the able-bodied men on relief, most of them unemployed men who had exhausted their extended benefits.

**The Financial Burden of Unemployment**    The burden on particular Unions was extremely heavy, and policy and rates of relief varied greatly between different parts. The rates levied also varied, from a few pence in the pound in the more prosperous areas to 10s.–15s. in the regions of heavy unemployment. Chamberlain in 1928 cited the Blackpool rate of 5d. and the Gateshead one of 10s. 5d. as examples of the range,[65] but in South Wales and the North-East more than 20s. in the pound was soon to be levied. In the middle 30s, when the financial burden of unemployment had to some extent been eased and conditions were in any case beginning to improve, although Gateshead's rate had fallen to 8s. 8d. Merthyr's still stood at 15s. and Blackpool's had risen to only 7d. There was obvious injustice in the fact that the heaviest rates had to be levied in the poorest and worst-hit centres, and it was to call attention to this fact, and to secure more assistance for Poplar from the other London boroughs, that Lansbury and the majority of his colleagues on the Poplar Council refused in 1921 to levy rates for the general purposes of the L.C.C., and were in due course imprisoned for contempt of court.

Although they had to clear their contempt, which was done by a special meeting of the Council held in Brixton prison, they won their point, and special regulations were made under which Poplar benefited to the extent of some £300,000 a year. Other authorities were less fortunate, however, having no wealthy neighbours on whom to draw. Money had to be borrowed, and this invited the exercise of the Ministry of Health's investigatory powers. In many areas, despite the inheritance of 'tests' of willingness to work, the numbers involved were so large that out-relief was given without any labour test or 'offer of the house', and 'relief scales' were drawn up, often based, for convenience, on unemployment benefit and allowances, inadequate though these were. Pre-war regulations had required that out-relief should not be given to able-bodied men except under conditions of urgent necessity and that the relief given should be such that the recipient was 'sufficiently fed, clothed and lodged'. With large numbers to provide for, anything but general out-relief was impossible in many areas, especially where families were involved, and the regulation permitting such relief on plea of urgent necessity was regularly invoked for years, without effective protest from the Ministry. The main problem, indeed, was as to the scale of help to be given and the means by which the necessary funds could be raised. A Ministry circular in 1921 required that relief should be 'on a lower scale than the earnings of the independent workman'. The advance on the standard of the 'lowest paid independent labourer', which had been imposed as a basis in 1834, perhaps represented some gain, but was small consolation to a man with a large family, who, having been earning reasonable wages during and immediately after the war, found himself, for no reason that he could fathom, reduced below the economic level of an unskilled labourer. Such a man, accustomed to the idea of honourable payments from public funds through social insurance, war-time maintenance grants, war pensions and the 'out of work donations' ('the golden showers', as the Webbs described them[66]), was far less unwilling than his predecessors to apply for relief. As an unemployed man in the Rhondda declared, 'I can remember the days when it was thought shame to accept poor relief. Now there's so many do it that there's nothing to it, and as far as I can hear, it all comes from the same place as the dole anyhow.'[67]

This was said in the middle 30s, when with the introduction of 'unemployment assistance' much of the help given to the unemployed was coming from national rather than, as in the case of the poor law, from local funds. It was still not quite true to say that 'it all comes from the same place', but to a man without hope of finding work the distinction between unemployment assistance from taxation after 1934, with a small contribution from the rates, the 'transitional payments' made from 1931 to 1934 through the poor-law authorities but paid for by the Treasury, and the poor law based on local rates (with supplementation from national taxation through Treasury grants to local authorities) was rather too nice to be grasped. Men who felt keenly their right to a livelihood were hardly more aware earlier, in the 20s, of the distinction between 'extended benefit' (the dole) paid by the State and poor relief from the guardians, except in so far as they had to be claimed from different places. Not unnaturally relief had already come to be regarded as a just due, though those who had to apply for it were as resentful as their fathers and grandfathers had been of the 'institution' or 'labour tests', and regarded them with no less horror. Yet there was no guarantee that when a man claimed relief it would provide him and his family with sufficient food, clothing and housing, however much might be done for his children, for instance, by way of school meals and gifts of boots and clothes. Often enough, too, where unemployment benefit was drawn it had to be supplemented by poor relief, unless the family were fortunate enough to possess other resources. Where there were resources, they were usually the result of war-time industrial prosperity— and disappeared even more speedily than they had come.

**Tightening Control** Under these circumstances there was for some years a minimum of central control, and the guardians pursued their statutory duty to relieve the poor according to their best lights, within the limits permitted by the official regulations, which were often stretched beyond their limits. In truth, unemployment was a problem beyond the power of the poor law to relieve. The tragedy was that the urgent necessity continued for so long, despite all the hopes that the blight would soon lift. Eventually, in 1926, the Ministry decided that the time had come to call a halt. There had been many complaints of laxity, and even of corruption, among guardians, inspectors had reported excessive leniency and ratepayers had demanded economy. The defeat of the General Strike, which brought to an end a long period of industrial tension, and the general policy of a return to normal conditions that was adopted by Baldwin's government, equally suggested a return to stricter administration. Guardians were encouraged, and if necessary warned, to examine claims more closely, to refuse help to single men, to continue relief to families only if the husband and father would enter the institution. This last device, though not commonly resorted to, meant in effect the break-up of the family, and was bitterly resented where it was adopted. A more reasonable requirement was the undertaking of some form of training, if only to preserve employability. Many guardians had long been attempting this, but could make little headway on their own.

Where guardians could levy adequate rates and made a show of keeping within the regulations, there was little that the Ministry could do, except apply rigorous auditing of their accounts. Where, however, money had to be borrowed, the Minister's consent was required, and could be withheld, in which case the guardians were unable to continue their functions. To meet such a contingency Chamberlain carried in 1926 the Board of Guardians (Default) Act, which empowered him to replace the elected guardians by nominees of his own, and this extreme treatment was resorted to in three instances, at West Ham, Chester-le-Street and Bedwellty, all three of them areas of high unemployment. Elsewhere there was a general tightening of administration, though where relief was refused, or an 'offer of the house' was rejected, little or no attempt was ever made to ascertain how the distressed family, if it were genuinely in distress, was managing. 'After care' was no part of poor-law provision, though it was more conspicuous in private charity, which was active enough in these years, even if its task were sisyphean.

The call for stricter administration, together with a gradual recovery from the effects of the troubles of 1926, brought the total number of people on relief from nearly a million and a half in 1927 to a million and a quarter in 1928, including some 100,000 unemployed men and their dependants, representing a not particularly impressive reduction of some 30,000. At that point the number was affected by the introduction of transitional benefit under the Unemployment Act of 1927, since many who had hitherto been on relief now qualified for benefit under the new unemployment regulations. The amount of poor relief provided to unemployed men fell from over £5 million in 1928 to £4 million in 1929 and £3 million in 1930. In 1931 the number involved was 60,000, of whom half were drawing both unemployment benefit and poor relief. With many years of this heavy burden of unemployment upon them, however, constant meetings to deal with the unceasing applications for relief, struggles to raise adequate funds and pressure from the Ministry of Health for strict attention to regulations, it is no wonder that in the end guardians in the hard-pressed areas urged upon the government the necessity for a national policy for the relief of unemployment.

## The Baldwin Government, 1924–9 : Chamberlain and Local Government Reform

Chamberlain eventually came to this opinion himself, even before it was adopted by the Royal Commission on Unemployment of 1931–2. In the middle 20s, however, when it was still believed that the situation must soon improve, his concern was rather with the enlargement of the areas of local government, including the poor-law unions, in order to increase their efficiency and resources. The local government boundaries and areas had remained untouched since 1888 and 1894, despite all the growth of population, the changes in its concentration that had taken place and the great developments in transport. The services provided by the authorities had expanded, and many of the smaller authorities lacked the population and resources for their efficient working, while where adequate services did exist there was a good deal of duplication and overlapping. This was particularly true in the health services, where local authorities might be short of hospital accommodation and yet have poor-law infirmaries standing nearby half empty or turned, to ensure their full use, into classic illustrations of the old trouble of the 'general mixed workhouse'. Chamberlain cited such an instance in the Commons, an institution in which seven cases of illness were jumbled with 35 of infirmity and senility, eight of lunacy and 27 of mental deficiency, with one fit man and three children thrown in for good measure.[68]

A reform of local government was overdue and there were the recommendations of the Maclean Committee of 1918, not forgotten, though still awaiting attention, to suggest methods. The strain of unemployment, unequal in its incidence through-out the country, made the case for reform even greater. Moreover, there were local authority services, such as roads and health, which needed encouragement, while the basis of Treasury grant-aid called for revision to remove the anomaly that gave the largest grants to the wealthiest areas. Chamberlain wished to experi-ment with a system of block grants, assessed on local needs and regularly revised. His desire to reform the poor law administration, which meant sweeping away the guardians, caused some consternation in the Government, however, and he was able to carry it only in association with a wider scheme of Churchill's.[69] Churchill wished to stimulate industrial recovery by reducing industry's contribution to local rates through 'derating', the lowering of rating assessments, and this would inevitably entail compensating Treasury grants to local authorities. All Chamber-lain's instincts were against so sweeping a measure of Treasury intervention in local affairs, which seemed to him 'fantastic',[70] and he had serious thoughts of resignation. He was eventually compelled to agree, however, as Churchill, that 'brilliant, erratic creature',[71] held the purse-strings for poor-law reform, though he managed to achieve a compromise. Out of a long struggle, the climax of several years of discussion and consultation, there emerged the great Local Government Act of 1929, the Act which introduced derating and block grants and at last began the reorganisation of the poor law. (See note, page 290.)

**The Passing of the Poor-Law Guardians**    The essence of the Act was the creation of rather fewer but larger authorities and the concentration of major services under the County Councils and County Boroughs. Eventually nearly 400 small authorities were abolished, but the most significant immediate result of the Act was the disappearance of the boards of guardians. The boards, which were within five years of their centenary, were swept away and their powers and duties handed over to the County Councils and County Boroughs, which were required to establish special committees to administer them. It there-fore became possible to spread the cost of relief over much wider areas and to pro-vide more efficient services by using scattered institutions to the best advantage. To mark the change, and to inculcate a new spirit, the poor-law service was re-named Public Assistance, and the new committees therefore became Public Assistance Committees. Authorities were encouraged (though, unfortunately, with the caution typical of new legislation, not obliged) to co-ordinate their various services and institutions, including those they took over from the guar-dians, and to use them in the best interests of the public: a great extension of hospital facilities therefore became possible. Authorities were also given the power, where help was required, to treat cases either under the public assistance committee or otherwise, through education or public health, for instance, as seemed most appropriate. This was perhaps the most significant innovation, for it implied acceptance of the principle of specialisation which the Minority Report had urged in 1909, and Sidney Webb, who had been in the Commons since 1922, hailed it with delight. When the Local Government Bill was introduced towards the end of 1928 it was just 19 years since the Minority Report had appeared, and he was able to point out, with lively satisfaction, that this was the almost invariable interval between the appearance of a Royal Commission's report and its translation into legislation.[72] As Beatrice Webb confided to her diary, 'the old Webbs' (they were both now 70) 'are chuckling over their chickens'.[73]

The Local Government Act did not break up the poor law, but it did at least reduce its scope, while for the present leaving the unemployed without other benefits to public assistance. Even the Unemployed Workmen Act of 1905, which had continued to operate on a small scale during the 20s, was repealed, so that, charity apart, the unemployed were the responsibility either of the Ministry of Labour, if they were 'in benefit', or of public assistance. Otherwise public assistance was still concerned with the aged and infirm, widows and orphans not entitled to pensions under the 1925 Act, deserted children, the mentally ill and all cases of 'sudden and urgent necessity', together with the numerous tramps and vagrants whom unemployment had sent wandering up and down the land in search of work or help. Sidney Webb complained that a national authority for the unemployed was more than ever required, and drew attention to the anomalous situation that had developed, whereby the poor law was maintaining some 100,000 unemployed and the Ministry of Labour a million of them, with, after the introduction of 'transitional benefit' in 1928, only a technical distinction between the two classes.[74]

However, the whole problem of unemployment, as Beatrice and he reflected, was left in such a tangle that the Minority Report's recommendation for a national authority to deal with it was bound to be carried out soon: 'To be able to *make* history as well as to write it—or to be modest—to have foreseen, twenty years ago, the exact stream of tendencies which would bring your proposals to fruition, is a pleasurable thought!'[75]

**Changes in the Treatment of the Unemployed**   After the shock of the great depression, with still more unemployment, and the report of the Royal Commission on Unemployment Insurance in 1932, such a central authority was at last constituted in 1934, in the form of the Unemployment Assistance Board. Meanwhile, as was seen at the beginning of chapter 2, an Act of 1930 restated the traditional poor law for the guidance of the new public assistance committees. The purposes of the poor law were restated in much the same terms as had been devised by the Elizabethans more than three centuries before: only the administrative machinery was refashioned, as it had already once been refashioned in 1834. There was, however, a significant change in the attitude to the unemployed, the 'able-bodied' who had been the principal target of the 1834 report, a change that reflected at long last the development of the agricultural labourers who once formed the majority of English working men into the industrial workers of a highly mechanised society. A new Relief Regulation Order laid down the conditions under which the unemployed could be relieved from public assistance. The requirement that relief should be given to an able-bodied man only in an institution, which had been inherited from the 1834 system, was at last withdrawn. It had not been pressed in recent years, though where it had been applied it had caused much bitterness, especially when it had meant taking a man from his family to keep him in an institution while they received out-relief. With it went also the old insistence on other deterrent tests. Where conditions had to be attached to relief they were now to have as their object not deterrence or the testing of destitution but the improvement of mental and physical condition so that a man could be the more ready to work when it offered. It would be fanciful to trace a connexion, but this was at least nearer the spirit of the Elizabethan intentions than the elaborate project of 1834, designed to force men back into the labour market and to leave them unaided to find a place in it.

**Public Health and Hospitals**    An important result of the merging of the poor law into local authority services by the Act of 1929 was the opportunity it provided for the linking of the public health services which had been urged by public health officials upon the Poor Law Commission 20 years earlier. This was straightforward in the case of the maternity and child welfare, tuberculosis and special services, but the hospital problem was more complex. The boards of guardians had created hospital services which were extensive, if lacking in adequate staff and equipment, but the local authorities had few hospitals apart from those for infectious diseases and tuberculosis. Although the Public Health Act of 1875 had empowered authorities to provide general hospitals, few had done so, most of them preferring the less expensive device of making grants to voluntary hospitals. The public had therefore come to rely on poor law and voluntary hospitals for treatment. Now authorities were able, if they wished, to plan the use and development of the hospital service as a whole, and even, with the encouragement of the Act, to arrange some co-ordination with the voluntary hospitals, an obviously desirable development which had been urged by medical opinion in 1920, soon after the Ministry of Health was founded. Progress was delayed by the economic crisis that followed so soon after 1929, but in many areas a good deal had been done by 1939, when the hospitals had to be ready to face the most serious testing-time in their history. Authorities were left a good deal of discretion by the Act, however, and progress and development were unequal. In 1939 there were nearly 60,000 beds in 400 hospitals and institutions which were still being maintained under the poor law, as against 70,000 in 140 hospitals under public health control and some 77,000 in voluntary hospitals. An estimate made at the end of the war, when new developments were being planned, suggested that in 1939 the country as a whole was short of hospital accommodation by one-third. Much of the accommodation, too, was antiquated and of low standard. Preparation for war made possible the first survey of resources undertaken by the Ministry of Health, which hitherto had not known what was available, and an official report confessed that the generally low standard came as a surprise.[76] Between 1930, when the Local Government Act came into effect, and 1939 there had been little enough time to do much and, in view of national economies, few enough resources with which to do it. A wider programme was called for, if all authorities were to bring their hospital service up to the standard that modern practice demanded, and by 1939 was at least being planned. Some of the voluntary hospitals had improved their facilities, the building of the Queen Elizabeth Hospital at Birmingham being an outstanding example, but others were facing serious financial difficulties, while the existence of voluntary and municipal hospitals, with poor-law institutions still in the background, was an obvious anomaly which hampered development. The rapid growth of hospital contributory schemes in the 30s was an indication of public concern, and many voluntary hospitals were kept going by the regular contributions thus provided. To some extent this was a reflection of the continued failure to include hospital treatment as a statutory benefit under National Health Insurance. Increasingly there was talk of regional groupings of public and voluntary hospitals to improve efficiency: this, first recommended in 1920, was again a recommendation of the Voluntary Hospitals Commission, under Lord Sankey, in 1937, and was to provide the basis for development under the National Health Service after the war. The general position of the hospital services before the war, however, was neatly, and frankly, stated in the National Health Service White Paper of 1944—'many people's business, but nobody's full responsibility'.

The changes in public health organisation under the Local Government Act were followed in 1936 by a new Public Health Act, replacing the great Act of 1875 and consolidating existing legislation. Under this Act public hospitals were given for the first time the power to provide out-patients' departments.

Ten years after the Local Government Act much had still to be done in the health services, but if progress was slow the deficiencies were becoming more apparent. The war, however, was to bring home the deficiencies more effectively than many years of peacetime administration could have done and to provide the will for developments far bolder than the cautious first steps of 1929. By 1941, three years before the appearance of plans for a National Health Service, the government was talking of 'a comprehensive hospital service' after the war.[77] Comprehensive the permissive powers of 1929 had certainly not been, but the Local Government Act had, of course, been more concerned with the reorganisation of the poor law than of public health provision. However, much had still to be done, the creation from 1930 of a single public health service, even if part of it was still administered under the poor law, was a step forward, and justifies the description of the Act as 'one of the important landmarks in the history of Public Health'.[78]

## 4 *The Problem of Unemployment*

We have now considered the operation in the post-war years of the social services created before 1914, with their later developments, and.the belated application of the lessons of the Poor Law Commission. We must now look more closely
at the condition of the unemployed and, as far as this is possible, of the people
generally. The 20s were a time of reasonable confidence, when, with the development of national insurance, it was expected that the 'circle of security' would
provide an adequate minimum of protection. In the 30s, however, the tone was
markedly different: it could hardly have been otherwise after the shock of the
great depression. Investigation after investigation then revealed how much was
still lacking, among not only the unemployed but all deprived of the means to
stand squarely up to difficult conditions, and the long and bitter debate on the
'means test' gave point to the discussion on what constituted, in effect, 'a national
minimum of civilised life'. The widespread interest in social work and the numerous
voluntary associations for help to the unemployed showed how much the public
conscience was stirred. Never again could there be complete ignorance about
conditions in 'Darkest England', and the will to improve matters was so sharpened
by the war and its aftermath that much that was unthinkable before 1939 is now
taken for granted as part of the natural and obvious order of things.

**'A Material Help'**   It had not been intended when unemployment insurance
was introduced that benefits should be more than a supplement to other resources
for tiding over a short period out of work. The trades originally selected had been
precisely those which, it was known, were particularly liable to fluctuations in
employment, and it was never expected that anyone should try to live on the 7s.
benefit of 1911. The rate for men was raised in 1920 to 15s., which hardly
matched the increase in the cost of living, and there was a brief rise to 20s. in 1921.
Afterwards the cost of living fell and the rate remained at 15s. until it was raised to
18s. by the Labour Government in 1924: this was equivalent to about 10s. (the
original National *Health* Insurance benefit) at 1911 prices. With a further fall in
the cost of living the rate was reduced in 1928 to 17s., and in 1931 there was the
notorious economy cut of 10 per cent, to 15s. 3d. Dependants' allowances began in
1921 with 5s. for a wife and 1s. for each child, the latter being raised in 1924 to 2s.
By 1930 a married couple were receiving 26s. a week, which was reduced to 23s.
3d. in 1931. The cut was restored in 1934 and the only increase thereafter was the
raising of the child allowance to 3s. in 1935. Unemployment Assistance benefits were
fixed in 1935 as 24s. for husband and wife, with a varying scale for children rang-
ing from 3s. to 6s. according to age and 7s. to 10s. for older members of the
family. (A reduction of 1s. each was proposed where there were more than five in
a family, but after the storm of protest at the amounts proposed for Assistance
this reduction was withdrawn in 1936.)

The rates laid down, the Minister of Labour, Sir Arthur Steel-Maitland, said in 1927, had never been intended to cover maintenance but to provide 'a help and a very material help indeed—for people to tide over a period of unemployment',[79] and the Blanesburgh Committee in the same year developed the argument: 'Ideal benefits . . . should certainly be so substantial that the insured contributor can feel that, if he has the misfortune to need them, then, taken in conjunction with such resources as may reasonably . . . be expected to have been built up, they will be sufficient to prevent him from being haunted while at work by the fear of what must happen to him if he is unemployed.'[80]

**The Pretence of Insurance** Unfortunately there were by this time many workers who were haunted not by the fear of unemployment but by anxiety lest they should never get back to work again. The number of long-term unemployed was perhaps not large, some 100,000 at this time out of a total insured population of more than 12 million. The number out of work at some time during any year was always, however, far larger than the average for the year (four million in 1927 as against something over one million for the year as a whole), and about one half of them were on 'extended benefit', having exceeded the statutory limit of benefit for which their past contributions provided. The Blanesburgh Committee made the reasonable comment that a fire insurance company when meeting a claim did not enquire how many contributions had been paid,[81] but the unemployment insurance scheme was, until the introduction of unemployment assistance after 1934, an *insurance* scheme, however tenuous the contribution link. It was therefore possible for a man to be out of benefit, and care was taken to bring that home by emphasising that extended benefits were a privilege, not a right. Since, however, they were an extension of the insurance scheme and regarded, until the Blanesburgh Committee swept away the pretence, as repayable, there was no test of means attached to them as there was in the case of poor relief. The means test was a later device, of 1931, when it was first acknowledged that for many people the insurance principle had gone by the board.

**Extending Benefits** To be on extended benefit, however, also meant, in all probability, that many men had exhausted such other reserves as they had possessed, and benefit then became a matter not of supplementation but of subsistence. Clearly it could not be paid at such a rate that it was more profitable not to work, but equally something more was required than 'a help for people to tide over', unless vast numbers were to be driven to the poor law, and the Blanesburgh Committee agreed that this should be avoided as far as possible: 'The dislike of most insured persons to resort to poor relief is natural and laudable. We would encourage it. . . . An Unemployment Insurance scheme should provide for the great bulk of genuine unemployment in a manner honourable to those whom it benefits.'[82]

Under these circumstances the Labour Government in 1924 took the view that some minimum of subsistence should be provided, and therefore increased the rates of benefit. In the words of the Minister of Labour, Tom Shaw, when presenting the new legislation, 'That is the principle of this Bill, that an honest man shall not starve though he be unemployed; neither shall he be driven to the Guardians; that he shall be paid a sum of money which at any rate will keep him from starvation.'[83] This consideration became increasingly important as the struggle to preserve the insurance principle became more difficult and the number technically 'out of benefit' grew larger. Until 1928, however, it was constantly and confidently expected that conditions were about to improve and that extended benefits were a temporary device which would cease as soon as the economy revived. Meanwhile, in the words of a report of 1923, 'it may not be possible to do more than meet current problems as they arise',[84] a bland statement that aptly sums up the bewildered fluctuations of policy in the 20s. The Blanesburgh Committee also believed in 1927 that improvement was coming. In recommending an easing of the statutory conditions for benefit so as to cover many of those hitherto drawing extended benefit, it proposed another temporary device of 'transitional benefit' for those who still could not qualify, in the confident expectation that it would not be needed by many or for long. In the event the number claiming transitional benefit was far larger than had been anticipated, 120,000, of whom nearly half had had no work for a year, and three-quarters had had no more than eight weeks of it. Unfortunately for the Blanesburgh Committee's recommendations, from the moment that transitional benefits were introduced unemployment began to rise again, and with an easing of regulations by the Labour Government in 1930 the number of benefits paid was soon more than 300,000. The worst was still to come, for unemployment did not reach its peak of nearly three million until the winter of 1932–3. Of this vast number some half million had been more than a year out of work, and the new 'transitional payments', with a means test, introduced in 1931, were paid to 800,000, representing, with their dependants, some 2,500,000 people in all. The Unemployment Assistance Board, when it assumed responsibility for those out of benefit in 1935, made allowances to a similar number, nearly 750,000, of whom 344,000 had been unemployed for more than one year, 139,000 for more than three years and 25,000 for over five years.[85]

Statistics are crude guides to the realities of distress and to these numbers must be added many more representing men whose last job was a short one and whose expectation of another was small. In the words of one investigator in the late 30s, 'There is not a small permanent chorus of 'really' unemployed and a huge revolving stage army who come on the scene again refreshed behind the scenes and full of beans. . . . Rather we must imagine the 2 million about equally divided into a standing army, that type of person whose main job is to be unemployed and the "stage army" of those whose main job is still to be in work but who are just now out of it'.[86] It is worth recalling, too, that in 1932 the number of people with incomes of over £250 a year, the limit for the insurance schemes, was not much more than two million, which was considerably less than the total of unemployment at the time. Similarly, the number of allowances made by the Assistance Board in 1935 was roughly equal to the number of incomes of £500 upwards, at a time when incomes below £500 numbered more than nine million.

**The Recognition of Failure, 1931** Although, therefore, even in the worst years of the depression there were millions of insured workers, rather more than one-third of the total, who made no claim for benefit, the number needing more than mere 'tiding over' was large, and led to a change of policy. From 1931 there was, in effect, a poor law outside the poor law, allowances not as of right but according to need, side by side with insurance benefit securely based on contributions. From 1934 these allowances were the responsibility of a special national authority, the Unemployment Assistance Board, and at the same time it was at last recognised, in the creation of the 'Special Areas', that certain parts of the country could never recover without assistance.

**Attitudes on Unemployment** We are not here concerned with the long, confused, deeply felt and often bitter—even savage—debate on the relief and cure of unemployment that went on unceasingly between the wars. The country settled down to a high degree of unemployment, even as many of the unemployed willynilly settled down themselves, and, while the Labour party demanded radical measures for a cure, there were many who refused to believe that relief and time for the international economy to recover would not produce a remedy. Many more went their way doubting the facts or ignoring all unpleasant reality: as late as 1938 the writer heard a prosperous tradesman argue that if unemployed men really wanted work they would tramp the country for it. Uncovenanted, extended and transitional benefits, transitional payments and unemployment assistance undoubtedly dulled the edge of distress and achieved Shaw's purpose in 1924 of preventing starvation, but while materially inadequate for more than a minimum standard of existence they also left unsatisfied the moral urges of life. A 'living death' was a grim comment in a notable report on unemployment among young men in the middle 30s: 'Unemployment due to conditions of world trade . . . meant nothing to them. . . . What mattered to most of them was that they were fit and able to work and wanted it badly, not so much as an end in itself as a means to an end.'[87] Still worse was the feeling that nothing mattered: 'To live in a state of unemployment or insecure employment seemed to involve the acceptance of a static universe. Nothing you can do appears to be worth while.'[88]

The general despair at the difficulty of coping with the situation struck one anxious and sympathetic observer, King George V, as he commented to Baldwin in 1925. Earlier he had urged upon Lloyd George the need to provide work: 'It is impossible to expect people to subsist upon the unemployment benefit. . . . The King appeals to the Government to meet this grave . . . difficulty with the same liberality as they displayed in dealing with the enormous daily cost of the war.'[89] The temptation to think in terms of a mobilising of resources was strong, and it was eventually only in this way, when war came, that the problem was solved. The country was too divided, however, and the Labour party not strong enough, while yet too strictly constitutional in outlook, to seize the initiative, even if it had been united on a remedy. Ramsay MacDonald and his Ministers were no revolutionaries, and in Philip Snowden the party had a Chancellor of the Exchequer of strangely orthodox stamp. Indeed, the Labour leaders, like Baldwin, had used all their influence against their less responsible followers to preserve the methods of parliamentary democracy. Nowadays, when those methods are so much taken for granted, earlier stresses, as a recent writer on inter-war politics has justly said, tend to be forgotten, and the debt to Baldwin and MacDonald is seldom acknowledged.[90] For the rest, the 20s were a time of Pecksniffian hopefulness and the early 30s too grim for risks: 'sitting it out' has aptly been suggested as the keynote of the years from 1931 to 1935.[91] Nor was there any substantial revolutionary activity among the unemployed, for all Wal Hannington's efforts in the National Unemployed Workers' Movement.[92] Low allowances, economy cuts, even delays over payment because of the awkward amounts to be paid out after the cuts, which often left an Exchange without small change—all was more or less patiently borne. As Dalton comments in his autobiography of an occasion when men were told to return to the Exchange next day because the pennies had run out, 'Such meekness is a mouldy miracle!'[93] There might be local protests, as in Poplar in 1921 and in Rotherham and County Durham in 1932, when the Public Assistance Committees refused to apply the Government's test of means, but at no time were there more than protests. The situation remained under control and special commissioners took the place of Public Assistance in the two recalcitrant centres, even as the guardians of West Ham, Chester-le-Street and Bedwellty had been set aside five years earlier. On the other hand, an economy-minded Government, clumsy and inept though much of its handling of the situation was, took care not to drive opposition too hard. Strong protests led to some modification of the means test in 1932, as of the Unemployment Assistance Board's rates in 1935.

**Attitudes among the Unemployed**   Nor was the lot of the unemployed unmitigated despair. As George Orwell wrote of his tour through the depressed areas in 1936, 'it makes a great deal of difference when things are the same for everybody'.[94] Another observer, who took part in the Pilgrim Trust enquiry of the same year which has already been quoted, found some with their compensations, a young man 'too busy' with his various interests, for instance, and another hugging his freedom: 'Isn't it marvellous to think of all those rich old men sweating their eyes out in their offices so that the likes of me can have a really good time?'[95] To this the present writer would add his own recollection of a young miner on a residential course in a stately country house, who saw the wry humour of his 'living like a Duke, on the dole'.

Equally, a wife might be relieved that there was regular money coming in from Assistance, though a cynic might see it as society's 'conscience money' and many reassert their own importance by 'playing a trick on society' through exploiting a loophole in the means test.[96] Yet 'of many skilled men it is no exaggeration to say that their whole life is centred upon their work', and the adjustment to unemployment in such cases was painful. On the other hand there was a general tendency, in psychological self-defence, to minimise the importance of work when it was no longer to be had,[97] though there was a pathetic pride in being 'on Benefit',[98] having, that is to say, a *right* to benefit instead of a claim upon allowance.

The worst aspect, surely, was the sense of not being wanted, of having nothing to offer society as a basis for self-respect. It is a matter for wonder and pride how the spirit of being at one again with the community in shared service returned with the coming of war in 1939, or, rather, with the disaster, the turning in of Britain upon herself, of 1940. This was the basis of the determined 'never again' of the war years and 1945, which Churchill, for instance, failed to appreciate, perhaps because in his intense dislike of Socialism he had not realised earlier the depth of the feeling about unemployment. His attitude to industrial problems had been coloured by the Bolshevik Revolution and the strikes of 1921, which, it has been said, he never managed to forget.[99] In 1931, for instance, in typical vein, he castigated the Labour Government for managing 'by every device and by every dodge . . . to keep on paying for the longest time in the loosest fashion the largest doles to the largest number'.[100] His handling of the Beveridge Report in 1942 revealed how little he had the sense of those who saw in the war their opportunity to break for ever with the unhappy past. By that time the true price of unemployment had become apparent. If starvation had been avoided, food had not been adequate to need, especially in view of the new science of nutrition. As recorded in the Ministry of Health's report on the war years, it was in 1942 that an American authority on deficiency diseases, with the aid of doctors from the colonial service, began the clinical examinations which demonstrated that, although the situation was then more satisfactory than had been expected, 'in districts which before the war had been subject to long periods of unemployment, many of the adults and adolescents, and particularly the women, showed that they had suffered severely'.[101] By then the higher wages of wartime, the sharing of foodstuffs through rationing and the various measures to ensure adequate nutrition had all contributed not only to improve nutritional standards but to reshape social policy.

**The Turning Point, 1931**   The turning point in the handling of the unemployment problem came in the year of financial crisis, 1931. The American slump of 1929 had already hit Europe and the crash began with the failure of the Austrian *Credit-Anstalt* in May 1931. Britain, with her international trade rapidly running down, became the victim of her position in international finance. Short-term loans were withdrawn by foreign investors and could not be offset by the mobilisation of long-term resources invested abroad, which were in any case seriously depreciated by the general depression. Confidence was shaken by the increase in the cost of unemployment benefit from £51 million in 1929 to £125 million in 1931, with only £30 million a year accruing from employers' and employees' contributions.

Britain's financial position, fundamentally sound though it probably still was, was thought to be seriously shaken, and in finance confidence is all. Hence the 'flight from the pound' and the crisis that followed from the difficulty of borrowing to meet urgent needs. The second Labour Government, which took office in June 1929, had added to the difficulties by introducing a more generous treatment of the unemployed at the very moment when the world economic crisis was about to add to their numbers. The Unemployment Insurance Act of 1930 made it easier for people with only a minimum of insured employment behind them to qualify for transitional benefit, and abolished the long-resented requirement that benefit should be paid only to those 'genuinely seeking work'. The condition was an obvious precaution, but had come to be regarded, in areas where the chances of work were slight, as adding insult to injury. Now it had only to be shown that no chance of work had actually been refused, and the result of the change, together with the relaxing of qualifying conditions, was a rapid increase in the number on transitional benefit, from 120,000 in 1929 to more than half a million in 1931.

Unexpectedly, many whose right even to inclusion in the insurance scheme had hitherto been uncertain and others whose claim to benefit was small—part-time and occasional workers, married women and the like—together with some whose means would not have stood the test of a poor-law investigation, now pressed claims which the new Act rendered perfectly legal. These 'anomalies', as they were discreetly called, were the subject of a special Act in 1931, and are known to have influenced Ramsay MacDonald's attitude. Although their incidence was usually exaggerated, they provided some of the justification for the imposition of the 'means test' from the autumn of 1931 and, when the test was applied, nearly 200,000 people who had been receiving transitional benefit dropped their claims, thereby relieving the Treasury to the extent of some £10 million. Whether the anguish and bitterness—and the evasions and doubtful practices—associated with the means test as it was applied were worth this saving is another matter. It was unfortunate that no better way could be devised of checking unnecessary claims without adding to the strain in cases of genuine need.

We are here concerned with the development of the welfare services, not with the intricacies of political controversy, and can therefore pass over the shocks and storms of the critical year, 1931, with the collapse of the Labour Government and the formation of the 'National' Government, which under various forms was to endure until the greater collapse of 1940. The whole tangled story of 1931 has been much investigated, and what is clear is the complexity of the situation and the narrow limits in which MacDonald and his colleagues had to manoeuvre. The left wing of the Labour party had long been pressing for stronger measures on behalf of the unemployed and had even been dissatisfied with the Act of 1930. It was the impossibility of agreeing on measures which, however distasteful, were necessary, under the conditions of the times, to restore financial confidence, that caused the Labour Government to throw in its hand. The financial strain was increased by the frankness of the revelations regularly published about the extent and cost of unemployment (thereby justifying the opinion of the economist already quoted who in 1929 had given the warning that the statistics would bring down the government), and still more by the economies demanded in the summer of 1931 by the Royal Commission on Unemployment and the May Committee. The latter, a special committee under Sir George May, appointed by Snowden to advise on economies, made sweeping recommendations which suggested imminent collapse and greatly influenced foreign opinion on Britain's economic position. Its report appeared at the end of July 1931, but was preceded by the first report of the Royal Commission, which had been appointed by the Government at the end of 1930 in answer to Opposition criticism of extravagance in the handling of unemployment.

**The Economy Orders**  The Commission's first report (its final report appeared late in 1932) proposed alterations in contributions and benefits, with the cautious application of a means test, but the Government, in the face of strong opposition from most of its supporters, hesitated to do more than bring in the Anomalies Act. With its resignation in August, however, and especially after the sweeping 'National' successes in the General Election in October, the refusal of the greater part of the Labour party to economise on unemployment benefits ceased to be a decisive factor. In October, by two 'National Economy Orders', unemployment insurance contributions were increased and benefits reduced, the period for receipt of normal benefit was limited, and, most significant of all, 'transitional payments', made under a test of means and paid through the Public Assistance Committees established in 1930, replaced the 'transitional benefits' of 1928. Public Assistance Committees, with their experience of poor-law administration, were the most convenient machinery for testing need, but the association with the poor law was little short of disastrous and caused bitter resentment. Nevertheless, under this new system the insurance principle was upheld and relief outside insurance cover finally made a national responsibility, although assessed by local committees. The establishment of a central organisation for unemployment assistance was the logical, if still unheralded, conclusion.

Under the Economy Orders over one million people were transferred to transitional payments, a quarter of a million hitherto receiving transitional benefits were refused further aid and half a million had their payments reduced. The results were seen in the reduction of the cost of unemployment payments of all kinds (administration and interest apart) from £110 million in 1931–2 to £104 million in 1932–3, with, despite an unemployment rate of nearly three million, a fall in the cost of unemployment insurance benefit (paid only to those who satisfied the more rigorous qualifying conditions) from £80 million to £54 million. The economies in assistance, being exercised by local authority committees, were applied unequally, and there was much resistance to the application of a means test, though in only two cases (Rotherham and County Durham) were the Public Assistance Committees set aside by the Government. Moreover, as local bodies the Public Assistance Committees were under considerable pressure in their areas and already in 1932 the Government was compelled to make some concessions: certain modest items of income were excluded from the assessment of means. This implied a retreat from the strict application of the principle of need, as assessed, for instance, under the poor law, but there is no doubt that it had the support of public opinion, stirred as it had been by the crisis of 1931 and the accompanying depression, with its dire effects on the livelihood of so many. Indeed, the combination of widespread concern with inability in governing circles to offer any practical remedy but relief is a phenomenon of these years which was to have its repercussions in the 40s. In the words of a contemporary comment on the condition of the unemployed, 'the amount of national goodwill is evidently in inverse proportion to the amount of national brain-power available to solve the problem'.[102]

The Royal Commission on Unemployment, 1930–2    The Royal Commission on Unemployment reported at the end of 1932. Its principal recommendations were that unemployment insurance should continue and, indeed, be extended to suitable occupations hitherto excluded from its operation, but that it should be regarded as a system of limited liability, with benefits restricted in time and, for those whose right to benefit had been exhausted, special assistance, outside insurance and based on ascertained need. This left unsolved the problem of those whose chances of a return to work were slight, even if it guaranteed them relief, though the report did recommend training schemes, at least for the young, if only to 'preserve their industrial quality'. To supervise the insurance system, and to preserve it from the pressure of political party interests, a statutory body was proposed. Assistance was to continue to be awarded by local committees, though as some of them, in the Commission's tactful phrase, had exercised their discretion in the matter 'to the point of not observing the requirements of the Statutes', there should be more central control. At the same time, however, in order to remove the unpopular association with the poor law, special Unemployment Assistance Committees of local authorities, separate from the Public Assistance Committees, were to be set up.

The need to draw a distinction between insurance and relief, which was the basis of the Commission's case, had already become plain to Neville Chamberlain, now Chancellor of the Exchequer in the National Government. Even before the Commission reported he had decided that assistance to the unemployed should be removed from local and national politics alike and entrusted to a statutory commission, which would 'avoid the danger of the relief being put up to auction by the parties'.[103] This was somewhat naive, for a century's experience had shown that Parliament would not leave such statutory bodies alone, and it would not be long before the lessons of experience were confirmed. Nevertheless, the fumblings and fluctuations in the handling of unemployment since 1920 had shown the desperate need for a settled policy and the removal of the issues as far as possible from the parliamentary battle: Chamberlain was feeling his way towards the Unemployment Assistance Board of 1934 which was so largely his own creation. He went further, for he saw the importance of 'providing some interest in life for the large numbers of men who are never likely to get work', and out of this realisation was to come the responsibility of the U.A.B. for the *welfare*, not merely the maintenance, of the unemployed.

**The Unemployment Act, 1934** A new Unemployment Act, the twenty-first since 1920, but the first definitive restatement of policy, followed the Commission's Report in 1934, after more than a year of cogitation and discussion. Unemployment Insurance, so long at the mercy of economic conditions and emergency legislation, was at last placed on a firm basis. To protect it, all those who had lost their entitlement to benefit were placed by Part II of the Act under the specially constituted Unemployment Assistance Board. The insurance scheme itself was committed to the care of another semi-independent body, the Unemployment Insurance Statutory Committee, which had the task of supervising the working of insurance, of ensuring its solvency, reviewing its finances and recommending to the Ministry of Labour such alterations in its operation as seemed necessary under changing conditions. The Committee was an ingenious device for keeping the operation of unemployment insurance flexible without submitting it, when changes were necessary, to the lengthy processes and wrangles of legislation, and it was to work well. As its Chairman Beveridge, who had been in academic life since 1919, was called back into the public service and was to hold office until he entered politics in 1944. A steady decline in unemployment of nearly one million between 1934 and 1937 enabled the Committee to build up a reserve fund of more than £60 million before the tide turned again in 1938, and, although Beveridge insisted on keeping a large reserve, it was possible to increase dependants' allowances in 1935 and to reduce contributions in the following year (the reduction being timed to coincide with the increase of contributions under the pensions scheme). Moreover, in 1936 a new scheme of unemployment insurance, drawn up by the Committee, was introduced for agricultural workers. This was a significant development, for it brought unemployment insurance more nearly into line with health and pensions insurance, with their more extensive coverage, and therefore strengthened the case for the overall unified scheme of insurance which Chamberlain had foreseen but rejected in 1925. By 1936 unemployment insurance covered 14,500,000 people, health insurance 18,000,000 and pensions insurance 19,600,000, the chief groups still outside unemployment insurance being domestic servants, nurses, civil servants and railwaymen. For normal fluctuations the insurance scheme was now solvent and likely to remain so, while the insurance principle was firmly established, approved alike by popular opinion, which infinitely preferred benefits as of right to the humiliations of a means test, and by the Treasury, which saved £2 million annually, for instance, through the reduction in contributions. By 1936, before the Unemployment

Assistance Board came into operation, rather more than 700,000 unemployed were receiving insurance benefit, and some 600,000 means-test assistance, while 330,000 were on poor relief. The figures covered serious variations, however, and although conditions were much improved there were still large parts of the country, especially in the North-East, North-West, Wales and Scotland, where the number on assistance and relief was greater than that covered by insurance. It was in these areas that means-test assistance was largely concentrated and that the Unemployment Assistance Board was to be most active.

**Unemployment Assistance**    The establishment of the Board, though based on the experience of national responsibility for the unemployed out of benefit which had been accepted in 1931, was a bold move which closed a chapter in poor-law history even more decisively than the Local Government Act of 1929 which had abolished the Guardians. The care of the able-bodied poor had long been the principal preoccupation of poor-law policy. The insurance schemes established since 1910 had shown how their numbers could be reduced, but heavy unemployment had revived the problem in a new form. By the middle 30s it was clear that the 'depressed areas' of heavy unemployment and certain of the older workers who had been long unemployed were unlikely to recover their industrial activity in full. It was obviously unthinkable under these conditions that a locally-raised poor law should be the only relief available, and, indeed, national resources had been committed since 1931. The Royal Commission had recommended that relief should continue to be administered by local committees, but the Act of 1934, in setting up the Unemployment Assistance Board, preferred to take the matter altogether out of local hands and to lay down a common national level of aid, thereby admitting, at least by implication, the principle of a 'national minimum'.

One problem was as to the extent of the Board's responsibilities, and it was eventually decided to include all those covered by the widest social insurance scheme, that for pensions, which meant all those normally employed who earned less than £5 a week. The Act therefore arranged that on two separate 'Appointed Days' the U.A.B. should assume responsibility, first for those who had been receiving transitional payments and later for those others, outside the scope of unemployment insurance, whose only recourse when unemployed had hitherto been to the poor law.

The new policy was an astute political move, aimed at removing assistance from political interference, both local and central, and the new Board was given considerable independence in its administration. Unfortunately, however, it was plunged immediately into a storm over its scale of allowances, and before it had even taken on independent life it found itself overruled by hasty legislative intervention in the manner so well known since 1920. When the new scales of assistance, which had been thought to be generous, were announced, it was discovered, amid a wave of indignation that ran through the country, that in most cases applicants would be worse off than under the local Public Assistance Committees.

This, though due largely to ignorance of the very varied scales paid by Public Assistance Committees, was a political and social blunder of the first order, and an unfortunate augury for a national against a local administration of relief. The case for an immediate revision of scales was so strong that, as Bevin declared, the Government 'must have the hearts of a Pharaoh' to ignore it.[104] A 'Standstill Order' was hastily passed and the second Appointed Day indefinitely postponed, in the event for nearly two years. Meanwhile payments were made on the new rates or the old Public Assistance rates, whichever were most favourable to individual applicants, and the rates themselves were raised. So much for the hopes of an independent Board untouched by political pressures, though after this ominous beginning, and with a more generous policy of assistance, the Board did establish itself. The second Appointed Day eventually occurred in April 1937, and the assimilation of the unemployed from the Public Assistance Committees was finally completed in the summer of the following year. It had been shown, however, in the words of a member of the Board, Violet Markham, that 'the idea that the Board could be taken out of politics and do its work in cloistered calm was of course ridiculous'.[105] The total payments made by the Board fell gradually from £42 million in 1935–6 to £35 million in 1938–9, though as unemployment was rising in the last year, with insurance payments increasing by £20 million, but for the war the pressure on Assistance might again have been intensified.

The Household Means Test   The U.A.B. was to continue until 1948, changing its title in 1940 to 'Assistance Board', and broadening its responsibilities: in the 13 years of its existence it dispensed in all some £221 million. The rates it paid have already been referred to. Basically 24s. for man and wife, with varying amounts for children and a small allowance for rent, they left when food had been bought little enough even for clothing, fuel and light. Yet, like the transitional payments since 1931, they were subject to a means test. The test was a 'household' one, taking into account the means of other members of the family in the household, and was therefore less exacting than the poor law, which as re-stated in 1930 maintained the traditional family responsibility for support. Moreover, it was applied at the home concerned by a visiting official (popularly—or, rather, unpopularly—known as the 'means test man'), not publicly before a poor-law committee, while after the enforced revision of the rates in 1936, and the accompanying modification of the tests, not all that came into the household was taken into account when assessing assistance (though the national total of family means taken into consideration exceeded £24 million). Yet, whatever the alleviations, the means test carried the poor-law implication of personal failure to people who were the victims of economic dislocation, and by compelling members of the same household to contribute from often slender resources to each others' support hardly encouraged family solidarity. Indeed, it provided occasion for family strife and even dishonesty, and, although instances were less common than rumour had it, young men in particular, if they did not completely move from home to ensure their full rate of assistance, sometimes provided themselves with accommodation addresses. As one such young man commented to an enquirer, 'It's a terrible business when you've got to tell lies to get a miserable 15s. a week'.[106] Much bitterness was brought into public life by the means test, bitterness among those who were subjected to it, and angry comment from others who resented—and exaggerated—the devices adopted to evade it. Of its very nature, as Bevin complained later, it was calculated to encourage 'a kind of "cleverness"' in evasion among the unemployed: 'they felt they had to "beat the State" and hence the whole spirit of the administration with all its conflict grew up'.[107] When eventually, and under Labour pressure, the means test was swept away by the war-time coalition, the 'personal test of means' that replaced it was intended, Bevin assured the Commons, to 'remove the temptation to people to be cunning in order to get assistance'.[108]

## 5 *Social Investigations and Standards of Living*

Low though they were, the Assistance Board's allowances were near enough to the lower wage-rates to tempt some to avoid any chance of work, and to make others feel the irony of working for the little extra that was all that some occupations could offer, especially when work was irregular. Disregarding agriculture, with its low standards, wages in the 30s varied in the main from £3–£3 10s. a week for skilled men to £2–£2 10s. for the unskilled. Only one wage-earner in seven received more than £5 10s.[109] and at the other extreme £2, even if the work were regular, was not much above what a family man might expect from the U.A.B. Wages had fallen since the high levels of 1920, but the cost of living had fallen with them and by 1935, when it reached its lowest point, was little more than half of what it had been in 1920 and even one-sixth lower than in 1929: this did something to mitigate the worst effects of the depression. It was estimated in 1936 that by comparison with pre-war conditions even an unemployed man with a family was better off than an unskilled labourer in full work had then been,[110] and taking into account increased wages and shorter working hours there had indeed been a rise of about one-third in the standard of living of the working classes. Yet large numbers were still in poverty, no less through low wages than on account of unemployment. As the 30s wore on this point was increasingly driven home, especially by a whole series of social investigations which were inspired by concern at the conditions of the unemployed. It is likely that even apart from the war, with its heightening of social sensibility, there would have been further developments in welfare policy. These would probably have come in the direction of family allowances, for which the dependants' allowances of unemployment insurance and assistance provided ample precedent, now reinforced by the findings of the social investigators, who showed how much any but the smallest of families could contribute to poverty when resources were small. Men with families that were still not large by nineteenth-century standards were often enough better off unemployed, when they did at least receive extra payments for their dependants. It was found in one survey in Bristol, for instance, that one-third of the poorest families, the father being in employment, received no help at all from the social services, whereas others who received assistance were actually better off.[111] The Unemployment Insurance Statutory Committee observed that it could not use its reserve funds to raise benefits to the unemployed unless wages for the lower-paid workers with dependants could somehow be increased. Regulation of wages was out of the question, but the case for family allowances, which Eleanor Rathbone had been pressing since 1918, was gradually driven home: 'By far the greatest cause of primary poverty is the failure of the wage system to adapt itself to the needs of the variously sized households actually dependent on the wage-earner.'[112] As *The Times* commented in a kite-flying article at the end of 1939, 'industry is failing, partly because of low rates for unskilled labour and partly because of intermittent employment, to provide an adequate standard of living for a large number of men and their families'.[113]

How large the number was the social investigators were to reveal. Rowntree in the middle 30s studied what he called, in the title of a re-issue of earlier conclusions, *The Human Needs of Labour*, and repeated his previous enquiries into conditions in York. What his careful and detailed investigations revealed was shown by the title of this 'second social survey of York', published in 1941 as *Poverty and Progress*, which a gloss might aptly convert into *Progress—and yet Poverty*. Of absolute grinding poverty, permitting only the merest and meanest subsistence, which Rowntree estimated as covering incomes for families with three dependent children of at most 30s. 7d. a week, without rent (the rate for unemployment insurance or assistance being about 35s.), he found only half as much as in 1899, but there was still seven per cent of it. The absolute minimum for a healthy life, which he based on estimates of nutritional standards prepared by the British Medical Association and fairly called a Spartan level, he set at 43s. 6d.—or 53s. with rent. (Beveridge in 1942, working on 1938 prices, arrived at exactly the same figure for a family of this size, and based his plans for subsistence allowances on it.) Of the working-class population of York Rowntree found that nearly one-third was living below this standard, most of them because of low wages (that is, wages inadequate for family or housing commitments) or unemployment. Significantly enough, as was also shown elsewhere, unemployment was not necessarily the principal cause of poverty: wages low in relation to commitments accounted for at least as much. Yet even 53s. was a bare minimum. 'To keep a family of five in health on 53s. a week, even when the income is guaranteed for fifty-two weeks in the year, needs constant watchfulness and a high degree of skill on the part of the housewife.'[114] These are sentiments which many, brought up between the wars, if only at rather higher standards, will confirm from their own experience. What long-term unemployment could mean was suggested by the Pilgrim Trust's *Men Without Work*, which showed 44 per cent of the unemployed on or below a bare subsistence level.[115]

Rowntree's findings were endorsed by others, notably by the Bristol survey of 1937, which showed that, even under the conditions of moderate prosperity that then obtained, and working to standards lower than those of Rowntree, one-third of the working classes, some 30,000 families, were on or near the poverty-line, while one-fifth of working-class children, 16,000 in all, were inadequately fed.[116] The birth-rate had fallen to such an extent that a family with more than three children was now large, but where there was such a family poverty through un-employment or low wages still made life a struggle and stunted the children's growth. Half of the country's children, in fact, lived in families whose income was less than £3 a week. Poverty told particularly on very young children. The great improvement in the infant mortality rate since the beginning of the century, as was shown by an important pioneer study of the returns of the 1931 census, affected poor families far less than those better-off: 'the infants of the poor are *relatively* worse off than they were before the 1914 war. They are, in other words, dying in relatively greater numbers.'[117] Actual undernourishment was much less than it had been a generation earlier, but there was still much of it where unem-ployment was rife or wages small. The numbers affected were difficult to calculate, but 'several million' was a common estimate. As *The Times* commented in a lead-ing article when the Bristol report appeared early in 1939, 'These statistics are compiled from . . . a prosperous city in a prosperous year. They disclose a dis-quieting amount of actual poverty.'[118]

Disquieting enough the statistics were, even to those who already knew the facts for themselves. Among the many other reports that appeared—to name only a single further instance—was one no less disquieting from Stockton-on-Tees, which revealed a significant increase of malnutrition on a new housing estate where rents were higher and left too little for adequate diets.[119] Through all the mass of evidence the comfortable part of the nation, which included no small part of the working classes, was gradually brought to accept the fact that neither the growth of the economy nor the social services were preventing involuntary poverty, though the final lessons were to be driven home during the war. If, as has been suggested, the 'National Government' of the 30s, in its progress towards the later Welfare State, seemed to the more old-fashioned among its supporters 'scanda-lously semi-socialistic',[120] there remained only too much still to be done. Progress there was, though it was unequal in its effects, but for all the schemes of social in-surance and welfare much avoidable poverty still clamoured for attention. The contrasts of comfort and penury were all the greater for the steady increase in the amenities of life that were now available.

## 6 Welfare, Special Areas and Industrial Balance

The functions of the U.A.B. went beyond assistance to people in need of work to 'the promotion of their welfare'. By this was meant such services as the provision of training courses, help in transference to other parts of the country, aid and advice on personal problems, especially matters of health and housing, and practical assistance, in the form of allotments and small holdings, to older men who could not hope for regular work again. 'The calculation of assessments', the Board's first report declared, 'is not the beginning and end of the work.' As trustees for the public conscience the Board's officials had the task of overcoming suspicion and rendering personal service to their clients: 'the act is the letter but the administration is the spirit'.[121] This was aiming high, and invited criticism of semi-socialism, but it was inspired by recognition of the fact that the problem of the maintenance, and still more of the rehabilitation, of men long unemployed was as much moral as physical. Unemployment Assistance alone would not solve the difficulties of a man who had lost his industrial tone. Equally the task was not one for a single government department to tackle unaided. The local authorities were responsible for many of the welfare services, and the still more personal approach of the Councils of Social Service up and down the country was essential. With all of these the U.A.B. co-operated, and the result was a remarkable out-pouring of social welfare activity far better organised and co-ordinated than anything attempted before.

**Training for Employment**  A substantial part of the welfare work was done in the Government Training Centres, which gave specific training for new work, and in the Instruction Centres, which aimed rather at keeping men fit for any work that offered. For young people there were Junior Instruction Centres under the Local Education Authorities. The disadvantage of these facilities, however, was that training did not—and under the circumstances could not—guarantee employment: most men got jobs after their courses, at least from the Training Centres, but it is doubtful if most kept them. The 20s had seen many attempts to create work for the unemployed on the old familiar lines of the poor law and the Unemployed Workmen Act, with the old familiar result—little achieved at great cost. As the final report of the Unemployment Commission showed in 1932, it cost four times as much to keep men on specially devised work as on unemployment benefit.[122] In the 30s the attempt to provide work was abandoned, but the training camps then came under the suspicion of being 'slave-camps' to keep the unemployed out of the way. Indeed, unless employment could be guaranteed, training seemed to many a mockery.

**The Special Areas**  The same kind of difficulty arose when the Special Areas were designated. At first the aim was to move away from them as many as could be persuaded to go, but it was speedily realised that, in conjunction with the steady movement of many on their own, this would only create derelict areas of unbalanced populations, with the younger and more hopeful elements all removed. After the Commissioner for Special Areas in England, Sir Malcolm Stewart, had resigned in 1936, in despair at the limited scope he was allowed and the lamentably poor response of industry to his efforts to attract new industrial development to the special areas, a rather more positive policy was adopted. Tax concessions and the erection of 'Trading Estates', in which industrial premises could be leased, were among the measures adopted, but their effect was small. Some £3 million were spent by 1938, but the number of people employed in new industrial development was only 15,000. Altogether the approach was too cautious to achieve much; 'amateurish slumming' it has been called, more in sorrow at lost opportunities than in anger, by one contemporary critic, himself a Conservative.[123] Something more dynamic and imaginative, on the lines of the Tennessee Valley Authority in America, was required: there was too little positive stimulation of interest, as against mere waiting on it. More was done by the social improvements and amenities that were fostered, the health services, community centres, holiday camps, agricultural holdings and the like. Yet it was out of the recognition of the inadequacy of the attempts to train the unemployed and to reconstruct the special areas that there was soon to emerge the conception of a policy of Full Employment, which by maintaining employment at a high level would render these desperate measures unnecessary.

**The Barlow Commission, 1937-40**    The new policy for the encouragement of industrial development in the special areas, which was adopted in 1937, was prompted by Sir Malcolm Stewart. In recommending it he stressed also the need for an embargo on further industrial development in the overgrown London area, which was attracting more than its fair share of the new industries that were springing up, and thereby not only upsetting the social and economic balance of the country, but adding to its strategic problems. The Government took up the point and decided to have it more closely examined. In 1937 a Royal Commission on the Distribution of the Industrial Population, with Sir Montague Barlow as Chairman, was appointed. This 'Barlow Commission', which reported in 1940, was the last of the inquiries into the problems of the inter-war period, and its report, appearing as it did in the year of the country's greatest crisis, was to prove the first of the basic reconstruction documents of the war years.

The Commission carried much further, and on wider grounds, the case for new industrial development which had already been adopted, albeit cautiously, for the special areas. It surveyed the concentration and congestion of British industry and pointed to the many disadvantages, social, economic and strategic, that arose from them. It urged government action to remedy the situation, seeing this as a counterpart of the contribution that the State already made to the welfare of the industrial population through national insurance in its various forms. 'A reasonable balance of industrial development, so far as possible, throughout the various divisions or regions of Great Britain', with redevelopment of congested areas and a dispersal of industry, were the main recommendations. Though mildly expressed, it was the most compelling plea for town planning that had yet appeared, and was to prove of decisive influence, especially in the development of the 'new towns' after the war. Apart from strategic considerations, however, it was the social rather than the architectural implications of past industrial and urban development that roused the Commission's concern, and especially the example of the special areas, left stranded as they had been by the tide of industrial change and depression. In its eighth recommendation the Commission advised 'anticipating cases where depression may probably occur in the future . . . and encouraging before a depression crisis arises the development . . . of other industries, or public undertakings'. Here, after long years of unhappy experience, are the rationalisation of the Elizabethan attempts to set the poor on work and the logical development of the efforts tardily made in 1886 and 1905 to find a remedy for the ills of involuntary unemployment. National planning, as Beveridge and the Majority Report of 1909 had long since urged (and the Labour Party constantly maintained), was an essential part of insurance against unemployment that had too long been neglected in the preoccupation with relief.

Of the disadvantages of unplanned urban development the Barlow Report had this to say: 'The standard of health in the large towns still tends to lag behind that of the country. . . . Associated with . . . the matter of health are slums and overcrowding; the absence of adequate provision for open air recreation and games; a lack of proper and regular contact . . . with the resources and amenity of country life; smoke and dirt, fog and general absence of sunlight; and noise. Not least grave . . . is transport congestion, which . . . often involves serious loss of time and money and probably some impairment of health.'[124]

## 7 Housing and Town Planning

With unemployment, housing had been a preoccupation of social policy since the war, but the Barlow Report here went beyond the mere problem of housing to the wider consideration of amenities, and in view of recent housing legislation the broadening of approach was timely. When Unemployment Assistance came into operation it had taken exactly a century to adapt to the needs of a highly organised industrial society the simple practices of a system of poor relief originally devised, and as late as 1834 re-shaped, to fit the needs of predominantly agricultural communities. At almost exactly the same time the housing conditions inherited from the earlier days of industrial development were at last tackled. The Housing Acts of 1930, 1933 and 1935 and the housing census of 1936, though owing to delays occasioned by the war their results were not to be seen to any great extent until the 50s and 60s, opened the final campaign against the century-old problem of the slums. Yet in no other aspect of social policy has the dichotomy of private enterprise and government action been more clearly revealed, or the dilemmas of social need exposed, and for all that has been done a final solution has still not been reached.

**The Situation in 1919—the Addison Act**   The problem of housing was one of those most obviously and immediately facing the nation in 1919. Housing development had always lagged behind the growth of population, and legislation had been mainly concerned with sanitary conditions. The Housing Act of 1890 had given local authorities the power to build, but little use had been made of it, and in fact the poorest people could not afford the rents of even the simplest decent accommodation. The main concern of authorities had been to ensure that private building kept to their standards, but standards, and costs, had risen steadily, until by the 20s working-class housing was becoming almost an impossibility for the private builder. Yet the problem was greater than ever before. New housing had been undertaken at a slow rate before the war, and building had then been almost entirely suspended, but the population was still growing and the demand for new houses increasing. By 1919 there was a deficiency of some 600,000 houses, which had to be met before any thought could be given to the improvement of poor-quality older housing, and with the rise of population demand could not but continue to increase during the 20s. Rent control had been introduced in 1915, to prevent war-profiteering, and obviously could not be relaxed until there was an adequate supply of accommodation, while the high hopes of better times had led to the rash promise of 'homes for heroes'. Under these circumstances only further action by the State was of any avail, and in the summer of 1919 the first post-war Housing and Town Planning Act was passed, commonly known as the Addison Act after the President of the Local Government Board (soon to be Minister of Health).

This Act introduced two important innovations. It both required local authorities to make good their deficiencies of housing, thereby strengthening the permissive powers of 1890, and provided the necessary assistance. A Treasury subsidy was to be paid to cover what was spent above the product of a penny rate, and a similar lump-sum subsidy was offered to private builders. Thus was introduced the combination of Treasury and local-rate financing of working-class housing which, except for a brief spell under Neville Chamberlain's influence in 1923-4, was to be the basis of social policy in housing. It was conceived, however, as a temporary measure, to tide over the period until the building industry itself could take over the task in full: there was little idea of the actual scale of the need, or of the time required to satisfy it.

Opinion was shocked, however, by the bill that was presented. The housing campaign started in the midst of the post-war building boom and was soon engulfed in the economic crisis of 1921. By that time nearly 170,000 local authority houses were building and the Treasury subsidy had already reached £12 million. A halt was called and a limit of 170,000 houses set. This was largely reached in 1923, by which time 40,000 subsidised houses had been erected by private builders and 54,000 other houses—but the national deficiency was even greater than ever.[125] Thus was revealed the dilemma of housing policy. Houses were urgently needed, but until costs fell could only be built at great expense: the Addison Act, in fact, imposed on the Treasury an annual charge of £7 million, which would fall only gradually over 40 years. Yet during the 20s private building could make little contribution to working-class housing. Not until the 30s did the combination of a large building industry, lower costs and government-sponsored cheap money make possible the great boom in small owner-occupier houses that produced more than 100,000 annually from 1931 and doubled that total from 1934.

**The Wheatley Act, 1924**   The main problem was, however, the provision of homes to rent. Chamberlain in 1923 reintroduced a small subsidy, though without permitting any charge on the rates. Wheatley, as Minister of Health in the Labour Government of 1924, increased this subsidy and by restoring rate-aid settled once and for all the responsibility of the local authorities for working-class housing. Above all, he introduced a long-term programme, extending to 1939, under which the building industry could confidently expand. Under his Act were built half of the houses constructed by local authorities between the wars, rather more than half a million in all, at a cost to the Treasury which eventually reached some £4 million a year. They are to be seen up and down the land, unmistakable 'Council Houses', unimaginatively planted in 'Estates' of dull uniformity, but far superior to what they replaced. Without them as pioneers the better planning of more recent years would hardly have been possible.

**Slum Clearance**   The Wheatley scheme was in operation until 1933, when it was brought to an end by the National Government, which, true to its mainly Conservative ideology, maintained that normal housing needs could now be met, especially in view of the fall in costs, by private enterprise. By this time a new aspect of the housing problem had been opened. As the housing situation improved attention turned to the condition of slums, for which nothing had yet been done. Consciences were roused by the contrast between the standards now possible and those still obtaining in many parts, especially in the depressed areas. There was more awareness, too, both of the need and of the possibility of improvement. In George Orwell's words, 'Talking once with a miner I asked him when the housing shortage became acute in his district; he answered, "When we were told about it"', meaning that till recently people's standards were so low that they took almost any degree of overcrowding for granted'.[126] Arthur Greenwood, as Minister of Health in the second Labour Government, introduced a new policy of slum clearance with the Housing Act of 1930 and it was continued by his successors in the National Government. The aim was no longer, as in the past, merely to pull down slum property but also to rehouse the inhabitants. Thus, policies of new housing and the destruction of old were to go on side by side: the essentially sanitary aims of nineteenth-century policy were to be combined with the new responsibilities accepted since 1919. To the National Government, however, when it took over the policy, the removal of slums was the only proper object of social policy in housing: for the rest private building must suffice. 'The Government', as one critic has said, 'had gone as near to rejecting responsibility for working-class housing as it could.'[127] In accordance with this policy, in 1933 a five-year limit was set for the clearance of the slums and a quarter of a million houses were declared to be involved.

**The Overcrowding Census**   Two years later, in 1935, a further Act at last tackled the problem of overcrowding, which was defined and made a legal offence. Like so many other aspects of Conservative social policy, this measure owed much to the concern with housing conditions which Neville Chamberlain had inherited from his father and carried with him from local into national politics. A special census undertaken by the local authorities in the following year revealed how much overcrowding actually existed, even on the modest scale laid down, and 341,000 houses were condemned, nearly four per cent of the total. Slum conditions and overcrowding are, however, capable of a variety of interpretation, and the estimates in both cases were certainly too small: at least a million houses, it was suggested by Sir Ernest Simon (Lord Wythenshawe), were in fact slums. Yet even the official estimates were not actually realised. Some authorities did better than others, but by 1939 only half even of the declared slums had been cleared. How serious the situation still was could be shown, for instance, by relating infant mortality rates to overcrowding in various centres of population. In the main, the higher the degree of overcrowding, the higher the infant death-rate.[128] It was the shock of the conditions revealed by evacuation in 1939 that finally brought home to the country, however, the inadequacy of all that had been done to improve the surroundings of a substantial part of the population in the more densely peopled and industrialised areas.

**New Housing**   In truth, housing policy since 1919, as before 1914, had mainly been of benefit to the better-off working man, whether through the provision of rented local authority accommodation or through the greatly extended possibilities of house purchase. And the benefit had gone principally to the favoured areas of new industry and greater prosperity. Hence, in the zones of rapid expansion, the long rows of smug-looking private enterprise housing that marked the 'ribbon development' of the 30s, usually easily distinguishable from council housing, but hardly less painful to the beholder in their sameness of design and arrangement. By 1939 the local authorities had built more than a million houses, three-quarters of them in the 15 years to 1934. Subsidised private builders had put up over 400,000 by 1930, and were to add a few thousands afterwards. The great spurt came, however, with unsubsidised private building, which produced in the 30s more than two million houses, of which about one-third were within the means of at least the better-off working man. In 1939 there were, in consequence, for all but the poorer elements in the population, more houses than were required. Yet slums and overcrowding were still common enough, and back-to-back housing, condemned for 50 years, was to survive into the seventh decade of the century, while in much older housing the lack of indoor sanitation and still more of baths was increasingly shown up by the rising standards of the new estates. Moreover, there remained other older property, better built but inadequately equipped, to threaten slum conditions in the future or demand replacement (or, as the event showed, re-equipment under the Acts of 1958–9). Soon war damage and wartime neglect were to intensify the problem: it would be nearly 20 years before the still unsatisfactory situation of 1939 was restored.

**Town Planning**  Most of the new housing undertaken in the inter-war years was suburban, much of it planted down, especially around London, with little consideration for the requirements of employment, or even of transport. Hence the melancholy 'dormitory suburbs' and the trials of 'strap-hanging', though there were exceptions, for instance, in Manchester's Wythenshawe. Too little attention was usually given to the possibilities of community development, and of over-all planning there was hardly any at all. In this last respect town-planning legislation, such as it was, was restrictive in scope. The Act of 1919 made planning obligatory, but confined it largely to new areas of development, while the Town and Country Planning Act of 1932, though it made it possible to extend planning over wider areas, reverted to permissive powers and achieved little. 'The general picture of urban development between the wars', it has justly been said, 'is one of confusion, of the predominance of the haphazard.'[129] Despite the example of such private developments as Welwyn Garden City, statutory town planning did hardly anything to remedy the confusion, being concerned rather with appearances than with the organisation of the business of living and working. Greater powers and a more imaginative grasp of the problems were required, and these the war years, beginning modestly enough with the Barlow Report, were to provide: after the devastation of wartime bombing planning at last came into its own.

# 8  *Education and Child Welfare*

Our final concern in this survey of social policy between the wars must be with the young, with education and other services touching their welfare. Lloyd George has spoken in his *War Memoirs* of the challenge and opportunity presented by the war to educational development in the national interest.[130] By 1914 illiteracy had almost vanished, and the elementary system, for all its limited chances of advancement, was soon to prove its worth on the battlefield: in the reluctant phrase of one senior officer during the war, 'There must be something in your damned elementary schools after all'.[131] A generation of parents had grown up accustomed to schooling and anxious to extend its children's opportunities. Secondary education for elementary schoolchildren, under the Act of 1902 and the 'free place' system of 1907, had not yet gone far: only some 56 children in every 1,000 were moving on in 1914, but the way was being prepared for the next advance. The greater prosperity for so many people of the war years, which made a child's earnings of less significance to the family budget, together with the hopes of a better and more just world with the return of peace, the realisation of the need for improved educational facilities to prepare young people for the heavy tasks of post-war recovery and the desire for equal opportunities to match the equal sacrifices of the war, all conspired to produce an outburst of demand which by 1921 had raised the 56 per 1,000 of 1914 to 97. By 1929 the proportion had further increased to double that of 1914, and the Hadow Report of 1926 had introduced a new, and wider, conception of secondary education. Though it was not until the Education Act of 1944 came into operation that the process was completed, the extension of the limited system of 1902 to the provision of secondary education of some kind for all was begun in the inter-war years. This was the 'silent social revolution',[132] though in view of the gradual nature of the process it was a matter of evolution rather than of revolution. The Labour Party's great statement of faith, *Secondary Education for All*, which was drawn up by R. H. Tawney, appeared in 1922, and the National Government in the general election of 1935 committed itself to the view that 'brains are the prerogative of no single class . . . wherever they are found it is essential in the interest of the State, as well as of the individual, that they should be given every opportunity of development'.[133] The driving force of the process was, however, as has well been said, 'the aspirations of the wage-earning classes, and the determination of those in receipt of small salaries themselves to equip their children to earn larger ones'.[134] Here the war, with its overturning of traditional barriers and its revelation of the possibilities of economic advancement, undoubtedly played its part. Respect for the established order could never be the same after 1918: too many thrones and castes had tottered, too many elementary schoolboys entered the once-charmed circle of the officer class.

**The Fisher Act, 1918**   To Lloyd George educational development was an essential part of reconstruction after the war. The greedy demands for men had exposed the poor physical condition of so many, and he hoped by improving the nation's schools both to improve the care taken of the nation's children and to prepare for the stern demands of peacetime recovery. When he formed his administration in 1916 he appointed as President of the Board of Education H. A. L. Fisher, then Vice-Chancellor of Sheffield University, who, though his own educational course had been run in pleasant places, deplored, like Lloyd George himself, the wastage of a State system which still cut short the education of so many children at the tender age of 12. To Fisher education was 'the most fundamental of all the social services',[135] and he was responsible for the second great advance since 1870, the 'Fisher Act' of 1918, the most significant sections of which, alas, were so soon to be balked by the economies of the early 20s.

The Education Act of 1918 made an imaginative, if in some respects hesitant, move forward by greatly extending the possibilities of education. The school-leaving age was at last set at 14, without the exceptions that had long been allowed, and powers, though only permissive ones, were given for the extension of the school years at both ends by the creation of nursery schools and the raising of the leaving age to 15. Moreover, part-time education up to 18 ('day-continuation') was introduced, a most significant innovation both for its social implications and for the opportunities it offered for further educational advancement. With more parents prepared to forgo temporarily their children's earnings it looked for a time as if the constricting bonds of elementary education might be burst. The Act certainly promised that no child should be debarred from educational opportunity because of inability to pay fees, abolished the half-time system of schooling, which still lingered in some parts from Victorian practice, and restricted the employment of schoolchildren to little more than newspaper delivery. It also extended medical inspection from the elementary to the secondary schools. It was, however, the placing on the statute book of the principle of continued education, in the interests alike of the pupils and of the community as a whole, that constituted the greatest advance. True, authorities were not obliged to make attendance compulsory: opinion, and especially much industrial opinion, was not yet prepared to accept that—indeed, it is not everywhere accepted even today. Within a few years, too, economy drives, particularly those associated with the 'Geddes Axe', made such cuts in the education services that 'day-continuation' was largely abandoned: only in Rugby was it kept going to point the way for its final acceptance, in principle, in 1944. Otherwise, for most young people continued education after 14 was still possible only in 'night-school'. In 1916 a departmental committee of the Board of Education had looked at the education of adolescents and shuddered at what it found: 'Can the age of adolescence be brought out of the purview of exploitation and into that of social conscience? Can the conception of the juvenile as primarily a little wage-earner be replaced by the conception of the juvenile as primarily the workman and the citizen in training?'[136] There was a wealth of social challenge in the questions, which marked a significant stage in the approach to that 'discovery of the child' which was to influence educational thought and policy between the wars. It was to be many years before answers to the questions even began to be made, but the Fisher Act did at least pose them as a challenge to the nation. Forty years later the now famous opening sentences of the Crowther Report of 1959 showed how much still remained to be done 15 years after the apparently decisive Act of 1944: 'This report is about the education of English boys and girls aged from 15 to 18. Most of them are not being educated.'[137]

Fisher's aims were frustrated by the immensity of the task he tackled and by the rapid onset of economic depression. In the hopeful spirit of 1918 too much was perhaps attempted too soon. The most enduring achievement was the great improvement in the status and conditions of the teaching profession, a cause which both Fisher and Lloyd George had much at heart.[138]

**The Hadow Report, 1926** The years that followed the Fisher Act were years of slow improvement and development in both elementary and secondary education. In 1926 appeared the Hadow Report, reporting on an assignment from the Labour Government of 1924. The principle of secondary education for all after the age of 11 was accepted in the report, with the almost derogatory term 'elementary' disappearing and the educational process being divided at 11 between 'primary' and 'secondary'. The secondary schools of the 1902 model were to become 'grammar schools', the upper forms of the old elementary schools and such higher elementary schools as existed (the 'central schools') being renamed 'modern' schools. These proposals were accepted and the reorganisation of the schools gradually put in hand, so that by 1939 about two-thirds of the school places available had been covered. So did a pattern familiar after 1944, with the much-debated break at '11-plus', begin to take shape. The Hadow Report also recommended the raising of the school-leaving age to 15, but this, though attempted by the Labour Government of 1929–31, was frustrated by the economic difficulties of the times and by the cost of providing the necessary teachers and places. Not until 1936 was the age raised by statute and the date then decided on for the change was the fateful one of 1 September 1939. Meanwhile the educational services concentrated on improving schools and lowering the size of classes: between 1924 and 1939 the number of classes with more than 50 pupils fell from 25,000 to 2,000 though there was little reduction in the number below 50. At the same time there took place a significant widening of the narrow curriculum that had been inherited from Victorian conceptions of the needs of working-class children: the period was one of considerable experiment.

'Special Places' In the grammar schools a new principle was introduced in the 30s. Under the economy drive of 1931 'free places' disappeared. Instead there were to be 'special places', with contributions from parents based on income, according to another kind of means test. This was a tacit recognition of the fact that the elementary schools, and the places reserved for some of their pupils in the secondary schools, were no longer the preserve of the poorest, but the change aroused a storm of understandable protest, and led to the adoption of a new principle of selection. Instead of merely reserving a small proportion of places for the brightest elementary pupils, the grammar schools were to be open to all according to ability (and, be it added, parental willingness): the parental contribution was to be settled according to means. The proportion of pupils who paid no fees fell only slightly as a result of this change, and was still in 1939 little short of one-half, though the number of working-class children in secondary schools remained disproportionately low.

The Spens Report, 1938 The gap in the reorganisation proposed by the Hadow Report was its failure to take technical education into account, a failure that reflected the popular preference (not without justification in the long years of industrial depression) for 'white collar' work as a means of advancement. In

1938, however, the Spens Report proposed a third type of secondary education, the technical, and even toyed with the notion of 'multilateral' schools (a first cautious approach to the later and much-debated 'comprehensive'). Whether the tripartite division is justified is a matter of controversy, but by 1939 a more effective educational pattern was slowly taking shape, and the decision to raise the school-leaving age in that year was at least a tardy recognition of the fact that more liberal measures were needed, though there was still a good deal of public indifference and especially of reluctance to spend more on a service that was soon to be seen, even more than in 1914–18, as a vital national investment. Very much remained to be done in the schools, and still more in higher education, but on the duly appointed day in September 1939, when the upper limit of the school age should have been raised, the nation was compelled to turn its attention to other and still more vital matters. Five years were then to pass before 'the most fundamental of all the social services' could be thoroughly overhauled in a new mood of hopefulness. The delay was only too typical of the way in which education, for all its fundamental importance, had so long been regarded as in practice the most expendable of the social services.

One thing in particular the schools had, however, achieved, the creation of a lower-middle class (to use a now outworn term), largely working-class in origin, which educational opportunity had made the functionaries of the community in such occupations as administration of all kinds and teaching, and the chief beneficiaries of social progress. Industry, commerce and the public services as they developed demanded more and more of such people and the schools provided them. From 'educating our masters' and training the raw material of industrial production, education was adapting itself, almost unconsciously, to meet the increasingly complex needs of social and industrial organisation, and there were sometimes complaints from the privately educated at this competition from tax-endowed sources. Only at the higher levels of direction, whether in administration, in science, or in technology, was the provision still lagging disastrously far behind the need.

**Child Health and Welfare** Whatever the limitations of the educational system in the 20s and 30s, despite the deprivations of economic depression the physical condition of the nation's children was in the main far better than it had ever been. The school medical services and the raising of general standards of health and cleanliness, which owed much to the example set in the schools, had together reduced considerably the incidence of ills caused by dirt or neglect. Between 1907 and 1934, for instance, the 30 children in every 1,000 examined who alone had been 'clean' had become only 30 who were 'dirty', and the death-rate among children of 5–15 years had fallen from 555 to 385 in every 100,000,[139] though evacuation in 1939 was to show how far the improvement had still to go. Nevertheless, that poorer children were no longer necessarily verminous was a factor making for greater unity among the social classes. School meals, though not everywhere provided, did something to relieve the strain of unemployment on children, and some authorities provided as much as three meals a day throughout the year. Free milk was made available to necessitous children from 1921, and as part of a national campaign to increase milk consumption the supply of milk to schools was subsidised by the Milk Marketing Board from 1934: the daily third of a pint became a feature of school life, with notable results in physique and growth, though not until after the war was the milk made free to all.

Yet, great though the improvement was from earlier conditions, it was, as war conditions were to reveal, far from enough: the first cursory examinations of recruits in 1939 proved seriously misleading in their optimism. Medical inspections in the early 30s showed that nearly one-quarter of the children in elementary schools were suffering, before the introduction of subsidised milk, from malnutrition in some degree, a proportion only exceeded by the incidence of defective eyesight and tonsils and adenoids.[140] The thin, starved children of the past were no longer seen, but, though actual starvation and even undernourishment had diminished, there was only too much evidence of malnutrition, the lack of those right types of food which medical research in these years was showing to be essential to health. It was now that 'vitamins' sank into general awareness. Yet the warnings of such pioneers of better feeding as Sir Edward Mellanby, with his passion for cod-liver oil, Sir John Boyd Orr and others were only slowly heeded, though the Ministry of Health set up in 1931 an Advisory Committee on Nutrition which was enlarged in 1935 and produced an influential report on the nutritive value of milk. School meals, however, increased only from 143,000 daily to 160,000 between 1935 and 1939: it was the war that was to raise the number to more than a million and a half by 1945. Insufficient attention was given, too, to the nutrition of expectant mothers. Milk was made available through Welfare Centres, but not free except to the necessitous, though the startling result of the feeding of undernourished mothers in the Rhondda Valley in 1935, which reduced the puerperal death-rate from 11 to four,[141] pointed the way to the revolution in policy from 1940, which made it possible to provide first milk and then orange-juice, cod-liver oil and vitamin tablets cheap or free to all expectant mothers and young children. In this connexion, as in so many aspects of social policy, the war and the evacuation from the great centres of population were to bring forward much that had long been hidden, and to upset much complacency. Above all, the wartime changes removed the last traces of poor-law provision and social condescension from the care of mothers and children. What was for all could not reflect upon its recipients, and in this, too, is to be found a 'silent social revolution', though in the 30s it lay still in the future. Certainly, one of the most serious gaps in welfare provision before 1946 was the exclusion of dependants from the National Health scheme, which kept, for instance, too many ailing mothers, and not merely the poorest among them, from the doctor, while having such effects as encouraging the vast sales of over-priced nostrums, poisoning many through neglected teeth and driving others to try to remedy defective vision with sixpenny spectacles.

**The Children and Young Persons Act, 1933**    Finally, in this review of the inter-war years, the attention given to children in need of care and protection and to the young delinquent. The epoch-making (it is hardly too strong a term) Children Act of 1908 has been described earlier. It remained in force until the early 30s, by which time experience of its working and a series of special enquiries, together with the reorganisation of local government in 1929, necessitated new legislation. In 1933 came the Children and Young Persons Act, which extended the responsibility of society up to the age of 17, and carried still further the provisions for the welfare of children in need of care for whatever reason, which had been established in 1908 and had now been extended by the modification of the poor law. The emphasis of the Act was laid on education and rehabilitation (remand homes, for instance, passed from the police to the local education authority, and new 'Approved Schools' were established) and on the alteration of the environment of the child in need of care. Section 44 of the Act expressed its essence: 'Every court in dealing with a child or young person who is brought before it, either as being in need of care or protection or as an offender or otherwise, shall have regard to the welfare of the child or young persons and shall in a proper case take steps for removing him from undesirable surroundings, and for securing that proper provision is made for his education and training.'[142] The desire to remove young people from the influence of the Fagins of society was commendable; the emphasis, even in cases of delinquency, on rehabilitation rather than punishment was in accordance with the best lights of the times. What was still missing, in the concern for the individual child, was a conception of the part that his family, given help, might still play. In the words of a Home Office report of 1938: 'The old theory, once very strongly held, that the parents having failed with their children, should be more or less ignored, has now given way to a realisation that whenever possible the co-operation of the parent in the training and disposal of the child is advisable and very helpful.'[143] In the 30s, with economic insecurity, the means test as a bitter threat to family unity and still inadequate social provision, the family was under a cloud.[144] It was to be left to the great Children Act of 1948, in the healthier circumstances of full employment and vastly improved welfare services, to complete the process and to restore the conception of the family as the constructive influence in social development.

## Conclusion—'Purposive Social Advance'

So far by 1948 had society come from the notion of a deterrent poor law, breaking up families to enforce economic independence, and insisting, as in the poor law report of 1834, that it was no business of the State's to prevent children from suffering for the sins of their fathers. So far doctrine and practice had not gone by the 1930s, but looking back we see the nation, in most matters of social policy, feeling its way forward then, slowly and painfully, as we have shown—too slowly and too painfully for the dispossessed—towards a wider sense of social responsibility. In the words used by a leading spirit of the Labour movement between the wars in a comment on the 20s and 30s, 'It is wrong, and false to historic fact, to forget that two decades of which we now think badly—and rightly, so far as international policies are concerned—were a period of steady and purposive social advance at home.'[145] This was also the conclusion, in distant retrospect, of a notable Conservative, Harold Macmillan, who had himself been much concerned with social problems in the two decades.[146] Steady and purposive advance was to give way in the war, however, to a Dunkirk-spirit of rescue and unity, with a new sense of the obligations of society to all its members.

*Note to page 259.* It is often overlooked that one of the decisive factors in the determination to abolish the guardians, was that de-rating would substantially reduce their resources. This is made clear in Ministry of Health reports of the time and is stressed by Professor Gilbert in his *British Social Policy 1914–1939*, ch. 5.

# 7 | Beveridge and Beyond

**The Final Stages** If, as was once claimed in a phrase that has become historic, the British Empire was created in a fit of absence of mind, the Welfare State has been no less the result of a fit of conscience, or, rather, as the story of its progress will have shown, of a whole series of fits of conscience. In this last stage, under the pressure of the great levelling influence of total war, conscience rounded-off, between 1940 and 1948, the long process by which an elaborate series of social services, most of them created to serve particular needs, was at last consolidated and extended into a pattern of welfare provision which could reasonably be styled a 'Welfare State'. Much was done, or prepared for, during the war, but the climax came in 1945, on what the Labour mover of the Address in the new Parliament of that year, John Freeman, called, with pardonable enthusiasm, 'D-Day in the battle of the new Britain'.[1] A new spirit was then abroad, the peacetime counterpart to the defiant resolution and endeavour which Winston Churchill had so magnificently embodied during the war. But no more than Churchill in war did the Labour Party in the electoral struggle *create* the spirit which brought victory. Churchill, in a majestic disclaimer, has seen himself during the war as but the focus of the courage of the British people, 'the lion's roar'. The Labour Party, in a similar simple concentration of emotion, was carried to victory in 1945 by a wave of distrust of those who had been in power before the war. For all his services, which none failed to recognise, Churchill was no more trusted than those in the Conservative Party who had earlier distrusted him to create the kind of England which so many wanted. The memory of the bright promises, and prompt disillusionment, of 1918 was strong, if only as part of the national folklore, and was reinforced by the clumsy handling of the Beveridge Report of 1942, which still rankled in 1945, especially in the Services. However much preparatory planning had been done during the war by the Coalition Government, there was suspicion of the Conservative Party's willingness to carry the plans into effect, and suspicion proved as fatal to Conservatism in 1945 as it had been to Labour in 1931. This it was, the desire for a new deal, for a breaking-away from the means-test approach to social problems, rather than for any experiments in Socialism, that coloured the electoral preference of so many. The result was the attempt, under the most difficult conditions of destruction and scarcity, to remedy many of the inherited ills of society, which the war years, and the 20 years before them, had brought before the country to a degree that permitted of no pusillanimity or half-measures. War and its revelations, however, had stirred consciences already uneasily aware of the inadequacy of the services that had been created by 1939. Conscience, and consciousness of this inadequacy, together with the egalitarianism of sacrifice, which brought the destruction of battle literally upon the homes of King and commoner alike, produced the war-time reports and proposals, and it was upon them, as the legacy of the years of unity in struggle, that the victors of 1945 were to build.

**A New Attitude**    The National Health Service White Paper of 1944 claimed, with a good deal of justice, that what was planned during the war years was 'not a matter of making good what is bad, but of making better what is good already'. The previous chapter will have shown that, however much truth there was in this, the benefits received from the social services before 1939 depended on many factors outside individual control. A young mother in one of the depressed areas, for instance, saw the services in a far less favourable light than even a moderately well-paid worker in an area of new and expanding industry. The gaps in 1939 were obvious enough; what the war did was not merely to begin to close them, but to introduce a wholly new attitude into social provision. In the past it had been accepted as axiomatic that the individual could usually, by the normal working of economic processes, provide for himself and his family, so that it was only in exceptionally difficult conditions that help was needed. Moreover, when help was given it was usually by means that stamped the recipient as in some way of inferior status. Experience and enquiry had shown, however, that difficulties were less exceptional, and less easily remedied, than had been assumed, and protective measures had therefore been devised and extended, measures in which, even when the principle of insurance was introduced, there lingered the taint of dependence, of poor law inferiority and charitable provision. Still more difficulties and limitations came to light and, in particular, the long record of unemployment between the wars showed that much more active intervention by the State was necessary. It was no longer a matter of helping individual cases of distress, but, as with the earlier revelations of poverty through old age, of assisting whole classes or groups who through no fault of their own could not hope to protect themselves against economic ills. There were, too, other groups, such as mothers and children, which needed attention that many could not provide for themselves even when they were aware of its necessity. If there was no longer the serious wastage of life that had been disclosed in earlier stages of development, there were still cramping poverty, uncertain employment, undernourishment, poor housing and lower standards of health than need be tolerated in the face of the advances in medicine. The war drove home the lesson that, considerations of sheer humanity and social concern apart, all this was a drain on human resources that the nation could ill afford. Expressed merely in material terms, there was serious wastage in lowered efficiency and productive capacity, both present, in the case of adults, and presumptive, as with children, no less than in the actual loss of producing and consuming power through unemployment. Expressed in terms of morale, of national unity and resilience in the face of the enemy, the weaknesses were potentially still more serious. It became part of the national war effort to remedy the deficiencies, and in the process new principles of social policy were to emerge.

Hitherto help had gone only to those who for one reason or another could not provide for themselves, and the limits had been narrowly circumscribed, so that, for instance, unemployment assistance had been restricted by the household means test. Under war conditions, however, it was not so much poverty as physical need that came to be the touchstone of national policy. All classes, and not merely the poor, were affected by the conscription of men and women, by bomb damage, by food shortages and by the stresses imposed on family life. Instead of being reduced as extravagant frills, as had at first been thought possible, the social services, in the interests of the efficiency of the war effort, had to be not only maintained, but adapted, extended and enlarged. Even before the further developments of 1945–8, the situation as it had existed in 1939 had changed almost beyond recognition. From assistance only to those most in need through poverty the responsibility of the community had been extended, without discrimination, to all who needed its help; from marginal provision to the destitute and helpless it had developed into a pooling of national resources to see all its members through any of the ills that social care could relieve. In particular did this apply to children, who were recognised as the community's most vital responsibility, and were ensured by wartime measures satisfactory physical and intellectual development regardless of the limitations of parental means. Elaborate arrangements were made for their health and nutrition, and even before the war ended the decisions had been made to introduce family allowances and to widen educational opportunity. 'Under something like conditions of siege the principle was accepted that "the child should be the first to receive relief in times of distress".'[2] It was a decision that was all the more urgent because of the steady decline in the birth-rate between the wars, a decline that seemed to threaten the nation in time with a catastrophic fall in population. As Beveridge wrote in his 1942 Report, 'the small families of today make it necessary that every living child should receive the best care that can be given to it'.[3] The prospect of heavy war casualties added point to the argument.

Furthermore, the spirit of assistance had become more humane. Deterrence, though long since past in policy, had lingered in memory and attitude, kept alive by the reluctance to provide more than a bare minimum, and had coloured reactions to the means test. With little enough new building done by 1939, for all the improvements in policy the bleakness associated with poor-law institutions (as with early school building) was still much in evidence, and was, for instance, to shock many evacuated during the war from the country's more modern hospitals to converted poor-law establishments. Despite the U.A.B.'s attempts to inculcate a new spirit among its officers there was much suspicion and distrust of officials, strengthened, of course, by the memory of the years during which no unemployed man who had exhausted his insurance benefit could expect extended help as of right, but had to accept it as an an act of grace from the mysterious *They* whose edicts made or marred. Where help had to be sought it was to the Relieving Officer, with all that that implied of poor-law practice, or to the U.A.B., with its household means test, that most people had to turn, and many felt keenly the humiliation involved. Not a few, especially among the elderly, whose modest means had been adequate before the war found themselves, owing to wartime economic strains, compelled to consider applying for assistance, and shrank from the prospect. Hence the 'remarkable discovery of secret need' among old people after the introduction of supplementary pensions in 1940, which in a few months raised the 275,000 pensioners granted supplementary allowances from the poor-law Public Assistance to more than a million receiving supplementary pensions through the Assistance Board.[4] The economic distress among pensioners proved, indeed, to have been seriously underestimated, the Government having assumed early in 1940, on the calm assurance of the Chancellor of the Exchequer (Sir John Simon), that there was no longer 'any very large number of old age pensioners who prefer destitution to the alleged indignity of applying for public assistance'.[5]

**The Significance of 1940**   It was the introduction of supplementary pensions, together with the abolition of the household means test in the following year, that marked the appearance of new spirit and attitude. 1940 represents a dividing line in social policy. It was symbolic both of the new spirit and of Britain's proud assurance in the face of a danger without parallel in her history that during all the dreadful summer of that year the preparations for the issue of supplementary pensions went quietly forward, so that on the appointed day, 3 August, with invasion almost hourly expected, everyone was duly paid. No less symbolic and significant was the decision, made within a week of the Dunkirk evacuation, to introduce a national milk scheme which ensured a supply of milk, at a reduced price or if necessary free, to all mothers and young children. Henceforth, it could increasingly be claimed that the State in the last resort accepted responsibility for all: there were no longer to be second-class citizens. The many further measures of welfare which followed during the war years reinforced the conception of a society organised to assist in time of need all its weaker members, whatever their circumstances or the occasion of their distress. How in practice this was worked out we must now consider. Underlying it was the tacit but general assumption that all the neglect which the years of peace and the impact of war had revealed should be remedied. In the words of the *Civil History of the War*, 'There existed, so to speak, an implied contract between Government and people; the people refused none of the sacrifices that the Government demanded from them for the winning of the war; in return, they expected that the Government should show imagination and seriousness in preparing for the restoration and improvement of the nation's well-being when the war had been won.'[6] By 1945 R. A. Butler could claim with some justice, in the opening debates of the new Parliament, that 'this country stands before the world as a living social experiment'.[7]

**Reconstruction Plans: (1) The Conditions for Change**  From its formation in May 1940, the Coalition Government, despite all its critical preoccupations, had in mind the problems of the return to peace when it should come, and the kind of Britain that should emerge from the war. Reconstruction in the First World War had been badly managed and had plunged the country into serious political and economic difficulties. This time, while it was unknown what the war casualties would be (mercifully they were to be far fewer), it was certain that there would be extensive damage in Britain itself: in the event, of course, nearly four million houses alone were destroyed or damaged, representing a formidable problem in physical reconstruction in themselves. Moreover, the very completeness of the nation's war effort and the immense scale of the call-up of men and women alike made it inevitable that the transition from war to peace would be a difficult and complex process, with controls of many kinds continuing well into the years ahead. To these practical considerations were added the shocks to national complacency, first of the revelations of evacuation and then of the sweeping German victories of the spring and summer of 1940. The resolution and uplifting of hearts that came with Dunkirk and all that it stood for brought also a mood of unity in sacrifice that was to colour the whole nation's attitude to social problems and ensure that things would never again be as they had been. Symbolic of the national unity was the presence as part of the Government of Labour leaders, not, as in the First War, as a gesture to the working-classes, but as equal partners in a Ministry that embodied the resolution in unity of the British people. The influence of these leading representatives of the Labour movement, Attlee, Bevin, Cripps, Morrison, Greenwood, Dalton and Alexander, and especially of the dominating figure of Bevin, the only one whose career had been made outside politics, was felt in social policy from the first, as well as in the over-all direction of the war. Indeed, for their influence on the shaping of events this might almost be called the third, as it was certainly the most constructive to date, of Britain's Labour Governments. The first legislative result of their entry into the government was the Determination of Needs Act of March 1941, which abolished the household means test against which the Labour Party had struggled so long and bitterly. It was an augury of what, with the revelations of continued economic distress, national unity could achieve. Bevin himself had accepted the Ministry of Labour because it would give him 'the chance to lay down the conditions on which we shall start again',[8] and the first general statement of peace aims, the 'Atlantic Charter' of August 1941, contained a reference to 'improved labour standards, economic advancement and social security' which was inserted by the War Cabinet into the draft prepared by Churchill and President Roosevelt and was in fact insisted on by Bevin.[9]

**Reconstruction Plans: (2) Beveridge Returns**  The first positive step in reconstruction policy was taken at the end of 1940, when one of the two members of the War Cabinet, Arthur Greenwood, who had been concerned in the reconstruction discussions of 1917-9 and had held the Ministry of Health in the Second Labour Government of 1929-31, was given the task of planning, in the Prime Minister's words, 'a number of practical steps which it is indispensable to take if our society is to move forward'. None could have foreseen how significant this assignment was to prove. It was Greenwood who set up in June 1941, as the result in the first place of representations from the T.U.C. on the inadequacy of the provision for social insurance, an Interdepartmental Committee on Social Insurance and Allied Services, 'to undertake, with special reference to the interrelation of the schemes, a survey of the existing national schemes of social insurance . . . and to make recommendations'.[10] By the happiest of chances the ideal man for the investigation, as it was to develop, was available in Sir William Beveridge, who in earlier years had been so much concerned with the origin of the schemes. Bevin had recently appointed him to the Ministry of Labour, but he had proved so difficult a colleague that Bevin passed him to Greenwood, who made him chairman of the committee, where his *prima donna* attributes had full play.[11] The committee, consisting as it did almost entirely of senior civil servants, was not intended to concern itself with more than administrative issues, but the chairman had other, and wider, views, and after the committee had been reconstituted to make him alone responsible for its findings he produced late in 1942 a major restatement of social policy which was to have the widest repercussions, the 'Beveridge Report'. This was to be the basis, two years later, of the Government's own proposals on Social Insurance and of the establishment of a Ministry of National Insurance.

**Reconstruction Plans: (3) Reith and Planning**  Even before Greenwood had started work another distinguished figure, Sir John Reith (Lord Reith), creator of the B.B.C., had been asked, largely at Bevin's prompting, to take charge of the Office of Works, promoted to the status of a Ministry in October 1940, and to concern himself with the physical aspects of post-war planning and reconstruction. The Barlow Report, with its important recommendations, had appeared in January 1940, but had been thrust aside by the desperate course of events. The blitz, however, with its devastation of whole areas of great towns, re-opened the whole question of future planning, and the report therefore assumed a new significance. Early in 1941 Reith appointed a committee under Mr Justice Uthwatt to advise on the public acquisition of land for reconstruction purposes and on the broader issues of development values which had so long plagued the country. Later in the same year a second committee was set up, with Lord Justice Scott as chairman, to study land utilisation in rural areas. The Scott Committee reported in August 1942, and the final report of the Uthwatt Committee appeared in the following month. The central planning authority which had been recommended by the Barlow Report came into existence when the Ministry of Town and Country Planning was established early in 1943.

**Churchill and Reconstruction**    Thus early in the war, almost before the Hinge of Fate (in Churchill's graphic phrase) had begun, in the latter months of 1942, to turn in the Allies' favour, appeared the first heralds of what, with victory assured, was in time to be. Churchill, as he showed in his handling of the Beveridge Report, deprecated the 'continual buzz of ardent discussion' about the future and was unduly, if understandably, concerned both to hold together his ministerial team, divided as it was on many political issues, and to keep the country aware of the economic difficulties it would have to face when peace came. As he told Reith on one occasion, when urging the importance of 'first-aid' to damaged houses, 'Do not let spacious plans for a new world divert your energies from saving what is left of the old'.[12] Yet, quite apart from the fact that preparations for orderly reconstruction had to be made in good time, the very discussion of proposals, as the public reception of the Beveridge Report showed, was a tonic in bleak times, and had therefore no small part to play in the war effort. It was necessary to have something to fight *for* as well as *against*, and there were many who felt that to the Britain they were defending they owed little enough. Moreover, few could share Churchill's satisfaction in being at the centre of things: most people were helpless pawns who were entitled to their hopes.

**Problems and Decisions: (1) The Cost of Living**    The Reports of 1942 introduced a whole series, and were in time to lead to legislation of the first importance. Meanwhile a host of practical problems had arisen, and the measures taken to cope with them proved no less far-reaching in the turn they gave to social policy. The most immediate issues were the direct outcome of the upheavals of war, economic difficulties through the rise in the cost of living and all the social strains brought about by evacuation and the separation of families. A rise in the cost of living followed directly on the outbreak of war: by January 1940 it had already reached 12 per cent and it was not checked until the summer of 1941, when it was nearly 30 per cent. Wage rates rose more slowly, but after initial hesitation largely kept pace and after 1942, indeed, outstripped the increase in living costs (actual earnings were, of course, still higher). For those on fixed incomes, old age pensions and U.A.B. allowances, however, there was grave hardship. Hence the decision in 1940 to supplement pensions from funds administered by the U.A.B., renamed, in view of this widening of its functions, the Assistance Board. This implied the withdrawal of yet another group from the operation of the poor law, and the response it attracted was a measure of the popular emotional reaction to the poor law and all it stood for. In the following year came the Determination of Needs Act, which eased the position of those receiving assistance subject to the household means test, and narrowed the enforceable family responsibility for support. This still further limited the traditional operation of the poor law, which, as shown earlier, had restated in Elizabethan terms, as recently as 1930, the duties of parents, grandparents, husbands and children to support those in want. Henceforth, Bevin pointed out in commending the measure to the Commons, the poor law was almost buried: in the words of another Labour contributor to the debate, responsibility had now been largely shifted from the family to the community.[13]

Under the scheme for the supplementation of pensions, people receiving non-contributory pensions under the arrangements that had been in operation from 1909 to 1926 received their basic pensions in the usual way from the Board of Customs and Excise and their supplementary allowances from the Assistance Board. In 1943 the procedure was simplified so that all supplemented pensions were handled by the Assistance Board alone. This was the final modification before its abolition in 1947 of the curious arrangement by which non-contributory pensions were the responsibility of the Customs and Excise. In 1943, also, there were further improvements in rates and conditions for all those receiving Unemployment Assistance and supplementary pensions.

These adjustments of the arrangements for assisting the needy were necessary in view of the economic difficulties of the early years of the war. Unemployment still stood at one million as late as the end of 1940, and did not reach its wartime minimum of 100,000 until 1943. Taking up the slack of the pre-war economy was a slow task even in the face of supreme danger, and when the economy was at full stretch, in 1943, there were still pockets of adjustment, in addition to the core of some 20,000 unemployables, amounting in all to about ½ per cent of the labour force: Unemployment Assistance was then still being paid to 16,000, though the vast majority of the total of nearly half a million who had been receiving it in 1939 were now at work. The war, for all Britain's immense effort, showed, however, that full employment was not a term to be taken too literally. Beveridge, in his Report of 1942, based his proposals on an unemployment rate of, at best, 8½ per cent,[14] though in his second, more specific, study, *Full Employment in a Free Society*, published in 1944, he defined full employment in terms that allowed for an irreducible minimum of three per cent[15] (in fact, the unexpected has happened and since 1946 the overall percentage had until 1966–7 only once risen as high even as two).

The demand for labour and the supplementation of pensions diminished the number of people receiving poor law assistance, but in 1942 there were still more than 300,000 (including dependants, nearly 500,000). Here, as with the continuance of some degree of unemployment, was evidence of the need for an adequate system of relief.

Far more than supplementation of rates of relief was required, however, to ensure both that the national economy would stand the strain of war and that the economic burdens would be fairly borne by all. The greatest menace to the economy was the possibility of a 'vicious spiral of inflation', with its calamitous effects on prices and wages, felt most by those least able to protect themselves. It was important, if wages were not to be forced up, that prices should be kept under control, and there was the memory of the profiteering of the First World War as a spur to action. The price of food was stabilised in December 1939, at first as a temporary measure, but from August 1940 on a permanent basis. Then, in his budget speech of April 1941, the Chancellor of the Exchequer (Sir Kingsley Wood) undertook to provide the means to keep the cost of living steady. This, associated as it was with the preparation of the first White Paper on the National Income and Expenditure, marked a most significant development in policy. Henceforth the full resources of the nation were to be mobilised in the interests of the economic security of State and citizen alike. It was a policy of wartime necessity, but had deliberate social implications, while the publication of statistical information was intended to explain and justify policy to all and to secure their understanding support for tough measures. The education of the public in economics and finance was highly necessary in view of a war-effort that demanded so much from all, but at the same time it was in itself evidence of a new conception of government.

(2) **School Milk and Meals**   Meanwhile supplies of essential foods were assured to those most in need, who were not necessarily the poorest. Concern at the possible effects of war shortages on the health of children led in 1940, and still more in 1941, to Treasury encouragement of the provision of school meals and milk, not only to those in financial need. 'There is no question of capacity to pay', urged an official report, 'we may find the children of well-to-do parents and the children of the poor suffering alike from an inability to get the food they need.'[16] In five years the number of school meals served daily rose from 130,000 to 1,650,000 while the proportion of children taking milk at school increased from 19 to 46 per cent. Both meals and milk were provided at subsidised prices, or free in cases of real need. From this great advance in social policy there could be no drawing back: the health and physique of the children of the war and post-war years are its best justification. It was, indeed, 'something very close to a revolution'.[17] Whatever their parents' circumstances, children were assured what was necessary for healthy development, without any thought of pauperisation or charity or any test of means or need except in so far as the poorest could get their allocation free. Since few parents hesitated to take advantage of what was made available for all, this was perhaps an even more significant stroke of policy than the Determination of Needs Act in speeding the lingering relics of the poor-law complex. It was a far cry from the days, only 40 years earlier, when the provision of meals for starving children from public funds had been hotly disputed.

(3) 'Putting Milk into Babies'   The national milk scheme, to ensure, again with Treasury aid, the supply of milk for mothers and babies, was another near-revolutionary step. It was introduced, as already recorded, in the dark days of July 1940, and by September 70 per cent of the mothers and children eligible were taking part. Churchill beamed approval in a notable broadcast in 1943: 'there is no finer investment for any community than putting milk into babies'. Nearly 30 per cent of the mothers received their milk free, though it is a measure of the rising prosperity of the war years that by 1945 this proportion had fallen to only three. The Government subsidies to the two milk schemes rose from little more than £500,000 in 1938 to £19,000,000 in 1945. In addition, there were sub-sidies to farmers, and steps were also taken, notably in the Milk and Dairies Act, 1944, to secure the safety and quality of milk. At the end of 1941 the milk scheme was followed by the provision of vitamin foods, eventually orange-juice, cod-liver oil (for those who could stomach it) and vitamin tablets. Mothers and children, it was said in the Commons in 1943, must have all they need: 'the raw material of the race is too valuable to be put to risk'.[18]

(4) Immunisation   One of the great risks for children in pre-war days had been diphtheria, which in 1938 killed nearly 3,000, and there were fears of epidemics in the difficult conditions of wartime, especially in view of the hours spent in air-raid shelters. Immunisation had been encouraged for some time and undertaken in some areas, but not intensively. At the end of 1940 it was decided to provide immunisation free, and a great programme of publicity was undertaken. By 1945 more than half the children of the country had been immunised, and the death-rate had fallen to 818, though it remained true that more children had been killed during the war by diphtheria than by bombs.[19] The immunisation cam-paign was a striking development in the personal health services which yet had most important social consequences. No compulsion was used, but again the advantages of State action were so obvious as to have lasting effects on the con-ception of the public health services. Health education, in particular, had its greatest boost. One lasting result of the war, indeed, was that the nation became health conscious, even as, through the White Papers on Income and Expenditure, it became economics conscious. Health education produced such striking slogans as 'coughs and sneezes spread diseases', which were put out by what the Ministry of Health's report on the war years called 'the full orchestra of propaganda', including that notable performer, Dr Charles Hill, the 'Radio Doctor' (later, Lord Hill of Luton), who, in the report's apt phrase, 'went on the air to bring health education down to earth'.[20]

All these measures undoubtedly contributed to the remarkable standard of public health during the war. Something was owed, of course, to the fact that a whole generation had grown up in better conditions of public health and with the school medical service to protect them. Much was due also to the higher incomes enjoyed by most people and to the rationing and price controls, which ensured them adequate supplies of food. To take only one illustration, many who before the war had relied on cheap condensed milk now turned to fresh milk: indeed, the great increase in milk consumption, not merely among mothers and children, was one of the real gains of these years. In the words of a leading authority on nutrition, it was 'strange that rationing should mean better food for the country at large, and stranger still that we should take this revolution so much for granted'.[21] The results of better feeding and the various preventive measures were seen in the fall in the infant and maternal mortality rates, in itself an indication of the higher general level of health and a sufficiently remarkable phenomenon under conditions of siege.

(5) **The Range of Government Intervention**    The steps so successfully taken to sustain the besieged garrison achieved much that had been called for in the 30s, and implied a more positive conception of government. How far intervention for purposes of welfare had to be carried can be simply but strikingly illustrated from one episode, the long discussion over the allocation, from desperately short stocks, of rubber for the making both of teats for feeding babies and of contraceptives to prevent their coming.[22] Concern with the supply of contraceptives was at first markedly reluctant and restricted to the case for the prevention of the social scourge of venereal disease, but wide social issues had soon to be taken into account. Here is epitomised much of the development of social policy, from the narrow concern with particular needs and difficulties to the broad interests of the whole community. Everywhere a higher standard of service came to be demanded and expected, without discrimination on financial or moral or any other grounds.

(6) **A National Health Service**    A widening of the National Health scheme was the inevitable outcome of the extension of social policy in matters of health. As the Ministry of Health frankly acknowledged in its survey of the war years, the arrangements for the care of the public health before the war 'constituted good services but a bad service'.[23] The limitations of National Health Insurance and the various other branches of the public health services have been touched on in the previous chapter. The war brought home the need, already acknowledged in many quarters, for a more comprehensive service, and public discussion was stimulated by the reports issued by the B.M.A. and the Medical Officers of Health, as well as by the Beveridge Report. Official discussions began in 1943, and early in the following year appeared the Government's White Paper, *A National Health Service*, which recognised the anomalies and inequalities of the existing services and aimed at preparing 'a comprehensive cover for health provided for all people alike': 'The Government believe that, at this stage of social development, the care of personal health should be put on a new footing and be made available to everybody as a publicly sponsored service. Just as people are accustomed to look to public organisation for essential facilities like a clean and safe water supply ... so

they should now be able to look for proper facilities for the care of their personal health to a publicly organised service available to all who want to use it.'[24]

(7) **The Assistance Board** At one with these developments were others in aspects of social care that were rendered more urgent by the war. In addition to the provision of supplementary pensions the Assistance Board was given the task of promoting the welfare of pensioners, and did much to relieve difficulties of many kinds that were not susceptible to cure by cash payment. This broke more new ground in social policy and, though much that was done might seem trivial, the Board realised, as recorded in its 1944 report, that the real value of its welfare work lay less in spectacular deeds than in the 'small and simple services that alleviate distress of mind and body'. Often enough, for instance, there was need for help in the home, even for those able in the past to employ servants, for the number of domestic servants fell during the war by some half million to 200,000. The Maternity and Child Welfare Act of 1918 had allowed authorities to set up 'home help' schemes for mothers during confinement, and many authorities had taken advantage of this, though the service was restricted to confinement cases and inevitably declined during the early years of the war. From 1942 it was recognised as being work of national importance, and in 1944 a similar 'domestic help' service for attendance on the elderly and the sick was authorised. Little progress could be made in either case owing to the shortage of possible staff, but, again, a national service, without discrimination for those in need, had been devised: it was to be greatly developed in the post-war years.

The Assistance Board also helped bombed-out families and other cases of distress. This wartime experience undoubtedly did much to eradicate in the public mind the memory of its earlier associations with the means test, and prepared the way for the important new functions as the reserve welfare service that it assumed, under the new name of 'National Assistance Board', in 1948.

**The Impact of Evacuation on Social Policy** The episode of the war that was at once the most dramatic, the most revealing and the most influential in its impact on social attitudes and policy was, however, evacuation, which held up a mirror to a society which had assumed, largely without thinking about it at all, that it was doing well enough by all its members. Loud were the cries of distress when homes were spoiled by dirty and incontinent children, shocked were hostesses by the poor and scanty clothing of many evacuees, which earned for their home towns the title of 'Plimsoll City', and worse still was the reaction to many mothers evacuated with young children. In the words of a notable study of the impact, *Our Towns: A Close-Up*, published in 1943, 'For once the mountain had come to Mahomet, and its aspect gave little satisfaction'.[25] It was, indeed, a 'close-up', revealing much of the worst about town conditions, often for the simple reason that it was the poorest and most congested areas that had to be evacuated, as they were closest to the probable targets, especially in the ports. And while the complaints about clothing were often sound enough, many homes in the danger areas had known unemployment for years and lacked the means to fit out their children. Clothing problems were in fact the easiest settled. Much was done by host families and voluntary organisations and something by official arrangement. A limited amount of money was made available by the Ministry of Health in 1939 and this was increased a year later.

What shocked most of all was less the actual conditions, the dirty habits, the bed-wetting and the like, of which so much was heard, than the realisation that such things could be in view of the services the State had been developing. 'What have we spent all this money for?' was a constant cry. Yet the worst conditions were found among small children of the very poor, who received no medical attention or social training, and on whom large sums would have to be spent by the school medical service when they eventually appeared at school—and all the harm had already been done. Family allowances to relieve family poverty, educational improvements, including nursery schools, school milk and meals and medical attention under a comprehensive health service were all obvious reforms, essential, *Our Towns* claimed, if the country was to ensure 'that John Smith's child becomes in truth John Bull's child, a cherished part of its country's capital'.[26] Better housing and surroundings and social facilities in community centres were among the other reforms advocated for older people. These were the lessons that were driven home by evacuation, and their influence on future policy is plain to see.

**Restoring the Family**  Underlying all the lessons learnt was a new recognition of the fundamental importance of the family. The failures of family life were painfully obvious from evacuation in neglected children and incompetent mothers, but no less striking was the pull of the family to evacuees who returned home in large numbers when danger seemed less imminent. Psychologists, studying the social phenomena of war, gave scientific warrant to the need for family life in development which mankind had always instinctively known, and the Ministry of Health, surveying the working of evacuation, acknowledged from its experience the impossibility of finding a substitute.[27] Where hitherto the failure of families, even if only through economic difficulties, had led to their being split up and their members divided, as under the old poor law, social policy aimed henceforth at maintaining the family intact, and, where necessary, restoring it and improving the quality of its care. Only in the last resort was a substitute sought, and then it had to bear the closest possible resemblance to the original. This was the policy that underlay the great Children Act of 1948.

**Infant Welfare**  During the war, despite many difficulties, the infant welfare services were maintained and developed, as, in a phrase used by the Ministry of Health, 'a bulwark in a system of national defence', until there were actually more centres than in pre-war days.[28] Residential and day nurseries were established to relieve mothers who, from war-work or other cares, were in need of help, and special hostels were opened for evacuated children who for any reason could not be billeted. The inevitable rise in the illegitimate birth-rate brought better provision for the unmarried mother and her child, who by a special circular of 1943 were no longer left to the poor law (and the limited resources of the voluntary societies), but were made the responsibility of local authorities. Here it was partly concern for young women away from home in the Services or war factories that wrought so significant a change after centuries of stern disapproval and neglect, but no less also an increasing interest in the welfare of all the nation's children, which eventually led in 1947, for instance, to the introduction of a modified birth-certificate which betrayed nothing of the origins of the illegitimate child.

**Child Care**   The concern for children, and especially for children in care, which culminated in the Act of 1948 was stimulated by wartime conditions and revelations and especially by the tragic death through neglect in 1945 of a 13-year-old boy, boarded-out with foster-parents. This event revealed the serious inadequacies of the arrangements by which authorities took children into care, and was followed by the appointment of the Care of Children Committee (the Curtis Committee), with the significantly worded assignment, to enquire into 'methods of providing for children . . . deprived of a normal home life'. The Committee's recommendations led first to the appointment of a Central Training Council in Child Care, to improve the quality and supply of child-care officers, and then, in 1948, to the new Act, which emphasised, first and foremost, the necessity of a family background for the child and gave local authorities new responsibilities, with special officials, the Children's Officers, to supervise them, and but one responsible Ministry, the Home Office. To sketch the new arrangements at this stage is to jump ahead, but the Act was so much a result of the re-thinking of the war years and owed so much to wartime experience that it is logical to treat it here. The changes it made can most simply be illustrated by comparing one of its clauses with the corresponding requirement of the last Poor Law Act of 1930.[29] The 1930 Act, restating Elizabethan policy, aimed, 'to set to work or put out as apprentices all children whose parents are not, in the opinion of the Council, able to keep them'. For this the 1948 Act substituted the following clause: 'Where a child is in the care of a local authority it shall be the duty of that authority to exercise their powers with respect to him so as to further his best interests, and to afford him opportunities for the proper development of his character and abilities.' The change reflected the complete *volte-face* that had taken place in the attitude to children and the family, and the recognition of the need for the full development of the child in the national interest which inspired also the Education Act of 1944.

**Other Developments**   To this wartime stirring of concern for children must be added other aspects of social policy which found themselves given new direction. Thus, the plight of many elderly people, especially those in institutions, who were pushed around to make room for the expected air-raid casualties, first gave the country the gerontological bias which, with the increasing proportion of old people in the community, it has since retained. Again, evacuation raised ticklish problems of the responsibility of local authorities, and the recovery of welfare costs between them, and exposed the irrationality of the lingering remnants of the poor-law settlement laws, thereby strengthening the case for an over-all national service of assistance.[30] In the health services the shortage of nurses led to the establishment, at long last, of a national nursing service, with a Nursing and Mid-wives Division within the Ministry of Health, and to the introduction, by the Nurses Act of 1943, of State Enrolled Assistant Nurses, as a service supplementary to the State Registered Nurses recognised under the Nurses Registration Act, 1919. This, though it did not solve the problems of recruitment, prepared the way for the still greater changes and needs of a National Health Service.

'Welfare, Not Warfare'  The development of services, as well as of the provision of help in cash or kind, was a necessary but impressive aspect of the war-time evolution of welfare. If so much could be done during the war, with so many other immense demands on the nation's resources, how much more, it was but natural to ask, could be done in peace. Put bluntly, the inevitable question was, 'If for warfare, why not for welfare?' This was the question that Sir William Beveridge, allotted a most congenial task, set out to answer in 1941, in the first of the great enquiries which were to set the social policy of the country on a new and more secure footing by 1948.

The Beveridge Report, 1942  It is a commonplace of comment on projects for reform that they are dismissed as visionary and impracticable. So it was with the Beveridge Report, the first comprehensive survey of the British system of social insurance ever made and a carefully reasoned scheme for the abolition of want, as it had been known before the war. 'The road to moral ruin', 'a seductive opiate', were typical comments on it, and Churchill himself lent his great name to the criticism. 'It is because I do not wish to deceive the people by false hopes and airy visions of Utopia and Eldorado', he observed in a note to the Cabinet soon after the report appeared, 'that I have refrained so far from making promises about the future.'[31] Yet, as Beveridge was at pains to show, his proposals were essentially practical ones, based on a diagnosis of known problems and on the services that had been built up over the years to improve conditions. 'The plan is based on a diagnosis of want,' he asserted firmly on an early page, 'it starts from facts[32] .... The scheme proposed here is in some ways a revolution, but in more important ways it is a natural development from the past. It is a British revolution'.[33] Nor did the proposals involve heavier expense than the country could bear. Beveridge showed that on the basis of pre-war conditions it would actually have been possible to abolish want by a redistribution of income, even within the wage-earning population alone: 'want was a needless scandal due to not taking the trouble to prevent it'.[34] His proposals entailed 'a method of re-distributing income, so as to put the first and most urgent needs first',[35] or, as he expressed it more succinctly on the eve of his lecture-tour in America, 'bread for everyone before cake for anybody'.[36] Moreover, the proposals themselves were scrutinised at length by the Government Actuary in a 38-page appendix to the report itself, while it was easy to show that some of them, such as the funeral-grant, merely transferred to a State insurance scheme, though at a lower cost, payments already made by most people through private insurance. The report was a long document, however, running in all to nearly 300 closely printed pages: as an American comment had it, like the best-seller of the day, *Gone with the Wind*, it covered life from the cradle to the grave, had an element of suspense—and was over-large for a single evening's reading.[37] Critics might therefore be excused for having failed to follow every lengthy turn of the argument. Like *Gone with the Wind*, however, it was a spectacular success on both sides of the Atlantic: queues formed to buy it and the Stationery Office made a handsome profit on its sale. As *The Times* commented in a leading article, 'SIR WILLIAM BEVERIDGE has succeeded in crystallising the vague but keenly felt aspirations of millions of people'.[38] The disappointment and resentment at the Government's equivocal handling of it was a measure of his success.

Basically, for all its length of argument and the wealth of statistical material gathered in support of it, Beveridge's case was a simple one. Taking as his starting-point the existing services and the surveys made in the 30s of living standards and conditions, he showed how, without any extreme measures, want could be abolished and a 'national minimum' be assured to all. Hence his insistence that social security was a matter not of politics but of common sense.[39] The plan was essentially an insurance scheme, 'giving in return for contributions benefits up to subsistence level, as of right and without means test'. In return for contributions which all would pay, and not merely certain limited, if increasing, classes, as in the past, a minimum income, known to be sufficient to meet basic needs, would be guaranteed for all periods of interruption of earnings, whether through sickness, disability, unemployment or old age. In addition there would be grants for the normal incidents of life that called for unusual expenditure; for birth maternity grants, for death funeral grants. The plan therefore substituted for all the anomalies and inadequacies of the existing arrangements, which had grown up in a haphazard way to meet *ad hoc* needs, a unified 'pooling of risks', which, being firmly based on insurance, removed all taint of poor law or means test and yet ensured adequate support in times of need. Moreover it covered the funeral expenses for which so many people had insured themselves at such high cost— and at such profit to the Industrial Assurance Companies—in the past, and which, as shown earlier, Lloyd George and others had wanted to cover by some national scheme. Beveridge brought together in this connexion the evidence which showed that, of the £73 million paid in premiums every year, £27 million, nearly 7s. 6d. in every £, went in costs and profits, while of the policies taken out some two-thirds lapsed, with total loss of premiums paid in about half the cases. A State funeral grant, he calculated, could be administered at a cost of only 6d. in the £, and as it would be covered by the one social insurance contribution paid throughout working life there would be no lapses.[40]

All this amounted to no revolutionary proposal. The Beveridge Plan, as it came to be called, rounded off and carried to their logical conclusion all the established services, but made no extravagant demands on the State. In fact it deplored the already accepted government responsibility for the long-term unemployed under the Assistance Board: 'the insured persons should not feel that income for idleness, however caused, can come from a bottomless purse'.[41] It argued that the State should protect the individual not by a system of doles but by ensuring the economic and health conditions that would make it possible for him to support himself and save through social insurance for the accidents of life and for old age: 'The place for direct expenditure and organisation by the State is in maintaining employment of the labour and other productive resources of the country, and in preventing and combating disease, not in patching an incomplete system of insurance.'[42] The plan was therefore one of co-operation between State and citizen, and it was only a minimum that would be provided. The individual would be free to add to his basic social insurance as his means and inclination permitted: the benefits were to be paid up to subsistence level, 'so that individuals may build freely upon it'.[43] True to his Liberal origins, in fact, Beveridge was concerned with the free development and enlargement of the individual: 'The plan is not one for giving to everybody something for nothing . . . or something that will free the recipients for ever thereafter from personal responsibilities . . . (it) leaves room and encouragement to all individuals to win for themselves something above the national minimum, to find and to satisfy . . . new and higher needs than bare physical needs.'[44] Above the minimum levels such voluntary associations as the Friendly Societies would still have an important part to play.

It was essential to the plan that, if the proper conditions of health and employment were to be ensured by the State, there should be more positive action than in the past. Hence the three *Assumptions* of the Report—a comprehensive health scheme, avoidance of mass unemployment and family allowances. The first two were aimed at preventing, or at least diminishing, all the waste of man-power and resources entailed in unemployment and bad health. Beveridge argued for them, but did not regard any detailed consideration of them as within the scope of his enquiry. (The avoidance of mass unemployment was to be the subject of his next study, *Full Employment in a Free Society*.) Family allowances he similarly took for granted, but he stated the case for them on several grounds. First there was the obvious need for a national minimum in employment no less than unemployment: the pre-war surveys had shown how much want was due, even when a wage-earner was in work, to the possession of a family even a little larger than usual. Next was the anomalous situation by which, without additional assistance for children, wages might be no more, or even less, than unemployment benefit. Lastly there was the need, with a falling birth-rate, for the utmost care for children and the greatest possible encouragement for having more of them: 'Children's allowances should be regarded both as a help to parents in meeting their responsibilities, and as an acceptance of new responsibilities by the community.'[45] The community responsibility was to be recognised by making family allowances a charge on the Exchequer, supported not by insurance contributions but by taxation. Parental responsibility was to be preserved by a sharing of the burden, with no allowances for the first child in a family.

The problems created by the falling birth-rate and the increasing proportion of old people in the community were much in Beveridge's mind. Provision for the elderly he saw as the most important and most difficult of all problems of social security, both because the number of the elderly, and therefore the cost of pensions, were increasing, and because their conditions varied so greatly. To keep down the cost of pensions in the early years of reconstruction Beveridge recommended, at official request conveyed by Keynes,[46] that by additions to the basic rate people should be encouraged to defer retirement and that the pension should be explicitly one for retirement rather than merely for old age. (When this idea was accepted and applied in 1948 two-thirds of the men eligible and one-half of the women elected to continue at work.) He urged, too, that pension rates should be kept as low as possible, in order to relieve the increasing financial burden, and that the full retirement-pension scheme should be put into effect only by gradual stages over 20 years, so that reserve funds might be built up.

There was much more of recommendation and comment in the report to excite the interest and enthusiasm which its appearance called forth. With the assumption of family allowances, for instance, went a significant recognition of the special status of the housewife, with her own right to benefits through her husband's insurance, her own special risks, particularly of widowhood, and her own contribution to society through the 'vital unpaid service' she rendered in her home.[47] For the first time, in fact, the place of the housewife in society was acknowledged. On her behalf Eleanor Rathbone had long been conducting her campaign and from the Beveridge Report the process of conversion was rapid to the day in 1945 when the Family Allowances Act decreed that allowances should be paid to the mother, not the father. Miss Rathbone had long since defined in more detail what Beveridge had summed up as the housewife's 'vital unpaid service'—'Potentially, the work of that woman is as highly skilled as that of half a dozen ordinary craftsmen. If the minds of Soyer, Eustace Miles, Paquin, and Liberty, Froebel and Mme. Montessori, Dr Coué, Mrs Carlyle and Mrs J. S. Mill were rolled into one and embodied in one working housewife, they would find scope in her job for their united abilities.'[48] The new attitude which the Beveridge Report helped to foster may not have converted everyone quite to this view, but the rapid acceptance of the principle of family allowances, stimulated as it was by the great part which women played in the war effort, demonstrated the recognition of the vital rôle of the housewife in what Miss Rathbone called 'the most essential of the nation's businesses', the family, and contributed to that new realisation of the importance of the family in society to which reference has already been made. .

For the achievement of his plan Beveridge proposed the establishment of a single Ministry of Social Security, though this proved to be one of his recommendations which was not for many years accepted. He did not, however, regard the plan as a complete scheme of social security in itself. It dealt only with Want, and 'Want is one only of five giants on the road of reconstruction'. Disease, Ignorance, Squalor and Idleness had still to be tackled; Disease by a new health service, Ignorance by educational reforms, Squalor by a housing programme and Idleness by measures for steadying and developing the economic system.[49] Want was perhaps, as Beveridge claimed, the easiest to tackle, but the great Report did at least turn the country to serious consideration of reconstruction and social improvement, at the moment when, after so many disasters and disappointments, the tide of war itself was at last beginning to turn. Recalling the significant fifth clause of the Atlantic Charter, Beveridge, in the penultimate page of the Report, sought the wider significance of his proposals: 'They are a sign of the belief that the object of government in peace and in war is not the glory of rulers or of races but the happiness of the common man. . . . That is a belief which, through all differences in forms of government . . . unites the United Nations and divides them from their enemies.'[50] The words, and the vision behind them, are still worth recalling.

**The Government White Paper, 1944** The publication of the Report was followed by what Beveridge, understandably gratified by its reception by the public, has called the period of 'Boom and Boycott'. Engrossed as he was with the war (and a period of illness early in 1943), and disconcerted by the Beveridge Boom, as also by some awkward premature publicity, Churchill did not take kindly to the Report.[51] The other dominating figure of the government, Bevin, was hardly less unfriendly: as a good trade-unionist he saw security in full employment and good wage standards rather than in any 'social ambulance scheme'. What the Report amounted to, he told the Scottish T.U.C. in April 1943, was 'the culmination of ideas on social services over the last 40 years . . . a co-ordination of the whole of the nation's ambulance services on a more scientific and proper footing', but by no means a complete answer to Britain's social and economic problems.[52] Beveridge, however, hoped for a speedy endorsement of his proposals, and when there was delay interpreted it as a slight. As Attlee commented, with typical pungency, he seemed to think the war should stop while his plan was put into effect.[53] Not unnaturally, he was not consulted about the consideration given to his proposals in official circles, and had no hand in the government's own *Social Insurance* White Paper of 1944. Indeed, in broadcasts in 1943 and again during the election campaign in 1945 Churchill went out of his way to disavow Beveridge by stressing his own earlier concern with social security, now, however, somewhat remote. In fact, of course, Beveridge had put the government in a dilemma. Churchill was interested only in the prosecution of the war, and the government was enabled to hold together by pursuing that aim and avoiding controversial issues of domestic policy.[54] Under these circumstances the Labour ministers were chagrined to have Beveridge steal their thunder, and were cool in their response, greatly to the concern of the Labour rank and file, while Churchill may well have been aiming to have the Plan up his sleeve for post-war reconstruction in which Labour, he hoped, would have no part.[55] Unfortunately the handling of the whole affair by the government was incredibly inept, and lent point to Beveridge's accusation of a boycott. There was a three-month delay before any declaration was made at all, and in the meantime the suspicions of the serving soldiers, always acute in matters of politics, had been aroused by the withdrawal of the original explanation of the Beveridge Plan prepared for educational discussion by the Army Bureau of Current Affairs (familiar to millions of serving men and women as ABCA) and its replacement by a watered-down version. The government seemed totally unaware of the boost to morale which the Report had administered, and of the hopes it had raised. Worse still, when in February 1943 a pronouncement was made, although it accepted much of Beveridge's case, it was couched in such terms by the government's spokesmen, Anderson and Kingsley Wood, neither of them inspiring speakers, that there was a storm of protest. Yet it was clear from the government's own proposals that, as Bevin insisted, there had in fact been much activity behind the scenes,[56] and when, three years later, the National Insurance Bill was before the Commons, Attlee was to point to the complexity of the measure as ample reason for the original delay.[57] The degree of agreement with Beveridge's proposals was indeed considerable.

The three basic assumptions concerning family allowances, the health services and unemployment were accepted in principle, though with family allowances at 5s. instead of the 8s. proposed in the Report. Accepted also were the universal contributory insurance scheme, with unemployment and sickness benefit on the same basis, funeral grants and improved old age and widows' pensions. Indeed, Anderson went one better than Beveridge in undertaking that pensions should not be subject to any 20-year delay, an obvious tactical political move which, however, cut across the insurance principle. On the other hand there was to be no over-all Ministry of Social Security. Yet, as *The Times* commented, 'no speech ever delivered in the House of Commons has committed a Government to more far-reaching measures of social advance'.[58] When, eventually, the Social Insurance White Paper appeared, the Government acknowledged in it 'their gratitude to Sir William Beveridge for . . . his comprehensive and imaginative Report': 'their main tribute', ran the final paragraph, 'is the embodiment of so much of his plan in the proposals set out in this White Paper.' Well might Beveridge, then himself in Parliament, wonder what his 'large and rather noisy baby' had been doing in Whitehall in the long interval.[59] Eighteen months later, when the

National Insurance Bill was before the House, Attlee declared unaffectedly that it was founded on the Report.[60]

**Hostile Opinion**   In the meantime, not all was approval in the world outside. The tone of much future comment on the Welfare State was set by such observations as the 'road to moral ruin' already quoted, though the failure of many critics to understand what the Report was about—or to get their facts right—was well illustrated by the American quoted by Beveridge in a speech, who objected that if there had been social security in the days of good Queen Bess there would have been no Drake, Hawkins or Raleigh.[61] Americans sometimes have fond illusions about the spur of want in the opening-up of their great country, and Beveridge was able to reply that the three great men of Devon had had social security from birth: 'Adventure came not from the half-starved, but from those who were well fed enough to feel ambition.' The debate has continued since, and whatever the criticisms of our present society Beveridge's practical idealism has proved not altogether misplaced.

**Churchill's Broadcast and the 'White Paper Chase'**   In March 1943, Churchill delivered a notable broadcast, which was obviously his answer to the Beveridge Boom, and in which, while promising a four-year plan of reconstruction after the war, he also deprecated too much talk of peace when the war was raging in Russia and North Africa, and refused to tell 'fairy tales' about the future. Yet he reminded his hearers of his own past share in Unemployment Insurance (while relegating Beveridge to the origins of Labour Exchanges) and of his phrase of 1911, 'bringing the magic of averages to the rescue of the millions'. 'You must rank me and my colleagues', he said in challenging style, but with another happy turn of phrase, 'as strong partisans of national compulsory insurance for all classes for all purposes from the cradle to the grave.' It was, as those who heard it will remember, a cool and discouraging statement, but it was nevertheless a commitment, if only for the future. Two years later the Government's proposals emerged from their long gestation and were set out in *Social Insurance*, published in September of 1944, the year of what Beveridge has called the 'White Paper Chase'.[62] Earlier in the year had appeared the Papers which dealt with two of his three assumptions, *A National Health Service* and *Full Employment*, while a new Education Act, introduced at the end of 1943, had become law in August 1944, when at long last a fully-fledged Ministry of Education had come into existence. The problems of post-war employment had been under consideration since 1941 and it was in the same year that further educational reforms had begun to be considered. Churchill himself, though as a triumphant advocate of self-education he had little interest in educational systems, set the tone of educational discussion in the address to his old school, Harrow, in 1941, in which he spoke in stirring terms of the great and stern days of the moment, 'the greatest days our history has seen', and looked ahead to social changes in victory: 'When the war is won, it must be one of our aims to work to establish a state of society where the advantages and privileges which hitherto have been enjoyed by the few shall be more widely shared by the men and youth of the nation.' There followed numerous representations and discussions, a White Paper in 1943 and finally the Education Bill, prepared and presented by the President of the Board of Education, R. A. Butler, in a way that has made the Act of 1944 as much the 'Butler Act' as the earlier great Acts have preserved the names of their chief promoters, Forster, Balfour and Fisher. Butler's own attitude was summed up in his view of education as the 'service of national self-fulfilment'. As such it was a vital aspect of reconstruction.

**Full Employment**    Fundamental to reconstruction was the conception of full employment, which because of the economic difficulties expected after the war, and the unhappy memory of all the years of unemployment since the end of the First World War, dominated the scene. Unemployment was expected—and feared—as almost unavoidable after the first flush of the return to peace: the comment of a responsible newspaper in 1940, 'When the war is over it will be upon us again with redoubled force',[63] was typical of a common view which could be understood only too readily. *Employment Policy*, however, changed all that, committing the Government, as in a notable phrase it did, to 'the maintenance of a high and stable level of employment', and setting out the policies necessary for the achievement of this aim, both in the short-term of transition from war to peace and in the long-term of restored activity. It started from the revolution in economic thought associated with the name of Keynes and the idea of an expansionist economy with a greater degree of government intervention to ensure steady employment. It recognised that slumps, once thought to be self-regulating, were too prolonged, and caused too much suffering, to be allowed to work themselves out, and it accepted 'a new approach and a new responsibility for the State'. In the short run of reconstruction there was to be a good deal of control, with cheap money and priorities in production to speed recovery. In the long run, control of capital investment, especially in the public sector, and pump-priming of various kinds, with regulation of the distribution of industry, mobility of labour and the training of workers for new jobs, were to maintain a steady level of employment. Public expenditure was to be encouraged at any threat of depression, and at such a time an ingenious system of varying rates of weekly insurance contributions, from both employers and employed, would feed back money into the economy and stimulate it to new activity. This last proposal, which had already been considered and rejected by Beveridge as too much like one of the 'fancy clauses' of the original insurance scheme of 1911, was not in fact to be adopted, though Keynes was enthusiastic for it. The idea of an automatic stimulation of public expenditure in times of depression, on the analogy, as the White Paper had it, of a thermostatic control, and in contrast to the budget-balancing of 1931, was equally strange to many. Churchill, who in 1908 had proposed similar measures to be brought into operation 'like organ stops', made the bright suggestion, in allusion to the current series of *Salute the Soldier* weeks, that at the onset of depression the Cabinet should set an example by 'Saluting the Stomach' with a series of banquets, a congenial notion.[64]

Like the Beveridge Plan *Employment Policy* did not promise anything for nothing. It stressed Britain's problems in international trade, and ended on a note that was both optimistic and cautious: 'If British industry carries into the peace the inventive power, technical skill and adaptability which it has shown during the war, we shall be able in due time to carry our burdens without a sense of excessive strain.' Much might be said of the progression from this to the 'never had it so good' of the late 50s, but that, of course, is another story. It is at least certain that, for all the ups and downs of policy, governments since the war in the spirit of the White Paper have intervened much more actively, and to better purpose in the maintenance of an astonishingly high degree of employment, than even the authors of the document can have thought possible. Something has probably been owed also to the social service payments which, whether adequate or not, have contributed significantly to many incomes and therefore indirectly to the level of employment.

**Social Insurance** *Employment Policy* dealt with one of Beveridge's assumptions. *Social Insurance* manifestly derived from his Report, but with significant differences. In brief, it proposed a single comprehensive insurance scheme for the whole population, with increased benefits for sickness, unemployment and retirement, family allowances and death grants. A Ministry of Social Insurance was to be established to launch the scheme and would also be responsible for National Assistance, which would continue to operate separately but would be extended to cover financial aid to all in need. Benefits, however, would not be on a subsistence basis; there would be no national minimum. The main difficulty here, in the Government's view, was the infinite variety of individual conditions, but there was also the size of the insurance contribution to be considered: 'Benefits must be paid for, and a high level of benefit must mean a high level of contribution. The Government therefore conclude that the right objective is a rate of benefit which provides a reasonable insurance against want and at the same time takes account of the maximum contribution which the great body of contributors can properly be asked to bear.'[65] So much for the hopes that went back to the Webbs, and all the careful work that Beveridge, with Keynes's assistance, had put into his estimates. The Labour Government in 1946 made a cautious modification of attitude, introducing 'a broad subsistence basis' (see note, page 325).[66] Since then any pretence at subsistence, whatever that may mean under present conditions, has, however, been abandoned, except in so far as National Assistance (now supplementary benefits) recognises certain minimum rates and gives assistance up to those levels.

Subsistence not being the object, the Government was able to put aside Beveridge's recommendation for the deferment of the new rates for retirement pensions, and to offer them from the inception of the scheme, though not at the levels he had proposed. This, however, served but to revive in a new form the old controversy about old age pensions, and with unemployment insignificant made retirement pensions a major issue of post-war policy. The rates offered have never been adequate, and became less so as the cost of living rose. Hence the many appeals to pensioners not to shrink from National Assistance, and thereby to avoid a general raising of pension rates, appeals which often fell on deaf ears owing to the lingering memory of the poor law and the means test.

**Family Allowances**    Similar difficulties faced Family Allowances. These were fixed at rates lower than Beveridge had wanted, as it was decided to develop the school meals and milk service and to regard them as allowances in kind. Like retirement pensions, however, family allowances have been affected by inflation and have had to be increased over the years. The case for the allowances for families in need was a strong one, and although there was something incongruous in granting them to families which did not really need them (and had to pay income-tax on them), unless there were to be a means test they could not but go to all. Moreover, the essence of the whole social insurance scheme was that it should be universal: 'Concrete expression is thus given to the solidarity and unity of the nation, which in war have been its bulwarks against aggression and in peace will be its guarantees of success in the fight against individual want and mischance.'[67] Unlike the other benefits family allowances were to be paid from national taxation and not based on insurance contributions, for the simple reason that 'it is in the national interest for the State to help parents to discharge (their) responsibilities properly'. The allowances were 'essentially for the benefit of the family', and were to be paid for each child after the first.[68] It was originally intended that, while the father should nominally receive them, special arrangements were to be made to allow the mother to collect them. It was in the Commons, after a free vote, that the decision was made to award them to the mother, and thereby to recognise that she had an economic position in her own right. Churchill himself would have liked the allowances to be tax-free and regarded as the property of the children, but this additional inducement 'to encourage the birth and extra nourishment of children' was too bold a conception to win Treasury approval.[69]

Family allowances became the first of the new services to be introduced. The necessary Bill was presented to Parliament in February 1945, in the last weeks of the Coalition Government, and actually became law during Churchill's short-lived second (Conservative) Ministry of May–July 1945, before the Labour Government took office. The first allowances were paid a year later, in August 1946, by which time 2,300,000 of the 2,600,000 claims made in 1946 had been received. By the end of the year allowances were being paid for more than four million children.

**Other Benefits**  With insurance becoming universal and comprehensive, sickness and unemployment benefit were brought into line and the anomaly by which no dependant's allowance was paid in the case of sickness benefit was at last tackled. Beveridge had hoped that some means would be found of associating with the administration of sickness benefit the Friendly Societies which had been concerned with it, under National Health Insurance, since 1912. He had hoped also to turn the Industrial Assurance Companies from 'their bad ways' into a public service.[70] The Government decided, however, to exclude the Friendly Societies, and to entrust all benefit payments to government departments. The Approved Societies were therefore to disappear, and the institution of a death grant similarly affected the position of the Industrial Assurance Companies. These were considerable changes, possible largely because many of the organisations concerned had other lucrative interests to occupy them. The changes were felt keenly, however, in the old Friendly Societies, which had long played no small part in the search for security by certain sections of the working classes, and the decision proved to be the chief point at issue when the Insurance Bill was debated in 1946.

One other significant change now introduced was the supersession of the Workmen's Compensation scheme of 1897, which had placed the responsibility for industrial injuries on the employer, by a social security scheme, based on insurance and a central fund. Beveridge had proposed such a scheme, but had wanted it to be assimilated to the general scheme of social insurance, with a special levy on industries with abnormal risks. The Government decided, however, to establish a separate scheme, which was described in Part II of the White Paper and was intended to secure for the vexed question of industrial injuries, with all its legal complexities, 'a happier and sounder foundation'.

Such were the proposals of *Social Insurance*, which before it could even be given legislative shape was renamed 'National Insurance' in deference to Conservative opinion. A new Ministry of National Insurance was devised and came into being in November 1944, with, as first Minister, Sir William Jowitt, who had long been concerned with reconstruction problems and to whom, indeed, as the responsible Minister, Beveridge had presented his Report two years before. The Act for the institution of the insurance scheme itself was passed by the Labour Government in 1946 and came into effect in July 1948.

**The National Health Service**  Still more important than the rationalisation of sickness benefit was the introduction of a comprehensive scheme of medical attention. As already recorded, the *National Health Service* White Paper promised 'a publicly sponsored service . . . available to all who want to use it'. It recognised that, however good the environmental services might be, the need for efficient medical attention of all kinds remained, but that in the past such attention had depended, for too many people, on a number of 'factors irrelevant to it', such as personal means and all too variable local conditions. There was therefore to be a National Health Service, 'free to all', and financed from taxation, with a new public service with a new responsibility— 'to make it in future somebody's clear duty to see that all medical facilities are available to all people'. This significant statement of policy, in itself a frank admission of the inadequacies of the existing system, was to lead to much difficulty and heart-burning. It pointed the need for effective local organisation of the health services, but even in its detailed proposals was somewhat vague as to how that might be achieved. In the event the problem of local organisation provided one of the principal causes of conflict between the Labour Government and Conservative Opposition over the plans actually made in 1946. What the White Paper proposed was a comprehensive service, both available to all who wished to make use of it (the wording was carefully devised so as to permit the continuance of private practice) and covering all forms of medical care, from the general practitioner and the local nurse to the hospital and the consultant (and including dental and optical services). In the general practitioner service the much talked-of 'family doctor', long out of reach for many people, was at last to become a reality with the extension of medical attention to the dependants of insured persons. It was recognised, however, in words quoted from a B.M.A. report, that 'the days when a doctor armed only with his stethoscope and his drugs could offer a fairly complete medical service are gone'. With all the great advances in medicine and surgery that had taken place in recent years, collaboration and access to consultant and hospital services were essential: as Aneurin Bevan said when presenting his Bill in 1946, the isolation of the G.P. had to be broken down.[71] Hence the White Paper's proposals for 'grouped practices' and Health Centres (with salaried medical staff) as essential parts of the new service. (Very few such Health Centres have in fact been opened, however.) The distribution of doctors, notoriously inadequate in the poorer parts of the country, was to be given consideration, as was the sale of practices. The hospital service had been severely tested by the war and found wanting in many respects. It was to be developed by co-operation between local authorities in 'joint authorities', which would have the task of framing, in co-operation with the medical profession, 'area plans' for securing complete health services in their several areas. The voluntary hospitals would be brought into the plans, and would participate as autonomous agencies. The area plan was to provide the basis for the 'new public service', and it was here that the divergences between Labour and Conservative ideas were to appear.

Such, in broad outline, was the White Paper scheme, a bold and simple project, based on the experience (if often conflicting) of 30 years' working of National Health Insurance and on the considered views of professional and governmental opinion. The application of the scheme was a much more complex matter, involving as it did local authorities in every part of the country, voluntary hospitals of almost every degree of size and efficiency and the most touchy of professions, acutely sensitive, especially when the Labour Party, with its theoretical notions of a salaried service, took office, to any suggestion of direction or salaried employment. Discussions that were intended to follow the publication of the proposals in 1944 were delayed by the flying-bomb attacks, and had not proceeded far before the Labour Government was formed. It therefore fell to that Government, with Bevan as Minister of Health, to frame the final proposals, which became law in November 1946. Apart from a reorganisation of the hospital service no great changes were made in the plans which had been under discussion so long. The ground had been worked over so much, and there were so many powerful and conflicting interests involved that there was little scope for anything radically new. Bevan, indeed, 'was less of an innovator than often credited: he was at the end, albeit the important and conclusive end, of a series of earlier plans. He "created" the National Health Service but his debts to what went before were enormous'.[72]

**The National Health Service Act, 1946**    The principal change made was that the service was to be organised on a functional, not a regional, basis. Thus, hospital autonomy was to disappear, and all hospitals, local authority and voluntary alike, were to be merged under Regional Hospital Boards, centred on the country's medical schools, though a shrewd gesture kept the teaching hospitals themselves still independent. The local authorities, though they were to lose their hospitals, were to develop their other health services, especially the preventive services, and to ensure close association with the Hospital Boards. The change, though many doctors welcomed the removal of the possibility of local authority control, roused Conservative ire, both because it overrode local authority responsibility and because of the disappearance of the voluntary principle. Some critics spoke, indeed, as if the voluntary hospitals were actually to be wiped off the face of the earth, and one went so far as to tell Bevan that his Bill 'saps the very foundation on which our national character has been built',[73] a statement only too typical of the criticisms levelled at the social services by some of the well-to-do since at least the days of old age pensions. Bevan justified his policy by arguing both that the voluntary hospitals were inadequately spread, with too few of them in the older industrial areas, and that it was 'repugnant' that medical care, which of all things should be independent of means, should have to rely on charity: 'We ought to have left hospital flag days behind.'[74]

**Bevan and the Doctors**    The Opposition resisted the changes, but Bevan's main difficulty was with the doctors and their Conservative supporters. Like Lloyd George 35 years earlier, he found himself condemned on suspicion, handicapped as he was by a political following that was openly in favour of the State salaried medical service, which, for all his reforming zeal and fire, he was too skilful a politician to press. He even dropped the White Paper suggestion of a salaried service in Health Centres, which his Conservative predecessor, H. U. Willink, had accepted (and which many doctors favoured), and eventually whittled down the controversial 'basic salary' element in doctor's remuneration to vanishing point. There were, however, only too many other points of disagreement or suspicion over conditions of pay and service. There were, also, too many wild men on both sides, and Bevan himself was hardly as yet tamed. Nevertheless, while firm he proved himself adroit by the concessions with which he won the support of many of the leaders of the medical profession; the exclusion of the teaching hospitals from the control of the Regional Boards and his conciliatoriness over the issue of 'private' beds in hospitals. Yet from the first he felt himself 'rather aggrieved', as he complained in the Commons, at the kind of thing that was said of his proposals,[75] and an aggrieved Bevan was more a spectacle of anger than of sorrow. Concessions were made, but they were laggard, and as *The Times* commented in a special article, while some of the disputed details may not have been explained with sufficient patience and clarity, 'all Mr Bevan's actions began to be interpreted as the first sinister steps in a Socialist conspiracy to rob doctors of their freedom. Hidden purposes were discovered in clauses of the Bill which Mr Willink would not have worded differently.'[76] The real objects of the measure, on which there was so much fundamental unity, tended to be forgotten in a welter of charges and counter-charges, with equivocal B.M.A. plebiscites, threats of strike action and exasperated Ministerial pronouncements. One major difficulty was Bevan's quite proper refusal, though he was willing to consult the doctors, to 'negotiate' with them.[77] This seemed to many in the profession to justify their worst fears. It was 1911 all over again, and on a larger scale, even if not quite so serious.

Eventually, only just in time, and aided by conciliatory action by Lord Dawson, Lord Moran and other medical leaders, Bevan in April 1948 made a notable effort to break down the barrier of suspicion by adjustments and assurances which, though they might have seemed superfluous, were clearly necessary: 'the word needed had been spoken, and with magnanimity'.[78] In 1949 he was to make a further gesture by an Amending Act which actually prohibited a salaried service. Honours were then about even. The 'appointed day' in July 1948, on which the service began, saw a message of goodwill from him to the doctors which was expressive of all that he and so many others hoped for from the new service: 'There is no reason why the doctor-patient relationship should not be freed from the money factor, the collection of fees or thinking how to pay fees. . . . My job is to give you all the facilities, resources, apparatus and help I can, and then to leave you alone . . . to use your skill and judgment without hindrance.'[79] By this time 8,000,000 people had applied to go on doctors' lists, making with the existing 'panel' lists, some 30,000,000 patients in all, and 18,500 of the country's 20,000 doctors had entered the new service. With the medical service there then began the dental and optical and the encouragement of aids for the deaf. The wave of demand that arose revealed the serious leeway that had to be made up, and caused some consternation both at home and abroad.

Whether the Health Service, as it has developed amid all the strains of the post-war situation, is quite as had been hoped, is another matter. The problem of local control has not been solved, and hospital development has lagged. On the other hand, doctors and patients have gained, and the sweeping charges of extravagance often heard have not only been disproved, but have failed to take into account all that the nation spent on health, for a less effective service, before the war, and all the suffering caused by neglect. One criticism which goes back to the White Paper still stands, however: the National Health Service is first and foremost a sickness service, 'designed to deal with those who have lost health'.[80] The prevention of ill-health is another, and larger, issue, though the success of the campaigns against diphtheria and poliomyelitis, administered by the local authorities, over the years since 1946, is a pointer, and there is much evidence of a more understanding public attitude to health matters.

**The Education Act, 1944**   Churchill in his famous broadcast of March 1943, had had much to say of the national need for great developments in education. The war, with its demands for skilled workers of all kinds, had revealed the gaps in the educational system and particularly the sorry state of technical education, the cinderella of cinderellas of a system that since the changes of 1902 had laid exaggerated stress on the traditional bias of the grammar schools. The long dichotomy of school and work, of which so many had complained in the past, was now made clear to all. Evacuation, too, with all the strains it imposed on education and all the weaknesses and shortcomings it revealed (and for which the country is still paying many years later) had roused opinion and interest. Once the first shock of the realisation of our island insecurity had passed, education became one of the most popular subjects of discussion, and there was widespread desire for improvement, particularly in the Labour party, which had so long been pressing for change. Bevin expressed the hopes of many in demanding that youth should be regarded no longer as a period of cheap labour for industry but as 'a preparatory age for industry, occupation and citizenship'.[81] Hence from 1941 the many plans and projects for reform, culminating in the White Paper of 1943, *Educational Reconstruction*, and the Butler Act of the following year. Butler himself became President of the Board of Education in the summer of 1941, and, unusual phenomenon in a position much subject to change (with an average term for Presidents of only two years), remained there for almost four years, through all the trials of war-time administration and rethinking. It was a happy choice and a happy chance for English education, though the new Act also owed much to Butler's Parliamentary Secretary, Chuter Ede, and to the lively interest and support of Bevin.

Churchill in his broadcast pointed the way of advance in two directions. On the one hand, the war's equality of sacrifice underlined the right of every child to opportunity for full development: 'it is in our power to secure equal opportunity for all . . . we must make sure that the path to the highest functions throughout our society and Empire is really open to the children of every family'. This, as one commentator has observed, was no more than was fair to the people of Britain, who had taken their shocks without flinching. 'Never in the history of human endurance', to rephrase more justly Churchill's famous comment on the Battle of Britain, 'had the Few owed so much to the Many.'[82] On the other hand, the great developments of science and industry demanded, as the war was showing, a high standard of education in the people if Britain were to hold her own. In Churchill's words: 'The future of the world is to the highly educated races who alone can handle the scientific apparatus necessary for preeminence in peace or survival in war. . . . You cannot conduct a modern community except with an adequate supply of persons upon whose education much time and money have been spent.' Of this second point much was to be heard from Churchill in the post-war years: it was the germ of the demand for a great increase of facilities in scientific and technical education. With it went the first public reference since the ill-fated Fisher Act to the idea of day-release for young workers, and a pledge for the extension of schooling which had been sacrificed in 1939 and for the necessary improvements in school building and in facilities for teacher-training.

The Act of 1944 imposed significant changes on the organisation of English education and established for the first time a comprehensive and progressive system of education for all. The President of the Board had hitherto had no other duty than 'the superintendence of certain matters relating to education'. Now there was to be a Minister, charged with the task 'to promote the education of the people of England and Wales', in accordance with 'a national policy for providing a varied and comprehensive educational service in every area', and with the power to secure the effective execution by the local authorities of their part in the national plan. Children were to be educated according to their 'age, ability and aptitude' in a special system of progressive schooling; local authorities were to make the necessary provision, and parents were required, for the first time, to see that their children were properly educated (hitherto parental responsibility had been limited to the minimum of 'elementary' instruction), though, within certain limits, in accordance with the parents' own wishes. This was a notable innovation, matched, however, by the duty laid on local authorities to contribute through efficient local arrangements to 'the spiritual, moral, mental and physical development of the community'. On the side of physical care the Act regulated the development of the School Medical Service and the provision of milk and meals, carrying further the important advances made during the war.

In the organisation of the schools the reforms of the Hadow Report of 1926 were at last to be completed, with the conception of elementary schooling disappearing and education reorganised in three progressive stages, primary, secondary and further, though there were also to be nursery schools for younger children. The school-leaving age was to be raised to 15 (this was actually done in 1947) and to 16 'as soon as the Minister is satisfied that it has become practicable', a situation not reached even in the 1960s. There was therefore to be, in practice, the long-sought ideal of secondary education for all. No directions were given in the Act as to the forms secondary education should take, but the White Paper had developed the Hadow and Spens recommendations tending towards a tripartite system of grammar, secondary technical and secondary modern schools, and this division was endorsed by the report of the Committee on the secondary school curriculum (the Norwood Committee), which appeared in 1943. The Norwood Committee also advocated the break between primary and secondary schooling at 'eleven-plus', and it was its proposals that were generally adopted in practice. The break at eleven and the arbitrary division into three types of secondary school have much against them, and have brought about new difficulties and tensions in the educational system since 1944. Of the tripartite division, alleged to reflect a similiar division of ability and aptitude among children, one commentator has neatly said that it suggests that 'the Almighty had benevolently created three types of child in just those proportions which would gratify educational administrators'.[83] 'Parity of esteem' was supposed to exist between the different types of school, but this was beyond the power of legislation or administrative regulation to command, and came only slowly, the more slowly because of the vast prestige of the grammar schools, a legacy from earlier days. With the eleven-plus examination and the secondary modern school had grown up, however, all the distress of 'failure to pass': 'For middle-class parents, in particular, eleven-plus day is a day of national mourning. Like King Aegeus they sit on the cliffs, waiting to see if the returning sails are white or black.'[84] Hence, for all the improvements in the national system and the decline expected in private schools, the great increase in the number of parents willing—and, thanks to the new affluent society, able— to pay privately for their children's education. The paying of school fees has remained a status-symbol despite all the social changes of recent years, and the educational system still has its divisions, though these are no longer the divisions between privilege and under-privilege. As Butler said, when justifying the continuance of fee-paying in the 'direct grant' schools, which are only partially within the State system, 'education cannot by itself create the social structure of a country.'[85] Education, indeed, is still more a reflection of social structure than a formative influence in creating it. Be it noted, however, that much of what is most criticised in the post-war educational system, in so far as it is not due to physical difficulties, is not necessarily in the Act itself, but has developed as something of a gloss upon it.

The Act of 1944 was also important for its proposals for further education. The day-continuation schools of the Fisher Act were taken up again and renamed County Colleges, but, although 'day-release' classes for young people have been one of the most important developments of the Act, their development was for some time slow, and of county colleges as planned there has been little sign. A significant innovation was the requirement that county-college work should include some preparation for 'the responsibilities of citizenship'. How far this particular task can be achieved is uncertain, and although many interesting experiments have been undertaken, the task is much more a matter for adult education, which traditionally has been much concerned with it, as well as with the enrichment of life. In addition to the provision for day-release students the

Act laid on local authorities the ambitious duty of providing full-time and part-time further education for all over school age, together with 'leisure-time occupation, in such organised cultural, training and recreative activities as are suited to their requirements' for all 'able and willing to profit by the facilities provided' (or, rather, the duty of 'securing its provision', which entails co-operation with other organisations). From this has stemmed a great broadening and liberalisation of many types of community activity and adult education, formal and informal alike.

**C.A.T.s and Universities**    The Act itself was followed by the establishment of a committee under Lord Eustace Percy to consider, in the light of wartime demands and experience, the development of technical education in general. From the report of this committee, which appeared in 1945, has come all the recent development of technical education, and especially the creation of the Colleges of Advanced Technology, the precursors of a new style of University. The post-war years have also seen, of course, a remarkable expansion of the Universities themselves, with State encouragement on a scale hitherto almost unthinkable. The 1944 Act was the greatest, to date, of the country's legislative measures for education, but its true significance lies in the fact that it caught up and expressed a surge of concern with all aspects of education, which when seen in perspective will make the middle years of the twentieth century some of the most constructive (literally as well as metaphorically) in our history. The provision of free education up to the age of 15–16 for all and 18 for some, with access and assistance beyond that, is certainly a major measure of welfare policy, and the numbers taking advantage of the higher levels are its best justification. There is still much to be done, and education still tends to be an easy field for economies, but the 'tradition of educating our children on the cheap', to which the McNair Report on the recruitment and training of teachers made reference in 1944, has happily been broken.

**The Third Labour Government, 1945**    Inevitably we have been drawn out of the strict sequence of events, and our story draws to a close. With so much preparatory work done it might have been thought best to continue the wartime Coalition beyond victory. Churchill, however, had other views and ambitious schemes of his own for tackling the problems of reconstruction. In his last short months of authority, after the Coalition had been abandoned in May 1945, he sketched his plans. National Insurance and National Health legislation were to be pressed forward, and a great drive, in the form of a military operation, was to be made on housing.[86] All this, however, was not to be. On 26 July came what was to him the 'quite effectively disguised blessing' of the results of the General Election,[87] and the Labour Party took over under Attlee.

**Labour Legislation**    Family allowances had already become law, but there followed an impressive stream of legislation. If we name only the principal measures, there were in 1946 Bills for Coal Nationalisation, National Insurance and National Insurance (Industrial Injuries), New Towns, Housing, Trade Union Law and the National Health Service; in 1947, for Industrial Organisation and Development, the Nationalisation of Transport and Electricity Production and for Town and Country Planning; in 1948, for National Assistance, the Nationalisation of Gas Production, Electoral Reform, Children and the Monopolies Inquiry. In most aspects of policy which concerned the social services much of the investigation and planning had, of course, already been done, and the decisions which had to be made were, therefore, essentially the political ones, which involved some changes. Something has been said, for instance, of the alterations made in the plans for the health service. In the case of National Insurance pensions were increased immediately, in 1946, while in the other services improvements were made and benefit and allowance rates (and contributions) increased. No subsistence-rates, such as Beveridge had urged, were explicitly accepted, but the figures decided on were, like his, based on 1938 minimum needs, with an allowance for the increased cost of living. They were rates, said James Griffiths, Minister of National Insurance, 'which can be justified broadly in relation to the present cost of living', and the intention was to review them at five-year intervals. If it was no more than a 'broad subsistence basis', it was at least 'the beginning of the establishment of the principle of a National Minimum Standard'.[88] For that matter, one might add, it was also the end, for the later rapid increase in the cost of living put an end even to the broad subsistence basis.

Contributions were heavy, but were in fact less than was usually paid, one way or another, for the various services now combined in one insurance scheme. It was, Griffiths declared, 'the best and cheapest insurance policy offered to the British people, or to any people anywhere',[89] and the inclusion of everyone made the Bill 'an epoch-making document'.[90] One unrepentant opponent, Sir Waldron Smithers, lamented, in characteristic vein, that it was a Bill 'against the natural law that if a man will not work neither shall he eat',[91] but Butler struck a happier note for the Opposition as a whole: 'I think we should take pride that the British race has been able . . . shortly after the terrible period through which we have all passed together, to show the whole world that we are able to produce a social insurance scheme of this character.'[92]

**The Administrative Tasks**    The passage of the various Acts was followed by vast preparatory labours in the departments concerned. For National Insurance itself staff had to be recruited from a number of sources, including the Approved Societies, whose staffs became redundant through the change in health insurance, and the local authorities' public assistance officials, who were similarly affected by the passing of the poor law and the coming of National Assistance. Some 30,000 applicants were interviewed, and from these and other sources the Ministry's staff was built up by 1948 to nearly 40,000 from the 5,600 taken over on the establishment of the Ministry in 1945. Special attention had to be given to training, especially in view of the spirit in which the work was to be performed, 'not merely efficiently but conveniently and courteously', as *The Times* commented,[93] in contrast to the cold carelessness of which much complaint had been heard in the past.

As part of a policy of avoiding the concentration of government work in London, the Ministry established its central headquarters at Newcastle, where special offices were built in 1946-7: this inevitably raised difficult problems of housing for some 7,000 staff involved. By 1948 there were also 912 local offices at work with a staff of more than 17,000, who in the first year handled 38,000,000 claims and enquiries and made 42,000,000 payments. Particularly numerous were the enquiries at seaside offices during the summer months of 1948, when the new service was being inaugurated. 'Holiday-makers', an entertaining note in a Ministry report commented, 'apparently filled in their spare time during wet weather by seeking shelter and information at the same time.'[94]

**National Assistance and the 'Appointed Day'**  Such were some of the practical tasks which arose from the passage of legislation, and which had to be completed before the services laid down could be put into operation. The 'appointed day' for National Insurance and the National Health Service came on 5 July 1948. Earlier in the year the National Assistance Act had been passed, and this new service, the successor to both the Assistance Board and the public assistance work of the local authorities (and ultimately, therefore, to the Elizabethan poor law) began to operate on the same day: the Welfare State had arrived. Under the terms of the 1948 Act the National Assistance Board has the duty 'to assist persons in Great Britain who are without resources to meet their requirements or whose resources . . . must be supplemented in order to meet their requirements'. Such is the successor to the old poor law.

Cash payments, such as were made by the poor law authorities as 'outdoor relief', were now transferred to a national authority, thereby spreading the local load over the whole nation. The long process which had seen the growth of responsibility from the parish to the nation was at last complete. To the local authorities were left the personal welfare services, which could only be administered by close contact. In Bevan's words, 'Where the individual is immediately concerned, where warmth and humanity of administration is the primary consideration, there the authority which is responsible should be as near the recipient as possible.'[95]

Some 800,000 recipients of assistance of various kinds were taken over by the N.A.B. in 1948, and by the end of the year had increased to more than one million. It had been hoped, as Thomas Steele, Parliamentary Secretary to the Ministry of National Insurance, said in the Commons, that National Assistance would not have 'an active future':[96] the insurance scheme and increasing prosperity, it was expected, would eventually leave it little to do. In the event, however, the failure to relate other benefits to subsistence costs has kept the N.A.B. only too well occupied. From just over one million at the end of 1948 the number of people receiving assistance rose steadily to nearly 1,800,000 in 1954 and 2,000,000 in 1962, falling but little below this last figure by 1966, when the N.A.B. was absorbed into the new Ministry of Social Security.

**Post-war Conditions**  While the new services were being prepared, controls, rent restriction and subsidies to food and housing, with all the work of reconstruction and redevelopment which had to be put in hand, and which, backed as it was by significant American help in international reconstruction, effectively guaranteed full employment, together created, with higher wages, conditions in which much of the pre-war distress that National Insurance and National Assistance in particular had been devised to prevent no longer threatened. By 1948, it has been calculated, the proportion of the total national purchasing power held by the five-sixths of the population who were wage-earners had probably risen by about one-quarter since 1938. For the pensioner, with his increased pension, the increase was of the order of one-half.[97] The steady rise in prices and the pressure of inflation were soon to upset the situation, however, and, although wage-earners could improve their position, if tardily, by negotiation, pensioners, and others on fixed incomes, were to feel the pinch. Soon even the 'broad subsistence basis', itself a reflection of the now outmoded standards of 1938, was to go by the board, and the result has been the constant pressure to do more for the elderly and the discovery of considerable pockets of need among other groups which, exactly as in the past, have been unable to keep up with their more affluent and comfortable contemporaries. 'Secret need', in fact, is still with us. Financial strain has also seriously affected the building programmes in health and education, and in many other respects the high hopes of 1942–8 have not been realised. Yet so much has been done, and the contrast with the position at earlier stages of development, as it has been described in the previous chapters, is striking enough. This is not the place, however, for an examination of the working of the Welfare State when it had been achieved. Here we have come full circle, and may take stock of the situation at the point of time at which the Welfare State had arrived by 1948.

*Note to page 313.* The basis was low, as, indeed, Beveridge's had been, and, although allowances were later raised to match the steady rise in the cost of living, it was not until 1959, amid conditions of general prosperity, that something more than 'broad subsistence' was offered.

# 8 | Conclusion

The decisive event in the evolution of the Welfare State was the Second World War, which, coming as it did after a long period of distress and puzzled endeavour at relief, challenged the British people to round off the system of social security that they had sketched and to maintain in peace the consideration for all which had so impressively marked the war period. The years of active thought and planning were those from 1941 to 1948: these mark an epoch in British history. Whatever may happen in the future to the services then planned and created, these years will stand out in our history, and not for the deeds of war alone: they provided the opportunity and the stimulus. In the words used by Beveridge towards the end of his Report, 'there are difficulties in planning reconstruction of the social services during the height of war, but there are also advantages in doing so. The prevention of want and the diminution and relief of disease—the special aim of the social services—are in fact a common interest of all citizens. It may be possible to secure a keener realisation of that fact in war than it is in peace, because war breeds national unity. It may be possible, through a sense of national unity . . . to bring about changes which, when they are made, will be accepted on all hands as advances, but which it might be difficult to make at other times.'[1]

So it was in Britain in these years. The war speeded changes and left a country markedly different and, for all its losses, markedly more humane and civilised than that of 1939, to face the different challenge of a period of unparalleled international difficulty, but to face it with a degree of unity and equality far beyond what had previously been possible. This is not to say that all the difficulties and differences had wholly disappeared, or that after submersion during the common perils of war they were not to re-emerge. The evolution of society during the 1950s and 60s, for all that had happened, revealed the social divisions that still existed, if often in new forms. What gave the social legislation its appeal was above all its universality,[2] the universality that was itself a reflection of wartime unity (and a disavowal of the 'means test' approach to social issues), but it was this very universality that from the fall of the Labour government in 1951 came increasingly under attack from critics who argued speciously against it. Nevertheless, the contrast with earlier periods was sufficiently impressive. Yet

Beveridge, closing on a gloomy note the study of his career that he published in 1953, wrote that 'the picture of yesterday's hopeful collaboration in curing evils of want and disease and ignorance and squalor . . . looks like a dream today'.[3] This was in part an old man's reaction against a world situation in which, under the shadow of the cold war and the Korean conflict (the latter an episode of immeasurable significance in the post-war era), peace and freedom seemed more insecure than ever. It was also, however, the reaction of one who felt that after his moment of glory the world had passed him by. If so much of the Beveridge Report had been adopted and put into practice, so many of the caveats that had been entered had been brushed aside, if not by the politicians then by the tide of events. What had emerged was hardly the combination of security, enterprise and social service, redolent of old-fashioned Liberalism, which Beveridge had favoured, but a vast State apparatus dedicated to welfare. And the very term 'Welfare State' inevitably suggested a degree of dependence unsuited to the relations between government and people in a free society. As one extreme critic put it, in a wild and sweeping denunciation, 'the inventors of the Welfare State have much to answer for. In its very essence, it is the most degrading political philosophy which has ever betrayed a country'.[4] This is characteristic of much of the criticism of State activity that has been noted in these pages. The old, stale argument, that State intervention is morally degrading to the individual, has been heard so often, too, without the course of events at any time providing conclusive evidence in its support, that it is easy to overlook the point, which was as disturbing to Beveridge as to any reactionary, that the delicate balance between individual liberty and State authority has to some extent been endangered by the very powers committed to government for individual welfare. On the other hand, full employment and high wages and profits are more likely to sap morale than 'free' schools and hospitals,[5] and it may be doubted in any case whether Beveridge's vision of an ideal society, the 'Social Service State', as he liked to call it, could ever be realised in practice. Part of Beveridge's appeal, as suggested above, was due to the simple fact that political programmes were in abeyance during the war. Putting his programme into effect, however, was a political exercise, and of politics he had little notion. At the other extreme the critics of State intervention stubbornly refused to look facts in the face and to recognise that the State alone had the power to right some of the more glaring wrongs of the social order. Yet what has emerged in practice is hardly what any of the pioneers of social reform set out to achieve. The *influence* of the Webbs, for instance, like that of Beveridge, has been immense upon ideas, but in practice severely limited: nor has the Labour Party seen directly realised many of the aims with which it set out.[6] The present mixed economy and social system of Britain is the result of many forces and influences, still in a state of flux, and likely long to continue so. In truth, it is of the essence of human growth, whether individually or in society, and of Johnson's 'vanity of human wishes', that as problems are solved they are forgotten, that conditions change and new issues arise. The tasks that have confronted the

British people since 1945 have been of immense difficulty and complexity. The country has come through them, so far, with a stability and a generally shared prosperity that few in 1945, could they have seen what lay ahead, would have dared to prophesy. And for all the anxieties of the times, and the stresses of adjustment to Britain's changed position in the world, any repetition of the overwhelming social despair of the inter-war years has been avoided. If the price of escape from a high rate of long-term unemployment is the constant threat of an overcharged economy, of inflation and 'stop-go', there are many who feel the price to be worth paying, at least among those with a memory of what went before. Of the contrast with the unhappy 1930s Harold Macmillan, for instance, has written, 'had we been told that overall unemployment would fall to something like two per cent . . . and that these almost Utopian conditions would bring with them novel and perplexing problems, we should have been incredulous. But we should unhesitatingly have closed with any offer on these lines.'[7] To him, ever conscious as he was in earlier years of the 'great gulf' fixed between Dives and Lazarus, 'the difficulties with which we must wrestle are almost precisely the reverse of those that beset us in the 30s. An overstrained economy with constant anxiety over the "balance of payments", shortage of labour, and an inflation that has generated a new insecurity . . . these are the problems with which contemporary statesmen must concern themselves. But, and we must be thankful for it, the "great gulf" is bridged.'[8]

The gulf is bridged, but many gaps remain. Quite apart from international tensions and the financial burdens they impose, there are still many problems of poverty, ignorance and squalor, still only too many 'casualties of the Welfare State'.[9] There is, too, much 'secret need' arising from the inadequacy of social security payments which have long remained tenuously linked to the modest requirements of mere subsistence in 1938. Above all there is the problem of the quality of our society, under conditions of affluence that bring new temptations and make earlier aspirations seem ingenuous. The 'I'm all right, Jack' attitude, the modern manifestation of a primitive human trait, has not diminished in significance in the affluent society, and Chadwick's revelation of the ignorance among the comfortably-off of the condition of many of their less-fortunate fellows could be repeated today. As Beveridge wrote in another context, 'the making of a good society depends not on the State but on the citizens'.[10] Earlier reformers were passionately convinced that only bad conditions stood in the way of good citizenship, and that these conditions it was the State's duty to improve. The general tone of British society has undoubtedly improved to a very great extent, and foreign observers pay frequent tribute to its maturity and tolerance. Yet the standard of citizenship is not always what the idealist would wish, and lapses are not all due to continued inadequacies of social provision. Those who felt hopefully that poverty and crime, for instance, were closely related and could largely be removed together, have had to make particularly painful adjustments. On the other hand, there is ample evidence of the idealism and sense of service of the youth brought up amid affluent conditions, and of the activity of innumerable adults in what has well been called 'a participating society'.[11] In the words of a report which used this phrase, 'Evidence from many quarters has confirmed the vital rôle played by volunteers in countless spontaneous acts of good neigh-bourliness, as well as corporately through organised schemes of help which augment, and extend, and often anticipate, the provisions of the public authorities.' Indeed it is not too much to claim that the Welfare State makes greater demands than ever on voluntary activity. Co-operation between voluntary and public bodies is actively encouraged, aided by the grants from public resources, both central and local, which have been possible since 1919,[12] and many of the deficiencies of the Welfare State have been eased or remedied by voluntary activity (often enough, up to the point when a public authority was able to take over). Moreover, the national services, especially Health and Assistance, call for much voluntary service on committees, appeal tribunals and the like. Despite all the increase of collectivism and State power, therefore, much scope for individual activity remains and many find their satisfaction in it. That this fruitful interplay of community and personal activity continues must not be overlooked in any assessment of the realities of the Welfare State.

Much has turned in the shaping of policy, as it has always done, on con-trasting views of the possibilities of human perfectibility. To the reformer, the emphasis is mainly on collective action; perfection would come with the im-provement of environment. Others, more conscious of human frailty, if not of 'original sin', have been more cautious, more conservative, even more cynical, and have demanded rather more individual responsibility, more improvement from within. The interplay of the two approaches can be traced throughout our story, and is with us yet. Broadly speaking they are reflected in the outlook of the two main political parties.

How much, in fact, has State provision, the Welfare State as spelt out in detail, helped to make the good society? It is impossible to say. More has been achieved, one might conjecture, by the continued high level of employment than by any other factor. Social security payments have provided a valuable margin, and have probably served to no small extent as stabilisers of the economy, contributing to the level of employment. Yet, as J. K. Galbraith has pointed out, it is production, and therefore employment, that has eliminated most of the tensions due to in-equality, not redistribution.[13] Inequalities remain, but full employment has avoided the wastage of manpower resources from which the country suffered so much be-tween the wars, and a high level of employment, as Beveridge insisted, is a pre-requisite of social advance. In making it possible to maintain employment, as governments have done, the State has contributed much, quite apart from Insurance and Assistance payments, Family Allowances and the Health Service. The effects of social policy, it has been pointed out, however, can easily be exag-gerated: 'The structure of society, and the pattern of economic inequality, de-pend primarily on the structure of the economy and the pattern of its rewards.'[14]

It is through full employment, too, that Britain has advanced to W. W. Rostow's stage of 'High Mass Consumption',[15] and inevitably the question has been raised whether under these conditions the services devised for an earlier and more restricted economy are any longer valid. It is certainly a matter for enquiry whether the vast resources collected from the community are necessarily spent to the most effective purpose in social security provision under prevailing conditions. 'The Beveridge revolution', in the words of a responsible Minister in 1964, 'spent itself some years ago',[16] and many of its assumptions and provisions are irrelevant to present needs. Hence the demands made from many different quarters, and reflecting many different attitudes, for more concentration on the areas of serious need which investigations have disclosed.

Whatever the inadequacies that have been revealed in the provision for such 'casualties' as the elderly, dependent on 'supplementary benefits', large families, widowed or abandoned mothers with young children, the chronically sick, the low-paid and the ill-housed, two major services stand out as the twin pillars of the system which seem certain to endure, the National Health Service and Social Security (as we must now call the combination of Pensions, National Insurance and National Assistance linked together in one Ministry in 1966). The N.H.S. has brought to all the most obvious and immediate benefits. To many it *is* the Welfare State, and every survey of public opinion on the subject has shown how much it is now valued and taken for granted as part and parcel of British life. Serious defects and deficiencies there still are, and many of the claims and high hopes of the White Paper of 1944 have yet to be realised. Critics, seeing no visible alternative concede, however, that it has come to stay, and devote their attention to improvement rather than to abolition: 'the very contemplation of denationalising it is enough to daunt the stoutest political heart'.[17] Close American observers, concerned at their own lack of a comparable system, have testified to the contribution it has made to social policy and practice, as one of the 'notable achievements of the twentieth century'.[18] Outside it there is surprisingly little of private general practice[19] (though much more of private hospital treatment), to suggest an alternative or even to compete in quality of care. Its best testimonial is the general standard of health of the British people, especially the health of mothers and young children, among whom, by comparison, the U.S.A., for all the affluence of its doctors, has fallen seriously behind since 1948.

Complaints about the cost of the service have been common enough, but have tended to overlook the fact that adequate medical care is now, with all the advances in diagnosis and treatment, a costly matter all the world over. The Guillebaud Committee, appointed by the Conservative Government in 1953 to enquire into the cost of the service, reported in 1956 that it saw no evidence of extravagance, and proposed, indeed, more expenditure, especially on hospitals, long the neglected sector of the service. More recent investigation has shown that Britain has actually fallen behind other countries since 1948 in the proportion of national resources spent on the health services.[20]

To co-ordinate the other services the Ministry of Social Security which Beveridge had sought was at last created in 1966, with National Assistance now renamed and administered by a 'Supplementary Benefits Commission' within the Ministry. Something was done at the same time to improve benefits and, with them, the Family Allowances that were of real significance to poorer families. In the matter of pensions and other insurance benefits a gradual change of policy from flat-rate to income-related contributions and benefits has been taking shape. Inflation has whittled away the value of past contributions, and a subsistence basis is in any case no longer adequate, while many employees, especially among white-collar workers, receive pensions from special schemes that are denied to others. Hence the fading of Beveridge principles: there is general agreement that all benefits should be more nearly adequate and should reflect rising standards of living. A first, limited graduated-contribution and pension scheme was introduced in 1959, and was extended in 1966 to other contributory benefits. As far as pensions are concerned a full superannuation scheme seems likely in time to follow, for those not otherwise covered. To attempt, in a State scheme, to cover differing needs and standards instead of, as Beveridge proposed, 'giving in return for contributions benefits up to subsistence level . . . so that individuals may build freely upon it',[21] indicates that another revolution, also a British one[22] in that it has gone through almost unnoticed, has overtaken that of 1942. The very creation of a Ministry of Social Security reflects the change. Beveridge advocated, on grounds of efficiency and economy, the administrative linking in this way of Insurance and Assistance,[23] but given the trend of policy, with the linking may come now something of a blurring of the distinction of function. Whether, with all the modern emphasis on casework practice, the supplementary benefits section of the Ministry can continue its somewhat mechanical methods of administration has yet, it would seem, to be considered.

The eventual significance of the changes and developments of recent years cannot yet be determined, and is in any case hardly matter for an historical study. If we try to sum up what had been achieved by 1948, what the term, the Welfare State, actually connoted, we find in it several elements:

There is, *first*, the guarantee to all of a minimum income at all times, not necessarily related to earning power and based on conceptions both of insurance and of assistance.

*Secondly*, there is protection, nominally entirely through insurance, against the accidents of life that interrupt or destroy the power of gaining a livelihood.

*Thirdly*, there is special protection for children through family allowances to ensure that family resources are adequate for their support.

*Fourthly*, there are services of universal provision, education and health, devised to provide a common standard higher than most individuals could provide for themselves, and offered in the interests of the community as a whole no less than in those of the individual.

*Finally*, there are the environmental and welfare services, providing goods and services rather than cash benefits—housing, old people's homes, child welfare, home helps, 'meals on wheels' and the like. Here, experience has shown, is a fruitful field of activity for voluntary and public services in co-operation.

Some of these derive from the traditional provision of a *minimum* that reaches back into the sixteenth century; others from a new conception of an *optimum*, the provision for all of the best service that modern developments make possible and financial resources permit.   The optimum is a conception evolved through the rapid improvement in conditions and opportunities during the past century and a half. Once it was admitted that people should be helped to take advantage of the improvement—in public health, education, personal health, etc.—the only limit was set by resources. Medical care can hardly be cut to size to suit individual incomes; nor is it in the national interest that education should be. The minimum is hardly less variable. The 'needs test' of today is not the 'means test' of yesterday, with all its lingering memory of the pre-war years, and today's minimum would have seemed luxurious then. There is now at least some attempt, within crude limits, to adapt aid to need. In matters of finance what has emerged is a combination of taxation with insurance contributions that have become increasingly an additional tax bearing only a limited relation to any eventual return.

The comparatively simple concepts of Beveridge have been left far behind, and what is developing is a highly complex bureaucratic system, slow to move and difficult to change, caught as it is in a somewhat antiquated framework of central and local government,[24] and subject to the activities of innumerable pressure groups. Britain's is not, of course, the only example of a Welfare State, though perhaps one, though only one, of the most fully developed. Its ideological basis, such as it is, is now generally accepted, if still reluctantly in some quarters, and millions are now growing up who have known nothing else. The problems of the present and future in the system, it has been said, are problems of social engineering rather than of ideology,[25] and there is only too much to be engineered to make a reality that fits present circumstances and is not merely a projection of past needs. The whole process of development, at least until the present, has been one of evolution, of uneven response to problems, of unexpected twists and turns of policy, of responsiveness to many pressures and indifference to others, of compromise, of political accident, of chance. There has been nothing inevitable about it, except in so far as a concern for the well-being of the population and an increase in the power of the State, growing *pari passu*, were bound eventually to produce some system of social welfare. But no-one ever dreamed up anything like what has emerged, and some past dreamers would regard it as little short of a nightmare.

Yet, despite what one distinguished authority on social policy has said,[26] the complicated historical process that has produced the Welfare State in Britain has about it something of romance. Placid the story is not, and looking back we may well be shocked at the length of time needed to improve conditions that seem to us unendurable, and at the devices needed to overcome prejudice and opposition. The process goes on, and if improvement is somewhat more speedy now it is not necessarily more certain. We can at least look back with some satisfaction, however, at the way we have come, even if satisfaction is tempered by the reflection that the way could well have been shorter, and straighter. We can take some satisfaction, too, in the preservation of political liberty, even though we may register concern at the enormous power wielded by an Executive which the very machinery of the Welfare State has helped to strengthen. Yet the point has already been made that to some extent at least individualism and collectivism have been reconciled. Perhaps the last word, which is on this theme, may rest with a skilled political practitioner who strove in his day for much that the Welfare State has achieved, and lived to preside, amid 'winds of change', over years of welcome, if uncertain, prosperity: 'To most people in Britain, because it affects their lives so closely, the coming of the Welfare State is perhaps the most marked of all the changes that the last fifty years have brought. Yet in this new growth of collectivism, the finer aspects of the individualism of the Reformation, the freedom of personal decision, initiative and responsibility, have not been forgotten. Indeed, much of the controversy in domestic politics has been generated by the fruitful interaction between these two philosophies.'[27]

The process of interaction has been evident enough in these pages. Where, if it is to continue, it will carry us next we can hardly yet see. Government is, at best, a crude process, and recent years have shown that, for all the efforts made, the common assumptions about welfare take too much for granted. Like Chadwick in his *Sanitary Conditions*, like Charles Booth, like the Royal Commission on the Poor Law (quoted on page 156 above) when we look into the facts we are often surprised at what we find. The end of the road is not yet.

# References

1 **The Ground Surveyed (pages 13-31)**
 1 W. W. Rostow, *The Stages of Economic Growth*, p. 11
 2 *ibid.*, p. 69
 3 From his budget speech, 19 April 1908, printed in a collection of his speeches, *Better Times* (1910), p. 143
 4 W. George, *My Brother and I*, p. 173
 5 R.C. (Royal Commission) on Poor Laws, Report (1909), Appendix, vol. viii, 77738
 6 *The Economic Journal*, 1892, pp. 374–9
 7 From the collection of his speeches, *The People's Insurance* (1911), p. 152
 8 J. M. Mackintosh, *Trends of Opinion about the Public Health, 1901–1951*, p. 29
 9 Speech at Glasgow, October 1906, printed in *Liberalism and the Social Problem* (1909), p. 81
 10 *The Times*, 15 January 1943
 11 *Liberalism and the Social Problem*, p. 82
 12 D. C. Marsh, *The Times*, 15 June 1959
 13 Minister of Pensions and National Insurance (J. Boyd-Carpenter), H. of C. (House of Commons), 24 June 1959
 14 *ibid.*
 15 Minister of Social Security (Mrs Judith Hart) in *Everybody's Guide to Social Security* (1967), foreword
 16 Report, Part I, p. 12
 17 *Law and Opinion in England in the Twentieth Century*, p. 20
 18 *Better Times*, pp. 52 and 55
 19 *Liberalism and the Social Problem*, p. 223
 20 *ibid.*, p. 377
 21 *Social Insurance and Allied Services*, para. 31
 22 Quoted by R. M. Titmuss, *Problems of Social Policy*, p. 516
 23 *ibid.*, p. 508
 24 R.C. on Unemployment Insurance, Final Report (1932), para. 62
 25 This section is based on information and suggestions kindly provided by Dr T. K. Derry, Dr W. H. Chaloner and the Editors of the *Supplement to the Oxford English Dictionary*
 26 S. Fine, *Laissez-Faire and the General-Welfare State*, preface
 27 *cf.* T. H. Marshall, 'The Welfare State: a Sociological Interpretation', *European Journal of Sociology*, II, 2 (1961), p. 284

2 **Background and Beginnings (pages 32-56)**
 1 H. of C., 29 April 1941, 371, col. 372

2  Sir C. Petrie, *Walter Long and His Times*, p. 71

3  R.C. on Poor Laws, Report (1909), Appendix VIII, 78461, 3

4  39 Elizabeth, c. 1, *Against the Decaying of Towns*

5  *The Agrarian Problem in the Sixteenth Century*, p. 264

6  C. Hill, *The Century of Revolution, 1603–1714*, p. 24

7  *The Agrarian Problem*, p. 268

8  Sir S. D'Ewes, *The Journals of all the Parliaments during the Reign of Queen Elizabeth* (1684), p. 555b

9  *ibid.*, p. 674b. The forms of poor relief already active before 1558 are well illustrated in J. Webb (ed.), *Poor Relief in Elizabethan Ipswich* (Suffolk Records Society)

10  1909 reprint, p. 36

11  J. E. Neale, *Elizabeth I and Her Parliaments, 1584–1610*, p. 345

12  *ibid.*, p. 337. The phrase, 'the Winning of the Initiative by the House of Commons', was coined by W. Notestein in a notable British Academy Lecture in 1924

13  *ibid.*, p. 343

14  D'Ewes, *Journals*, p. 674b

15  *cf.* A. L. Beier, 'Poor Relief in Warwickshire, 1630–1660', *Past and Present*, no. 35

16  W. K. Jordan, *Philanthropy in England, 1480–1660*, ch. V, especially p. 139

17  *ibid.*, p. 118

18  *ibid.*, p. 124

19  *ibid.*, p. 182

20  R. H. Tawney, *Religion and the Rise of Capitalism*, Pelican edn, p. 214

21  E. Lipson, *The Economic History of England*, III, p. 270

22  Quoted in M. James, *Social Problems and Policy during the Puritan Revolution*, p. 284

23  See, for instance, 'Poor Relief in Warwickshire'

24  *Philanthropy in England*, p. 201

25  C. Hill, *Society and Puritanism in Pre-Revolutionary England*, pp. 129–37

26  Quoted in C. Hill, 'Puritans and the Poor', *Past and Present*, no. 2, p. 40

27  V. Kiernan, 'Puritanism and the Poor', *Past and Present*, no. 3, p. 47

28  *ibid.*, quoting Perkins

29  Quoted in *Social Problems and Policy during the Puritan Revolution*, p. 16

30  M. Walzer, *The Revolution of the Saints*, p. 211

31  Quoted in *Society and Puritanism in Pre-Revolutionary England*, p. 125

32  *ibid.*, p. 276. A further element in the situation was the common law, which in its concern for personal and property rights against the extension of the royal prerogative was to prove a factor in political and economic resistance and a pointer to economic liberalism: *cf.* B. Malament, 'The Economic Liberalism of Sir Edward Coke', *Yale Law Journal*, June 1967

33  Quoted in *Religion and the Rise of Capitalism*, p. 232

34  *The Wealth of Nations*, ed. Cannan, I, p. 477

35  Quoted in *Religion and the Rise of Capitalism*, pp. 238–9

36  Quoted in S. and B. Webb, *The Old Poor Law*, p. 110

37  *ibid.*, p. 115

38  E. Lipson, *The Economic History of England*, III, p. 268

39  *Introductory Lectures on Political Economy*, 4th ed. (1855), p. 98

40  *Religion and the Rise of Capitalism*, pp. 227–8

41  Quoted in *Philanthropy in England*, p. 200

42  *Society and Puritanism in Pre-Revolutionary England*, p. 510

43  D. Marshall, *The English Poor in the Eighteenth Century*, p. 161

44 *The Wealth of Nations*, I, p. 157

45 *An Essay on the Principle of Population*, ch. V

46 Minority Report, ch. IX (A)

47 The current interest in local history has made instances familiar. A Cambridgeshire study has estimated that two-thirds of parish records were concerned with removals (E. M. Hampson, *The Treatment of Poverty in Cambridgeshire, 1597–1834*, p. 267). For a typical forced marriage see J. Woodforde (ed. J. Beresford), *The Diary of a Country Parson*, II, p. 297, the entry for 28 January 1787

48 *The Old Poor Law*, p. 322

49 *The English Poor in the Eighteenth Century*, pp. 11–12

50 *The Old Poor Law*, p. 347n

51 See the B.M.A. publication, *Porphyria—a Royal Malady*

52 cf. E. P. Thompson, 'Time, Work Discipline and Industrial Capitalism', *Past and Present*, no. 38

53 *The Wealth of Nations*, I, ch. VIII

54 The case put briefly here is developed in three important papers: J. D. Chambers, 'The Vale of Trent, 1670–1800', *Economic History Review Supplement*, 1957; A. W. Coats, 'Changing Attitudes to Labour in the Mid-Eighteenth Century', and 'Economic Thought and Poor Law Policy in the Eighteenth Century', *Economic History Review*, 1958–9 and 1960–1

55 e.g. in his *Political Arithmetic* (1774)

56 Sir J. Clapham, *An Economic History of Modern Britain*, I, p. 371

57 quoted *ibid.*

58 *ibid.*, p. 372

59 Quoted in K. de Schweinitz, *England's Road to Social Security*, p. 61

60 D. Marshall, 'The Old Poor Law, 1662–1795', *Economic History Review*, 1937–8, p. 45

61 J. D. Chambers and G. E. Mingay, *The Agricultural Revolution, 1750–1880*, p. 119

62 *ibid.*, pp. 119–20. See also *Land, Labour and Population in the Industrial Revolution*, ed. Jones and Mingay, p. 246

## 3 The Impact of the Industrial Revolution (pages 57-88)

1 Owing to the vast amount of building and re-development that has taken place within in the last decade this is becoming increasingly less true

2 W. P. Alison, *Observations on the Management of the Poor in Scotland* (1840), p. 38

3 *Political Arithmetic* (1774), p. 66

4 K. F. Helleiner, 'The Vital Revolution Reconsidered', in *Population in History*, ed. D. V. Glass and D. E. C. Eversley, ch. 4, p. 86

5 C. F. G. Masterman, *The Heart of Empire* (1907), preface, p. vii

6 A. Ure, *The Philosophy of Manufactures* (1835), pp. 312 and 365

7 *Hard Times* (1854), Book I, ch. X

8 3rd ed. (1806), Book IV, ch. III and VIII

9 Book II, ch. XVI

10 *ibid.*

11 *Report on the Sanitary Condition of the Labouring Population*, Local Reports, England (1842), p. 337

12 J. Haywood and W. Lee, *A Report on the Sanatory Condition of the Borough of Sheffield* (1847)

13 S. E. Finer, *The Life and Times of Sir Edwin Chadwick*, pp. 211–2

14 *English Local Government : Statutory Authorities*, p. 400
15 R. Lambert, *Sir John Simon*, p. 380
16 For a general account of cholera and its visitations see N. Longmate, *King Cholera*
17 *Sir John Simon*, p. 124
18 Edith Mosley (ed.), *The Correspondence of Crabb Robinson with the Wordsworth Circle*, I, p. 225
19 *Report on the Sanitary Condition of the Labouring Population*, p. 3
20 *ibid.*, ch. IV
21 *ibid.*, p. 190
22 *ibid.*, p. 369
23 Fourth Annual Report of the Poor Law Commissioners (1838), p. 94
24 *Report on the Sanitary Condition of the Labouring Population*, p. 340
25 Fifth Annual Report of the Poor Law Commissioners (1839), App. C2
26 Fourth Report, p. 94
27 *Report on the Sanitary Condition of the Labouring Population*, pp. 207–9
28 *ibid.*, p. 43
29 ch. XI
30 *Report on the Sanitary Condition of the Labouring Population*, p. 342
31 ch. XX
32 see p. 143 below
33 *Observations on the Management of the Poor in Scotland*, p. 49
34 Quoted by M. B. Simey, *Charitable Effort in Liverpool in the Nineteenth Century*, p. 40
35 *Report on the Sanitary Condition of the Labouring Population*, p. 371
36 *ibid.*, p. 262
37 *Observations on the Management of the Poor in Scotland*, p. 49
38 *Local Reports—England*, p. 339
39 First Report of the Commissioners for inquiring into the State of Large Towns and Populous Districts (1844), I, p. 32
40 *Sir John Simon*, p. 150
41 *Our Partnership*, p. 442
42 Book III, ch. VIII
43 *Report on the Sanitary Condition of the Labouring Population*, p. 206
44 Quoted in H. Lynd, *England in the Eighteen-Eighties*, p. 160
45 *Report on the Sanitary Condition of the Labouring Population*, ch. VII
46 *ibid.*, p. 201
47 R.C. on the Housing of the Working Classes, p. 12
48 *Charitable Effort in Liverpool*, p. 150
49 *Report on the Sanitary Condition of the Labouring Population*, p. 236
50 Children's Employment Commission, First Report (Mines) (1842), App. part 2, p. 258
51 *ibid.*, p. 256
52 *ibid.*, p. 258
53 Second Report (Trades and Manufacturers) (1842), App. I, E13
54 *cf.* A. Cobban, 'Carlyle's French Revolution', *History*, 1963
55 Book III, ch. IV
56 Factories Inquiry Commission, Supplementary Report (1834), part II, CI, 15
57 Speech at Swansea, October 1908, *Better Times*, p. 56
58 Book I, ch. XI

59  p. 179
60  See the article by S. Pollard, 'Investment, Consumption and the Industrial Revolution', *Economic History Review*, 1958–9
61  Book I, ch. XIII
62  Quoted by C. Driver, *Tory Radical. The Life of Richard Oastler*, p. 43
63  N. Senior, *Letters on the Factory Act* (2nd ed., 1844), p. 4
64  Factories Inquiry Commission, Supplementary Report (1834), Part II, CI, 17
65  A. Kydd, *The History of the Factory Movement* (1857), I, p. 154
66  J. L. and Barbara Hammond, *Lord Shaftesbury*, p. 276
67  *ibid.*, p. 156, quoting Sir James Graham
68  Book IV, ch. XIV
69  F. Hill, *Crime: Its Amount, Causes and Remedies* (1853), p. 49
70  M. Longfield, *Lectures on Political Economy* (1834), quoted in G. S. L. Tucker, *Progress and Profit in British Economic Thought*, p. 165
71  N. W. Senior (ed. S. L. Levy) *Industrial Efficiency and Social Economy*, II, pp. 292–3
72  N. W. Senior,*Historical and Philosophical Essays*, II, p. 67, quoted in H. L. Beales, 'The New Poor Law', in E. M. Carus-Wilson (ed.), *Essays in Economic History*, III, pp. 185–6
73  *Industrial Efficiency and Social Economy*, pp. 292–3
74  H. of C., 6 July 1908, 191, col. 1334
75  Children's Employment Commission, Mines, App. part 2, pp. 257–8
76  *My Apprenticeship*, ch. VI
77  Report, p. 13
78  *Life and Labour of the People in London*, Poverty, I, p. 155
79  Book II, ch. I
80  Book I, ch. I
81  (1831–2), p. 209
82  Quoted in J. H. Morris and L. J. Williams, *The South Wales Coal Industry, 1841–75*, p. 209
83  *Letters on the Social Condition of the Operative Classes*, p. 480
84  Book I, ch. III
85  A. R. Schoyen, *The Chartist Challenge*, p. 180
86  *ibid.*, p. 287
87  Quoted in A. Briggs (ed.), *Chartist Studies*, p. 34
88  Book IV, ch. 4
89  Book II, ch. IV
90  *The South Wales Coal Industry*, p. 129
91  A. Redford, *Labour Migration in England*, new ed. (ed. W. H. Chaloner), p. 161
92  *ibid.*
93  ch. XVIII and XXII
94  *Autobiography*, ch. VII
95  Report, p. 30
96  M. Hewitt, *Wives and Mothers in Victorian Industry*, p. 153, quoting R. W. Cooke Taylor (1874)
97  Book I, ch. XI
98  D. Roberts, *The Victorian Origins of the British Welfare State*, p. 315
99  Quoted in F. Smith, *The Life and Work of Sir James Kay-Shuttleworth*, p. 33
100 *The Moral and Physical Condition of the Working Classes employed in the Cotton Manufacture of Manchester* (1832), p. 10

101 *A Report on the Sanatory Condition of the Borough of Sheffield*
102 *Social Insurance and Allied Services*, paras. 8 and 456

## 4 The Victorian Poor Law (pages 89-153)

1 *English Local Government: Statutory Authorities*, p. 483
2 D. Roberts, *The Victorian Origins of the British Welfare State*, p. 319
3 Second Annual Report of the Poor Law Commissioners (1836), p. 147
4 Quoted in T. Mackay, *A History of the English Poor Law*, III, p. 196
5 Poor Law Report (1834), p. 279
6 R.C. on Aged Poor, Report, p. xxvi
7 Sir G. Nicholls and T. Mackay, *A History of the English Poor Law*, III, p. 20. Vol. III, dealing with the period 1834–98, was the work of Mackay, a prominent member of the Charity Organisation Society, of whom *The Times* said on his death in 1912 that he was 'an individualist of the old-fashioned school', an opinion which is amply illustrated in the passages from his book quoted in these pages, and which can be summed-up in his comment, 'We cannot, alas! write of the Poor Law as a thing of the past' (III, p. 155)
8 *English Poor Law History: The Last Hundred Years*, I, p. 84
9 Pelican ed., p. 242
10 Poor Law Report (1834), p. 264
11 S. E. Finer, *The Life and Times of Sir Edwin Chadwick*, pp. 74–5. The relevant section of the 1834 report is on p. 228
12 Poor Law Report (1834), p. 262
13 *ibid.*
14 *ibid.*, p. 264
15 *ibid.*, p. 263
16 'World's Classics' ed., p. 167
17 Poor Law Report (1834), p. 53
18 *ibid.*, p. 307
19 *ibid.*, p. 59
20 R.C. on Poor Laws, Report (1909), Appendix I, 3184
21 *ibid.*, 3219
22 G. Lansbury, *My Life*, p. 165
23 *A History of the English Poor Law*, III, p. vi
24 R.C. on Poor Laws, Report, Appendix I, 2782
25 *A History of the English Poor Law*, III, p. 19
26 Book III, ch. VIII
27 *The Life and Times of Sir Edwin Chadwick*, p. 70
28 *ibid.*, p. 182
29 S. Pollard, *A History of Labour in Sheffield*, p. 40
30 C. Driver, *Tory Radical. The Life of Richard Oastler*, p. 332
31 *ibid.*, p. 339
32 S. Kydd, *The History of the Factory Movement* (1857), quoted in A. Briggs (ed.), *Chartist Studies*, p. 11, n. 3
33 A. Redford, *Labour Migration in England*, new ed. (ed. W. H. Chaloner), p. 162
34 R.C. on Poor Laws, Report, Appendix I, 2443
35 See D. Roberts, 'How Cruel was the Victorian Poor Law?', *Historical Journal*, 1963
36 Quoted in Sir J. Clapham, *An Economic History of Modern Britain*, I, p. 582
37 *A History of the English Poor Law*, III, p. 6

38  *Voyages en Angleterre* (1835), p. 90
39  *The People's Budget*, preface, p. ix
40  Book III, ch. VIII
41  Book I, ch. XXXI
42  Book III, ch. I
43  *My Life*, pp. 135–6
44  *ibid.*, p. 136
45  *ibid.*, p. 133
46  *The Island Pharisees* (1908)
47  Open criticism of workhouse practice, and its effects, is recorded in R.C. on Poor Laws, Majority Report, Part IV, ch. 5, and Minority Report, Part I, ch. I
48  How far this can be ascribed to the poor law is considered in P. H. J. H. Gosden, *The Friendly Societies in England, 1815–1875*, pp. 205–9
49  Quoted in *History of the English Poor Law*, III, p. 589
50  Quoted in *The Friendly Societies in England*, p. 209
51  Dean Stanley, *The Life and Correspondence of Thomas Arnold*, ch. IX, letter 195, 20 Jan. 1839
52  *History of the English Poor Law*, III, p. 231
53  *ibid.*, pp. 33–4
54  The Poor Law Commissioners issued a circular on the subject in 1840: *The Friendly Societies in England*, pp. 202–4
55  Quoted in K. de Schweinitz, *England's Road to Social Security*, p. 166
56  H. of C., 4 May 1911, XXV, col. 609
57  *Voluntary Action*, p. 55
58  H. of C., 4 May 1911, XXV, col. 610
59  Sir A. Wilson and H. Levy, *Industrial Assurance*, p. xi
60  H. of C., 4 May 1911, XXV, col. 609
61  Report, p. XV
62  Quoted in M. Richter, *The Politics of Conscience. T. H. Green and His Age*, p. 338
63  *Thrift*, p. 165
64  *The Last Hundred Years*, II, p. 470
65  See the discussion in H. of C., 11 March 1886, 303, col. 469, and Chamberlain's reply
    For an example of the special provision now made for elderly married couples, see A. R. Neate, *The St. Marylebone Warehouse and Institution, 1730–1965*, p. 29
66  *Candleford Green*, p. 52
67  H. House, *The Dickens World*, p. 100
68  P. F. Aschrott, *The English Poor Law System* (1902), p. 121
69  Part IV, para. 438
70  ch. XX. Salaries in fact differed greatly from Union to Union, and were a constant source of professional complaint, while medical relief was often begrudged, partly from suspicion of the doctors' self-interest, partly from an unwillingness to provide what many independent workers could not afford: see Ruth Hodgkinson, *The Origins of the National Health Service. The Medical Services of the New Poor Law, 1834–1871*
71  *The Last Hundred Years*, I, p. 324
72  See the account of the political manoeuvres that preceded this Act in B. Rodgers, 'The Medical Relief Disqualification Removal Act, 1885. A Storm in a Political

Teacup', *Parliamentary Affairs*, 1955–6. The first suggestion that medical relief
alone should not pauperise, was made in 1844: *The Origins of the National Health
Service*, pp. 15–16
73 R.C. on Poor Laws, Report,—Appendix 1, 3225
74 Majority Report, p. 264. (The expression 'state hospitals' for workhouse infirmaries
seems first to be used in 1867: *The Origins of the National Health Service*, p. 689)
75 *ibid.*, p. 255
76 *Rich and Poor* (1896), p. 36
77 R.C. on Poor Laws, Report, Appendix IX, pp. 267 and 274
78 *ibid.*, Appendix IA, p. 445
79 R.C. on Poor Laws, Majority Report, Part IV, ch. 6, para. 245
80 Report (1895), p. xxi
81 R.C. on Poor Laws, Majority Report, Part IV, ch. 6, para. 256
82 Report (1895), p. xx
83 For a recent account of the Society see C. L. Mowat, *The Charity Organisation
Society, 1869–1913*
84 *My Life*, p. 129
85 D. Owen, *English Philanthropy, 1660–1960*, p. viii
86 Una Cormack, *The Royal Commission on the Poor Laws, 1905–9, and the Welfare
State*, p. 28
87 *Rich and Poor*, preface
88 B. Kirkman Gray, *Philanthropy and the State* (1908), p. 113
89 B. Kirkman Gray, *A History of English Philanthropy* (1905, new ed. 1967), p. 290
90 J. F. Wilkinson, *Pensions and Pauperism* (1892), p. 88
91 Quoted in *England's Road to Social Security*, p. 159
92 *Unemployment. A Problem of Industry*, p. 158
93 Majority Report, Part IV, ch. 10, para. 552
94 H. of C., 12 March 1886, 303, col. 661
95 *Unemployment. A Problem of Industry*, p. 157. R.C. on Poor Laws, Minority Report,
quotes a similar case on pp. 331–2
96 Minority Report, Part II, ch. 1 (B), p. 464
97 Speech at Dundee, May 1908, *Liberalism and the Social Problem*, p. 159
98 *The Last Hundred Years*, I, p. 234
99 *The Economic Journal* (1892), pp. 189 and 375
100 *The Last Hundred Years*, I, p. 354
101 *Lark Rise*, p. 100
102 *The Last Hundred Years*, I, p. 363n.
103 Report, Appendix I, 128, 2310
104 Report, Part VI, para. 201
105 Minority Report, Part II, ch. 5, section (F)
106 *History of Labour in Sheffield*, p. 11
107 C. Fraser Brockington, *Public Health in the Nineteenth Century*, p. 149
108 Quoted in Sir A. Newsholme, *Fifty Years in Public Health*, p. 43
109 Quoted in R. Lambert, *Sir John Simon*, p. 150
110 Sir J. Simon, *English Sanitary Institutions*, p. 444
111 *ibid.*
112 *ibid.*, p. 445
113 *Sir John Simon*, p. 182
114 Quoted in W. M. Frazer, *A History of English Public Health, 1834–1939*, p. 93

115 *Sir John Simon*, p. 522
116 *The Life and Times of Sir Edwin Chadwick*, pp. 472 and 467
117 *Sir John Simon*, p. 223, n.3
118 *Public Health in the Nineteenth Century*, p. 163
119 *Sir John Simon*, p. 273
120 *Public Health in the Nineteenth Century*, pp. 156 and 187, referring to Dr F. Cooper of Southampton
121 *English Sanitary Institutions*, p. 299
122 *Sir John Simon*, p. 423
123 For names and careers see *Public Health in the Nineteenth Century*, pp. 201–3 and 238–69
124 *Sir John Simon*, p. 501
125 *ibid.*, p. 502
126 *ibid.*, p. 456, n. 91
127 *ibid.*, p. 367
128 J. L. and Barbara Hammond, *James Stansfeld*, p. 103
129 *Sir John Simon*, pp. 559–60. See also P. Smith, *Disraelian Conservatism and Social Reform*, a critical study of the legends surrounding Disraelian 'social policy'
130 *English Sanitary Institutions*, p. 476
131 *Sir John Simon*, p. 561
132 *A History of English Public Health*, p. 120
133 The title of an article by R. Lambert in the *Historical Journal* (1962)
134 R.C. on Poor Laws, Report, Appendix IV, 37927, 31
135 J. M. Mackintosh, *Trends of Opinion about the Public Health, 1910–51*, p. 6
136 *The Card*
137 Report, pp. 7–8
138 Report, Appendix XVI, *Report on the Relation of Industrial and Sanitary Conditions to Pauperism in London*, p. 57
139 *Life and Labour of the People in London: Poverty*, I, p. 30
140 *London: a Pilgrimage*, p. 116
141 *My Apprenticeship*, pp. 262–3
142 'Realities at Home' in *The Heart of Empire* (1901), p. 16
143 *My Apprenticeship*, p. 263
144 Report, p. 19
145 *My Apprenticeship*, p. 265
146 E. Moberly Bell, *Octavia Hill*, p. 86
147 *ibid.*, p. 78
148 Octavia Hill, 'The Homes of the London Poor', *Macmillan's Magazine*, vol. XXX (1874), pp. 131–2
149 *London: A Pilgrimage*, p. 142
150 A. Briggs, *History of Birmingham, Borough and City, 1865–1938*, p. 86
151 W. Ashworth, *The Genesis of Modern British Town Planning*, pp. 98–9
152 Under the Manchester Police Act, 1844: A Redford and I. S. Russell, *The History of Local Government in Manchester*, II, pp. 86–7
153 C. W. Boyd (ed.), *Mr Chamberlain's Speeches* (1914), I, p. 63
154 *History of Birmingham*, p. 86, and K. Feiling, *Life of Neville Chamberlain*, ch. vi
155 G. R. Sims, *How the Poor Live*, p. 35
156 Report, p. 12
157 *ibid.*, p. 54

158 *Octavia Hill*, pp. 257–8
159 E. R. Dewsnup, *The Housing Problem in England* (1907), p. 186
160 J. Hole, *The Homes of the Working Classes* (1866), p. 34
161 R. C. K. Ensor, *England, 1870–1914*, p. 518
162 B. Simon, *Studies in the History of Education, 1780–1870*, p. 365
163 From an early report to the University of Cambridge Board of Extra-Mural Studies
164 *Final Volume*, p. 202
165 *The New Survey of London Life and Labour* (1930–32), I, *Forty Years of Change*, p. 249
166 *At the Works* (1907), p. 143
167 Part II, ch. V (F)
168 *How the Poor Live*, p. 29
169 H. of C., 18 April 1905, 145, col. 534
170 Lord Percy, *Some Memories*, p. 95
171 Quoted in G. A. N. Lowndes, *The Silent Social Revolution*, p. 90
172 C. F. G. Masterman, *The Condition of England* (1909), p. 73
173 H. of C., 18 April 1905, 145, col. 539. *Cf* the letter of H. M. Hyndman quoted on p. 224 below
174 Quoted in J. B. Brebner, 'Laissez Faire and State Intervention in Nineteenth-Century Britain', *Journal of Economic History*, supplement VIII, 1948, p. 73
175 A. V. Dicey, *Law and Public Opinion in England during the Nineteenth Century*, introduction to 2nd ed., 1914, p. lxxiv
176 See p. 14 above
177 See p. 16 above. Engels put it more forcefully: see the quotations in R. N. Carew Hunt, *The Theory and Practice of Communism*, p. 101

## 5  The Turning Point: Social Reform 1905–14 (pages 154–227)

1 *Our Partnership*, p. 321
2 Lord George Hamilton, *Parliamentary Reminiscences and Reflections, 1886–1906*, p. 330
3 *ibid.*, p. 329
4 see p. 67 above
5 *Our Partnership*, p. 462
6 Part IX, para. 173
7 *Round about a Pound a Week*, p. 2
8 Part IX, para. 172
9 G. R. Sims, *How the Poor Live* (1889), p. 35
10 *The Condition of England* (1909), p. 177
11 Part IX, para. 173
12 *ibid.*
13 *ibid.*
14 Part VI, para. 12
15 R.C. on Poor Laws, Report, Appendix, vol. viii, p. 565
16 Part IX, para. 170
17 *Better Times*, p. 93
18 *Round about a Pound a Week*, p. 146
19 *The Condition of England*, p. 177. A new edition of this significant book, which went through six editions in 1909–10, was published in 1960, ed. J. T. Boulton
20 *The Journals of Arnold Bennett*, 2 January 1910, Penguin ed. by F. Swinnerton, p. 207

21 A. L. Bowley, *The Changes in the Distribution of the National Income, 1880–1913*, p. 27
22 Lady Bell, *At the Works* (1907), p. 47
23 *English Sanitary Institutions*, p. 444
24 ed. A. Briggs, *Fabian Essays* (1962), p. 286
25 *ibid.*, p. 78
26 Sir J. Clapham, *An Economic History of Modern Britain*, III, p. 398
27 p. xxxv
28 p. xxiv
29 p. 263
30 *cf.* O. MacDonagh, 'The Nineteenth-century Revolution in Government: a Reappraisal', *Historical Journal*, 1958
31 see p. 28 above
32 *The Condition of England*, pp. 72–3
33 H. M. Hyndman
34 R.C. on Labour, Minority Report, p. 146
35 Fabian Tract No. 70, July 1896, p. 5
36 *The Relation between Law and Public Opinion in England*, pp. lxii–iii
37 *ibid.*, p. xxxvii
38 *ibid.*, p. 465
39 *The People's Insurance* (1911), p. 152
40 H. of C., 4 May 1911, xxv, col. 609
41 Speech at Penrhyndendraeth, Sept. 1906, *Slings and Arrows*, ed. P. Guedalla, p. 8
42 *Better Times*, p. 52
43 Speech at Bangor, January 1906, *Slings and Arrows*, p. 5
44 Blanche Dugdale, *Arthur James Balfour*, II, p. 20
45 C. T. King, *The Asquith Parliament* (1910), p. 9
46 *My Apprenticeship*, p. 184
47 *ibid.*, p. 179
48 The best study of Green is M. Richter, *The Politics of Conscience. T. H. Green and His Age*
49 Quoted from Mrs Humphrey Ward in *The Politics of Conscience*, p. 29
50 Quoted from Green's *Works*, III, p. 372 in *The Politics of Conscience*, p. 283
51 Quoted in T. W. Hutchinson, *A Review of Economic Doctrines, 1870–1929*, p. 11n
52 H. Barnett, *Canon Barnett*, p. 308
53 *My Life*, p. 130
54 *A History of English Philanthropy*, new imp. 1967, p. 289
55 T. S. and M. B. Simey, *Charles Booth, Social Scientist*, pp. 69–70
56 *ibid.*, p. 105
57 *ibid.*, p. 125, n. 2
58 *ibid.*, p. 92
59 *My Apprenticeship*, p. 245
60 C. Booth, *Life and Labour, Religious Influences*, II, p. 52 (the comment is dated 1898). The significance of this conclusion of Booth's was stressed by Beatrice Webb, *My Apprenticeship*, p. 252
61 See p. 166 above
62 *Life and Labour, Poverty*, I, p. 154
63 *The Aged Poor in England and Wales* (1894), pp. 53–4
64 *ibid.*, p. 43

65 *Life and Labour, Poverty*, I, p. 151
66 *Poverty*, p. 304
67 R. S. Churchill, *Winston S. Churchill*, II, *Young Statesman, 1901–14*, pp. 32 and 276; *Liberalism and the Social Problem*, p. 361
68 Albert Hall speech, 1905, printed in *Speeches by the Right Honourable Sir Henry Campbell-Bannerman, 1899–1908*
69 Speech at Bangor, May 1891, *Slings and Arrows*, p. 4
70 9 December 1909. Quoted in W. George, *My Brother and I*, p. 17. This extract is translated from the Welsh original; the English text quoted in the contemporary press, and in *Better Times*, is less colourful
71 *My Brother and I*, p. 27
72 *Better Times*, p. 51
73 A. M. Gollin, *The Observer and J. L. Garvin, 1908–14*, p. 209
74 Speech at Dundee, May 1908, *Liberalism and the Social Problem*, p. 155
75 *My Early Life*, p. 363
76 Speech at Glasgow, October 1906, *Liberalism and the Social Problem*, p. 78
77 'A Gentleman with a Duster' (H. Begbie), *The Mirrors of Downing Street*
78 *Better Times*, p. 68
79 *Liberalism and the Social Problem*, p. 78
80 *ibid.*, p. 82
81 For a detailed discussion of the origins of old age pensions see B. B. Gilbert, *The Evolution of National Insurance in Great Britain*, ch. 4
82 W. J. Braithwaite (ed. Sir H. Bunbury), *Lloyd George's Ambulance Wagon*, p. 71
83 *The Evolution of National Insurance*, p. 196
84 *ibid.*, p. 194
85 Report (1895), p. xiv
86 The phrase is quoted from the Minority Report
87 *The Aged Poor in England and Wales*, pp. 330–1
88 R.C. on Aged Poor, Report, p. xxvi
89 Annual Report, 1908, quoted in B. Kirkman Gray, *Philanthropy and the State* (1908), p. 118
90 *Life and Labour, Final Volume*, p. 145
91 J. F. Wilkinson, *Pensions and Pauperism*, p. 88
92 *Better Times*, p. 145
93 Speech at Manchester, May 1909, *Liberalism and the Social Problem*, p. 312
94 *The Evolution of National Insurance*, p. 210
95 Professor Gilbert sees the introduction of pensions rather too much as an electoral manoeuvre, 'a matter of buying votes', *ibid.*, p. 219. See also C. H. Pelling, *Popular Politics and Society*, pp. 144–5
96 *My Brother and I*, p. 220
97 *ibid.*
98 This is Snowden's claim in *An Autobiography*, I, p. 190, but it does not altogether agree with the record in H. of C., 9 July 1908, col. 153
99 Speech at Dundee, October 1908, *Liberalism and the Social Problem*, p. 210
100 H. of C., 25 May 1911, XXVI, col. 509
101 H. of L., 20 July 1908, 192, col. 1415
102 *Encyclopaedia Britannica*, vol. V, p. 885b
103 *Liberalism and the Social Problem*, p. 236
104 *Lark Rise*, p. 100

105  *Liberalism and the Social Problem*, p. 193
106  *ibid.*, pp. 196–7
107  H. of C., 4 May 1911, XXV, col. 640
108  R.C. on Poor Laws, Majority Report, Part VI, para. 469
109  *Unemployment. A Problem of Industry. 1908 and 1930*, p. 104
110  Select Committee on Distress from Want of Employment, Report (1896), p. vii
111  *ibid.*, p. vi
112  *ibid.*, p. xv
113  R.C. on Poor Laws, Report, Appendix, vol. VIII, p. 578
114  H. of C., 19 July, 1906, 161, col. 423
115  *Unemployment. A Problem of Industry. 1909 and 1930*, p. 72
116  *ibid.*, p. 70
117  F. Owen, *Tempestuous Journey. Lloyd George, His Life and Times*, p. 162
118  Sir H. Fairfax-Lucy, in a letter to *The Times*, 27 August 1908
119  H. of C., 20 June 1905, 147, col. 1191
120  H. of C., 19 July 1906, 161, col. 437
121  R.C. on Poor Laws, Report, Appendix, vol. VIII, 78461, 11
122  *My Life*, p. 145
123  R.C. on Poor Laws, Report, Appendix, vol. VIII, 78461, 8
124  H. of C., 18 April 1905, 145, col. 460
125  H. of C., 20 June 1905, 147, col. 1183
126  R.C. on Poor Laws, Report, Appendix, vol. VIII, 77832, 46
127  H. of C., 20 June 1905, 147, col. 1172
128  H. of C., 7 August 1905, 151, col. 433
129  H. of C., 7 August 1905, 151, col. 432
130  *My Brother and I*, p. 173
131  H. of C., 19 July 1906, 161, col. 432
132  *Unemployment. A Problem of Industry. 1909 and 1930*, pp. 448–9. The last account of the working of the Act, by this time principally concerned with farm colonies, is in the Annual Report of the Ministry of Health for 1922/3, pp. 94–5
133  R.C. on Poor Laws, Report, Appendix, vol. VIII, p. 534
134  *ibid.*, p. 533
135  *Power and Influence*, p. 24
136  *ibid.*, p. 53
137  *Unemployment. A Problem of Industry. 1909 and 1930*, p. 216
138  The heading of Part VI, ch. 1, section (15)
139  Part VI, para. 201
140  *Our Partnership*, p. 402
141  See his tribute to Lloyd George in H. of C., 28 March 1945, 409, col. 1378
142  *Liberalism and the Social Problem*, p. 198
143  *ibid.*, p. 199
144  H. of C., 25 May 1911, XXVI, col. 509
145  R. C. Davison, *The Unemployed*, p. 68
146  *Liberalism and the Social Problem*, p. 309
147  H. of C., 19 May 1909, V, cols. 499–512
148  *ibid.*, col. 525
149  *ibid.*, col. 519
150  *An Economic History of Modern Britain*, III, p. 427
151  *Unemployment. A Problem of Industry. 1909 and 1930*, pp. 304–5

152  Speech at Dundee, October 1908, *Liberalism and the Social Problem*, p. 199
153  *Power and Influence*, pp. 90–1
154  Speech at Glasgow, October 1906, *Liberalism and the Social Problem*, p. 82
155  *Power and Influence*, p. 81
156  *Unemployment*, p. 264
157  H. of C., 25 May 1911, XXVI, col. 508
158  Speech at Manchester, May 1909, *Liberalism and the Social Problem*, p. 315
159  H. of C., 4 May 1911, XXV, cols. 610–11
160  *Our Partnership*, p. 480
161  H. of C., 25 May 1911, XXVI, col. 496
162  *Power and Influence*, pp. 83–4
163  *ibid.*, p. 83
164  Unemployment Insurance Committee, Report (1927), para. 49
165  *Social Insurance and Allied Services*, para. 21
166  *Lloyd George's Ambulance Wagon*, pp. 121–2
167  *Our Partnership*, p. 470
168  Sir C. Petrie, *Walter Long and His Times*, p. 70
169  Sir A. Newsholme, *Fifty Years in Public Health*, p. 260. J. M. Mackintosh, *Trends of Opinion about the Public Health*, pp. 192–5, quotes another typical instance. In fairness it must be said that the Local Government Board was always seriously understaffed. How much the Board's narrow conception of its functions and unwillingness to give a lead were due to cramping Treasury control and to the mass of legislation and regulations which had to be administered by an overburdened staff, restricted in any case by the still-pervading conceptions of limited government intervention, is suggested in several papers by R. M. MacLeod: 'Social Policy and the "Floating Population", 1877–99', *Past and Present*, 35; 'The Frustration of State Medicine, 1880–99', *Medical History*, 1967; *Treasury Control and Social Administration. A Study of Establishment Growth at the Local Government Board, 1871–1905*. Christopher Addison, who had to contend with the Board when the Ministry of Health was being established in 1918–19, has written of its 'invertebrate' quality in *Politics from Within*, II, ch. XV
170  *Our Partnership*, p. 322
171  *Parliamentary Reminiscences and Reflections, 1886–1906*, p. 329
172  *ibid.*, p. 233
173  *Our Partnership*, p. 369
174  For a valuable discussion of the similarities between the Majority and Minority Reports, and a defence of the former, see Una Cormack's Loch Memorial Lecture, 1953, *The Welfare State. The Royal Commission on the Poor Laws, 1905–9, and the Welfare State*
175  Majority Report, Part IX, para. 3
176  *ibid.*, para. 168
177  *ibid.*, para. 145
178  *ibid.*, para. 107
179  *ibid.*
180  Part VI, para. 623
181  The case is set out in full in Part IX; ch. 6 is a criticism of the Minority's proposal to break up the Poor Law
182  Una Cormack, *The Welfare State*, p. 21
183  *ibid.*, p. 25

184 *ibid.*, p. 21
185 Sir A. Newsholme, *The Last Thirty Years in Public Health*, p. 72
186 *The Last Hundred Years*, II, p. 514
187 Majority Report, Part V, para. 226
188 *ibid.*, para. 227
189 See the criticism directed at it in Part V, paras. 206-10
190 Una Cormack, *The Welfare State*, p. 25
191 Quoted *ibid.*, p. 27
192 *ibid.* The quotation is from the C.O.S. *Review* for 1910
193 See p. 102 above
194 Majority Report, Part IX, para. 71
195 *Our Partnership*, p. 425
196 *The Last Hundred Years*, II, p. 546
197 Minority Report, Part I, ch. XII, (B), iii, (a)–(f)
198 Minority Report, Part II, ch. I, p. 517
199 *Our Partnership*, p. 419
200 *ibid.*, p. 430
201 *The Evolution of National Insurance*, p. 272
202 From a letter from Beveridge to his mother, 12 March 1908: reference kindly provided by Professor Gilbert
203 *Our Partnership*, p. 419
204 *ibid.*, p. 482
205 *ibid.*, p. 435
206 H. of C., 19 May 1909, V, col. 500
207 *Canon Barnett*, p. 677
208 Una Cormack, *The Welfare State*, p. 24
209 *Our Partnership*, p. 426
210 C. L. Mowat, *The Charity Organisation Society, 1869-1913*, p. 163
211 The jibe was Bonar Law's: W. Kent, *John Burns. Labour's Lost Leader*, p. 222
212 H. of C., 8 April 1910, XVI, col. 845
213 *ibid.*, col. 838
214 *Lloyd George's Ambulance Wagon*, p. 72
215 H. of C., 8 April 1910, XVI, col. 838
216 *ibid.*, col. 840
217 *Canon Barnett*, p. 678
218 *The Asquith Parliament*, p. 8
219 *The People's Budget*, preface, p. xi
220 *My Brother and I*, p. 232
221 Closing words of the Budget speech, 29 April 1909
222 *The People's Budget*, preface, p. ix
223 *Better Times*, p. 146
224 Speech at Newcastle, October 1909, *Better Times*, p. 159
225 Speech at Norwich, July 1909, *Liberalism and the Social Problem*, pp. 352-3
226 Speech at Abernethy, October 1909, *ibid.*, p. 400
227 Speech at Leicester, September 1909, *ibid.*, pp. 373-4
228 *Better Times*, p. 72
229 Quoted in *The Evolution of National Insurance*, pp. 252-3
230 *Better Times*, p. 53
231 *The People's Budget*, preface, p. ix

232 H. of C., 4 May 1911, XXV, col. 626
233 Quoted by R. M. Titmuss in *Law and Opinion in England in the Twentieth Century*, p. 312
234 H. of C., 29 May 1911, XXVI, col. 763
235 *The Evolution of National Insurance*, ch. 6-7
236 See p. 252 below
237 *The Evolution of National Insurance*, p. 327
238 ibid., p. 328
239 ibid.
240 ibid., p. 359
241 *Lloyd George's Ambulance Wagon*, p. 96
242 ibid., p. 168
243 ibid.
244 R. W. Harris, *National Health Insurance in Great Britain, 1911-1946*, p. 8. For an account of this lively episode, and its significance, from another who took part in it, see Lord Salter, *Memoirs of a Public Servant*, ch. III
245 *The Observer and J. L. Garvin*, p. 331
246 *Lloyd George's Ambulance Wagon*, commentary by R. M. Titmuss, p. 46
247 H. of C., 25 Feburary 1914, LVIII, cols. 1899-1900
248 *Our Partnership*, p. 475
249 *Lloyd George's Ambulance Wagon*, p. 140
250 ibid., p. 177
251 *Power and Influence*, p. 295. Cf A. Bullock, *The Life and Times of Ernest Bevin*, II, p. 326
252 *The Evolution of National Insurance*, p. 416
253 Quoted in *Trends of Opinion about the Public Health*, p. 66
254 H. of C., 28 March 1945, 409, col. 1378
255 Violet Markham, 'Robert Morant—Some Personal Reminiscences', *Public Administration*, 1950
256 Lord Addison, *Four and a Half Years*, p. 35
257 G. F. McCleary, *The Early History of the Infant Welfare Movement*, pp. 158, 167
258 *Fifty Years in Public Health*, p. 323
259 *The Early History of the Infant Welfare Movement*, p. 165
260 C. Tsuzuki, *H. M. Hyndman and British Socialism*, p. 148
261 *The Evolution of National Insurance*, ch. 3
262 Lord Samuel, *Memoirs*, p. 53
263 Part II, ch. V (F)
264 *Liberalism and the Social Problem*, p. 210
265 *The Evolution of National Insurance*, pp. 451-2

## 6 Between the Wars (pages 228-290)

1 C. L. Mowat, *Britain between the Wars, 1918-40*, p. 125, quoting the *Economist*
2 *The Times*, 28 February, 1940. The early chapters of Lord Birkenhead's *Halifax* portray life as it was before 1914 for the aristocratic Edward Wood and his circle. The Ministry of Reconstruction in 1918 also assumed that there would be a return to the conditions of 1914: D. Abrams, 'The Failure of Social Reform, 1918-20', *Past and Present*, 1963
3 W. A. Lewis, *Economic Survey, 1919-39*, ch. V

4  W. A. Orton, *Labour in Transition* (1921), p. 158. On the frustrations of many of these hopes see 'The Failure of Social Reform, 1918–20'

5  Quoted in *Disinherited Youth* (Carnegie U.K. Trust), p. 10

6  In the experience of the writer, shared no doubt by many of his generation

7  'A Gentleman with a Duster' (H. Begbie), *The Mirrors of Downing Street*, p. 15

8  Sir H. Clay, *Lord Norman*, p. 168

9  Lord Beveridge, *Full Employment in a Free Society*, p. 61

10  *Men Without Work* (Pilgrim Trust, 1938), p. 22

11  *Full Employment in a Free Society*, pp. 316–20

12  A. Bullock, *The Life and Times of Ernest Bevin*, I, p. 541; cf H. Macmillan, *Winds of Change*, pp. 508–9

13  H. of C., 18 May 1925, 184, col. 107

14  *ibid.*

15  Mary Hamilton, *Remembering My Good Friends*, p. 98

16  G. Orwell, *The Road to Wigan Pier*, p. 90

17  F. Brockway, *Socialism over Sixty Years*, p. 182

18  R. F. Harrod, *The Life of John Maynard Keynes*, p. 348

19  p. 112

20  H. of C., 18 May 1925, 184, col. 112

21  VI, p. 3335

22  Beatrice Webb, *Our Partnership*, p. 420 n

23  R.C. on National Health Insurance, Report, p. 300

24  *ibid.*, p. 73

25  H. of C., 19 December 1919, 123, col. 890

26  *Social Insurance and Allied Services*, para. 233

27  H. of C., 18 May 1925, 184, col. 79

28  *ibid.*, col. 92

29  *Social Insurance and Allied Services*, para. 26

30  H. of C., 28 April 1925, 183, col. 82

31  *ibid.*, col. 71–2

32  See P. J. Grigg, *Prejudice and Judgment*, pp. 180–4, and R. S. Sayers, 'The Return to Gold, 1925' in *Studies in the Industrial Revolution*, ed. L. S. Pressnell

33  H. of C., 6 March 1925, 181, col. 841

34  H. Nicolson, *King George the Fifth*, p. 403

35  L. S. Amery, *My Political Life*, II, p. 480

36  A. W. Baldwin, *My Father: the True Story*, p. 127

37  Lord Salter, *Personality in Politics*, p. 67

38  Lord Snell, *Men, Movements and Myself*, p. 248

39  K. Feiling, *The Life of Neville Chamberlain*, p. 132

40  Quoted in *Prejudice and Judgment*, p. 110

41  A. J. P. Taylor, *English History, 1914–1945*, p. 237

42  Lord Percy, *Some Memories*, p. 189

43  *ibid.*, p. 17

44  T. Jones, *A Diary with Letters*, p. 422

45  *The Life of Neville Chamberlain*, p. 128

46  *ibid.*, p. 104

47  *ibid.*, p. 142

48  *Winds of Change*, p. 174

49  *The Life of Neville Chamberlain*, p. 131

50  H. of C., 18 May 1925, 184, cols. 76–7
51  *ibid.*, col. 92
52  H. of C., 28 April 1925, 183, col. 82
53  H. Dalton, *Call Back Yesterday*, p. 159, and H. of C., 30 April 1925, 183, col. 419
54  H. of C., 18 May 1925, 184, col. 132
55  *ibid.*, cols. 119–20. In fact Lloyd George had not dared
56  H. of C., 28 April 1925, 183, col. 94
57  T. Barna, *Redistribution of Incomes through Public Finance in 1937*, p. 233
58  *ibid.*
59  C. Clark, *National Income and Outlay*, p. 148
60  *Social Insurance and Allied Services*, para. 445
61  *Redistribution of Incomes*, p. 236
62  *Social Insurance and Allied Services*, para. 236
63  R. M. Titmuss, *Essays on 'The Welfare State'*, p. 67
64  B. Abel-Smith in *Law and Opinion in England in the Twentieth Century*, p. 362
65  H. of C., 26 November 1928, 223, col. 71
66  *The Last Hundred Years*, II, p. 825
67  *Men Without Work*, p. 186
68  H. of C., 26 November 1928, 223, col. 74
69  The story is told in *The Life of Neville Chamberlain*, ch. XI. See also *Winds of Change*, ch. 8
70  *The Life of Neville Chamberlain*, p. 144
71  *ibid.*
72  H. of C., 28 November 1928, 223, col. 457
73  ed. M. Cole, *Beatrice Webb's Diaries, 1924–32*, p. 188
74  H. of C., 28 November, 1928, 223. col. 466
75  *Beatrice Webb's Diaries*, p. 188
76  R. M. Titmuss, *Problems of Social Policy*, p. 64
77  *ibid.*, p. 504
78  W. M. Frazer, *A History of English Public Health*, p. 393
79  Quoted in R.C. on Unemployment Insurance, Final Report, p. 23
80  Report of the Unemployment Insurance Committee (1927), I para. 67
81  *ibid.*, para. 80
82  *ibid.*, para. 81
83  Quoted in R.C. on Unemployment Insurance, Final Report, p. 22
84  Report on National Unemployment Insurance to July 1923, para. 53
85  Report of the Unemployment Assistance Board, 1935 (1936), App. VI
86  H. W. Singer, *Unemployment and the Unemployed*, p. 4
87  *Disinherited Youth*, p. 5
88  *ibid.*, p. 79
89  *King George the Fifth*, p. 342, *cf* also p. 414
90  R. Bassett, *Nineteen Thirty-One*, p. 19
91  *Britain between the Wars*: the title of ch. 8
92  See W. Hannington, *Unemployed Struggles, 1919–36* and *Never on our Knees*
93  *Call Back Yesterday*, p. 296
94  *The Road to Wigan Pier*, p. 88
95  *Unemployment and the Unemployed*, p. 72
96  See the comments by Bevin quoted on p. 274 below
97  These illustrations are all drawn from *Unemployment and the Unemployed*

98 *Disinherited Youth*, p. 56
99 *Men, Movements and Myself*, p. 247
100 *Nineteen Thirty-One*, p. 43
101 Ministry of Health, Report on the state of the Public Health during six years of war (1946), p. 119
102 L. Beales and R. S. Lambert (ed.), *Memoirs of the Unemployed* (1934), p. 51
103 *The Life of Neville Chamberlain*, p. 230
104 *The Life and Times of Ernest Bevin*, I, p. 541
105 *Return Passage*, p. 194
106 *Disinherited Youth*, p. 56
107 *The Life and Times of Ernest Bevin*, II, p. 241
108 H. of C., 29 April 1941, 371, col. 368
109 *Redistribution of Incomes*, p. 285
110 *National Income and Outlay*, p. 270
111 H. Tout, *The Standard of Living in Bristol* (1938), p. 48
112 E. Rathbone, *The Disinherited Family*, p. 27
113 *The Times*, 11 December 1939
114 *The Human Needs of Labour*, p. 125
115 *Men Without Work*, p. 109
116 *The Standard of Living in Bristol*, pp. 28 and 36
117 R. M. Titmuss, *Birth, Poverty and Wealth*, p. 99
118 *The Times*, 10 January 1939
119 G. M'Gonigle and J. Kirby, *Poverty and Public Health*, ch. VII
120 *Nineteen Thirty-One*, p. 357
121 Report of the Unemployment Assistance Board, 1935, p. 19
122 R.C. on Unemployment Insurance, Final Report, para. 644
123 Lord Percy, *Some Memories*, p. 150
124 paras. 395–6
125 M. Bowley, *Housing and the State, 1919–44*, p. 24. For an examination of the frustrations and failures of housing policy see 'The Failure of Social Reform, 1918–20'
126 *The Road to Wigan Pier*, p. 65
127 *Housing and the State*, p. 140
128 P.E.P., *The British Health Services*, p. 37
129 W. Ashworth, *The Genesis of Modern British Town Planning*, p. 212
130 *War Memoirs*, VI, ch. LXXXVI
131 G. A. M. Lowndes, *The Silent Social Revolution*, p. 242
132 The title of Lowndes's pioneer study, first published in 1937: an important and more recent study is G. Bernbaum, *Social Change and the Schools, 1918–44* (1967)
133 *The Silent Social Revolution*, p. 122
134 *ibid.*, p. 125
135 H. A. L. Fisher, *An Unfinished Autobiography*, p. 98
136 Quoted in *15 to 18* (Crowther Report, 1959), p. 14
137 *ibid.*, p. 3
138 Lloyd George's father had been a schoolmaster before his illness and early death
139 *The Silent Social Revolution*, pp. 221–5
140 *Poverty and Public Health*, pp. 48–9
141 P.E.P., *The British Social Services*, p. 95n
142 Quoted in Jean Heywood, *Children in Care*, p. 131

143 *ibid.*, p. 132
144 *ibid.*, p. 131
145 *Remembering My Good Friends*, p. 97
146 *Winds of Change*, p. 516


7 Beveridge and Beyond (pages 291-325)
  1 H. of C., 16 August 1945, 413, col. 73
  2 S. Ferguson and H. Fitzgerald, *Studies in the Social Services* (History of the Second World War), p. 157
  3 *Social Insurance and Allied Services*, para. 413
  4 R. M. Titmuss, *Problems of Social Policy* (History of the Second World War), p. 516
  5 *ibid.*
  6 W. K. Hancock, and M. M. Gowing, *British War Economy* (History of the Second World War), p. 541
  7 H. of C., 17 August 1945, 413, col. 207
  8 A. Bullock, *The Life and Times of Ernest Bevin*, I, p. 653
  9 *ibid.*, II, p. 69; cf Winston Churchill, *The Second World War*, III, p. 392
 10 These were the Committee's terms of reference
 11 *The Life and Times of Ernest Bevin*, II, p. 225
 12 *The Second World War*, III, p. 638
 13 F. W. Pethick-Lawrence, H. of C., 13 February 1941, 368, col. 1557
 14 *Social Insurance and Allied Services*, para. 441
 15 p. 128
 16 *Problems of Social Policy*, p. 509
 17 *ibid.*, p. 510
 18 *Studies in the Social Services*, p. 162
 19 Report on the state of the Public Health during six years of war, p. 3
 20 *ibid.*, ch. XV
 21 *Studies in the Social Services*, p. 160, quoting J. C. Drummond
 22 *ibid.*, pp. 12-13
 23 Report on the state of the Public Health, p. 252
 24 p. 6
 25 *Our Towns*, p. 1
 26 *ibid.*, p. 106
 27 *Problems of Social Policy*, ch. XX-XXI and pp. 181-2; Jean Heywood, *Children in Care*, pp. 134-5
 28 *Studies in the Social Services*, p. 153
 29 *Children in Care*, p. 158
 30 The problems presented to the poor law by wartime conditions are illustrated in *Problems of Social Policy*, ch. XII
 31 *The Second World War*, IV, p. 861
 32 *Social Insurance and Allied Services*, para. 15
 33 para. 31
 34 para. 445
 35 para. 457
 36 Speech on 10 March 1943, *The Pillars of Security*, p. 178
 37 *The Times*, 11 March 1943
 38 *The Times*, 16 February 1943

39  *The Times*, 15 January 1943. The full quotation is given on p. 26 above
40  *Social Insurance and Allied Services*, para. 158 and Appendix D
41  *ibid.*, para. 22
42  *ibid.*
43  para. 10
44  para. 455
45  para. 413
46  Lord Beveridge, *Power and Influence*, pp. 309–10
47  *Social Insurance and Allied Services*, para. 107
48  *The Disinherited Family*, p. 78
49  *Social Insurance and Allied Services*, paras. 8 and 456
50  para. 459
51  Lord Moran noted his churlish behaviour to Beveridge on an Atlantic crossing, *Winston Churchill. The Struggle for Survival*, p. 94
52  *The Life and Times of Ernest Bevin*, II, p. 242
53  F. Williams, *A Prime Minister Remembers*, p. 57
54  *The Life and Times of Ernest Bevin*, II, pp. 226–7
55  This was Attlee's interpretation, *A Prime Minister Remembers*, p. 57
56  *The Life and Times of Ernest Bevin*, II, p. 242
57  H. of C., 7 February 1946, 418, col. 1895
58  *The Times*, 17 February 1943
59  Janet Beveridge, *Beveridge and His Plan*, p. 215
60  H. of C., 7 February 1946, 418, col. 1896
61  *The Times*, 20 January 1943
62  *Power and Influence*, p. 330
63  *Manchester Guardian Weekly*, 31 May 1940
64  H. Dalton, *The Fateful Years*, p. 428
65  *Social Insurance*, Part I, para. 13
66  H. of C., 6 February 1946, 418, col. 1742
67  *Social Insurance*, Part I, para. 8
68  *ibid.*, para. 50 and 59
69  *The Second World War*, VI, p. 627
70  *Power and Influence*, p. 302
71  H. of C., 30 April 1946, 422, col. 50
72  A. J. Willcocks, *The Creation of the National Health Service*, p. 104
73  Lady Davidson, H. of C., 30 April 1946, 422, col. 91
74  H. of C., 30 April 1946, 422, col. 47
75  *ibid.*, col. 61
76  *The Times*, 6 January 1947
77  H. of C., 30 April 1946, 422, col. 60
78  J. S. Ross, *The National Health Service*, p. 125. For a succinct but informative statement of the dispute see G. Forsyth, *Doctors and State Medicine*, ch. 2, 'Launching the N.H.S.' and A. J. Willcocks, *The Creation of the National Health Service*. Fuller accounts are given in A. Lindsay, *Socialized Medicine in England and Wales* and H. Eckstein, *The English Health Service* and *Pressure Group Politics*. Lord Platt, sometime President of the Royal College of Physicians, has described some of the B.M.A. opposition as 'paranoid': *Doctor and Patient*, p. 53
79  *ibid.*, p. 127
80  J. M. Mackintosh, *Trends of Opinion about the Public Health*, p. 168

81 *The Life and Times of Ernest Bevin*, II, p. 282
82 W. K. Richmond, *Education in England*, p. 147
83 S. J. Curtis, *Education in Britain since 1900*, pp. 144–5. See also G. Bernbaum, *Social Change and the Schools, 1918–44*, ch. 6: '1944—Promise Unfulfilled'
84 D. V. Glass in *Law and Opinion in England in the Twentieth Century*, p. 338
85 Quoted in H. C. Dent, *The Education Act, 1944*, p. 58
86 *The Second World War*, VI, pp. 652–53
87 *ibid.*, p. 583
88 H. of C., 6 February 1946, 418, col. 1741–42
89 *ibid.*, col. 1751
90 *ibid.*, col. 1738
91 H. of C., 11 February 1946, 419, col. 45
92 H. of C., 30 May 1946, 423, col. 1380
93 *The Times*, 25 February 1952
94 The details in this paragraph are from the Report of the Ministry of National Insurance for the period 1944–9
95 H. of C., 24 November 1947, 444, col. 1604
96 H. of C., 5 March 1948, 448, col. 716
97 D. Seers, *The Levelling of Income since 1938*, pp. 56 and 67

## 8 Conclusion (pages 326–333)

1 *Social Insurance and Allied Services*, para. 460
2 *cf* T. H. Marshall, in 'On the Welfare State', *European Journal of Sociology*, II, 2 (1961), p. 297
3 *Power and Influence*, pp. 360–1
4 J. Gibson-Jarvie, Chairman of United Dominions Trust, quoted in *The Observer*, 'Sayings of 1958', 21 December 1958
5 T. H. Marshall, *Social Policy*, p. 182
6 For a study of the influence of the Labour Party on developments see A. Marwick, 'The Labour Party and the Welfare State in Britain, 1900–1948', *American Historical Review*, December 1967
7 H. Macmillan, *Winds of Change*, p. 286
8 *ibid.*, p. 511
9 The title of a Fabian report published in 1960
10 *Voluntary Action*, p. 320
11 The National Council of Social Service, 46th Annual Report, 1964–5, p. 3, from which comes also the quotation that follows
12 *cf* M. Rooff, *Voluntary Societies and Social Policy*
13 *The Affluent Society*, p. 76
14 *Social Policy*, p. 182
15 *cf* W. W. Rostow, *The Stages of Economic Growth*
16 Mr D. Houghton, Chancellor of the Duchy of Lancaster, H. of C., 10 November 1964
17 J. Enoch Powell, *A New Look at Medicine and Politics*, p. 67. Mr Powell was Minister of Health, 1960–63, and his book has much shrewd comment based on his experience of the working of the N.H.S. at the centre
18 *cf* S. E. Harris, *The Economics of American Medicine*, and A. Lindsey, *Socialized Medicine in England and Wales. The National Health Service, 1948–61*. The quotation is from the latter, p. 474
19 *cf* S. Mencher, *Private Practice in Britain*

20 B. Abel-Smith, *An International Study of Health Expenditure* (*W.H.O.*, Public Health Papers, 32), p. 92. Critics of the N.H.S. who earlier complained of overmuch spending have tended more recently to argue that private spending would produce more for health services

21 *Social Insurance and Allied Services*, para. 10

22 *ibid.*, para. 31

23 *ibid.*, para. 44

24 For a sharp indictment see D. C. Marsh, *The Future of the Welfare State*

25 *Social Policy*, p. 89

26 R. M. Titmuss, foreword to B. B. Gilbert, *The Evolution of National Insurance in Great Britain*, p. 8

27 *Winds of Change*, p. 2

# A Guide to Further Reading

This is not intended to be a full bibliography. It includes works which are essential to the study of the historical process described in this book, and many others which will enable the reader to look further into particular aspects, but it does not pretend to be complete. It can be supplemented to some extent from the references to each chapter, and, to help the reader further, books which themselves incorporate bibliographies have been marked (B). The titles are grouped under subject headings, though many of them could appropriately appear in several sections. Within the main sections subdivisions will be found, and special sections are devoted to the works of such pioneers as Beveridge and the Webbs. Reports of Royal Commissions and Parliamentary Committees have not been included, as they are referred to in the text and the index, and are listed in full in the Breviate of Parliamentary Papers in the first section. A short list of important articles in periodicals follows at the end.

## Works of Reference

D. Butler and J. Freeman (B), *British Political Facts, 1900–1960* (1962)
P. Deane and W. A. Cole (B), *British Economic Growth, 1688–1959* (1662)
B. R. Mitchell and P. Deane (B), *Abstract of British Historical Statistics* (1962)
P. and G. Ford, *Select List of British Parliamentary Papers 1833–1899* (1953)
    *A Breviate of Parliamentary Papers: 1900–1916. The Foundation of the Welfare State*
    (1957), *1917–1939* (1951), *1940–1954: War and Reconstruction* (1961)
The Annual Reports of Government Departments are, of course, an important source, particularly those of the Ministry of Health, the Ministry of Pensions and National Insurance and the National Assistance Board (now combined as the Ministry of Social Security), and their predecessors before 1948. Special Departmental Reports are also published at intervals: H.M.S.O. lists should be consulted.

## Primary Works

*Collections of Speeches:*
J. Chamberlain (ed. C. W. Boyd), *Mr Chamberlain's Speeches* (1914)
W. S. Churchill, *Liberalism and the Social Problem* (1909)
W. S. Churchill (ed. F. B. Czarnomski), *The Wisdom of Winston Churchill* (1956)
D. Lloyd George, *Better Times* (1910) (ed. P. Guedalla), *Slings and Arrows* (1929)

William Beveridge, *Unemployment, a Problem of Industry* (1909)
    *Unemployment, A Problem of Industry. 1909 and 1930* (1930)
    *Social Insurance and Allied Services* (Beveridge Report) (1942)
    *The Pillars of Security* (Speeches) (1943)
    *Full Employment in a Free Society* (1944)

*Voluntary Action* (1948)
*Power and Influence* (autobiography) (1953)
Janet Beveridge, *Beveridge and His Plan* (1954)
Charles Booth, *Life and Labour of the People of London* (17 volumes, 1889–1903)
  *The Aged Poor in England and Wales* (1894)
Seebohm Rowntree, *Poverty: A Study of Town Life* (1901)
  *Poverty and Progress* (1941)
  *Poverty and the Welfare State* (1951)
  *The Human Needs of Labour* (1937)
Sidney and Beatrice Webb, *The Minority Report of the Poor Law Commission* (1909): Part 1—*The Break-up of the Poor Law*; Part 2—*The Public Organisation of the Labour Market.*
  *English Local Government from the Revolution to the Municipal Corporation Act*: vol. iv—*Statutory Authorities for Special Purposes* (1922); vols. vii-ix—*English Poor Law History*: Part 1—*The Old Poor Law* (1927); Part 2—*The Last Hundred Years* (1929)
  *The State and the Doctor* (1910)
Beatrice Webb's Diaries, *My Apprenticeship* (1926)
  *Our Partnership* (ed. B. Drake and M. I Cole, 1948)
  *Beatrice Webb's Diaries 1912–1924* (ed. M. I. Cole, 1952)
  *Beatrice Webb's Diaries 1924–1932* (ed. M. I. Cole, 1956)

## Background Studies

*(i) General:*
A. Briggs, 'The Welfare State in Historical Perspective' in M. N. Zald (ed.), *Social Welfare Institutions* (1965)
G. D. H. Cole and R. Postgate, *The Common People, 1746–1946* (1961)
K. de Schweinitz, *England's Road to Social Security* (1943)
D. C. Marsh, *The Future of the Welfare State* (1964)
T. H. Marshall, *Social Policy* (1965)
G. Myrdal, *Beyond the Welfare State* (1960)
D. Owen, *English Philanthropy, 1660–1960* (1965)
E. P. Thompson, *The Making of the English Working Class* (1963)
R. M. Titmuss, *Essays on 'The Welfare State'* (1958)
  *Commitment to Welfare* (1968)

*(ii) Historical Series:*
ed. T. S. Ashton, *An Economic History of England*:
  T. S. Ashton, *The Eighteenth Century*
  W. Ashworth, *1870–1939*
ed. A. Briggs, *Social and Economic History of England*:
  C. Wilson, *England's Apprenticeship, 1603–1763* (B)
  S. G. Checkland, *The Rise of Industrial Society in England, 1815–1885* (B)
ed. Sir G. Clark, *The Oxford History of England*:
  E. L. Woodward, *The Age of Reform, 1815–1870* (B)
  R. C. K. Ensor, *England, 1870–1914* (B)
  A. J. P. Taylor, *English History, 1914–1945* (B)
ed. W. N. Medlicott, *A History of England*:
  D. Marshall, *Eighteenth Century England*
  A. Briggs, *The Age of Improvement*

W. N. Medlicott, *Contemporary England, 1914–1964*
Home University Library (now Oxford Paperbacks University Series):
T. S. Ashton, *The Industrial Revolution, 1760–1830* (B)
J. D. Chambers, *The Workshop of the World, 1830–1880* (B)
R. S. Sayers, *A History of Economic Change in England, 1880–1939* (B)

(*iii*) *The Nineteenth Century:*
Sir J. Clapham, *An Economic History of Modern Britain:* I *The Early Railway Age, 1820–1850* (1926); II *Free Trade and Steel, 1850–1886* (1932); III *Machines and National Rivalries, 1887–1914* (1938)
A. V. Dicey, *The Relation between Law and Public Opinion in England during the Nineteenth Century* (1905)
G. P. Jones and A. G. Pool, *A Hundred Years of Economic Development in Great Britain* (1940)
H. M. Lynd, *England in the Eighteen-Eighties* (1945) (B)
M. Richter, *The Politics of Conscience. T. H. Green and His Age* (1966)
D. Roberts, *The Victorian Origins of the British Welfare State* (1960) (B)
K. B. Smellie, *A Hundred Years of English Government* (2nd edn. 1950)

(*iv*) *The Twentieth Century:*
G. Dangerfield, *The Strange Death of Liberal England* (1935)
ed. M. Ginsberg, *Law and Opinion in England in the Twentieth Century* (1959)
A. F. Havighurst, *Twentieth-Century Britain* (1962) (B)
W. A. Lewis, *Economic Survey, 1919–1939* (1949)
A. Marwick, *Britain in the Century of Total War* (1968)
C. L. Mowat, *Britain between the Wars, 1918–1940* (1955) (B)
S. Pollard, *The Development of the British Economy, 1914–1967* (2nd ed., 1969)
F. M. G. Willson, *The Organisation of British Central Government, 1914–1956* (1957)

## Social Problems and Policies

*Earlier Periods:*
(i) Contemporary:
P. F. Aschrott (trans. H. Preston-Thomas), *The English Poor Law System* (1902)
Lady Bell, *At the Works* (1907)
H. Bosanquet, *Rich and Poor* (1896)
  *Social Work in London, 1869–1912. A History of the Charity Organisation Society* (1914)
B. K. Gray, *A History of English Philanthropy* (1905, reprinted 1967)
  *Philanthropy and the State* (1908)
C. F. G. Masterman, *The Condition of England* (1909)
  *England after War* (1922)
Sir G. Nicholls and T. Mackay, *A History of the English Poor Law* (3 volumes, 1898–99)
M. S. Reeves, *Round about a Pound a Week* (1913)
Sir J. Simon, *English Sanitary Institutions* (1890)
G. R. Sims, *How the Poor Live* (1889)
J. F. Wilkinson, *Pensions and Pauperism* (1892)

(ii) Recent Studies:
ed. S. D. Chapman, *The History of Working-class Housing* (1971)
P. H. J. H. Gosden, *The Friendly Societies in England, 1815–1875* (1961)
R. Hodgkinson, *The Origins of the National Health Service. The Medical Services of the New Poor Law, 1834–71* (1967)

R. M. MacLeod, *Treasury Control and Social Administration, 1871–1905* (1966)
D. Marshall, *The English Poor in the Eighteenth Century* (1926)
E. C. Midwinter, *Social Administration in Lancashire, 1830–1860* (1969)
C. L. Mowat, *The Charity Organisation Society, 1869–1913* (1961)
A. R. Neate, *The St Marylebone Workhouse and Institution, 1730–1965* (1967)
J. R. Poynter, *Society and Pauperism. English Ideas on Poor Relief, 1751–1834* (1970)
M. B. Simey, *Charitable Effort in Liverpool in the Nineteenth Century* (1951)
P. Smith, *Disraelian Conservatism and Social Reform* (1967)
J. N. Tarn, *Working-class Housing in Nineteenth-century Britain* (1971)


*Between the Wars:*
ed. L. Beales and R. S. Lambert, *Memoirs of the Unemployed* (1934)
Carnegie Trust, *Disinherited Youth* (1943)
G. D. H. and M. I. Cole, *The Condition of Britain* (1937)
R. C. Davison, *The Unemployed. Old Policies and New* (1929)
   *British Unemployment Policy since 1930* (1938)
P. B. Johnson, *Land Fit for Heroes. The Planning of British Reconstruction, 1916–1919*
   (1968)
D. C. Jones, *Social Survey of Merseyside* (3 volumes, 1934)
   *New Survey of London Life and Labour* (9 volumes, 1930–1935)
W. A. Orton, *Labour in Transition* (1921)
G. Orwell (E. Blair), *The Road to Wigan Pier* (1937)
P.E.P. *The British Social Services* (1937)
Pilgrim Trust, *Men Without Work* (1938)
H. W. Singer, *Unemployment and the Unemployed* (1940)
R. M. Titmuss, *Poverty and Population* (1938)
   *Birth, Poverty and Wealth* (1943)
H. Tout, *The Standard of Living in Bristol* (1938)


*General Studies:*
A. B. Atkinson, *Poverty in Britain and the Reform of Social Security* (1969)
G. Bernbaum, *Social Change and the Schools, 1918–44* (1967)
M. Bowley, *Housing and the State, 1919–44* (1945)
U. Cormick, *The Royal Commission on the Poor Laws and the Welfare State* (Loch
   Memorial Lecture, 1953)
S. Ferguson and H. Fitzgerald, *Studies in the Social Services* (*History of the Second
   World War*) (1954)
V. George, *Social Security: Beveridge and After* (1968)
B. B. Gilbert, *The Evolution of National Insurance in Great Britain* (1966) (B)
   *British Social Policy, 1914–39* (1970) (B)
M. P. Hall, *The Social Services of Modern England* (1952)
J. S. Heywood, *Children in Care* (1959)
G. Ince, *The Ministry of Labour and National Service* (1960)
G. S. King, *The Ministry of Pensions and National Insurance* (1958)
G. A. N. Lowndes, *The Silent Social Revolution. Public Education in England and Wales,
   1895–1935* (1937)
D. C. Marsh, *National Insurance and Assistance in Great Britain* (1950)
E. H. Phelps Brown, *The Growth of British Industrial Relations* (1955)
H. Pelling, *Popular Politics and Society in Late Victorian Britain* (1968)
E. Rathbone, *The Disinherited Family* (1924)

B. Simon, *Education and the Labour Movement, 1870–1920* (1965)
R. M. Titmuss, *Problems of Social Policy (History of the Second World War)* (1950)
K. Woodroofe, *From Charity to Social Work* (1962)

## Public Health

B. Abel-Smith, *A History of the Nursing Profession* (1960)
   *The Hospitals, 1800–1948* (1964) (B)
E. Moberly Bell, *The Story of Hospital Almoners* (1961)
C. Fraser Brockington, *Public Health in the Nineteenth Century* (1965)
J. C. Drummond, *The Englishman's Food* (1957)
H. Eckstein, *The English Health Services* (1959)
   *Pressure Group Politics* (1960)
G. Forsyth, *Doctors and State Medicine* (1966)
W. M. Frazer *A History of English Public Health, 1834–1939* (1950)
R. W. Harris, *National Health Insurance in Great Britain, 1911–1946* (1946)
H. Levy, *National Health Insurance. A Critical Study* (1944)
A. Lindsey, *Socialized Medicine in England and Wales. The National Health Service 1948–61* (1962)
N. Longmate, *King Cholera* (1966)
J. M. Mackintosh, *Trends of Opinion about the Public Health, 1901–51* (1953)
G. M'Gonigle and J. Kirby, *Poverty and Public Health* (1937)
A. Newsholme, *Fifty Years in Public Health* (1935)
   *The Last Thirty Years in Public Health* (1936)
P.E.P., *The British Health Services* (1937)
R. Platt, *Doctor and Patient. Ethics, Morale, Government* (1963)
J. S. Ross, *The National Health Service in Great Britain* (1952)
A. J. Willcocks, *The Creation of the National Health Service* (1967)

## Biography and Autobiography

C. Addison, *Politics from Within, 1911–18* (1924)
M. Foot, *Aneurin Bevan, 1897–1945* (1962)
A. Bullock, *The Life and Times of Ernest Bevin,* I, *1881–1940* (1960); II, 1940–45 (1967)
T. S. and M. B. Simey, *Charles Booth, Social Scientist* (1960)
ed. H. N. Bunbury, *Lloyd George's Ambulance Wagon. Being the Memoirs of W. J. Braithwaite, 1911–12* (1957)
W. Kent, *John Burns, Labour's Lost Leader* (1950)
S. E. Finer, *The Life and Times of Sir Edwin Chadwick* (1952)
R. A. Lewis, *Edwin Chadwick and the Public Health Movement, 1832–54* (1952)
K. Feiling, *The Life of Neville Chamberlain* (1946)
I. Macleod, *Neville Chamberlain* (1961)
R. S. Churchill, *Winston S. Churchill. Young Statesman, 1901–14* (1967)
H. Dalton, *Call Back Yesterday. Memoirs 1887–1931* (1953)
   *The Fateful Years. Memoirs 1931–45* (1957)
   *High Tide and After. Memoirs 1945–60* (1962)
M. A. Hamilton, *Remembering My Good Friends* (1944)
F. Smith, *The Life and Work of Sir James Kay-Shuttleworth* (1923)
G. Lansbury, *My Life* (1928)
R. Postgate, *Life of George Lansbury* (1951)
W. George, *My Brother and I* (Lloyd George) (1958)
H. Macmillan, *Winds of Change, 1914–39* (1966)

L. Masterman, *C. F. G. Masterman* (1939)
Lord Morrison, *Herbert Morrison. An Autobiography* (1960)
C. Driver, *Tory Radical. The Life of Richard Oastler* (1946)
A. Briggs, *Social Thought and Social Action. A Study of the Work of Seebohm Rowntree, 1871–1954* (1961)
A. Salter, *Memoirs of a Public Servant* (1961)
  *Slave of the Lamp* (1967)
G. F. A. Best, *Lord Shaftesbury* (1964)
J. L. and B. Hammond, *Lord Shaftesbury* (1925)
R. Lambert, *Sir John Simon, 1816–1904, and English Social Administration* (1963) (B)

## Some Articles in Periodicals

A small selection of papers of interest and importance
*American Historical Review:*
   1967—'The Labor Party and the Welfare State in Britain, 1900–48' (A. Marwick)
*Economic History Review:*
   1937—'The Old Poor Law, 1662–1795'* (D. Marshall)
   1953–4—'Some Influences affecting the Development of Sanitary Legislation in England' (B. Keith-Lucas)
   1962–3—'The Reduction of Unemployment as a Problem of Public Policy, 1920–29' (K. J. Hancock)
   1966—'The Allowance System in the new Poor Law' (M. E. Rose)
*European Journal of Sociology:*
   1961—'On the Welfare State'
*Historical Journal:*
   1958—'The Nineteenth Century Revolution in Government: a Reappraisal' (O. MacDonagh)
   1960—'A Reappraisal Reappraised' (H. Parris)
   1962—'A Victorian National Health Service: State Vaccination, 1855–71' (R. Lambert)
   1963—'How Cruel was the Victorian Poor Law?' (D. Roberts)
   1967—'State Intervention at the Local Level. The New Poor Law in Lancashire' (E. C. Midwinter)
   1968—'How Cruel was the Victorian Poor Law?' (Ursula Henriques)
*History:*
   1931—'The New Poor Law' (H. L. Beales)
   1960—'Progress and Poverty in Britain, 1780–1850'* (A. J. Taylor)
*Journal of Economic History:*
   1948—'Laissez-Faire and State Intervention in Nineteenth-Century Britain' (J. B. Brebner)
   1963—'The Myth of the Old Poor Law and the Making of the New' (M. Blaug)
   1964—'The Poor Law Report Re-examined' (M. Blaug)
*Medical History:*
   1967—'The Frustration of State Medicine, 1880–99' (R. M. MacLeod)
*Northern History:*
   1966—'The Anti-Poor Law Movement in the North of England' (M. E. Rose)
*Parliamentary Affairs:*
   1955/6—'The Medical Relief Disqualification Removal Act, 1885' (B. Rodgers)

*Past and Present :*
  1953—'Lloyd George and the Labour Movement' (W. S. Adams)
  1961—'Cholera and Society in the Nineteenth Century' (A. Briggs)
  1963—'The Failure of Social Reform, 1918–20' (P. Abrams)
  1965—'Nineteenth Century Social Reform: a Tory Interpretation of History' (J. Hart)
  1966—'Poor Relief in Warwickshire, 1630–60' (A. L.,Beier)
  1967—'Bastardy and the New Poor Law' (U. R. Q.Henriques)
*Political Science Quarterly :*
  1963—'Is there a Welfare State?' (B. Wootton)
*Public Administration :*
  1959—'The Genesis of the Ministry of Labour' (J. A. M. Caldwell)
*Transactions of the Lancashire and Cheshire Antiquarian Society*:
  1960—'The New Poor Law in North-East Lancashire, 1834–71' (R. Boyson)
  * Reprinted in *Essays in Economic History*, ed. E. M. Carus-Wilson

# Index of Subjects

All Statutes referred to are entered under ACTS OF PARLIAMENT; Ministries and Government Departments under GOVERNMENT, CENTRAL; Reports of Commissions and Committees under COMMISSIONS AND COMMITTEES. All aspects of the operation of the Poor Law are similarly entered under the heading, POOR LAW

# Index of Persons